# Origen's Revenge

# Origen's Revenge

The Greek and Hebrew Roots of Christian Thinking on Male and Female

Brian Patrick Mitchell

◆PICKWICK *Publications* · Eugene, Oregon

ORIGEN'S REVENGE
The Greek and Hebrew Roots of Christian Thinking on Male and Female

Copyright © 2021 Brian Patrick Mitchell. All rights reserved. Except for brief quotations in critical publications or reviews, no part of this book may be reproduced in any manner without prior written permission from the publisher. Write: Permissions, Wipf and Stock Publishers, 199 W. 8th Ave., Suite 3, Eugene, OR 97401.

Pickwick Publications
An Imprint of Wipf and Stock Publishers
199 W. 8th Ave., Suite 3
Eugene, OR 97401

www.wipfandstock.com

PAPERBACK ISBN: 978-1-6667-0015-2
HARDCOVER ISBN: 978-1-6667-0016-9
EBOOK ISBN: 978-1-6667-0017-6

*Cataloguing-in-Publication data:*

Names: Mitchell, Brian Patrick, author.

Title: Origen's revenge : the Greek and Hebrew roots of Christian thinking on male and female / Brian Patrick Mitchell.

Description: Eugene, OR: Pickwick Publications, 2021 | Includes bibliographical references and index.

Identifiers: ISBN 978-1-6667-0015-2 (paperback) | ISBN 978-1-6667-0016-9 (hardcover) | ISBN 978-1-6667-0017-6 (ebook)

Subjects: LCSH: Sex differences—Religious aspects—Christianity | Sex—Religious aspects—Christianity | Women—Religious aspects—Christianity | Men—Religious aspects—Christianity | Maximus, Confessor, Saint, approximately 580–662 | Origen

Classification: BT708 M58 2021 (print) | BT708 (ebook)

09/17/21

Unless otherwise indicated, all Scripture quotations are taken from The Authorized (King James) Version. Rights in the Authorized Version in the United Kingdom are vested in the Crown. Reproduced by permission of the Crown's patentee, Cambridge University Press.

Scripture quotations marked (NRSV) are from the New Revised Standard Version Bible, copyright © 1989 the Division of Christian Education of the National Council of the Churches of Christ in the United States of America. Used by permission. All rights reserved.

To George Gilder,
whose early work on male and female
opened my eyes to a great mystery
half a century ago.

"So God created man in his own image,
in the image of God created he him;
male and female created he them."

Genesis 1:27

# Contents

*Acknowledgments* | xi
*Abbreviations* | xiii
*Introduction: Tradition Against Tradition* | xvii

1 **The Known and the Not Known** | 1
   Enduring Debates | 5
   Maximian Scholarship | 8
   Unexamined Tensions | 12
   Image as Relation | 14
   Person and Nature | 17

2 **The Greek View of Male and Female** | 22
   Myth as History | 23
   Men Imitating Myth | 26
   Love and Lust | 31
   Sex and the Single Philosopher | 36
   Plato: The Lonely Soul | 42
   Aristotle: Married with Children | 47
   After Aristotle | 54
   Conclusion: Intellection vs. Relation | 60

3 **The Hebrew View of Male and Female** | 63
   Creation and Fall | 64
   First Families | 70
   Gender Order and Disorder | 73
   Sexual Order and Disorder | 81
   Hebrew Hellenism | 88
   Philo of Alexandria | 92
   Conclusion: Carnal Israel | 97

4  **The Greek Christian View of Male and Female** | 101
   New Testament Support for the Greek View | 102
   Early Encratism | 105
   The Valentinian Gnosis | 109
   Origen on the Body | 112
   Origen on the Soul | 116
   Origen and Valentinianism | 119
   The Cappadocians | 124
   Ambrose and Augustine | 132
   Maximus the Confessor | 140
   Maximus, Gregory, and Aristotle | 147
   Conclusion: The Ascent of Alexandrian Anthropology | 149

5  **The Hebrew Christian View of Male and Female** | 154
   "What God hath joined together" | 156
   "The head of every man is Christ" | 159
   "For Adam was first formed, then Eve" | 163
   "There is neither male nor female" | 168
   The Good of Marriage | 173
   The Challenge of Virginity | 178
   Distinction, Relation, Separation | 183
   Last Adam, New Eve | 189
   Conclusion: Continuity and Consensus | 193

6  **"That They May Be One, Even as We Are One"** | 195
   The Greek Way | 196
   The Hebrew Way | 199
   Remaining Differences | 201
   The Image of God | 204
   Archy Versus Hierarchy | 207
   "That they may be one, even as we are one" | 211
   "Male and female created he them" | 214
   Conclusion: Archē kai Telos | 217

*Bibliography* | 223
*Subject Index* | 243

# Acknowledgments

THIS BOOK IS THE result of many years of research begun nearly a quarter of a century ago, yet it would not exist today but for the interest, assistance, and persistently cheerful encouragement of Dr. Andreas Andreopoulos of the University of Winchester, to whom I owe my success as a scholar and with this book. I was especially blessed to have him as my director of studies. He made it possible for me to do what no one would be advised to do—write a doctoral thesis of broad scope on a dangerously controversial topic.

Many others contributed significantly to this book in other ways: My thesis examiners, Dr. Robin Baker of the University of Winchester and Dr. Mark Edwards of the University of Oxford, provided invaluable criticism and guidance that greatly improved both my thesis and this book. My editors, EJ Davila and Dr. Robin Parry of Pickwick Publications, along with the Wipf and Stock staff—Matt Wimer, George Callihan, Joe Delahanty, Kara Barlow, and Rachel Saunders—gave the book the utmost attention at a professional level far above that of all my other publishers. Dr. Mitzi Budde and the staff of the Bishop Payne Library at the Virginia Theological Seminary were always extremely helpful over the years. Dr. Joel Kalvesmaki at Dumbarton Oaks corrected my Greek and challenged some of my early assumptions to good effect.

Professor David Bradshaw of the University of Kentucky; Professor Claes Ryn of the Catholic University of America; Archpriest David Pratt of Georgetown University; Archpriest Alexander F. C. Webster, former dean of Holy Trinity Orthodox Seminary; Archpriest John Behr, former dean of St. Vladimir's Orthodox Theological Seminary; and Professor Patrick Viscuso of the Antiochian House of Studies all provided advice or encouragement over the years, no doubt never knowing how much their help meant to me. The interest and encouragement of a few friends—Bob

Miller, Andrew Berry, Andrew Van Sant, and Kelly Kehrer—also sustained me.

Finally, I could hardly have imagined, much less written, so much about male and female without close acquaintance with five godly women very dear to me: my mother Jean, my grandmother Alma, my daughters Alma Jean and Paula, and, most of all, my wife of thirty-eight years, Cindy. To each I owe more than I can possibly repay.

# Abbreviations

## General Abbreviations

| | |
|---|---|
| ANF | *Ante-Nicene Fathers* |
| CSEL | *Corpus Scriptorum Ecclesiasticorum Latinorum* |
| FC | *Fathers of the Church* |
| Fr. | Fragment |
| HTR | *Harvard Theological Review* |
| JBL | *Journal of Biblical Literature* |
| JTS | *Journal of Theological Studies* |
| JECS | *Journal of Early Christian Studies* |
| JSP | *Journal for the Study of the Pseudepigrapha* |
| LSJ | *Liddell-Scott-Jones Greek-English Lexicon* |
| LXX | Septuagint |
| NPNF1 | *Nicene and Post-Nicene Fathers, Series 1* |
| NPNF2 | *Nicene and Post-Nicene Fathers, Series 2* |
| PG | *Patrologia Graeca* |
| PL | *Patrologia Latina* |
| SPCK | Society for Promoting Christian Knowledge |
| ZAC | *Zeitschrift für antike Christentum (Journal of Ancient Christianity)* |

## Ancient Sources

### Aristotle

| | |
|---|---|
| EE | *Eudemian Ethics* |
| EN | *Nicomachean Ethics* |
| Meta. | *Metaphysics* |
| Pol. | *Politics* |
| AP | *Prior Analytics* |
| GA | *Generation of Animals* |
| HA | *History of Animals* |

## Clement of Alexandria

| | |
|---|---|
| *Paed.* | *Paedagogus* |
| *Strom.* | *Stromata* |

## Diogenes Laertius

| | |
|---|---|
| D.L. | *Lives and Opinions of Eminent Philosophers* |

## Eusebius

| | |
|---|---|
| *Ecc. Hist.* | *History of the Church* |

## Evagrius Ponticus

| | |
|---|---|
| KG | *Kephalaia Gnostika* |

## Gregory of Nyssa

| | |
|---|---|
| *An et res* | *De anima et resurrectione* |
| *Cant.* | *In Canticum canticorum* |
| *HO* | *De hominis opificio* |
| *Virg.* | *De virginitate* |

## Hesiod

| | |
|---|---|
| *Op.* | *Works and Days* |
| *Th.* | *Theogony* |

## Homer

| | |
|---|---|
| *Il.* | *Iliad* |
| *Od.* | *Odyssey* |

## Irenaeus

| | |
|---|---|
| *Adv. Haer.* | *Against Heresies* |

## Josephus

| | |
|---|---|
| AJ | *Antiquitates Judaicae* |

## Maximus the Confessor

| | |
|---|---|
| *Amb.* | *Ambigua to John* |
| *Char.* | *Four Centuries on Charity* |
| QD | *Questions and Doubts* |
| *Thal.* | *Responses to Thalassius* |
| *Theo.* | *Two Hundred Chapters on Theology* |

## Origen

| | |
|---|---|
| *ComJn* | *Commentary on John* |
| *ComMatt* | *Commentary on Matthew* |
| *ComRom* | *Commentary on Romans* |
| *ConCel* | *Contra Celsus* |

| | | | |
|---|---|---|---|
| Dial. Her. | Dialogue with Heraclides | Plato | |
| HomGen | Homilies on Genesis | Cra. | Cratylus |
| Prin. | De Principiis | Leg. | Laws |
| selPs | Selecta in Psalmos | Phd. | Phaedo |
| | | Phdr. | Phaedrus |
| | | Rep. | Republic |
| **Philo of Alexandria** | | Smp. | Symposium |
| Agri. | De Agricultura | Ti. | Timaeus |
| Her. | Quis Rerum Divinarum Heres | | |
| Legat. | De Legationem ad Gaium | **Porphyry** | |
| | | Abst. | On Abstinence from Animal Food |
| Legum | Legum Allegoriae | Mar. | Letter to Marcella |
| Migr. | De Migrationes Abrahami | Cav. | On the Cave of the Nymphs |
| Mos. | De Vita Mosis | Sent. | Sententiae |
| Opif. | De Opificio Mundi | | |
| QG | Quaestiones et Solutiones in Genesin | **Pseudo-Dionysius** | |
| Quod | Quod Omnis Probus Liber Sit | CH | Celestial Hierarchy |
| | | DN | Divine Names |
| Sacr. | De Sacrificiis Abelis et Cain | EH | Ecclesiastical Hierarchy |
| Somn. | Quod a Deo Mittantur Somnia or De Somniis | | |
| Spec. | De Specialibus Legibus | **Xenophon** | |
| Virt. | De Virtutibus | Mem. | Memorabilia |
| | | Oec. | Oeconomicus |
| | | Smp. | Symposium |

# Introduction
## Tradition Against Tradition

THERE IS AN INHERENT tension in traditional, historical Christianity on matters of male and female. The Church of the first seven centuries has handed down what appear to be two contradictory imperatives—insisting on the distinction of male and female yet obliging us to transcend it, blessing marriage as natural and good yet honoring celibacy as more spiritual and therefore better. Despite these tensions, Christianity's regard for male and female remained relatively stable until the modern age, when many Christians began assuming a more positive view of sexual relations and also, paradoxically, a more negative view of sexual distinction, abandoning clerical celibacy and monasticism along with, more recently, the constraints of traditional sexual morality and sex roles.

Even the most traditional Christian communions are now challenged to defend Christianity's traditional sexual and gender order. Eastern Orthodox Christians[1] are especially challenged, for several reasons: Their church is overtly hierarchic and patriarchal; their ultimate authority in matters of faith is "Holy Tradition"; they are extremely reluctant to admit errors, inconsistencies, or even change within Holy Tradition; they are also extremely reluctant to find fault with those they venerate as "saints"; and yet one of their saints, Maximus the Confessor (+662)—long venerated by the Orthodox and Catholic Churches as a champion of orthodox Christology and now touted by many Orthodox, Catholic, and Evangelical scholars as a philosopher and theologian of the first rank—has said

---

1. "Eastern Orthodox" and afterwards "Orthodox" are here understood to mean the communion that identifies as "Orthodox" on the basis of the Seven Ecumenical Councils, including Greeks, Slavs, some Arabs, and assorted others, but excluding the so-called Oriental Orthodox (Copts, Armenians, Ethiopians, Indians, and other Arabs).

the hardest things about the difference of male and female, disparaging it as a temporary "division" that must be "shaken off" so that men and women are no longer men and women but merely human beings. This, according to Maximus, is the first step in the renewal of creation.

What Maximus says about male and female has seemed so out of step with even modern Christian thinking that most scholars have tended to minimize its significance in various ways, but others have recently begun reading Maximus more literally and drawing out the obvious and quite radical implications for gender relations today. No one, however, has yet made the case for or against Maximus based on a thorough examination of Christian tradition demonstrating how what Maximus says about male and female does or does not fit.

This book will attempt such an examination, tracing the evolution of "anti-sexual" philosophy, originating among the early Greeks and culminating with Maximus the Confessor, and contrasting that philosophy against the more "pro-sexual" view evident in Holy Scripture and in the doctrine and discipline of the early Church.[2] This examination will demonstrate that Christians in general, not just the Orthodox, have in fact inherited two traditions that are fundamentally inconsistent on male and female: a speculative "Greek" tradition minimizing the significance of sexual distinction on the assumption that male and female is all about the body and only for the sake of procreation and therefore has no part in the "image of God" as well as no place "in Christ," per Gal 3:28; and a dogmatic "Hebrew" tradition that abominates the blurring of male and female and obliges Christians to practice this difference daily in dress and demeanor, understanding the "image of God" as a matter of relation, according to which the man is the "head" of the woman as the Father is the "head" of the Son, per 1 Cor 11:3.

Today more than ever, the words *sex*, *sexual*, *sexuality*, and *gender* mean different things to different people. In this book, I will speak mostly of *male and female* to avoid misunderstandings and to focus on the fundamental issue, which is the different ways this binary was understood by early Christians. The word *sex* will still be used as needed, both in its original Latin sense meaning male or female and in its common modern sense meaning carnal relations. However, the characterization of the two traditions as either *pro-sexual* or *anti-sexual* will be based, not on how

---

2. Except where otherwise indicated, all mentions of "the Church" will refer to the Church of the first ten centuries as defined by the bishops of the Seven Ecumenical Councils held between 325 and 787.

the traditions viewed carnal relations, but on their different views of the nature and purpose of the differentiation of human beings as male and female. In a sense, I will be asking each tradition two questions: (1) Is the distinction of male and female an essential aspect of human nature such that a human being must always be either male or female? (2) Is the purpose of the distinction of human beings as male and female solely for the sake of procreation? To these questions, the pro-sexual "Hebrew" tradition will answer yes and no, while the anti-sexual "Greek" tradition will answer no and yes.

The anti-sexual "Greek" tradition on male and female owes its lasting establishment within Christianity to Origen of Alexandria. Others before him preached the descent of the soul into the body and prophesied an end to male and female in the soul's ascent from the body, despising marriage, associating sex not with union but with division, and blaming it for the cycle of sin and death, but these Christians were condemned as heretics by the early Church. Some of Origen's speculations in this direction were also condemned, and yet they survived in modified forms denying the preexistence of souls and affirming a bodily resurrection, but still greatly stressing the discontinuity of the soul's embodied existence before, during, and after this life. Today, Origen's basic vision can be seen to have been already largely vindicated in the seventh century by Maximus the Confessor's great synthesis of Christian and Neoplatonist philosophy. But it is only in the twentieth century, with the revival of interest in Neoplatonism, in the Greek Fathers, in Maximus in particular as well as in his major Origenian influencers, namely Gregory of Nyssa and Evagrius Ponticus, that Origen's reputation has begun to be rehabilitated. And it is only in the past half-century that Origen may be said to be at last taking his revenge upon the Church that condemned him, through the present popularity of anthropological theories based on the eschatological vision of Origen as expressed by Maximus.[3]

This Maximized but still essentially Orgienist anthropological theory now directly threatens much of traditional Christianity's understanding

---

3. Beliefs attributed to or inspired by Origen were the subject of ten anathemas issued by the emperor Justinian in 543 and fifteen anathemas issued by the Fifth Ecumenical Council (II Constantinople) in 553. Some modern scholars believe the council stopped short of condemning Origen himself, doubting the texts that have come down to us, but the council was widely understood afterwards to have done so, as attested by the Definition of Faith of the Sixth Ecumenical Council (III Constantinople) in 681, by Canon 1 of the Quinisext Council in 692, and by the Decree and the Letter to the Emperor and Empress of the Seventh Ecumenical Council (II Nicaea) in 787.

of not just male and female but virtually all personal relationships. Consider, for a moment, the thinking of just two living Orthodox theologians, John Zizioulas and John Manoussakis.

If the non-Orthodox of today have heard of any modern Orthodox theologian, they have probably heard of John Zizioulas, metropolitan bishop of the titular see of ancient Pergamon. Claiming Maximus the Confessor as his chief patristic authority, Zizioulas has put forth a philosophy of personhood and otherness based on freedom from nature, denying the relevance of nature to communion so as to allow persons in communion absolute freedom of being: "This means that a person is not subject to norms and stereotypes; a person cannot be classified in any way; a person's uniqueness is absolute."[4] Zizioulas's enthusiasm for the freedom of uniqueness leaves him with little good to say about nature as a basis for categorization and discrimination. He is especially hard on our sexual nature and sounds most like Maximus when speaking of it. Sex is a "mechanism of death."[5] Marriage and childbearing are said "only to supply matter for death."[6] Human fatherhood is about "division" and "individuality," both bad, whereas divine fatherhood is "relational and totally inconceivable in human terms, which are conditioned by individualism." Divine fatherhood "has nothing in common with human fatherhood; no analogy between the two is possible."[7]

Such thinking in the late twentieth century—stressing the radical discontinuity of this life and the next, and, on that basis, denying the significance of personal differences in this life—has set the stage for an even more radical rethinking of Orthodox belief and practice in this century by John Panteleimon Manoussakis, professor of philosophy at the (Jesuit) College of the Holy Cross in Worcester, Massachusetts. Citing Zizioulas on the eschaton, Manoussakis writes, "Nothing undermines our freedom more than a predetermined and given nature, our fixed facticity." He therefore asserts an "anarchic principle of Christian eschatology" that focuses on our end (*telos*) instead of our beginning (*archē*), to argue against "narcissistic nostalgia" and "patristic Talmudism," understanding eschatology as "in essence a 'liberation' theology (freeing us from the

---

4. Zizioulas, *Communion and Otherness*, 9.
5. Zizioulas, *Communion and Otherness*, 59.
6. Zizioulas, *Being as Communion*, 47.
7. Zizioulas, *Communion and Otherness*, 122–23.

moralistic and sociological constellations of this world)."[8] Among the "moralistic and sociological constellations" from which Manoussakis says we need freeing is the Orthodox Church's heterosexual conception of marriage, which supposedly grounds marriage in the selfish, egotistical desire for procreation. He argues that marriage is not truly a Christian sacrament because it does not "effect" the Church but is rather dissolved by the Church.[9] He calls it a "sacrament of sin," borrowing the label from Hans Urs von Balthasar, who used it critically to characterize Maximus the Confessor's view of marriage.[10] Citing Maximus in support of the "problematic connection of marriage with the fallen nature," Manoussakis faults the Church for failing to "dissociate marriage from sexuality and sexuality from procreation" and concludes, "The ensuing condemnation of any sexual expression that does not lead to procreation as sinful remains ungrounded."[11]

It is certainly true that the Orthodox Church and Christianity in general have *associated* marriage with sexuality and sexuality with procreation, but it is the anti-sexual "Greek" tradition within Christianity that has done this most, to the point of declaring that the absence of marriage in heaven means also the absence of male and female. The pro-sexual "Hebrew" tradition within Christianity, including Orthodox Christianity, has seen other purposes for marriage as well as greater meaning in male and female. That tradition does *dissociate* marriage, sexuality, and procreation to some degree, enabling us to put each into its proper perspective, and thus it is to that tradition that traditional Christians appeal to defend marriage, while Manoussakis appeals, rather ironically, to the anti-sexual Greek tradition—the tradition responsible for the fault he finds—to question the Church's approval of heterosexuality and condemnation of homosexuality.

Some Orthodox scholars have argued that the thinking of Zizioulas and Manoussakis relies too much on modern Western philosophical methods and concepts (especially Idealism and Personalism) and reads too much of twentieth-century European personalism into Maximus and other early Church Fathers.[12] But, as this book will show, the anti-sexual

8. Manoussakis, "The Anarchic Principle of Christian Eschatology," 30, 44.
9. Manoussakis, "Marriage and Sexuality in the Light of the Eschaton," 2–4.
10. Balthasar, *Cosmic Liturgy*, 199.
11. Manoussakis, "Marriage and Sexuality in the Light of the Eschaton," 11.
12. See, for example, Loudovikos, "Person Instead of Grace and Dictated Otherness," 684–99; and Turcescu, "Person Versus Individual," 527–39.

tradition of Origen, Gregory of Nyssa, Evagrius Ponticus, and especially Maximus does in fact provide patristic precedent for radically revisioning human nature in ways that disregard prominent features normally considered natural, like the distinction of male and female. This is a problem traditional Christians must face if they are to successfully resist the innovative anthropologies supporting anti-traditional beliefs, practices, and policies.

Much has been written in the past half-century against the traditional Christian understanding of male and female. Taking a literary-critical approach to Scripture, supplemented with ethnographic and archeological research, feminists have offered revisionist readings of the Bible amplifying the "female voice" supposedly hidden in biblical texts; emphasizing the strength, power, and status of women in the Bible; and re-imaging God on the basis of Judean pillar figurines, feminine metaphors in Scripture, and the cult of the "Queen of Heaven" mentioned in Jeremiah 7 and 44. More recently, "third wave" feminists have taken an even more radical, postmodern, poststructural, multicultural, and multigenderal approach to Scripture consistent with New Historicism, which assumes that truth cannot be known and that claims of truth are essentially assertions of self aimed at establishing dominance over others, which makes demonstrating attempts at domination the aim of scholarship. Thus, in her critique of what others say about the book of Hosea, Yvonne Sherwood warns the reader, "I shall be attacking commentaries on Hos 1.2 not because they are erroneous, but because they are dominant, and legitimate dominance with untenable claims to 'objectivity.'"[13]

This book will not take that approach or deal much with the scholarship of those who do, for three main reasons. First, contrary to the epistemological assumptions of New Historicism, I am writing as a traditional Orthodox Christian, believing that truth can be known to some degree, that men and women are not so different that they cannot share the same knowledge of truth, that scholarship is appropriately a search for truth, that scholars are obliged to be honest in their claims of truth, that the utility of language is not limited to selfish assertion but also includes truthful description, that language itself is inherently traditional

---

13. Sherwood admits that her own commentary is not "ideology-free" but says that it is nevertheless of value because "it brings different ideological interests into play and relativizes the dominant (apparently natural) descriptions of Hosea 1.2 by introducing an alternative, more marginal perspective." See Sherwood, *The Prostitute and the Prophet*, 38–39.

*Introduction*

and loses its utility when alienated from its tradition, that a text only means something within a tradition, and that therefore the meaning of Holy Scripture must be found in Holy Tradition.[14]

Second, the feminist prejudice against patriarchy creates problems in biblical interpretation that exist only for feminists of biblical religions. What must be done, they ask, about the "texts of terror" and other passages suggesting an unwelcome difference between men and women? Their answer: Passages read simply and accepted without qualm by Christians for two millennia must be "problematized" and then "depatriarchalized," if only because they suggest what feminists refuse to accept.[15] Some feminists have done their depatriarchalizing modestly and decently, proposing alternative readings worth considering by any Christian, but others have attempted much more ambitious projects of little relevance to traditional Christianity. In explaining the title of her 1999 book *Jesus: Miriam's Child, Sophia's Prophet*, Elisabeth Schüssler Fiorenza writes:

> By naming Jesus as the child of Miriam and the prophet of Divine Sophia, I seek to create a "women"-defined feminist theoretical space that makes it possible to dislodge christological discourses from their malestream frame of reference.[16]

Traditional Christians—meaning those who still uphold the authority of tradition in matters of faith and discipline, who therefore refer respectfully to Scripture, saints, synods, creeds, and customs of the early Church for guidance, and who therefore also assume order in nature, shared human nature, and the providential goodness of some degree of economical subjection of persons to persons—can only understand Fiorenza to be talking about another religion, one whose adherents read the same Bible but very strangely, as do Mormons and Muslims, who will also not be consulted here for their opinions on early Christianity.

Third, inasmuch as the subject of this thesis is early Christian thinking about the nature and purpose of the distinction of male and female, the main sources of which were Greek philosophy and Hebrew Scripture, discussion will concentrate on what Greek philosophers, the Old Testament, and early Christians said about male and female. This means that many issues that have attracted much scholarly attention in recent decades—for example, how the Greeks in their golden age viewed

---

14. For the Orthodox approach to Scripture, see Breck, *Scripture in Tradition*.
15. See, for example, Trible, "Depatriarchalizing in Biblical Interpretation," 30–48.
16. Fiorenza, *Jesus*, 1.

homosexuality, what life was really like for the Israelites beyond what is said in the Old Testament, which of the three civilizations in view was most or least oppressive of women, and whether Origen was justly or unjustly condemned by the Church—lie beyond our scope. I am not writing a social history of the ancient Greeks, Hebrews, or Christians, neither am I writing a general indictment of influence of Hellenism on Christianity or of Origen, Maximus the Confessor, or anyone else; I am writing merely to prove the existence of a particular problem within traditional Christianity and to propose a possible solution to the problem consistent with traditional Christian faith.

My methods of examination will be primarily literary and secondarily historical, relying heavily on literary analysis of primary sources in translation, with reference to Greek, Latin, and Hebrew texts as needed, supplemented when helpful with historical information mainly from secondary sources, and with limited use of source criticism, applied mainly to the later books of the Hebrew Bible that seem to show Greek influence. Since the significance of the problem is not merely literary or historical but also, for today's traditional Christians, moral and theological as well as directly relevant to current social, political, and religious issues, my methods of putting forth the alternative understanding in the last chapter will take a more philosophical and theological approach, including some exegesis of Holy Scripture, consistent with Christian tradition, and some philosophizing on the various bases of personal relationships, with discrete definitions of current terms and some new terms to provide greater clarity to our understanding.

The book consists of six chapters. Chapter 1 will provide a review of literature on Greek, Hebrew, and early Christian views of the nature and purpose of male and female, as well as literature attempting variously to explain the difference of male and female on the basis of the Christian Trinity. Chapter 2 will then review the evolution of Greek philosophical speculation on male and female from the pre-Socratics, through Plato and Aristotle, to the Neoplatonists Plotinus and Porphyry. Chapter 3 will then examine key portions of the Old Testament as the main source of "Hebrew" thinking on male and female among early Christians, marking the putative influence of Hellenism in the later books and in some early Jewish extra-biblical works, examining Philo of Alexandria's Platonizing allegorizations of the Old Testament relevant to male and female, and concluding with a brief look at Rabbinic literature demonstrating a clear contrast between Rabbinic thinking and contemporary Greek and Christian thinking on male and female.

Chapter 4 will then trace the appearance of recognizably Greek ideas about male and female in Christian literature of the first through the seventh centuries, with a look first at New Testament passages seen as supporting the Greek view, then at Encratite and Gnostic thinking, and then at the parade of leading patristics authorities of the allegorizing Philonian/Origenian/Alexandrian tradition, concentrating on Origen, Gregory of Nyssa, and Maximus the Confessor, with briefer consideration of Origen's influence on Evagrius Ponticus, Ambrose of Milan, Augustine of Hippo, and others. Chapter 5 will then demonstrate the difficulty of reconciling the Greek view of male and female with Christian tradition by marking the many ways early Christians insisted on the distinction of male and female, citing Hebrew Scripture as their authority for doing so. This chapter will look at key passages of the New Testament and how they were understood by Church Fathers and at the general practice of the early Church in blessing marriage and maintaining a gender order based on Mosaic law and apostolic tradition.

Chapter 6 will then address the problem of reconciliation by challenging the key Greek assumption that the distinction of male and female is all about the body, exists solely for the sake of sexual reproduction, and therefore has no part in the image and likeness of God. The challenge will consist in demonstrating a way in which sexual distinction can be said to resemble personal distinction within the Trinity based on different ways of relating, according to both biblical and patristic authorities, developing more fully an explanation proposed by me in *St. Vladimir's Theological Quarterly* in 2010.[17] This explanation will not tell us what will become of male and female in the next life, but it will eliminate the necessity of "shaking off" male and female, provide a much firmer theological basis for traditional gender identities and roles, and support a more positive regard for marriage, conjugal relations, procreation, and family life than one commonly finds among Church Fathers of the Alexandrian tradition.

Throughout the book, the words *pagan* and *Greek* will be used as the word *Hellēn* was used by early Christians and ancient *Hellēnes* themselves—to mean someone who identified with ancient pagan philosophy and culture and was therefore not a Christian. The word *Hebrew* will be used as a general term for the perspective conveyed to early Christians

---

17. Mitchell, "The Problem with Hierarchy," 189–217.

through the Old Testament, some extra-biblical Jewish literature, and the written and unwritten traditions of the apostolic Church consistent with Jewish scripture and custom. Traditional authorship of the books of the New Testament will be assumed, just as it was by early Christians. Except where noted, quotations from the Old and New Testaments will come from the King James Version for three reasons: (1) because more recent translations, including the New Revised Standard Version, often obscure the gendered thinking of biblical writers to encourage genderless thinking among modern readers;[18] (2) because the KJV's New Testament, based as it is on the *Textus Receptus*, is closer to the New Testament most widely used by both the ancient Church and the Orthodox Church today; and (3) because I value the utility of distinctive language in making the communication of Holy Scripture more recognizable, memorable, and reverential.

Finally, whenever comparing two complex phenomena, the finite human mind tends toward simplistically binary thinking. This is true for both writers and readers: Writers will naturally stress differences when making a case for difference and sometimes neglect important similarities and qualifications; readers will naturally focus on the writer's argument for difference and sometimes miss obvious similarities or assume unwarranted simplicity on the part of the writer. As the writer in this case, I can only hope that I have not missed any necessary qualifications and that the reader will not think I am making more of the differences of Greek and Hebrew and of male and female than I intend.

To avoid the latter, at least at the outset, it might help to consider, very briefly, a third example of thinking about male and female: Chinese philosophy is based on the concept of *yinyang*, according to which the world is governed by two conceptually opposite yet mutually dependent and dialogic forces, the balance of which is the basis of harmony and goodness. In their earliest usages, the characters of *yin* and *yang* represented merely darkness and light, respectively. Other associations came later. *Yin* came to represent night, moon, water, rest, passivity, softness, earth, and femininity; *yang* came to represent day, sun, fire, movement,

---

18. See, for example, 1 Cor 11:3, where the KJV says "the head of the woman is the man," and the NRSV says "the husband is the head of his wife"; 1 Cor 13:11, where the KJV says "when I became a man [*anēr*], I put away childish things," and the NRSV says "when I became an adult"; and Jas 1:7–8, where the Greek uses *anthrōpos* and *anēr* in parallel verses, which the NRSV rewrites as one verse that speaks only of "the doubter," thus avoiding the KJV's use of "man" for both Greek words.

activity, hardness, heaven, and masculinity. *Yin* and *yang* were personified in myth as the gods Nüwa and Fuxi, twin sister and brother seen as the progenitors of the human race. Nüwa and Fuxi were often depicted with human heads, arms, and serpentine bodies intertwined to symbolize their cooperation in bringing order to both heaven and earth. Chinese philosophers later theorized that all illness and disorder are caused by an imbalance of *yin* and *yang*. Flooding, for example, was seen as an excess of *yin*; its remedy was to close the *yin* and open the *yang*: Women were to stay indoors while men stayed outdoors, avoiding sexual intercourse, in which *yin* conquered *yang*. Drought was an excess of *yang* and required the opposite response: Men indoors, women outdoors, and frequent copulation to make women happy and release more *yin*.[19]

For whatever reasons, neither the Greeks nor the Hebrews made so much of male and female. Other oppositions mattered more to them. Greek philosophy, particularly Platonism and Pythagoreanism, based everything on the ontological oppositions of one and many, mind and matter, soul and body, and intelligible and sensible, positing a fall of souls into bodies followed by the soul's escape from the body and reunion with its impersonal source, and relegating the distinction of male and female to the body as a strictly material difference for the purpose of material reproduction, otherwise relevant only in that the physical inferiority and child-bearing responsibility of women required some accommodation in social roles. In contrast, Hebrew Scripture tells the story of the dialogical relationship of Creator and creation, God and man, Jehovah and the house of Israel, with very little to say about the oppositions that mattered most to the Greeks and much more to say about the necessity of sexual distinction and traditional sex roles based on the creation of the man and the woman in the image of God, their commandment to "be fruitful and multiply," their subsequent fall, and their divinely intended and assisted multiplication thereafter.

Early Christians combined these two ways of thinking but not always easily or evenly. Many Christians followed the allegorizing tradition of Alexandria, adopting the Greek scheme of souls descending and ascending; assuming the significance of the philosophers' favorite oppositions; stressing the dissimilarity of bodies before, during, and after this life; and implying if not declaring the complete disappearance of male and female "in Christ." Many other Christians, including but not limited

---

19. Wang, *Yinyang*, 95–96.

to those typically identified with the more literal Antiochene tradition of biblical exegesis, continued to insist on distinction according male and female on the basis of Holy Scripture and apostolic tradition, analogizing the dialogical relationship of male and female to Christ and the Church as well as to the Father and the Son, reacting against the idea that men and women would no longer be men and women in the resurrection, and effectively suppressing the plain statement of that idea among sainted Church Fathers, St. Maximus the Confessor's *Ambiguum* 41 being the sole exception.

Now, however, Origen is again popular and Maximus's *Ambiguum* 41 is again being read, often quite literally, posing a much greater challenge to traditional Christianity than it did in the Church's early centuries on account of our present world's hostility to traditional sex roles and gender identities. Whatever one's preferences, fuller examination and development of the pro-sexual thinking of the early Church will enable today's Christians to better weigh the two traditions against each other and thus to better decide what in each tradition—the Greek or the Hebrew—Christians today should keep or lay aside, for only when a tradition is fully understood are we safe to discard it.

# 1

# The Known and the Not Known

IN *AMBIGUUM* 41, MAXIMUS the Confessor writes that man was meant to heal five divisions by first "completely shaking off from nature . . . the property of male and female, which in no way was linked to the original principle of the divine plan concerning human generation," so that "instead of men and women" we will be shown "properly and truly to be simply human beings, thoroughly formed according to Him, bearing His image intact and completely unadulterated, touched in no way by any marks of corruption."[1]

Where did Maximus get this idea that the difference of male and female is an adulteration, a "mark of corruption" that Christ does away with?

His immediate source is Gregory of Nyssa, who speaks not quite so bluntly but in the same direction, as will be shown. But where did Gregory get the idea? The Scriptural basis is Gal 3:28: "There is neither Jew nor Greek, there is neither bond nor free, there is neither male nor female, for ye are all one in Christ Jesus." There are also the words of Christ to the Sadducees that "in the resurrection they neither marry, nor are given in marriage, but are as the angels of God in heaven" (Matt 22:30; cf. Mark 12:25; Luke 20:34–36). But quite a few early Church Fathers understood these verses very differently, with many assuming if not insisting that in the resurrection men and women will still be men and women. Among those regarded as saints by the ancient Church, only Maximus dares to declare that they will not. Why did he think that? And why is he the only sainted Father to plainly say so?

---

1. Maximus, *Amb.* 41, in *On Difficulties*, 2:105–7, 115.

The answer to the first question is hardly a mystery. For some time, the standard view has been that Christianity profoundly reformed the sexual culture of the Greco-Roman world but was also profoundly influenced by trends in Greek philosophy stretching back several centuries before Christ. Derrick Sherwin Bailey notes at the beginning of his 1959 book *The Man-Woman Relation in Christian Thought* that though much had been written about Christian marriage, very little had been written about the development of Christianity's regard for relations between the sexes in general.[2] He then gives a brief summary of the historical background identifying three factors presumed to have influenced early Christian sexuality: the high regard of Jews for marriage and childbearing, the rampant sexual immorality of ancient Greeks and Romans, and the anti-sexual reaction to that immorality among Greek and Roman philosophers. Bailey saw evidence of the first factor in Paul's practical approach to sexual ethics and high regard for the marital bond, but he lamented that Paul's insight into the union of man and woman had a "negligible influence" on the early Church, which was instead "profoundly affected by the ascendency of Hellenistic dualism over Hebraic naturalism."[3]

Subsequent scholarship has generally supported Bailey's judgment. Paul Veyne has argued that a fundamental shift in sexual and marital ethics occurred in the Roman empire in the early Christian era "independent of all Christian influence."[4] Eric Fuchs's *Sexual Desire and Love* contrasts the negative "Stoic" Christian view of sexuality against the more positive biblical view based mainly on the New Testament, strangely ignoring the influence of Platonism. Peter Brown's influential *The Body and Society* contrasts pagan and Christian views of sexuality while also noting the influence of Platonism and Stoicism on the Alexandrians Clement and Origen as well as the influence of Origen on Ambrose of Milan, Gregory of Nyssa, and the Desert Fathers. Michel Foucault credits Veyne and Brown with major contributions to his thinking on ancient Greek sexuality and demonstrates both continuities and discontinuities between Greek and Christian sexual ethics in the second volume of his *History of Sexuality*, even while following Kenneth Dover in stressing a major discontinuity in attitudes toward homosexuality. Daniel Garrison contrasts the "high sexual culture" of the Greeks and the "low sexual culture" of "virulently

---

2. See Bailey, *The Man-Woman Relation in Christian Thought*, vi.
3. Bailey, *The Man-Woman Relation in Christian Thought*, 100.
4. Veyne, "La famille et l'amour sous le Haut-Empire romain," 35.

anerotic" Christianity, blaming the latter on Christianity's "Hebraic traits" but also on "antierotic feelings in the Greek world that took hold during the Classical period."[5] Bruce Thornton concentrates on the latter to counter the popular myth of "sunlit pagan Greeks indiscriminately and uninhibitedly delighting in the sexual body," faulting "fashionable scholars" for paying too much attention to pornographic pottery and not enough to the Greeks' "relentless negative characterizations of sexuality."[6] Marilyn Skinner acknowledges a dramatic shift in sexual mores in the Christian era, attributing it to both Christianity and the growth of "pre-Christian attitudes extending all the way back to sixth-century BCE Pythagoreanism."[7] William Loader also notes the influence of Pythagoreanism as well as Platonism and Stoicism on both first-century Christians and Philo of Alexandria.[8]

Some scholars have challenged this standard view. Kathy Gaca's *The Making of Fornication* takes aim at Foucault's claim of continuity, alleging "no connection whatsoever between ancient Greek sexual morality in any form, popular or philosophical," and the Apostle Paul's "cardinal dictate" against fornication (*porneia*).[9] She also alleges "no transparent connection" between Paul and Rabbinical Judaism on sexuality, repeatedly implying (but not demonstrating) that differences between the Septuagint and the Hebrew Bible account for differences between Christian and Jewish sexuality.[10] More recently, and more convincingly, Kyle Harper has argued that the Roman empire "was not careening toward a repressive

---

5. Garrison, *Sexual Culture in Ancient Greece*, viii–ix, 246–47.

6. Thornton, *Eros*, 213, xii–xiii.

7. Skinner, *Sexuality in Greek and Roman Culture*, 283.

8. Loader, *The New Testament on Sexuality*; Loader, *Philo, Josephus, and the Testaments on Sexuality*.

9. Gaca, *The Making of Fornication*, 13–14. Gaca argues that Paul equated "sexual fornication" with "religious fornication," i.e., apostasy, concluding that he considered even marital relations by non-Christians as fornication. See Gaca, *The Making of Fornication*, 151–52. For a more sensible explanation of *porneia* as it appears in the Septuagint and early Christian literature, see Harper, "*Porneia*," 363–83.

10. Gaca, *The Making of Fornication*, 8, 14, 18, 207, and 121–22. Gaca's writing is highly polemical and prone to overstatement. She says that Philo "urges" the execution of adulterers, when he merely relates the biblical penalty; she suggests, on the basis of 1 Cor 5:5, that Paul might have meant to incite the Corinthians to murder the man who bedded his father's wife; she also judges Paul's condemnation of the man "at odds" with Christ's "unqualified principle" of "unconditional forgiveness"—as if God's forgiveness is not conditioned on a sinner's repentance. See Gaca, *The Making of Fornication*, 209, 140, 142.

future" of "stern conjugal morality" under the influence of either Greek philosophy or Christianity until the early fifth century, when Christian emperors began cracking down on the use of slaves (men, women, and children) as prostitutes.[11] Harper contrasts the pagan *laissez-faire* regard for sex, which assumed the body must be obeyed, against Christian belief in free will and consequent efforts to regulate sexual behavior. He supports this by contrasting ancient pagan novels, in which lovers fend off threats and temptations to remain true to each other and finally marry, against Christian hagiographies, in which women and sometimes men resist marriage, defilement, and torture to remain true to God and die as martyrs.

Scholars have also challenged the standard view of what early Christians learned from Greek philosophers from a different angle, taking issue with Anders Nygren's classic contrast between the Christian conception of *apapē* as a "downward," "self-giving" love and the Platonic conception of *erōs* as a strictly "upward," "appetitive" love.[12] John Rist detects hints of another form of *erōs* in Plato, one that "overflows" downward from the lover to the beloved, which Proclus developed many centuries later, possibly under Christian influence.[13] More recently, Kevin Corrigan makes a broader case on the same and other grounds against the common opinion that the philosophers undervalued the love and pleasure of personal relationships. Corrigan's complaint is not against the Christian critique of Nygren but against the postmodern critiques of Richard Rorty, Martha Nussbaum, and others who see Greek philosophy as espousing "essentialism, universalism, abstract idealism, and intellectualism over the much more obvious desires and needs of individuals."[14] Corrigan argues that the problems and principles of divine and human love laid out by Plato and Aristotle were synthesized by Plotinus, perfected by Proclus, and Christianized by Pseudo-Dionysius.

This book will also challenge the standard view but from a different angle, arguing that although the philosophers' disdain for male and female did contribute significantly to the cult of virginity, growth of monasticism, and anti-sexual philosophical speculations of early Christians, the early Church nevertheless preserved, encouraged, and, indeed, insisted upon the more positive view of male and female inherited from the Jews,

---

11. Harper, *From Shame to Sin*, 2–3.
12. Nygren, *Agape and Eros*, 30–34.
13. See Rist, *Eros and Psyche*, 213.
14. Corrigan, *Love, Friendship, Beauty, and the Good*, 114.

condemning the tendency of the more Greek-minded to deny the difference, although without fully reconciling the discordant themes within Christian tradition—and this explains both why Maximus thought as he did and why he was the only sainted Father to plainly say so.

## Enduring Debates

The case naturally begins with the Greeks, whose regard for male and female has been the subject of bitter debates in the past half-century. Until the twentieth century, Europeans typically likened the ancient Greek gynaeceum to the Turkish harem and credited Christianity with raising women out of "oriental seclusion." Then scholarly consensus shifted toward the view that the status of women in ancient Greece approximated that of women in modern Europe, such that Moses Hadas could write in 1936 that "the attitude toward women among the Athenians was much the same as among ourselves."[15] This new consensus was then challenged later in the same century by Sarah Pomeroy and others, prompting the polarization of scholarship between feminists such as Eva Keuls pressing an indictment of the Greeks as extraordinarily sexist, misogynistic, and oppressive of women, and Hellenists such as Mary Lefkowitz stressing the opposite characteristics in defense of a more critical version of the early twentieth-century consensus.[16] In the same decades, the works of Dover and Foucault generated claims that homosexuality was normal in ancient Greece, that shame attached only to the person penetrated, and that whether one preferred a male or female partner was merely a matter of taste, like a preference for chicken.[17] Such claims have since been refuted by many critics, but Foucault's analytical approach to sex, sexuality, and gender, pitting "essentialism" against "constructivism" and seeing all "constructions" as attempts at domination, still deeply divides scholars.[18]

---

15. Hadas, "Observations on Athenian Women," 100.

16. Marilyn Katz names Keuls and Lefkowitz as representing the poles of opinion in her overview entitled "Ideology and 'The Status of Women' in Ancient Greece," 80. See also Keuls, *The Reign of the Phallus*; Lefkowitz, *Women in Greek Myth*; and Pomeroy, *Goddesses, Whores, Wives, and Slaves*.

17. The analogy of sexual preferences to dietary preferences appears in Halperin, "The Social Body and the Sexual Body," 135-36.

18. Ruth Mazo Karras surveys criticism of both Dover and Foucault in "Active/Passive, Acts/Passions," 1250-65. See also Cohen, "Law, Society and Homosexuality in Classical Athens," 151-66; Hubbard, "Popular Perceptions of Elite Homosexuality

Both of these debates are beyond our scope, however, because the chosen approach is not Foucault's and because we are not comparing Greek, Hebrew, and Christian stances on the status of women or the ethics of homosexuality, but rather tracing the influence of Greek philosophy and Hebrew scripture on Christian thinking about the nature and purpose of male and female.

On the subject of Greek influence, the debates are much older but still very much alive. It is now generally agreed, since Antoine Guillaumont's publication of the unexpurgated *Kephalaia Gnostika* of Evagrius Ponticus in 1962, that many ancient attacks on Origen were really attacks on Origenism as elaborated by the likes of Evagrius. But even Origen's advocates disagree as to Origen's responsibility for Origenism. Mark Edwards has vigorously defended Origen against virtually all charges of heresy, past and present, as well as against Origen's dependence on pagan sources, denying that Origen can be called a "Platonist" without serious qualification and holding that Origen himself was first and last a "Biblical philosopher" and orthodox Christian, at least by the standards of his day.[19] In contrast, Ilaria Ramelli has declared Origen a Christian Platonist, not to condemn him as a heretic but to commend him as the mastermind behind the Christianization of Hellenism.[20] Ramelli's case is a contradiction of Origen's ancient pagan and Christian critics, both of whom considered "Christian Platonist" a contradiction in terms. In making her case, she belabors the very similarities and associations Edwards belittles, arguing, for example, for one Ammonius, teacher of both Origen and Plotinus, and for one Origen, not a Christian Origen and a Neoplatonist Origen as in Eusebius; Edwards argues for two of each, putting as much distance as possible between Origen and Platonism.[21]

Origen is still generally believed to have taught the preexistence of souls and a fall of souls into bodies, but whereas some scholars like Benjamin Blosser have stressed the Platonist basis of such thinking, others

---

in Classical Athens," 48–78; Davidson, "Dover, Foucault and Greek Homosexuality," 3–51.

19. See, for example, Edwards, *Origen against Plato*; Edwards, *Catholicity and Heresy in the Early Church*; Edwards, "Origen's Platonism," 20–28; Edwards, "Origen in Paradise," 163–85.

20. See Ramelli, "Origen, Patristic Philosophy, and Christian Platonism," 217–63.

21. See Eusebius, *Ecc. Hist.* 6.19.4; Ramelli, "Origen, Patristic Philosophy, and Christian Platonism," 239–45, and "Origen the Christian Middle/Neoplatonist," 98–130; also Edwards, *Catholicity and Heresy in the Early Church*, 64–65, "One Origen or Two?" 81–103, and Edwards, "Ammonius, Teacher of Origen," 169–81.

like Mark Scott have stressed the Scriptural basis of the same.[22] Scholars also disagree on how to reconcile Origen's fall of souls into bodies with his scattered comments on Gen 1–3. Caroline Bammel, elaborating on the thought of Marguerite Harl, suggests that a "double fall," rather than a "double creation," might be the easiest way to "systematize" Origen's reading of Genesis—a fall of the soul into a body per Gen 2 and a fall of the ensouled body into a grosser body per Gen 3.[23] Peter Martens, however, sees no need to systematize Origen's understanding of Gen 1–3, considering how freely and often Origen uses Scripture, including Gen 1–3, to support his basic scheme of descent from the intelligible realm into to the sensible realm.[24] Edwards argues that there is no need for a "double fall" because Origen's "double creation" was logical rather than chronological, allowing for, at most, an "instantaneous pre-existence in the hand of God before embodiment."[25] Panayiotis Tzamalikos also denies that Origen taught a fall of souls into bodies, systematizing Origen's thinking by distinguishing between the creation of *logoi* in Christ and the subsequent creation of embodied souls based on the *logoi*.[26] Without attempting to settle the issue of how Origen understood Gen 1–3, this book will follow the standard view of the Platonist basis of Origen's scheme of the descent and ascent of sexless souls and argue in favor of indirect influence through Philo of Alexandria and Valentinian Christians also of Alexandria, as proposed by Gilles Quispel and others.[27]

Although the influence of Plato on Origen is still hotly debated, the influence of Origen on the Cappadocians—Basil of Caesarea and Gregory of Nazianzus but especially Gregory of Nyssa and Evagrius Ponticus—has been much less controversial. Gregory of Nyssa is generally considered to be the most Platonist and Origenist of sainted Church Fathers, while Evagrius is now seen as the source of the Origenist doctrines condemned

22. Blosser, *Become Like the Angels*; Scott, *Journey Back to God*. Others who have argued that Origen taught the preexistence of souls include Crouzel, *Origen*; Daniélou, *Origen*; Butterworth, *Origen On First Principles*; and Faye, *Origen and His Work*.

23. Bammel, "Adam in Origen," 62–141. Also Harl, "La préexistence des âmes," 244–46.

24. Martens, "Embodiment, Heresy and the Hellenization of Christianity," 594–620; Martens, "Origen's Doctrine of Pre-Existence," 516–49; Martens, "Response to Edwards," 186–200.

25. Edwards, *Origen against Plato*, 160.

26. Tzamalikos, *Origen*.

27. Quispel, "Origen and the Valentinian Gnosis," 29–42; Boersma, "Nuptial Reading," 227–58; Brown, *The Body and Society*, 171–74; Crouzel, *Origen*, 121–26.

by the Fifth Ecumenical Council (II Constantinople) in 553. Mark Hart and John Behr have tried to modernize Gregory's comments on marriage by arguing that in praising virginity Gregory is slyly justifying marriage and defending human sexuality as angelic when governed by reason, but Warren Smith and Hans Boersma have effectively refuted this notion.[28] Kevin Corrigan and Ilaria Ramelli have argued convincingly for a closer connection between Gregory of Nyssa and Evagrius Ponticus than between Evagrius and Gregory of Nazianzus and Basil of Caesearea.[29] Gabriel Bunge and Augustine Casiday have doubted Evagrius's authorship of the Syriac *Kephalaia Gnostika* known as S2, arguing for the originality of the more orthodox Syriac version known as S1, but many more scholars, including Corrigan, Ramelli, Brian Daley, Rubén Peretó Rivas, and Elizabeth Clark, have accepted Guillaumont's conclusion that S1 is a sanitized version of S2 and that Evagrius's authorship of S2 explains his condemnation by the Sixth Ecumenical Council (III Constantinople) in 681, the Quinisext Council in 692, and the Seventh Ecumenical Council (II Nicaea) in 787.[30]

## Maximian Scholarship

The influence of both Gregory and Evagrius on Maximus the Confessor is well established, as is Maximus's debt to Gregory on the matter of male and female. Scholars have, however, disagreed on what Maximus means when he writes that male and female must be "completely shaken off." Hans Urs von Balthasar took a dim view of Maximus's regard for male and female, writing that the narrowness of Maximus's understanding of male and female ties the difference too closely to sin to allow its continued existence, "not in the realm of personal relations, first of all, but not

---

28. Hart, "Reconciliation of Body and Soul," 450–78; Hart, "Gregory of Nyssa's Ironic Praise of the Celibate Life," 1–19; Behr, "The Rational Animal," 219–47; Behr, "Marriage and Asceticism," 24–50; Smith, "The Body of Paradise and the Body of the Resurrection," 207–28; and Boersma, *Embodiment and Virtue in Gregory of Nyssa*.

29. Corrigan, *Evagrius and Gregory*; Ramelli, "Evagrius and Gregory," 117–37.

30. Casiday, *Reconstructing the Theology of Evagrius Ponticus*; Corrigan, *Evagrius and Gregory*; Ramelli, *Evagrius's Kephalaia Gnostika*; Daley, "Evagrius and Cappadocian Orthodoxy"; Rivas, "The Two Versions of Evagrius Ponticus' *Kephalaia gnostika*," 485–92; Clark, *The Origenist Controversy*. For the condemnations of Evagrius, along with Origen and Didymus the Blind, see the Definition of Faith of the Sixth Ecumenical Council, Canon 1 of the Quinisext Council, and the Decree and the Letter to the Emperor and Empress of the Seventh Ecumenical Council.

even in the bodily realm." He goes on to say that "metaphysics, at this point, must systematically take on a monastic character! It is therefore no accident that in Maximus' great syntheses, no exalted place is reserved for Mary as the New Eve, the Bride of Christ."[31]

Lars Thunberg reaches a rather different conclusion in which "an overcoming of differences" between the sexes "does not imply an elimination of them as such, but their proper use," merely noting without explanation that von Balthasar "does not explicitly arrive at our conclusion."[32] Thunberg bases his own conclusion on a survey of Maximus's philosophical predecessors: Philo of Alexandria, Clement of Alexandria, Evagrius Ponticus, Gregory of Nazianzus, and Gregory of Nyssa, whom Thunberg says account for two main aspects of Maximus's view of male and female: the Greek association of male and female with anger and concupiscence and the belief that sex is an inessential difference added to human nature in expectation of the Fall solely for the sake of procreation. To these, according to Thunberg, Maximus adds three features: his "dialectic of pleasure and pain" perpetuated by sexual intercourse; his concept of mediation, whereby sexual distinction represents the mean between divine intention and eternal achievement; and his scheme by which the five fundamental "divisions" in creation are overcome in Christ. Thunberg adds it all together to conclude that Maximus understands salvation in Christ to mean the revelation of common human nature in both sexes and an end to the selfish desire for carnal relations in men and women.[33]

Throughout his discussion of sex, Thunberg seems not only eager to defend Maximus against the charge of Encratism, but also sensitive to the complaint that Maximus sees man's destiny as utterly androgynous. He avoids quoting Maximus's own words on the subject and does not acknowledge the vehemence of Maximus's treatment of male and female compared to his treatment of four other divisions: paradise and the inhabited world, heaven and earth, the intelligible and the sensible, created and uncreated. These four are all said by Maximus to be "united" by Christ, but male and female are said to be "removed," "driven out," and "completely shaken off from nature," so that people can be united as "simply human beings" "instead of men and women."[34]

---

31. Balthasar, *Cosmic Liturgy*, 204.
32. Thunberg, *Microcosm and Mediator*, 380–81.
33. Thunberg, *Microcosm and Mediator*, 373–81.
34. Maximus, *Amb.* 41, in *On Difficulties*, 2:103–15.

Most scholars have followed Thunberg in denying the absolute elimination of sexual distinction and downplaying Maximus's animus against male and female. Andrew Louth touches only briefly on Maximus's division of male and female, differing from Thunberg only in following Polycarp Sherwood in explicitly attributing to Maximus the double creation of Gregory of Nyssa, whereby sexual distinction is added to humanity after its creation in the image of God.[35] Paul Blowers has more to say than Louth and follows Thunberg, but stresses Maximus's negative regard for sexuality, saying that Maximus's view of male and female is "largely that of the ascetical tradition from which he came," which associates sexuality with the selfish struggle to "sustain pleasure and escape pain."[36] Even so, Blowers credits Maximus with "upholding sexual distinction in paradise" and merely questions in passing von Balthasar's contrary opinion.[37] Adam Cooper goes further in quoting Maximus's own words, but he also denies the absolute abolition of sexual distinction and speaks euphemistically of the "reconciliation or union between male and female"—words very unlike Maximus's own—which Cooper says is merely "a matter of recognizing the single human nature common to all, male and female, and of practicing the dispassionate relating to one another such recognition entails." He then quotes Maximus saying that he who is "perfect in love . . . knows no difference . . . between male and female . . . [and] regards all people equally, and is disposed equally toward all."[38] Neither Cooper nor Blowers nor Thunberg nor Louth draw out the implications of such words for non-carnal, strictly social relations between the sexes, traditionally entailing for Christians the headship of the man, the subjection of the woman, and the obligation of all to live according to one's strictly binary biological sex.

Doru Costache does draw out the implications somewhat. Granting Maximus's sometimes "chastising" and "strident" phraseology on the subject of sex, Costache assures us that Maximus "never envisaged a schematized, literally asexual, disembodied human nature";[39] instead, he envisaged merely virtuous living in a "state above gender, yet without

---

35. See Louth, *Maximus the Confessor*, 72–74; Thunberg, *Microcosm and Mediator*, 151–53.

36. Blowers, *Maximus the Confessor*, 219.

37. Blowers, *Maximus the Confessor*, 220–21.

38. Maximus, *Centuries on Love*, 2.30, quoted in Cooper, *The Body in St. Maximus the Confessor*, 222.

39. Costache, "Living Above Gender," 261–62.

eliminating the gender division."⁴⁰ To Costache, "living above gender" means that there are two ways toward the same goal, marriage and celibacy, which are represented by Moses and Elijah in Maximus's allegorical interpretation of the transfiguration of Christ on Mount Tabor.⁴¹ But it also means living without the "complications, prejudices, and discriminations entailed in the division into female and male."⁴² Costache has much more to say about the legitimacy of married life than about living without "complications, prejudices, and discriminations" and indeed only signals the direction of his thinking about the latter in brief mentions of the "oppression of gender," the "liberation of humankind from the rule of gender," and the "liberation of humankind from the tyranny of gender categories."⁴³

More recently, Sotiris Mitralexis has returned the discourse back to the conclusion of von Balthasar, carefully parsing Maximus's *Ambiguum* 41 and concluding that for Maximus the difference of male and female is "not even part of humanity's logos of nature, of God's prelapsarian (or rather a-lapsarian) will and intention for humankind—quite contrary to Genesis."⁴⁴ Similarly, Dionysios Skliris sums up Maximus's "rather peculiar view on genders and sexuality" as denying that they "belong to the *logos* of human nature"; this, he says, entails even a "rejection of heteronormativity," which "paves the way for an *apophaticism of gender and of the unchartered human body*."⁴⁵ Karolina Kochańczyk-Bonińska, however, concludes that we cannot say with certainty where Maximus's philosophizing leaves male and female, given the "tremendous ambiguity" and many "inconsistencies" in Maximus's thought.⁴⁶

---

40. Costache, "Mapping Reality," 384.

41. Costache, "Living Above Gender," 287–88; Costache, "Gender, Marriage, and Holiness," 356–60.

42. Costache, "Mapping Reality," 287.

43. Costache, "Mapping Reality," 287.

44. Mitralexis, "Rethinking the Problem of Sexual Difference in *Ambiguum* 41," 384.

45. Skliris, "The Ontology of Mode," 57. Emphasis original.

46. Kochańczyk-Bonińska, "The Philosophical Basis of Maximus' Concept of Sexes," 229–38, esp. 237.

## Unexamined Tensions

Missing from the aforementioned scholarship is a thorough survey of early Christian teaching and practice enabling judgments as to how Maximus's view of male and female is or is not consistent with authoritative Church tradition, meaning, tradition that actually governed behavior within the early Church. Most Maximian scholars seem to have presumed Christian belief in the essentiality of sexual distinction, which would explain their assurances that its persistence is at least allowed if not required by Maximus's reasoning, but they have avoided broadening the scope of their inquiry beyond Maximus's philosophical predecessors and left the question of consistency with Christian tradition largely unexamined. Feminist scholars have also presumed early Christian beliefs and practices at odds with Maximus's view, but have attributed such beliefs and practices to historically contingent cultural influences (Greek and Jewish) and treated Maximus's view as more authentically Christian. Thus, Valerie Karras writes of a "generally unexamined tension" in Christian tradition between the Orthodox Church's "theoretically egalitarian theological anthropology and a history of earlier liturgical practices based in inegalitarian historical social and cultural norms."[47]

The related tension between marriage and monasticism has received considerable attention, much of it emphasizing the "anerotic" aspect of early Christianity (as already noted), and much of it also focusing on Augustine. Two Orthodox scholars, David Ford and Josiah Trenham, have attempted to correct this apparent Western bias using John Chrysostom to represent ancient Eastern and modern Orthodox Christianity. Ford, writing with the aim of absolving Chrysostom of the charge of misogyny made by Peter Brown and others, first contrasts the views of several ancient Western Christians (Tertullian, Ambrose, Jerome, and Augustine) against the views of other ancient Christians (Clement of Alexandria, Methodius of Olympus, Cyril of Jerusalem, Lactantius, Gregory of Nazianzus, and Paulinus of Nola) to argue that the former but not the latter viewed sexual relations even among the lawfully wedded as inherently shameful and even sinful if not for the purpose of procreation.[48] Ford then presents Chrysostom's views on men and women in the best possible light, arguing along the way that whereas Augustine's view of marriage

---

47. See Karras, "Orthodox Theologies of Women and Ordained Ministry," 147.

48. Ford, *Women and Men in the Early Church*, 12–37. For Ford's criticisms of Brown, see 28n73, 45n27, 50n48, 78, 100n44, and 241n3.

hardened in the course of his campaign against Pelagianism, Chrysostom's view of marriage softened after his ordination to the priesthood.

Trenham writes from the same perspective and makes many of the same arguments, although with greater emphasis on the consistency of belief about sexuality among early Church Fathers.[49] He differs with Ford on the question of change in Chrysostom's beliefs about marriage and virginity, but he agrees with Ford on Chrysostom's and Augustine's differences, citing the latter's emphasis on procreation as contributing to clerical celibacy in the West.[50] The implication in both Ford and Trenham is that modern Western scholars have attended too much to Augustine, and too much to his personal struggle against the flesh and his anti-Pelagian polemics, while attending too little to evidence of a more positive view of male and female in the works of Eastern Fathers, and thus allowed the literature of Western Christian asceticism to unduly darken their view of early Christian life.

But where does Maximus the Confessor fit in this supposedly more positive view of human sexuality? Neither Ford nor Trenham have much to say about Maximus. Trenham cites him several times in support of other Fathers without dealing directly with Maximus's harder sayings. Ford mentions Maximus only once and only to criticize another Orthodox scholar, Philip Sherrard, for writing in his brief book *Christianity and Eros*, "Where the eastern tradition [of sexuality] is concerned, two authors—Gregory of Nyssa and Maximos the Confessor—may be taken as representative."[51] Sherrard sees the Eastern tradition as very similar to the Western tradition and hardly more positive, inasmuch as "generic sin is always at work within the sexual relationship [according to Maximus] and this can be extirpated only on condition that sexuality itself is extirpated."[52] Ford objects, declaring that Nyssa "is simply not in the mainstream of Eastern Christianity" on sexuality on account of his Origenist tendencies; he does not, however, include Maximus in his objection and never mentions him again.[53]

---

49. Trenham sets up his argument for the consistency of Chrysostom's views by first summarizing the views of Tertullian, Clement of Alexandria, Origen, Methodius of Olympus, Athanasius the Great, and Ephrem the Syrian. See Trenham, *Marriage and Virginity*, 20–82.

50. Trenham, *Marriage and Virginity*, 170–75, 213–15.

51. Sherrard, *Christianity and Eros*, 5.

52. Sherrard, *Christianity and Eros*, 8.

53. Ford, *Women and Men in the Early Church*, 28n73.

Past scholarship has therefore left us with a gap: Scholars who have offered explanations of Maximus's view of male and female have not attempted explanations of early Christian sexuality, while scholars who have offered explanations of early Christian sexuality have not attempted explanations of Maximus's view of male and female and do not agree among themselves as to what constitutes the Christian tradition such that we can easily see where Maximus fits in it.

This book will attempt to fill the gap by contrasting the two main sources of presumed influence—the generally negative Greek philosophical view of male and female fundamental to the Alexandrian tradition of Philo, Origen, Gregory of Nyssa, and Maximus the Confessor, and the much more positive and personal Hebrew view of the man and the woman evident in Hebrew Scripture, Christian Scripture, the canons of the early Church, and the teaching of other early Church Fathers. Explication of the Hebrew inheritance of the early Church will rely primarily upon literary analysis of the Old Testament, supported by ancient and modern commentary as needed, and also on the extensive work of William Loader on sexuality as it appears in late Jewish and early Christian literature.[54] Loader shares the general perspective of this book in viewing the Hebrew tradition as more sex-positive than the Greek philosophical tradition. This view is also supported by recent scholarship on Rabbinic literature of the early Christian era, including that of Daniel Boyarin and Naomi Koltun-Fromm, which clearly contrasts early Rabbinic sexuality against ancient Greek and Christian sexuality.[55] Rabbinic scholars, in fact, disagree as to whether Rabbinic Judaism even has a truly ascetic tradition. Steven Fraade and Eliezer Diamond say that it does; Paul Heger argues against them that it does not.[56]

## Image as Relation

Our contrast of the "Greek" Christian and "Hebrew" Christian traditions will reveal a key difference between them on the image of God. Greek Christians will view the image ontologically, as the human soul—rational,

54. Loader, *Making Sense of Sex*; Loader, *The New Testament on Sexuality*; Loader, *Philo, Josephus, and the Testaments on Sexuality*; Loader, *The Dead Sea Scrolls on Sexuality*.

55. Boyarin, *Carnal Israel*; Koltun-Fromm, *Hermeneutics of Holiness*.

56. Fraade, "Ascetical Aspects of Ancient Judaism"; Diamond, *Holy Men and Hunger Artists*; Paul Heger, *Women in the Bible, Qumran and Early Rabbinic Literature*.

immortal, free-willing, and sexless. Hebrew Christians will view the image dialogically, as man in relation to others, including the sexes in relation to each other, based on the Pauline analogies of the man and the woman to Christ and the Church (Eph 5) and to God and Christ (1 Cor 11).

In the past century, Christians have taken a renewed interest in the Trinity as the model of human relations, with mixed results. Karl Barth, combining the Thomist definition of God as "pure act" with the Johannine saying that "God is love" (1 John 4:8), defined the Persons of the Trinity as "modes of being" but always "being-in-relation," saying of God, "He is Himself the One who loves eternally, the One who is eternally loved, and eternal love; and in this trinity He is the original and source of every I and Thou."[57] This then is the basis of the "covenantal" relationships of God and Israel and of Christ and the Church, as well as of the "structural and functional" relationship of the man and the woman, in which the man is by nature the "inspirer, leader and initiator" and the woman is by nature his assistant, supporter, and subordinate.[58]

Hans Urs von Balthasar is less modalist in his Trinitarianism but also relates the man and the woman to the Trinity, describing God the Father as "(supra-)masculine," the Holy Spirit as "(supra-)feminine," and the Son as "(supra-)feminine" toward the Father and "(supra-)masculine" toward the Holy Spirit.[59] Clergy and laity are also understood to take masculine and feminine roles, the clergy as spiritual seed-bearers and the laity as spiritual seed-receivers. Like Barth, von Balthasar stresses the sexes' difference and complementarity, terming the woman the "counterimage" of the man and describing the sexes as "two distinct but inseparable realities, each fulfilling the other."[60] But whereas Barth, the Reformed theologian, stresses the masculine over the feminine, von Balthasar, the Catholic theologian, stresses the femininity of the "Marian Church" and even "the precedence of the feminine aspect of the Church over the masculine," identifying the Church with Mary as the mother of all Christians and their co-redemptrix.[61]

Pope John Paul II also stresses the Marian character of the Church, basing his view of human sexuality on the "nuptial" relationship of Christ

---

57. Barth, *CD* III/2:218. See also Deddo, *Karl Barth's Theology of Relations*.

58. Barth, *CD* III/4:117, 170, 181.

59. Balthasar, *Theo-Drama*, 4:80. See also Schindler, *Heart of the World, Center of the Church*, 240–58.

60. Balthasar, *Theo-Drama*, 2:365–66.

61. Balthasar, "Women Priests?" 168.

and the Church. He explicitly relates the "image of God" to man's creation as male and female, declaring man "essentially the image of an inscrutable divine communion of Persons."[62] He does not, however, distinguish different roles for human persons in communion except the maternal vocation of women, about which he has much to say in his *Theology of the Body*, though very little to say about the paternal vocation of men. John Paul is much more egalitarian than Barth and von Balthasar, stressing the "reciprocal submission" of husband and wife by which the "communion of persons" is realized, denigrating the obedience required of wives by the Apostle Paul in Eph 5:23 as "a concept rooted in the mentality of his time," and strangely avoiding all reference to 1 Cor 11.[63]

Jürgen Moltmann has shown even less respect for traditional Christian theology and ethics, advancing his doctrine of a "social Trinity" based on the concept of *perichōrēsis*, a word sometimes used by early Church Fathers to describe the union of Christ's divine and human natures, the mutual indwelling of the Father and the Son per John 10:38, or the movement of angels about the throne of God like the dancing of the chorus in Greek theater, the usage closest to the word's origin.[64] Moltmann uses *perichōrēsis* to critique Christianity's traditional "monotheistic way of thinking," blamed for papism and authoritarianism, and to argue that the Church "is not the monarchy of a ruler that corresponds to the triune God; it is the community of men and women, without privileges and without subjugation."[65] Moltmann's "social Trinitarianism" has proved especially appealing to Christian feminists, helping them past the problem of patriarchy within the Godhead. Patricia Wilson-Kastner writes:

> Because feminism identifies interrelatedness and mutuality—equal, respectful and nurturing relationships—as the basis of the world as it really is and as it ought to be, we can find no better understanding and image of the divine than that of the perfect and open relationships of love.[66]

---

62. John Paul II, *Man and Woman He Created Them*, 163. See also Sutton, "The Complementarity and Symbolism of the Two Sexes," 418–33.

63. John Paul II, *Man and Woman He Created Them*, 472–78.

64. See Lampe, *A Patristic Greek Lexicon*, 1077–78; Harrison, "Perichoresis in the Greek Fathers," 53–65.

65. Moltmann, *The Trinity and the Kingdom of God*, 143, 198–201.

66. See, for example, Wilson-Kastner, *Faith, Feminism and the Christ*, 127.

# The Known and the Not Known

Moltmann's Social Trinitarianism has been criticized by Karen Kilby for putting too much of a contemporary human face on God, and by John Behr for misrepresenting the patristic use of *perichōrēsis*.[67] Nevertheless, Social Trinitarianism in some form—seeing the image of God in the "communion of persons" and thus basing human relations on divine relations (or vice versa) à la Barth, von Balthasar, John Paul, or Moltmann—has become, as Behr laments, "almost the consensus position."[68] It is now found even in a conservative Evangelical form advancing a hierarchical model of gender "complementarity" based on the "eternal submission of the Son to the Father."[69] This has prompted charges of heresy from feminist Evangelicals, who accuse conservative Evangelical "complementarians" of subordinationism.[70]

The age-old problem of reconciling Christ's "equality with God" (Phil 2:6) with his obedience to the Father (Phil 2:8) and acknowledgement that "the Father is greater than I" (John 14:28) is thus once again at issue. This time, however, some advocates of divine equality have gone so far as to deny the Father his causal character, identifying divinity with the perichoretic relationship of the Father, Son, and Holy Spirit rather than with the essence imparted by the Father to the Son and the Holy Spirit. Alan Torrance, for example, questions "the Cappadocian projection of causal notions into the internal life of God," which, he says, "has the effect of reducing the unity of the Godhead to the personal singularity of the Father."[71] Colin Gunton also objects to the Father as the "cause" of the Son and Holy Spirit, stressing the "mutual constitution" of the Trinity and saying that "the priority of the Father is not ontological but economic."[72]

## Person and Nature

Such developments pose serious problems for Orthodox Christians, who are firmly committed by dogma and doctrine to the equality of the Father, Son, and Holy Spirit; to the Father as the *archē* and *aitia* ("source" and

---

67. Kilby, "Perichoresis and Projection," 432–45; Behr, *The Nicene Faith: Part 2*, 425–26.

68. Behr, *The Mystery of Christ*, 176.

69. See, for example, Ware and Starke, *One God in Three Persons*.

70. See, for example, Giles, *The Trinity & Subordinationism*.

71. Torrance, *Persons in Communion*, 290–91.

72. Gunton, *The Promise of Trinitarian Theology*, 196–97.

"cause") of the Son and Holy Spirit; to the distinction of essence (*ousia*) and person (*hypostasis*) as they pertain to the Trinity; to the distinction of the *ousia* and the *energeia* of the Trinity; to hierarchy as a "sacred order" of angels and the Church; and to subordination as an economic necessity in the fallen world.

Even so, some Orthodox theologians have joined in the search for alternatives to traditional conceptions of God and man. Early in the twentieth century, following a romantic trend in Western spirituality, Sergei Bulgakov formulated a doctrine of the "Divine Sophia" as the "pre-eternal self-revelation of the Most Holy Trinity," the "fulfillment of which is the Mother of God," who is herself the "personal revelation of the Holy Spirit."[73] Bulgakov's "sophianism" was condemned by the Russian Orthodox Church, both in Moscow and in exile, in 1935, but the association of femininity with the Holy Spirit survived in the thinking of Paul Evdokimov, who posited an "ontic link" between the woman and the Holy Spirit and a "profound connection among the Holy Spirit, Sophia, the Virgin, and the feminine."[74] Such thinking was briefly popular in the late twentieth century but has since been overtaken in popularity among less traditional Orthodox by the more radical and more widely influential theology of John Zizioulas.[75]

The thrust of Zizioulas's Social Trinitarianism advances two paradoxical theses. On one hand, Zizioulas has defended the *monarchia* of God the Father based not only on the Father being the *monē archē* or sole source of the Son and Holy Spirit but also on the "a-symmetry" of relationships within the Trinity. There is, he says, "a kind of subordination of the Son to the Father," suggesting also a kind of subordination of the Holy Spirit to the Son on account of the Spirit's procession from both the Father and the Son.[76] Even more fundamentally, the Trinity is a "hierarchy," he says, because "otherness is, by definition, 'hierarchical' . . . since persons [*prosōpa*] are never self-existent or self-explicable, but in some sense 'caused' by some 'other.'"[77] This "Patro-centric" Trinitarianism

---

73. Bulgakov, *The Burning Bush*, 105–9.

74. Evdokimov, *Woman and the Salvation of the World*, 219–22.

75. For critical but not entirely dismissive comment on the association of femininity with the Holy Spirit, see Hopko, "God and Gender," 141–83, esp. 154–59; Ware, "Man, Woman and the Priesthood of Christ," 19–20.

76. Zizioulas, *Being as Communion*, 89; Zizioulas, *Communion and Otherness*, 192–200.

77. Zizioulas, *Communion and Otherness*, 131–34, 143–49.

supports Zizioulas's strongly monarchical ecclesiology, in which the hierarch constitutes the Eucharistic communion by causing others to be included (an ecclesiology conveniently supporting the novel claim of Zizioulas's own primate, the Patriarch of Constantinople, to being *primus sine paribus* among Orthodox primates).[78]

On the other hand, Zizioulas effectively denies any other order among persons by basing personhood on absolute freedom from nature. He writes that personhood "belongs to an entirely different category from nature—it belongs to the realm of freedom and is in no way a natural category, or a part of nature."[79] The freedom he means is not merely "freedom of will" but "freedom to be other in an absolute ontological sense," which means being accepted for who you are just as you are; it is "not freedom *from* the other but freedom *for* the other" and is thus "identical with love."[80] He writes:

> Person implies not simply the freedom to have different qualities, but mainly the freedom simply to be yourself. This means that a person is not subject to norms and stereotypes; a person cannot be classified in any way; a person's uniqueness is absolute.[81]

Again: "Personhood is not about qualities or capacities of any kind: biological, social or moral. Personhood is about hypostasis, that is, the claim to *uniqueness* in an absolute sense of the term, and this cannot be guaranteed by reference to sex or function or role, or even cultivated consciousness of the 'self,'" for all such things allow one to be classified and classification denies uniqueness.[82] The basis of communion is not likeness but uniqueness; it the loving acceptance of "authentic" otherness, permitting one exclusion only: "the exclusion of exclusion itself."[83] Zizioulas's enthusiasm for the freedom/love of uniqueness/otherness as the basis of being/communion leaves him with little good to say about nature. He calls it "unredeemable," saying it "not only precedes particular

---

78. See Lambriniadis, "First without Equals." Zizioulas is cited in footnote 7 as "Metropolitan John of Pergamon."

79. Zizioulas, *Communion and Otherness*, 277.

80. Zizioulas, *Communion and Otherness*, 9. Emphasis original.

81. Zizioulas, *Communion and Otherness*, 9.

82. Zizioulas, *Communion and Otherness*, 111. Emphasis original.

83. Zizioulas, *Communion and Otherness*, 7.

beings and dictates its laws to them, but also finally swallows them up through death."[84]

In Zizioulas's opposition of person to nature, Nikolaos Loudovikos has seen an analogy to grace and sin, but a more obvious analogy is to soul and body.[85] For Zizioulas, it is the "human person" who needs saving, not the human soul, and the salvation of the "human person" is achieved not by putting off the body (mortally or ascetically) but by denying human nature so as to make communion with other persons possible. This denial, however, is not self-denial, which is anti-personal as well as anti-other inasmuch as it deprives others of one's own otherness, which is essential for Zizioulas's conception of being as communion.[86] Instead, the denial that enables communion is the denial by others of the limitations that nature might impose on one's self. Zizioulas's claim of freedom for uniqueness is thus a claim *against* others, obliging them to disregard any aspect of one's nature that might inhibit communion by limiting one's freedom to be unique, thus securing for one's self, paradoxically, the right to refuse to be bound by nature but also the right to claim nature as an excuse for "authentic" otherness.

Zizioulas is not the first to recast the opposition of soul and body as an opposition of person and nature. Among the Orthodox, this also appears in Christos Yannaras, Vladimir Lossky, and Nikolai Berdyaev—and I will argue, Maximus the Confessor, who begins his work calling for the eradication of male and female with a line from Gregory of Nazianzus saying that in the Incarnation, "The natures are innovated, and God becomes man."[87] Maximus is the patristic authority on whom Zizioulas relies most, the saint Zizioulas lauds as "perhaps one of the greatest and most creative geniuses in history," the man Zizioulas credits with the "most developed and complete reconciliation between the Greek, Jewish and Christian concepts of truth."[88] Many scholars have questioned Zizioulas's use of patristic sources, including Maximus, but that is not at issue here and will

---

84. Zizioulas, *Communion and Otherness*, 63.

85. See Loudovikos, "Person Instead of Grace and Dictated Otherness," 684–99.

86. See also Reid, "Patristics and the Postmodern in the Theology of John Zizioulas," 308–16, esp. 313–14.

87. Maximus, *Amb.* 41, in *On Difficulties*, 2:103, quoting Gregory of Nazianzus, Oration 39, 13. For Zizioulas's intellectual roots, see Loudovikos, "Person Instead of Grace and Dictated Otherness," and Petra, "Personalist Though in Greece in the Twentieth Century," 1–48.

88. Zizioulas, *Being as Communion*, 52n46, and 92.

not be argued.[89] At issue here is Maximus's own denial of human nature as male and female, which is supported by a long-standing Christian tradition with Greek roots but is opposed by an equally long-standing Christian tradition with Hebrew roots. In the latter, it is possible to discern the basis of a more traditional version of Social Trinitarianism firmly rooted in Holy Scripture as understood by many early Church Fathers and posing far fewer challenges to Orthodox belief and practice than previous attempts to relate male and female to the Trinity. Chapters 2 through 5 will contrast the two Christian traditions to pose the problem facing traditional Christians; chapter 6 will offer a possible solution.

---

89. See, for example, Torrance, *Persons in Communion*, 288–95; Gunton, *The Promise of Trinitarian Theology*, 196–97; Loudovikos, "Person Instead of Grace and Dictated Otherness"; Turcescu, "Person versus Individual," 527–39.

# 2

# The Greek View of Male and Female

MENTION WAS MADE IN the introduction of the Chinese *yinyang* tradition, according to which the world is governed by two conceptually opposite yet mutually dependent and dialogic forces, the balance of which is the basis of harmony and goodness. Such thinking befitted the stable agrarian communities dotting China's great river valleys, but neither the Greeks nor the Hebrews lived in such a setting, and neither made quite so much of male and female. The ancient Hebrews were semi-nomadic, desert-dwelling hunters and herders, while the ancient Greeks were a warrior race that arose amid the chaos caused by the collapse of the Mycenaean and Hittite civilizations in the late Bronze Age, before 1100 BC. The Greek word *polis* (cf. *polemos* "war" and *polemizo* "to wage war") originally meant a citadel, beginning as a fortified camp about which a town formed.[1] Athenians habitually referred to the Acropolis as their *polis* and to Athens as their *astu* ("town").[2] From their fortified *polis*, armed *politai* ("citizens") dominated the town and the countryside, subjugating the local populace and warring against the *politai* of other *poleis*.

Centuries of struggle among themselves and against outsiders induced among the Greeks what the ancient Chinese would no doubt have considered an extreme excess of *yang*, the result being a hyper-masculinized civilization that modern historians have likened to Japan and that

---

1. See Toynbee, *Hellenism*, 38–41.
2. LSJ, 263, 1434.

some feminists have condemned as a "phallocracy."[3] Scholars disagree on the degree to which women were oppressed in ancient Greece, but there is no denying the impact of war on Greek culture. The Greeks themselves, in their earliest writings, bear witness to their war-scarred psyche. The *Iliad* is a tale of war and its ravages; the *Odyssey*, an epilogue about a warrior's travail of return and recovery. Homer's epics together with Hesiod's violent creation myths colored the imagination of later Greeks such as Heraclitus, the "weeping philosopher" of the fifth and sixth centuries before Christ, who declared war to be "the father of all things." This was true for many Greeks in a very personal way: Their mothers were trophies of war hauled home by their victorious fathers as wives, concubines, or slaves.

Greek sexual culture was deeply conflicted as a result of the violent beginnings of Greek civilization, which caused the Greeks to associate sex with violence in such a way that it engendered both an extraordinary permissiveness in male sexual behavior and a prudish disdain for sexual passion. On one hand, law and custom allowed Greek men to indulge their desire for sex with men, women, and children through sexual slavery, prostitution, and pederasty; on the other hand, a main theme of Greek literature was the disastrous effect of sexual passion on both the soul and the social order, and a main goal of Greek philosophy was to achieve self-mastery, self-sufficiency, immunity from the passions of soul and body, and ultimately union with the source of all good. Having unleashed the tiger of sexual desire by permissive custom, the Greeks were obliged to either tame the tiger through discipline or escape its grasp through transcendence. Their experience, outlook, and efforts would greatly influence early Christian thinking about sex for many centuries, especially in monastic settings. The first half of this chapter will document the Greeks' troubled regard for the difference, purpose, power, and pleasure of sex; the second half will examine the Greeks' philosophic response.

## Myth as History

The history of Greek sexuality begins with the familiar stories invented or collected by Homer and Hesiod in the seventh or eighth centuries before Christ. Hesiod's *Theogony* preserves for us as for the Greeks their fullest

---

3. For similarities to Japan, see Toynbee, *Hellenism*, 36; Garrison, *Sexual Culture in Ancient Greece*, 120–21, 140. For an extreme feminist view, see Keuls, *The Reign of the Phallus*.

account of creation in the form of a poetic genealogy of gods and goddesses. First came Chaos, says Hesiod, then "broad-breasted Earth" and then Tartarus and then Eros, "the most handsome among the immortal gods."[4] The first to come from Earth was "one equal to herself, starry Heaven, so that he should cover her all about."[5] Then, out of the union of Heaven (Ouranos) and Earth (Gaia) came a gang of unruly children called Titans, meaning "strivers" or "strainers," who were hated by their father and were therefore hid from him in Gaia's belly such that she was greatly discomfited and pled with them to relieve her of her cruel and ugly husband. The "crooked-schemer" Kronos, youngest of the Titans, rose to the task and ambushed Ouranos while he was copulating with Gaia, severing his father's genitals with a sickle and casting them into the sea. Drops of blood and semen sprinkled earth and ocean, from which spring other gods and goddesses, the greatest among them being Aphrodite, so named, says Hesiod, because she was "formed in foam (*aphros*)."[6] Kronos then begets Hestia, Demeter, Hera, and Hades by Rhea, daughter of Ouranos and Gaia, but swallows them all at birth. Fearing that he will swallow her next child, Rhea conspires with Gaia to trick him into swallowing a stone instead, which allows the child, Zeus, to be born free. Upon reaching maturity, Zeus overpowers Kronos, who then throws up the stone and Zeus's siblings. Zeus then frees the Titans and becomes king of the immortals, but only after a long struggle against the Titans, which ends with them imprisoned forever in Tartarus.

Hesiod's account shares several features with Near Eastern creation myths, including the overthrow of older gods by younger gods, a war between the forces of order and disorder, and the notion that the world began as a watery abyss of formless matter.[7] Feminist scholars have stressed an active role for Hesiod's Gaia, who gives birth to Ouranos as well as to the mountains and the sea on her own, "apart from delightful affection" (*ater philotētos ephimerou*).[8] Prudence Allen contrasts this with the strictly passive role Plato assigns Gaia as primordial matter in the *Timaeus* to claim that Hesiod gives evidence that the Greeks originally worshiped a great mother goddess like the Phrygian Cybele and only

---

4. Hesiod, *Th.* 120–22.
5. Hesiod, *Th.* 126–27.
6. Hesiod, *Th.* 197.
7. See Fontenrose, *Python*, 211–22; also West, *The East Face of Helicon*, 101–6.
8. Hesiod, *Th.* 132.

later came to identify femininity with passivity.[9] But even in Hesiod the feminine Gaia is preceded by the neuter Chaos, personified in Hesiod but also imagined by the Greeks as a deep, dark pool of formless matter in which many things are lost. Other Greek accounts of creation begin with Oceanus and Tethys, whom Homer names the father and mother of all the gods, without saying where they came from.[10] The first philosopher, Thales of Miletus, believed water to be the first principle, which his younger contemporary, Pherecydes of Syros, called *chaos*, and this was how the later Stoics Zeno and Carnutus read Hesiod.[11] Gaia's primacy in Greek thinking was therefore limited, as is also her activity in Hesiod. Gaia is devious, devising the plots to overthrow both Ouranos and Kronos, but both she and Rhea are powerless to resolve their conflicts with their husbands without the vigorous collaboration of a male.

The Greeks did worship a mother goddess, "bountiful Demeter," goddess of the harvest.[12] Demeter is the only goddess remembered for her motherly affection, which she demonstrates in attempting to rescue her maiden daughter Persephone from Hades. There was also Hestia, goddess of the hearth, who refused to marry and was therefore confined to the home by Zeus, but of Hestia very little can be said; she was a strictly household goddess. Homer never mentions Hestia and barely mentions Demeter (five times in the *Iliad* and just once the *Odyssey*, compared to Athena's ninety-eight mentions in the *Iliad* and ninety-three mentions in the *Odyssey*). Otherwise, the Olympian goddesses appear as products of a male imagination—contentious consorts (Hera), objects of desire (Aphrodite), virginal daughters who take after their fathers (Athena, Artemis), inspiring spirits (Muses), or disturbing passions (Fates, Furies).[13] As goddesses, they rarely behave with the modesty and submissiveness expected of Greek women, leading some moderns to remark on how unfeminine

9. Plato, *Tim.* 50c–51b. See Allen, *The Concept of Woman*, 13–14, 59–60.

10. Homer, *Il.* 14. In Hesiod, Heaven and Earth are the first father and mother of the gods, including Oceanus and Tethys as well as Kronos and Rhea. Hesiod, *Th.* 133–36.

11. On the Greek conception of Chaos, see Fontenrose, *Python*, 222–28.

12. Hesiod, *Th.* 912.

13. Garrison (*Sexual Culture in Ancient Greece*, 72) writes, "The goddesses of nature, sex, and fertility who were so plentiful in the Near East . . . are nowhere to be seen in Homer's world. Male gods are in control, and even though the goddesses have their place as divine consorts, quarrelsome spouses, spiteful enemies, or personal patrons, they are (with the exception of Athena) characteristically subordinated in a patriarchal system."

they are, but they often misbehave in stereotypically feminine ways.[14] Hera is contentious toward her husband Zeus and vindictive toward his children by other females. Aphrodite is frivolous, deceitful, and unfaithful. Demeter is vengeful and promiscuous. Hera, Athena, and Aphrodite vainly bare themselves before Paris to win the title of the fairest. The best-behaved goddesses are the manly virgins, Athena and Artemis, although among male gods there are no virgins—and also no happy marriages: Male gods are all extremely promiscuous and often violently so. With justice, Sarah Pomeroy writes that Greek myth is an "endless catalogue of rape."[15] No god stains his honor when forcing himself on a female of any species. No matter what the circumstances, the act of copulation seems only to confirm a god's divinity: That's what gods do.

## Men Imitating Myth

Mortal men often followed the gods' promiscuous example, although with more respect for the institution of marriage. Greek society was organized by household, and citizens were expected to marry and raise legitimate offspring to maintain the social order and ensure the survival of the *polis*.[16] Adultery (*moicheia*) was therefore severely punished and sometimes treated as worse than rape because it defiled not just the woman's body but her morals and affections and also called into question the legitimacy of her children.[17] But only citizens were protected by laws against adultery, leaving plenty of opportunity for Greek men to imitate

---

14. Nicole Loraux even declares that among the Greeks "the divine cannot be expressed in the feminine," except in feminine groups like the Muses, Fates, and Furies. See Loraux, "What Is a Goddess?" 15, 43. Also Eller, *The Myth of Matriarchal Prehistory*, 103–4.

15. Pomeroy, *Goddesses, Whores, Wives, and Slaves*, 12.

16. Claudine Leduc ("Marriage in Ancient Greece," 278) writes, "No law required a father or brother to marry off daughters over whom they exercised authority. But if they allowed daughters to grow into spinsters, they risked losing face in the eyes of the community and being judged stingy or impoverished."

17. An adulterer caught in the act could be killed, beaten, or imprisoned pending payment of a hefty fine, while an adulteress might have her head shaved and be forced to dress and even work as a prostitute. See Dover, "Classical Greek Attitudes to Sexual Behavior," 117–18; Herter, "The Sociology of Prostitution in Antiquity," 69–70. Lysias, *On the Murder of Eratosthenes*, 1.32–33, notes that death was permitted for the adulterer but not the rapist, and Aristophanes often treats adultery more seriously than rape. See Marre, "Aristophanes on Bawds in the Boardroom," 52–53.

the gods among a city's resident alien and slave populations. Slaves could be used sexually by their owners regardless of age or sex. Prostitution was legal, ubiquitous, a source of public revenue, an acceptable alternative to adultery, a sacrifice to the goddess Aphrodite, and a principal driver of the slave trade.[18] Some resident aliens also worked as prostitutes, either independently or for brothel owners. Above the common prostitute (*pornē*) was the *hetaira* (literally, "female companion," or, as Kyle Harper suggests, "lady friend"), whose beauty, cultured graces, and seductive skills attracted an elite clientele for either the occasional dalliance or a long-term relationship.[19] These were the courtesans and mistresses of the rich and famous, the *geisha* girls for their symposia, and sometimes the mothers of their children, as in the case of Pericles, who divorced his wife to live openly with the talented and intellectual hetaera Aspasia, who bore him a son, Pericles the Younger.[20] A cheaper alternative was the simple concubine, who might be a slave, a former hetaera, or a foreigner who could not by law marry a citizen.[21] A married man might partake of all of these opportunities, limited only by his wife's patience. Demosthenes has a client explain: "Mistresses we keep for the sake of pleasure, concubines for the daily care of our persons, but wives to bear us legitimate children and to be faithful guardians of our households."[22]

Greek men of course viewed marriage (*gamos*) with ambivalence, but not with the same ambivalence as men might today. The warlike Greeks saw wives as a dangerously softening influence that young men still in military service were wise to avoid. Marriages in ancient Greece were usually arranged by parents. Love figured much less in the matter, and the desires of men for sex, companionship, and even love could be satisfied in other ways.[23] The principal benefit of marriage to Greek men

18. Kyle Harper writes, "The demand for sex was a major impetus behind the circulation of human chattel in the Roman world." See Harper, *From Shame to Sin*, 196, and 45–50. Also Herter, "The Sociology of Prostitution in Antiquity," 61; Dover, "Classical Greek Attitudes to Sexual Behavior," 118–20; Thornton, *Eros*, 151–52.

19. Herter, "The Sociology of Prostitution in Antiquity," 91–106; Harper, *From Shame to Sin*, 47.

20. Plutarch, *Life of Pericles*; Garrison, *Sexual Culture in Ancient Greece*, 149–52.

21. Wives who had already fulfilled their obligation to bear legitimate children were sometimes inclined to tolerate concubinage because it spared them further risk of death in childbirth. See Rousselle, "Body Politics in Ancient Rome," 296–336.

22. Demosthenes, *Against Neaera*, 59, 122.

23. Juha Sihvola writes that although marriage was sometimes depicted more favorably, especially by women, "it is not misleading to say that it was often thought that

was legitimate offspring, necessary for the future prosperity of the family and the community. The word *gamos* might indeed be better translated as "mating" or "breeding," for the principal benefit of "marriage" today is more likely to be companionship, often without breeding.[24] For the benefit of breeding, Greek men faced a loss of personal freedom, the cost of maintaining a household, and the difficulty of living with a wife. Instead of viewing wives as both a blessing and a curse, Greek men were prone to viewing them more negatively as both a curse and a necessity. Women existed, in the Greek mind, for the purpose of procreation, but procreation for the ancients was itself a costly, painful, and dangerous endeavor. Thus Hesiod, after declaring that Zeus made women to be "an evil to mortal men," speaks not of a counterbalancing blessing brought by women but of a "second evil" decreed by Zeus that men who avoid marriage must die alone, with no one to care for them in their old age or remember them when they are gone.[25] Wives were, first and foremost, as Martine de Marre says, "a necessary biological entity but accompanied by a Pandora's box of liabilities."[26] The curse of Zeus was therefore unavoidable.

Slaves, prostitutes, mistresses, concubines, and wives did not complete the Greeks' list of permissible options as sexual partners, for at some point they adopted the peculiar custom of allowing even the sons of citizens to be abused sexually by adult male citizens. The accepted protocol assumed an active role on the part of the older male *erastēs* ("lover"), who plied his chosen *erōmenos* ("loved one") with gifts, guidance, and protection, in exchange for which the *erōmenos* allowed his *erastēs* sexual favors. Tradition traced the institution of Greek pederasty (from *paiderastēs*, "boy-lover") to the rape of Chrysippus by Laius, the mythical founder of Thebes, but Plato attributed the custom to the strict segregation of males from females for the purpose of military training.[27] The custom was therefore often blamed on the Dorians of Sparta and Crete, who were the most extreme in segregating the sexes and training

---

pleasure, passion, and even companionship should rather be sought in other types of sexual relationships." Sihvola, "Aristotle on Sex and Love," 205.

24. LSJ, 337, suggests a connection between the Greek *gamos*, the Latin *geminus* ("twin, double"), and the Sanskrit *jamis* ("brother, sister").

25. Hesiod, *Th.* 600–610.

26. Marre, "Aristophanes on Bawds in the Boardroom," 47.

27. Plato, *Leg.* 636b–c, 836c–840e. Many modern scholars agree. See Cohen, "Law, Society and Homosexuality in Classical Athens," 163–64; Evans-Pritchard, "Sexual Inversion among the Azande," 1428–35.

boys with men.[28] The Spartans were also said to have been the first to strip naked for athletic competitions, at the fifteenth Olympiad in 730.[29]

But what explains the embrace of pederasty, public male nudity, and homosexuality in general by other Greeks? Kenneth Dover resists blaming the Dorians, arguing that homosexuality first appears in literature in the sixth-century Ionian poets Sappho and Alcaeus, both of Lesbos, and that segregation of the sexes merely "fortified and sustained the acceptance and the practice" of homosexuality, which the Greeks considered "natural and normal"; he concludes that homosexuality satisfied "a need for personal relationships of an intensity not commonly found within marriage" or anywhere else in Greek society.[30] Bruce Thornton, on the other hand, credits Dorian militarism as a contributing factor but concludes that Greek homosexuality was "a result of the depraved human imagination and vulnerability to pleasure," which together tended to sexualize behavior beyond what had been traditionally allowed.[31]

The progress of this sexualization is not difficult to trace. The absence of obvious references to homosexuality in any form in Homer, Hesiod, Archilochus, and Tyrtaeus, whose works span the eighth and seventh centuries, testifies against both the prevalence and approval of homosexuality before the sixth century.[32] But already in the eighth century we find the Spartans competing in the nude and the first apparently homoerotic artefacts: a bronze figurine of two helmeted men with erect penises holding hands, and a storage jar found at Thera, a Dorian settlement, carved with these words: "Erpetidamus, son of a lover of boys."[33] Then in the seventh century the first male nudes appear in Greek monumental art—highly stylized statues of beardless men or boys (hence the modern name *kouros* meaning "youth" or "boy") modeled on Egyptian statues but with their genitals fully exposed, in contrast to contemporary female *korai*,

28. Strabo, *Geographica,* 10.4.20–21, describes the regimented life and pederastic recruitment of Cretan boys. For a discussion of various explanations of the origin of Greek pederasty, see Skinner, *Sexuality in Greek and Roman Culture,* 62–71.

29. Thucydides, *History of the Peloponnesian War,* 1.6.5.

30. Dover, "Classical Greek Attitudes to Sexual Behavior," 121–22; Dover, *Greek Homosexuality,* 194–203.

31. Thornton, *Eros,* 101–3, 194.

32. Archilochus (680–645 BC) is significant because he is quite explicit about heterosexuality; Tyrtaeus (mid- to late-seventh century) is significant because he was a Spartan writing for Spartans during their Second Messenian War. See Skinner, *Sexuality in Greek and Roman Culture,* 69; Dover, *Greek Homosexuality,* 195.

33. See Skinner, *Sexuality in Greek and Roman Culture,* 68.

which are all fully clothed.[34] We are so familiar with Greek art that we miss how truly unusual it was for men to appear and be depicted entirely naked in public. Only corpses appear naked in the *Iliad*, and when the shipwrecked Odysseus is washed up naked in the *Odyssey*, he does not shamelessly strut himself before Nausica and her maids, but covers himself with a leafy branch before asking them for help.[35] Yet the nakedness of athletes and *kouroi* is followed in the sixth century by the homoerotic poetry of Sappho and Alcaeus, carved pillars called *herms* used as boundary markers and displaying just the head and genitals of a god or man, and a plethora of pornographic pottery that moves from comically obscene and homoerotic toward more artful and more heterosexual depictions in the late sixth and early fifth centuries.[36] Garrison writes that pottery from 530 to 470 BC provides "the fullest record of erotic life in all Greek art; outside Japan, there is little to rival it for sheer bulk or variety."[37] Then in the fifth century, we find, in Dover's words, "the steady importation of homosexual themes" into myth and history: Aeschylus portrays Achilles and Patroclus as lovers in his lost work *Myrmidons*; Thucydides does the same for Harmodius and Aristogeiton, which his predecessor Herodotus did not do; Heracles's son Hyllus, nephew Iolaus, and rival Eurystheus are all re-cast as his *erōmenoi*; and Ganymede is said to have been raped by Zeus before being made Zeus's cupbearer.[38] Dover also speculates that Euripides may have invented the rape of Chrysippus by Laius, noting that though the myth of Laius is much older, "no trace of the rape of

---

34. Garrison, *Sexual Culture in Ancient Greece*, 177.

35. Homer, *Od.* 6.127–29.

36. Dover, *Greek Homosexuality*, 194–96. Garrison (*Sexual Culture in Ancient Greece*, 135–38) writes, "The old black-figure vases emphasized love scenes between males, but by the fourth quarter of the sixth century, heterosexual scenes came into their own." See also Skinner, *Sexuality in Greek and Roman Culture*, 80.

37. Garrison, *Sexual Culture in Ancient Greece*, 140. Erotic themes fall suddenly out of favor after 470, perhaps as a casualty of the social disruptions caused by the Persian wars, but also perhaps as a casualty of the changing fortunes of their Etruscan owners in central and southern Italy. Skinner (*Sexuality in Greek and Roman Culture*, 80) notes that the "overwhelming majority" of Greek earthen artifacts bearing erotic scenes come from Etruscan graves, cautioning against assuming Greeks shared the same interest in pornographic pottery as Etruscans on the grounds that much of it might have been made for export.

38. Thucydides, *History of the Peloponnesian War*, 6.54–59; Herodotus, *Histories*, 5.55; Dover, *Greek Homosexuality*, 199; Garrison, *Sexual Culture in Ancient Greece*, 95, 120; Thornton, *Eros*, 195. Plato blames the Cretans for inventing the rape of Ganymede, *Leg.* 1.636c.

Khrysippos can be identified with assurance before Euripides."[39] Also in the fifth century, the modesty of the fully clothed *korai* gives way to more revealing female statuary through the technique known as "wet drapery." Nude females then appear in private sculpture before becoming the norm in public art in the fourth century after the success of Praxiteles's Aphrodite of Cnidus in 364.[40] In the same century, the depiction of nude males becomes typically more boyish and feminine, especially for the gods Hermes, Apollo, and Dionysus.[41]

## Love and Lust

The specific claims and counterclaims about pederasty and homosexuality, mentioned in the previous chapter, are of less concern here than the general tendency of much modern scholarship to overlook the problems that unrestrained sexuality caused for individual Greeks and Greek society. The ancient Greeks did indeed often follow the gods' promiscuous example—but not without consequences, as the Greeks themselves were well aware. Their literature bears them record.

In Homer, the sexual incontinence of men is a foundational fault. The Trojan War is fought over a woman, Helen, who has been seduced by Paris, who is berated by his own brother, Hector, as "Paris, Disaster-Paris, superbly beautiful, woman-crazed seducer!"[42] The *Iliad* begins *in medias res* with bad behavior by both Agamemnon and Achilles in a quarrel over female captives, which must be resolved before the Trojans can be defeated.[43] Its sequel, the *Odyssey*, continues the story not as a tale of triumph in battle but as an accounting of the calamities wrought by war: Troy is sacked, its homes are broken up, and its women are hauled away as captives; Agamemnon brings home the Trojan princess Cassandra as his concubine, but both are murdered by his jealous wife Clytemnestra and her lover Aegisthus; Menelaus recovers Helen, but although she is penitent, happiness eludes them and she bears him no heir; Penelope

---

39. See Dover, *Greek Homosexuality*, 199–200. See also Thornton, *Eros*, 102.
40. Garrison, *Sexual Culture in Ancient Greece*, 129, 190–99, 206.
41. Garrison, *Sexual Culture in Ancient Greece*, 197, 207; Thornton, *Eros*, 106.
42. Homer, *Il.* 13.769.
43. When Agamemnon is forced by Apollo to give up the captive Chryseis, he takes the captive Briseis from Achilles as compensation; Achilles then refuses to fight the Trojans to teach Agamemnon a lesson. Homer, *Il.* book 1.

must keep 108 self-interested suitors at bay until her husband, Odysseus, returns; he must first fend off the temptations of the nymph Calypso, the sorceress Circe, and the head-strong princess Nausica, each of which would prevent him from returning home and deny him his rightful place as lord and king.[44] Odysseus would seem to pronounce the moral of both epics when he tells Nausica that "nothing is greater or better than this, when man and wife dwell in a home in one accord, a great grief to their foes and a joy to their friends; but they know it best themselves."[45] It is then that Nausica declares that Odysseus is neither evil nor insane.

But the same forces that bring a man and a woman together can pull them apart, so it should not surprise us that the Greeks regarded the goddess Aphrodite with ambivalence. For the high-minded, there was the Heavenly Aphrodite (*Aphroditē Ourania*), a personification of perfect love and beauty, but for everyone else there was the Vulgar Aphrodite (*Aphroditē Pandēmos*), "not the Goddess of Love, as we call her today," writes Thornton, "but the goddess of *sex*, the sheer amoral drive of all life to reproduce."[46] Indeed, what is "sex" to us was "*ta aphrodisia*" to the Greeks. The distinction between the two Aphrodites predates the philosophers' use of the distinction, as Xenophon acknowledges in noting the existence of "separate altars and temples for the two, and also rituals, those of the 'Vulgar' Aphrodite excelling in looseness, those of the 'Heavenly' in chastity."[47] Plato says Heavenly Aphrodite is the older.[48] The epithet *Ourania* does appear to predate the epithet *Pandemos*, but the original significance of *Ourania* is uncertain.[49] Pausanias says the cult of Heavenly Aphrodite was first established by the Assyrians and introduced to the Greeks by the Phoenicians.[50] Thornton sees the epithet *Ourania* as

---

44. Skinner, *Sexuality in Greek and Roman Culture*, 37. See also Felson and Slatkin, "Gender and Homeric epic," 91–114.

45. Homer, *Od.* 6.183–85.

46. Thornton, *Eros*, 50. Emphasis original. C. S. Lewis makes the same point about Venus vs. Eros in *The Four Loves*, 131–32.

47. Xenophon, *Smp.* 8.9.

48. Plato, *Smp.* 181a–d.

49. Pausanias, *Description of Greece*, 3.23, writes that the temple of Heavenly Aphrodite at Cythera was the most holy and most ancient of all temples of Aphrodite among the Greeks.

50. Pausanias, *Description of Greece*, 1.14.7.

an indication of Near Eastern influence on Aphrodite, noting that the fertility goddesses Inanna and Ishtar also had "astral connections."[51]

What is certain is that in her earliest appearances in Greek literature Aphrodite is anything but chaste. In Homer, she is often called "smile-loving Aphrodite," an indication of her flirtatiousness and possibly also a *double-entendre* playing on the similarity of *meidēma* ("smile") and *mēdea* ("genitals").[52] Hesiod plainly names her *philommēdea* "because she sprang from the genitals [*oti mēdeōn exephaanthē*]" of Ouranos.[53] Her chief power is the power of seduction. In the Iliad, she lends her magic breast-band to Hera so she can seduce Zeus to get the better of him.[54] In the *Odyssey*, Aphrodite commits adultery with Ares and is denounced by her husband, Hephaestus, as "dog-eyed" (shameless) and "beautiful but out of control."[55] In the Greek imagination, the irascible Ares and the lustful Aphrodite served as archetypes of male and female, displaying the stereotypical passions of anger and desire, but often the two passions were combined in Aphrodite. Of her many names, including *Kypris* on account of her birth in the surf of Cyprus, Sophocles says, "Kypris is not Kypris alone, but is called by many names. She is Death and undecaying life, she is the rage of madness."[56] She had a jealous, violent side and was sometimes shown armed and armored like Ares, being worshiped as Aphrodite *Areia* (Warlike) at Sparta, Aphrodite *Nikēphoros* (Bringer of Victory) at Argos, Aphrodite *Androphonos* (Manslayer) in Thessaly after the hetaera Laïs was murdered by jealous wives in her temple, and Aphrodite *Melainis* (Dark, Black) at Corinth, Mantineia, and Thespiae because, according to Pausanias, whereas beasts mate in the daytime, men do so at night.[57] Perhaps in jest, Pausanias names *Mēchanitis* (Deviser) as the goddess's most apt epithet because "many are the devices and most varied are the forms of speech invented by men because of Aphrodite

---

51. Thornton, *Eros*, 55.

52. Homer calls Aphrodite "golden" nine times, "fair" five times, and "smile-loving" (*philomeidēs*) six times (*Il.* 3.424, 4.10, 5.375, 14.211, 20.40; *Od.* 8.362).

53. Hesiod, *Th.* 200. Hesiod also mentions "smile-loving Aphrodite" (*philommeidēs Aphroditē*, *Th.* 989) and "Glauconome the smile-loving" (*Glaukonomē te philommeidēs*, *Th.* 255). In the *Iliad*, Aphrodite is the daughter of Zeus and Dione.

54. Homer, *Il.* 14.199.

55. Homer, *Od.* 8.319-20.

56. Sophocles, Fr. 855N. See Thornton, *Eros*, 49-50.

57. Pausanias, *Description of Greece*, 3.17.5, 8.31.3, 2.19.6; Athenaeus, *Deipnosophists*, 589A; Pausanias, *Description of Greece*, 8.6.5, cf. 2.2.4, 9.27.5.

and her works."[58] She was often attended by the goddess Peitho ("Persuasion"), as at Athens, where the cult of Aphrodite Pandemos was said to have been established either by the legendary Theseus or by the historical Solon, funded in the latter case by the brothel he ordered built.[59] Her cult was sometimes combined with that of Dionysus, as at Mantineia, and was often supported by the work of temple prostitutes, as at Corinth and Comana Pontica.[60]

But Aphrodite at least had a popular following, which cannot be said of Eros. Eros was recognized as a powerful force of life driving many human affairs, and here and there were images of Eros, often in temples of Aphrodite, but temples of Eros were exceedingly rare. Pausanias says Eros was worshiped at Thespiae and Parium on the Hellespont, but he never mentions a temple to the god there or anywhere else.[61] At Athens, he finds a trace of ambivalence toward Eros like that toward Aphrodite: an altar of Eros at the entrance to the Academy, where Plato taught a higher love of the good, and an altar of "Love Requited" (*Anterōtos*) inside the city conveying more of the sense in which the Greeks typically held Eros. According to Pausanias:

> [T]he Athenian Meles, spurning the love of Timagoras, a resident alien, bade him ascend to the highest point of the rock and cast himself down. Now Timagoras took no account of his life, and was ready to gratify the youth in any of his requests, so he went and cast himself down. When Meles saw that Timagoras was dead, he suffered such pangs of remorse that he threw himself from the same rock and so died. From this time the resident aliens worshiped as Anteros the avenging spirit of Timagoras.[62]

In the words of the fifth-century sophist Prodicus, "Desire doubled is love, love doubled is madness."[63] This association of *erōs* with *mania*

---

58. Pausanias, *Description of Greece*, 8.31.6.

59. Pausanias, *Description of Greece*, 1.22.3; Thornton, *Eros*, 56. Also Herter, "The Sociology of Prostitution in Antiquity," 61.

60. Pausanias, *Description of Greece*, 8.6.5; Strabo, *Geographica*, 8.6.20. See also Garrison, *Sexual Culture in Ancient Greece*, 110–11, 289; Herter, "The Sociology of Prostitution in Antiquity," 61. Strabo, *Geographica*, 12.3.36, also describes Comana Pontica as a "lesser Corinth" because of its abundance of temple prostitutes.

61. Pausanias, *Description of Greece*, 9.27.1. According to Pausanias, Eros was worshipped at Thespiae in the form of an "unwrought stone."

62. Pausanias, *Description of Greece*, 1.30.1.

63. Prodicus, Fr. 7.

*The Greek View of Male and Female* 35

seems to have grown over time. In Homer, *erōs* is neither personified nor strictly sexual nor especially troublesome. In Hesiod, Eros is an elemental force of nature, the fourth in order of existence (after Chaos, Earth, and Tartarus), and is characterized by Hesiod as the "limb-loosener [*lusimelēs*], who overpowers reason and resolve in the breasts of all gods and all men."[64] Loosening limbs and joints is how Homer speaks of death; Hesiod and later writers attribute the same effect to Eros.[65] In the early fifth century, the pre-Socratic philosopher Empedocles (c. 490–430) constructed a cosmogenic theory based on four elements (fire, water, earth, and air) and the effect on them of the forces of attraction and repulsion, calling attraction *philotēs* ("friendship," "love," "affection") and repulsion *neikos* ("quarrel," "strife"); he often personified *philotēs* as Aphrodite, but he never personified *philotēs* as Eros or used the word *erōs* to speak of *philotēs*.[66] The reputation of *erōs* was too negative for Empedocles's benign force of attraction. The Greeks associated *erōs* with *pathos*, just as we today associate love with passion, but whereas to us passion means merely intense interest, to the Greeks passion (*pathos*) meant suffering. *Erōs* was a "disease," a "destroyer," a "tyrant of gods and men," a "beast on all fours," a team of "maddened horses" threatening to wreck the chariot of the soul.[67] In later myth, Eros is the bastard of Ares by Aphrodite, a child born of lust and violence armed with a weapon of war greatly feared by the ancients because of its cowardly stealth and the excruciating pain it caused.[68] In the third-century *Argonautica* by Apollonius of Rhodes, Eros is the mischievous brat of Aphrodite who wreaks havoc in the heart of Medea. Garrison writes that Apollonius's depiction of Medea's madness constitutes a "*summa erotica*" of anti-erotic Greek poetry, "reaffirming the sinister nature of love's affection."[69] As Pausanias says, "Love [*erōs*] is

---

64. Hesiod, *Th.* 120–22. Eros is said by later writers to be the child of Night and Darkness (Acusilaus Fr. 1; Aristophanes, *Av*, 690–99), Heaven and Earth (Sappho, Fr. 198C), Iris and Zephyr (Alcaeus, Fr. 327C), and Ares and Aphrodite (Simonides, Fr. 575C.). See Thornton, *Eros*, 13.

65. E.g., Homer, *Il.* 13.412; Homer, *Od.* 18.212, 18.238, 14.69. See also Thornton, *Eros*, 26–27.

66. See Allen, *The Concept of Woman*, 31; Thornton, *Eros*, 125–26.

67. Euripides, *Hippolytus*, 765–66; Apollonius of Rhodes, 3.296–97; Euripides, Fr. 136N; Sappho, Fr. 130C; Callimachus, *Iambi*, Fr. 195T. See also Thornton, *Eros*, 38–40.

68. See Thornton, *Eros*, 28–29.

69. Garrison, *Sexual Culture in Ancient Greece*, 219. See also Thornton, *Eros*, 38–40.

wont to bring many calamities upon men."[70] Little wonder, then, that the god Eros was not often worshiped by the Greeks.

## Sex and the Single Philosopher

Greek philosophy almost begins with the pre-Socratic notion that the opposites hot and cold and wet and dry determine the nature of things, first proposed by Anaximander (c. 610–546) and then by Anaximenes (c. 585–28). Heraclitus (c. 535–475) added male and female to the list, speculating on the harmony produced by the combination of opposites.[71] The Pythagoreans later produced a table of opposites associating male with limit, odd, one, right, rest, straight, light, square, and good, and associating female with unlimited, even, left, many, motion, curved, dark, oblong, and bad.[72] A similar table of opposites appears in Chinese philosophy, but whereas the cooperative Chinese sought balance as the basis of harmony and goodness, the contentious Greeks thought less in terms of equal pairs of opposites than of dichotomies of domination: soul over body, mind over matter, cosmos over chaos, culture over nature, and male over female.[73] As Bruce Thornton explains, the feminine noun *physis*, "nature," comes from the verb *phuô* meaning to "grow" or "spring up," the basic sense being that of unplanned, uncontrolled, organic growth.[74] Nature by itself is *ataktos*—"disorderly," "irregular," "lawless." Like an untended garden, it wants cultivation. The feminine *physis* must be brought under the control of the masculine *nomos*—"law," "custom," "habit."[75]

The association of *nomos* and *physis* with male and female was seen by the ancient Greeks in the mythical dominance of Ouranos over Gaia, in the order created by Father Zeus after his defeat of the Titans, in the division of labor of all ancient societies according to which men ruled and women raised children, and in the struggle between the rationality

---

70. Pausanias, *Description of Greece* 1.10.3.

71. Aristotle, *EE* 7.1235a. Also Allen, *The Concept of Woman*, 17–20.

72. Aristotle, *Meta.* 1.986a.20.

73. On ancient Chinese thinking, see Wang, *Yinyang*.

74. Thornton, *Eros*, 1–2. For a standard treatment of the opposition of *nomos* and *physis*, see Guthrie, *A History of Greek Philosophy*, 111–30.

75. Pederasts even argued that the love of males for females was beastly and effeminate, whereas the love of males for males was cultured and manly (and also, paradoxically, that a boy's beauty is natural whereas a woman's beauty is fake). See Hubbard, "The Paradox of 'Natural' Heterosexuality and 'Unnatural' Women," 249–58.

of men and the sexuality of women experienced firsthand by husbands in the challenge of domesticating their much younger wives. Daniel Garrison writes:

> The old myths had kept alive the tradition of mother earth and father sky; fifth-century rationalism had new myths of its own that contrasted a feminine *physis* and masculine *nomos*. These sexual linkages were not just a matter of noun gender: they were seen as extending to the natural affinities and social roles of men and women, justifying the traditional assignment of political roles to men and nutritional, procreative roles to women.[76]

Thornton concurs, writing that this is why women figure so prominently in Greek literature, "because in them this fundamental human problem, this conflict between nature's chaos and culture's order, is magnified."[77] Similarly, David Sedley sees "isomorphism" in the accounts of the origin of matter and of evil in Hesiod and Plato, writing that the creation of woman "represents the planned intrusion of moral badness into the world," not because women are themselves bad, but because their existence poses problems for men, in the same way that the body poses problems for the soul.[78]

In Hesiod, the order of creation is the race of men and then the "deadly race and tribe of women," beginning with Pandora, created by Zeus to punish men for the theft of fire. In relating the myth of Pandora, Hesiod has little good to say about women, "who live amongst mortal men to their great trouble, no helpmeets in hateful poverty, but only in wealth."[79] They are "an evil to mortal men, with a nature to do evil."[80] Pandora herself is said to possess "a shameless mind and a deceitful nature."[81] She is "a plague to men who eat bread."[82] Such words are heard in Homer only from the ghost of Agamemnon, who complains bitterly that women are not to be trusted, but in Homer Agamemnon himself is not to be trusted, and Penelope proves him wrong.[83] Nowhere in Homer

---

76. Garrison, *Sexual Culture in Ancient Greece*, 211.
77. Thornton, *Eros*, 97.
78. See Sedley, "Hesiod's *Theogony* and Plato's *Timaeus*," 256.
79. Hesiod, *Th.* 590–91.
80. Hesiod, *Th.* 601.
81. Hesiod, *Op.* 67.
82. Hesiod, *Op.* 82.
83. Agamemnon says Clytemnestra's treachery "has shed shame on herself and on

are all women declared shameless, as they are in Hesiod, and only after Hesiod does such abuse of women becomes a standard feature of Greek literature.[84] The seventh-century BC poet Semonides named ten types of women: pig, fox, dog, earth, sea, donkey, ferret, mare, monkey, and bee, of which only the bee is beneficial.[85] Women are the "greatest evil" in Semonides, a "foul tribe" in Menander, and a "plague" in Sophocles, Euripides, and Aristophanes.[86] A popular saying of the sixth-century satirist Hipponax declared that there are only two days in which a wife pleases her husband: the day he marries her and the day he buries her.[87]

The pre-Socratic philosophers had little if anything good to say about marriage. When a man asked Pythagoras when he should take a wife, the philosopher is said to have replied, "When you want to lose what strength you have."[88] Empedocles might be expected to view marriage more positively, given his emphasis on the power of attraction, but his dualism of Love and Hate made love and marriage merely a part of an endless cycle of union and disunion.[89] Parmenides spoke of the "cruel" process of mating and birthing.[90] Antiphon warned that "marriage is a great gamble for a man" because divorce is difficult and so is living with a difficult woman, and with marriage come children and all of the troubles they entail.[91] Democritus opined that a man should not have children, advising the man who wants them to choose them from his friends' children to get the kind he wants.[92] Socrates, who married late in life, is said to have advised a young man asking if he should marry, "Whichever you

---

women yet to be, even upon her that doeth uprightly" and that "no longer is there faith in women," but these are the words of a selfish, suffering soul whose lust for women (first Chryseis, then Briseis, and finally Cassandra) repeatedly caused calamity. See Homer, *Od.* 11.405-56.

84. The chastened Helen calls herself "dog-eyed" (*kynōpidos*) in both the *Iliad* and the *Odyssey*, and Agamemnon calls Clytemnestra "dog-eyed," but all women are not said to be "dog-eyed" in Homer as they are in Hesiod. See Homer, *Il.* 3.180, 6.344, 6.356; Homer, *Od.* 4.145, 11.424, 11.434.

85. Semonides, Fr. 7.

86. Semonides, Fr. 7.115E; Menander, Fr. 535K; Sophocles, Fr. 187N; Euripides, Fr. 496N, Aristophanes, Fr. 10K.

87. Hipponax, Fr. 68W.

88. D.L. 8.9.

89. See Allen, *The Concept of Woman*, 30-34.

90. Parmenides, Fr. 12.

91. Antiphon, Fr. 123.

92. Democritus, Frs. 276-77.

do, you will repent it."[93] The same dilemma is expressed comically by the chorus of old men in *Lysistrata*: "You wheedlers. Still, the saying's true—we can't live with you, we can't live without you!"[94]

Two early schools of philosophy lent sexual licentiousness an air of intellectual respectability by treating sex lightly and flouting traditional sexual mores. The hedonistic Cyreniacs valued sensual pleasure above all else and therefore advocated sex without emotional attachment or marital commitment, with Aristippus of Cyrene famously saying of his mistress, "I possess Laïs; she does not possess me."[95] The Cynics advocated natural living according to their own very low view of human nature, which Diogenes of Sinope demonstrated by masturbating in public, saying, "Would that we could relieve hunger by rubbing the belly."[96] He is also said to have advocated the sharing of both wives and sons, the only requirement being consent by both parties, but also to have advised his students not to marry or raise children on the grounds that such attachments limit a philosopher's freedom.[97] When his student Crates married Hipparchia, they consummated their marriage, *sans* ceremony, in a public portico in broad daylight, shielded only by the cloak of Crates's student Zeno of Citium.[98] Thereafter Hipparchia kept company with Crates in the stoas of Athens, wore the same clothes, and dined with him and other men, sparring verbally with them and caring little for her modesty.[99]

After the death of Socrates, two new schools continued the thinking of the Cynics and Cyreniacs, but more respectably and with a much lower regard for sexual relations. The Epicureans, building on the materialism of Democritus and the hedonism of the Cyreniacs, also valued pleasure above all else, but they defined pleasure as an absence of pain, both sensual and emotional. Since sex was not necessary for survival, they saw it

---

93. D.L. 2.5.33. In both Plato's *Apology* (34d) and his *Phaedo* (116b), Socrates, at the time of his death at age 70, is said to have had two young sons and an older son. The *Phaedo* (60a) also mentions his wife Xanthippe sitting next to Socrates with her a son in her arms. She must have been much younger than Socrates.

94. Aristophanes, *Lysistrata* 1039, quoted by Marre, "Aristophanes on Bawds in the Boardroom," 59.

95. D.L. 2.8.75; Garrison, *Sexual Culture in Ancient Greece*, 172.

96. D.L. 6.46, 6.69.

97. D.L. 6.72, 6.29.

98. The tale is told by Apuleius, *Florida*, 14. Such is also how Garrison (*Sexual Culture in Ancient Greece*, 307) understands Diogenes Laertius's "*en tō phanerō syneginetō*" in D.L. 6.97.

99. D.L. 6.97–98.

as rarely worth the trouble, with Epicurus himself famously saying, "No one was ever the better for sexual indulgence, and it is well if he be not the worse."[100] Epicurus thought even less of *erōs*, dismissing it as "an intense longing for sex accompanied by smarting and distress."[101] Friendship was necessary to achieve the goal of fulfillment (*ataraxia*), but love made fulfillment impossible by inhibiting self-sufficiency (*autarkeia*). A wise man would therefore never fall in love or marry or raise children, except when circumstances such as civil law make bachelorhood more painful than marriage.[102] He need not, however, swear off sex altogether; it was, after all, a natural physiological desire that could be satisfied painlessly if one were careful. Later Epicureans were more in favor of sex but just as opposed to romance. The Epicurean poet Lucretius considered monogamy unnatural and casual sex more pleasurable, recommending promiscuity as a cure for love.[103]

Zeno of Citium, founder of the Stoic school, was a student of Crates the Cynic and followed the Cynics in advocating the sharing of wives, unisex attire, and nude athletics for both sexes.[104] His followers repudiated such practices but kept his definition of passion as an irrational and unnatural movement of the soul; he who would be happy must strive for *apatheia* (dispassion).[105] Diogenes Laertius summarizes the Stoic teaching on *erōs* with the words, "The passion of love is a craving from which good men are free, for it is an effort to win affection due to the visible presence of beauty."[106] From Chrysippus onward, Stoics differed from Cynics in their emphasis on fate and in their belief that living in accordance with nature meant accepting one's fate and using one's natural reason to avoid mental disturbance. Sex and love both disturbed the mind, causing reason to lose control of the body; both were therefore morally suspect, but whereas the desire for sex can be easily satisfied and quickly over, love is demanding and persistent. Many later Stoics valued marriage as an institution in accordance with reason, but the danger of feeling too

---

100. D.L. 10.131–32, 10.118–19.

101. Epicurus, Fr. 483, in Skinner, *Sexuality in Greek and Roman Culture*, 163.

102. D.L. 10.118–19.

103. Lucretius, 4.1058–90. See Skinner, *Sexuality in Greek and Roman Culture*, 229–33; Stephens, "What's Love Got to Do with It?" 19.

104. D.L. 7.33, 7.131. See also Skinner, *Sexuality in Greek and Roman Culture*, 161–62; Gaca, *The Making of Fornication*, 59–81.

105. D.L. 7.110.

106. D.L. 7.113.

fondly for someone was such that Stoics practiced *premeditatio malorum* (premeditation of evils), with Epictetus saying, "If you are kissing your child or wife, say that it is a human being whom you are kissing, for when the wife or child dies, you will not be disturbed."[107]

Disdain for the body appears very early in the history in Greek philosophy. Empedocles spoke of the body as the "clothes" of the soul; to the fifth-century Pythagorean Philolaus, it was the tomb of the soul; to Xenophon, it was a net that entraps the soul.[108] Plotinus quotes Empedocles saying sinful souls descend into bodies as punishment, attributing this view also to Pythagoras.[109] Diogenes Laertius names Pythagoras as the first to teach that souls migrate from body to body.[110] He also alleges that Pythagoras taught that only reason is immortal, that the "most momentous thing in human life is the art of winning the soul to good or to evil," that sexual pleasures are "always harmful and not conducive to health," and that husbands and wives must copulate only with each other to ensure the orderly reincarnation of souls.[111] Pythagoras is also said to have accepted women as students, one of them being his own wife, Theano.[112] Many scholars have seen Pythagorean influence in the sexual ethics of Plato's *Laws* as well as in Plato's speculations concerning metempsychosis and numerology, but many also discount such influence.[113] Because many of our sources on Pythagoras post-date Plato, it is difficult to tell how much Plato borrowed from Pythagoras and how much later Pythagoreans borrowed from Plato. At any rate, it is Plato and not Pythagoras who is commonly considered, in Thornton's words, "our most important source of the long-lived prejudice against the body and its appetites that dominates the philosophy of the West."[114]

---

107. Epictetus, *Enchiridion*, 3.

108. Empedocles Fr. 126; Philolaus Fr. 14; Xenophon, *Mem.* 3.11.9; See Thornton, *Eros*, 124.

109. Plotinus, *Ennead* IV.8.1, IV.8.5.

110. D.L. 8.1.14.

111. D.L. 8.30, 8.32, 8.9, 8.21.

112. D.L. 8.42.

113. On sexual ethics of Plato and the Pythagoreans, see Skinner, *Sexuality in Greek and Roman Culture*, 155–58; Gaca, *The Making of Fornication*, 94–116.

114. Thornton, *Eros*, 128.

## Plato: The Lonely Soul

The foundational conceit of Plato's understanding of soul and body is his notion of another world beyond the world of our physical senses—an immaterial, strictly intelligible world of divine Ideas or Forms, which the soul has seen before its descent into a material body. Confinement in the body inhibits the soul's memory of the forms and its perception of the forms in the world sensible to the body. In book seven of the *Republic*, in what is called the Allegory of the Cave, Plato likens the soul to a prisoner chained in a cave whose only experience of the world is the movement of shadows on the wall, cast by a fire behind him that he cannot see. The prisoner's fetters are the body. Only when loosed from his fetters can the prisoner leave the cave and ascend into the light of day, which is more than his eyes can at first bear. The vision of reality seen by the soul above ground is true knowledge (*gnōsis*); the shadows mistaken for reality by prisoners in the cave, merely opinion (*doxa*). Upon returning to the cave, the prisoner can neither see in the darkness as he once did nor convince those who have not left the cave of what he has seen in the sunlight.[115]

In other works, Plato likens the body to a tomb, a prison, chains of slavery, and an oyster's shell.[116] As matter, the body is impure and contaminates the soul with "passions and desires and fears, and all sorts of fancies and foolishness."[117] The body cannot be trusted. Its sensory organs are unreliable and deceitful, and its genital organs are "disobedient and self-willed, like a creature that is deaf to reason."[118] Thus, "if we are ever to know anything absolutely, we must be free from the body and must behold the actual realities with the eye of the soul alone."[119] For this reason, "the soul of the philosopher greatly despises the body and avoids it and strives to be alone by itself."[120] True philosophers "are in every way hostile to the body and they desire to have the soul apart by itself alone."[121] They "practice dying" because death frees the soul from the body.[122]

---

115. Plato, *Rep.* 514a–517b.
116. Plato, *Phd.* 82e, 66d, 83d; Plato, *Ti.* 69d–71e; Plato, *Phdr.* 250c.
117. Plato, *Phd.* 66a–c.
118. Plato, *Tim.* 91b.
119. Plato, *Phd.* 66d–e.
120. Plato, *Phd.* 65d.
121. Plato, *Phd.* 67e.
122. Plato, *Phd.* 67e.

While in the body, the soul is aided in its search for truth by occasional recollections of divine reality that astonish the soul, causing a kind of "divine madness."[123] In the *Phaedrus*, the character of Socrates names four forms of divine madness associated with different divine patrons: the prophetic madness of Apollo, the mystic madness of Dionysus, the poetic madness of the Muses, and the erotic madness of Aphrodite and Eros.[124] The greatest of the four is erotic madness because it is more often experienced and drives men to great feats for that which is good.[125] When souls "see here any likeness of the things of that other world, [they] are stricken with amazement and can no longer control themselves."[126] They desire to possess the beauty they perceive so as to be happy, and this desire for the good is called *erōs*.[127] Plato reasons that because no one wishes to be happy only for a time, *erōs* naturally seeks the perpetuation of the good through procreation, either physical or spiritual. "All men," says Plato through the character of Diotima in the *Symposium*, "are pregnant both in body and in soul."[128] Those who are pregnant more in body produce other bodies; those who are pregnant more in soul produce first prudence and virtue and then art, inventions, justice, and spiritual children. Those who produce such products of the soul "enjoy a far fuller community with each other than that which comes with children [of the body], and a far surer friendship, since the children of their union are fairer and more deathless."[129]

The aim of Diotima's lecture and of the *Symposium* is to show that physical attraction is properly just a starting point for progressive enlightenment leading to a purely rational love of goodness itself. Thus, in contrast to the stock excuse for pederasty as a higher love, already offered in the *Symposium* by Pausanias, Diotima advocates a purely intellectual tutelage that enables an "escape from the mean, meticulous slavery of a single instance" of beauty in one person and that begins the step-by-step ascent from love for one person to love for all persons, all good things,

---

123. Plato, *Phdr.* 265a; Plato, *Sym.* 202e–203a.
124. Plato, *Phdr.* 265a–b. Cf. 244d–245a, 249d–e.
125. Plato, *Phdr.* 245b–c, 249e, 265b; Plato, *Symp.* 207b–208d.
126. Plato, *Phdr.* 250a. Cf. 250e–251a.
127. Plato, *Smp.* 204d–206a.
128. Plato, *Smp.* 206c. Cf. Plato, *Phdr.* 250e–251a.
129. Plato, *Smp.* 209c.

and ultimately the essence of goodness.[130] This, says Diotima, is the "right method of boy-loving" [*to orthōs paiderastein*] and "right approach to love-making" [*to orthōs epi ta erōtika*].[131]

But why is this "right approach to love-making" said to be only a "right method of boy-loving" not also a right method of marriage? The difference between the two is that Plato's "right method of boy-loving" is strictly intellectual, whereas marriage exists for the purpose of procreation and is necessarily carnal. The former is therefore purer than the latter by definition. Plato plainly ranks the former over the latter in both the *Symposium* and the *Phaedrus*. In the *Symposium*, the love of women is said to be the work of Aphrodite Pandemos: "this is the Love we see in the meaner sort of men; who, in the first place, love women as well as boys; secondly, where they love, they are set on the body more than the soul."[132] The love of boys is the work of Aphrodite Ourania and is "untinged with wantonness: wherefore those who are inspired by this Love betake them to the male, in fondness for what has the robuster nature and a larger share of mind."[133] In the *Phaedrus*, Plato attributes the love inspired by "the beauty of the boy" to "he who is newly initiated [and] who beheld many of those realities" in the world of Forms, while attributing the love that leads to sexual intercourse and the begetting of children (*paidosporein kai hubrei prosomilōn*) to "he who is not newly initiated or has been corrupted, [and] does not quickly rise from this world to that other world and to absolute beauty when he sees its namesake here."[134]

The contrast between pederasty and marriage provides a convenient context for a discussion of Plato's theory of *erōs*. Given Plato's audience's experience with pederasty and its familiarity with the arguments in pederasty's defense, Plato's exaltation of love inspired by "the beauty of the boy" allows him to explain the attraction of men to boys in a way that flatters the men for feeling the attraction but shames them for acting on it physically and also exhorts them to a higher love for philosophy, whereas a similar exaltation of love inspired by the beauty of a woman would make the contrast between of two loves—one intellectual and one carnal—less clear, because marriage mixes them, and also less convincing, given the

---

130. Plato, *Smp.* 180c, 210a–210e. Cf. Plato, *Leg.* 837c–d.
131. Plato, *Smp.* 211b–c.
132. Plato, *Smp.* 181b.
133. Plato, *Smp.* 181c.
134. Plato, *Phdr.* 250e–251e.

## The Greek View of Male and Female

audience's low regard for women and marriage. Plato shares this low regard, ranking women a step lower on the scale of being from divine ideas to formless matter. He likens the separation of the head and heart from the loins to the separation of the men's and women's quarters in a Greek house.[135] He writes of the womb as an "indwelling creature" that becomes vexed and ill when unused for long periods and restlessly invades other organs until it is satisfied by sexual intercourse.[136] He associates maleness with form and femaleness with matter, the former active and the latter passive, speaking of matter as the "Mother and Receptacle" of all creation that is itself "invisible and unshaped [and] all-receptive" to the forms imparted by the Demiurge.[137] He strongly implies that the souls of men and women are essentially sexless, attributing to both men and women the same basic virtues such as temperance, justice, courage, intelligence, memory, and magnanimity.[138] But if, as he says, wicked or cowardly men are reincarnated as women, then women at least begin life farther from the philosophic goal, as weaker souls in weaker bodies that make their recollection of forms, exercise of virtue, and philosophic ascent more difficult.[139] A right-loving man therefore naturally prefers young men over women "as having robuster nature and a larger share of mind."[140]

Plato allows that some women may surpass some men in virtue, and on that basis he says the nature of men and women is the same with regard to guardianship of the State, but he nevertheless regards masculinity as superior to femininity and men better than women as a class.[141] Arguing against any distinctively feminine virtue, Socrates asks in the *Republic*:

> Do you know, then, of anything practiced by mankind in which the masculine sex does not surpass the female on all these points? Must we make a long story of it by alleging weaving and the

---

135. Plato, *Ti.* 69e–70a.
136. Plato, *Ti.* 91c.
137. Plato, *Tim.* 50c–51b.
138. Plato, *Tim.* 42a–b, 90e–91a; Plato, *Meno* 71e–73b, 88a.
139. Plato, *Tim.* 42a–b, 90e–91a.
140. Plato, *Smp.* 181c.

141. Plato, *Rep.* 5.455c–456a. Cf. Plato, *Tim.* 42a, and Plato, *Leg.* 805c–d. A. W. Price writes that in the *Republic*, "He is willing to pretend, unseriously, that the philosopher should resemble a well-bred dog (2.375d4–376c2), but not seriously to propose that the philosophic mind should be half feminine." See Price, *Love and Friendship in Plato and Aristotle*, 170.

watching of pancakes and the boiling pot, whereon the sex plumes itself and wherein its defeat will expose it to most laughter?[142]

Glaucon answers, "You are right that the one sex is far surpassed by the other in everything, one may say. Many women, it is true, are better than many men in many things, but broadly speaking, it is as you say."[143] Plato has nothing good to say about femininity and little good to say about women except that with effort they can become men. A. W. Price notes that Plato could have consoled women with some recognition of their distinctively feminine virtues; "Instead, the best prospect he is willing to hold out to women is of a transformation into she-men."[144] The woman's path to the divine is thus through the man. But for the man, the woman is a lesser beauty, and the love of a lesser beauty draws souls in the wrong direction—downward toward matter instead of upward toward the divine.

Plato therefore cannot hold heterosexual *erōs* in high regard. Love of the female form serves only the purpose of procreation, which is of no interest to a philosopher in his ascent toward the divine, except as a political good, about which he might advise his less enlightened companions in the allegoric cave. Thus, it is only in Plato's political works that he deals directly with relations between men and women. In the *Laws*, the very first law to be laid down by the lawgiver would require men and women to marry and have children.[145] Couples would be monitored to ensure they are trying to have children, and those who fail to do their duty would be punished.[146] "The bride and bridegroom must set their minds to produce for the State children of the greatest possible goodness and beauty," he writes.[147] Women of childbearing age would be exempt from military service.[148] All alternatives to procreative sex—homosexuality, masturbation, fornication—would be condemned and punished.[149] In the earlier and more fanciful *Republic*, Plato even proposes the sharing of wives and children of the guardian class, as well as the use of secrecy and deception to match the best men to the best women and to prevent

---

142. Plato, *Rep.* 5.455c–d.
143. Plato, *Rep.* 5.455d.
144. Price, *Love and Friendship in Plato and Aristotle*, 170.
145. Plato, *Leg.* 720e–721e, 785b.
146. Plato, *Leg.* 784a–784e.
147. Plato, *Leg.* 783d.
148. Plato, *Leg.* 6.785b.
149. Plato, *Leg.* 838e–839a, 841a–e.

parents from finding out whose children are whose.[150] He also stresses sexual equality more in the *Republic*, arguing at length that male and female differ only in that one begets and the other bears, and that this difference is irrelevant to the duties of guardians.[151] Women guardians must therefore exercise naked like men, go to war alongside men, assume other civic duties like men, and have no other occupation—yet he still allows them lighter tasks "because of their weakness as a class."[152]

Opinions differ as to how and how much Plato means what he writes, especially in the *Republic*. Many modern readers believe he is merely demonstrating the absurdity of utopian theory.[153] Even so, his lack of interest in sexual distinction and the most natural, necessary, and intimate of human relations is undeniable.

## Aristotle: Married with Children

Aristotle stood almost alone among leading philosophers in viewing marriage positively. He was a devoted husband and father, a fact used against him by his philosophical critics.[154] So partial was he to the married state that when his wife Pythias died, he took a concubine named Herpyllis, who became the mother of his son, Nicomachus. No extant work of Aristotle's focuses mainly on marriage, but Aristotle comments often enough on it in his surviving works for us to outline his view of it.[155] He writes in the *Nicomachean Ethics* that "man is by nature a social being" and furthermore that "man is by nature a pairing creature even more than he is a political creature, inasmuch as the family is an earlier and more fundamental institution than the State, and the procreation of offspring a more general characteristic of the animal creation."[156] The affection (*philia*) of husbands and wives is therefore a natural instinct, but

150. Plato, *Rep.* 5.457c–e, 5.459c–460d.

151. Plato, *Rep.* 454d–e.

152. Plato, *Rep.* 457a–b.

153. See, for example, Forde, "Gender and Justice in Plato," 657–70.

154. See D.L. 5.1.3–4; also Price, *Love and Friendship in Plato and Aristotle*, 173; Sihvola, "Aristotle on Sex and Love," 205.

155. Diogenes Laertius (D.L. 5.1.22) names several non-extant works by Aristotle that might have focused on or touched upon marriage, including works entitled *Concerning Love*, *Theses on Love*, and *Symposium*. See also Sihvola, "Aristotle on Sex and Love," 202.

156. Aristotle, *EN* 1.1097b.6, 8.1162a.7. Cf. Aristotle, *EE* 1242a.

not an instinct solely for the purpose of procreation, as it is among other animals, for the man and the woman also need each other to ensure their own survival:

> So whereas with the other animals the association of the sexes aims only at continuing the species, human beings cohabit not only for the sake of begetting children but also to provide the needs of life; for with the human race division of labor begins at the outset, and man and woman have different functions; thus they supply each other's wants, putting their special capacities into the common stock.[157]

Xenophon, a contemporary of Plato, also writes of the importance of the division of labor and the naturalness of the sexes' differences, as well as of the moral and legal obligation of men and women to live according to their sex. But in relating his thinking on marriage in a dialogue on estate management, *Oeconomicus*, Xenophon seems to recommend marriage mainly as a matter of optimal organization, whereas Aristotle makes his case for marriage mostly in his discourses on ethics, in which the focus is often on the social bonds that raise man above the level of beast.[158] Marriage is the first of those bonds. Aristotle writes (mistakenly) that only humans form lasting couples.[159] He notes that the distinction of male and female is more pronounced in higher beings.[160] He also criticizes Plato for proposing that women take the same roles as men in imitation of other animals, which fails to recognize that beasts have no households to manage.[161] Aristotle even recommends marriage for the sake of virtue because it brings together the peculiar virtues of both sexes to form a more fully virtuous unit. In this way, he says, "love [*philia*] of the opposite is also love of the good," for a greater good results from bringing opposites together.[162]

---

157. Aristotle, *EN* 8.1162a.7.

158. Xenophon identifies two chief purposes of marriage: children, to be "the very best of allies and the very best of support in old age," and joint management of the household, seeing the ideal marriage as a "perfect partnership in mutual service." Xenophon, *Oec.* 7.10–13, 19; 7.18–26.

159. Aristotle, *EE* 7.10.1242a22–26. See also Price, *Love and Friendship in Plato and Aristotle*, 172.

160. Aristotle, *HA* 9.608b.4–8.

161. Aristotle, *Pol.* 2.1264b. Cf. Plato, *Rep.* 5.451d–e.

162. Aristotle, *EE* 7.1239b. Cf. Aristotle, *EN* 8.1159b, 8.1162a.

Thus, says Aristotle, marriage serves three basic interests: utility, pleasure, and virtue.[163] Procreation is part of the utility of marriage, but instead of recommending marriage for the sake of children, Aristotle recommends children for the sake of marriage, noting that, "Children, too, seem to be a bond of union, and therefore childless marriages are more easily dissolved; for children are a good possessed by both parents in common, and common property holds people together."[164] Sexual intercourse is not an end in itself but a means to an end, and the end Aristotle names is not children but friendship (*philia*), or as it is rendered here, affection:

> Therefore in love [*erōs*] to have one's affection [*philia*] returned is preferable to intercourse [*synousia*] with the beloved. Therefore love aims at affection rather than at intercourse; and if affection is the principal aim of love, it is also the end [*telos*] of love. Therefore intercourse is either not an end at all, or only with a view to receiving affection.[165]

Aristotle treats sexual desire as a natural appetite like hunger and thirst. It is more complex than other appetites, but as with other appetites the pleasure experienced in its satisfaction is a natural good serving a greater good. Its purpose is not just procreation, for it also brings and binds a man and a woman together for their mutual benefit. The same is true of *erōs*, which is also not an end in itself but a means to an end. It begins as a pleasure of the eye but leads in marriage to an especially intense form of *philia* that one can share with only one person, which has its own beginning not in desire but in goodwill.[166] Aristotle does not speculate on any form of divine *erōs*, as Plato does, and instead treats *erōs* as a strictly human emotion also serving the purpose of bringing and binding together one man and one woman for their mutual benefit. As such, it is not inherently shameful or especially dangerous; it is a natural good serving an essential purpose and only needs to be properly directed and disciplined, like all other emotions.

Ironically, despite the practical importance of sexual distinction in Aristotle's anthropology, he was himself responsible for contributing to

163. Aristotle, *EN* 8.1162a.24–26.

164. Aristotle, *EN* 8.1162a.27–29.

165. Aristotle, *AP* 2.68b1–10. See also Sihvola, "Aristotle on Sex and Love," 200–201.

166. Aristotle, *EN* 8.1158a.12–13, 9.1167a.1, 9.1171a–b; Aristotle, *EE* 7.1245a–b.

philosophy a notion that tended to diminish the philosophical significance of sexual distinction for many centuries to come. He did so accidentally, by setting forth both a theory of animal generation and a system of categorization that together made the distinction of male and female technically inessential to human nature. Let us look first at his theory of animal generation and then at its impact on his system of categorization.

Like Plato and others, Aristotle associated maleness with form and femaleness with matter, the former active and the latter passive. Plato did this at the cosmic level, calling matter the "Mother and Receptacle" of the forms imparted by the Demiurge.[167] Aristotle does the same at the biological level, rejecting the double-seed theories of animal generation put forth for Anaxagoras, Empedocles, and Democritus, in favor of a single-seed theory according to which the male alone provides the "principle of both movement and definition" (*archē kai kinēsontos kai dioriountos*), the "principle of movement" (*archē kinēseōs*), the "principle of the form" (*archē tou eidous*), the "principle of the soul" (*tēs pyschēs archē*) as the "essence of a particular body" (*hē gar pscyhē ousia sōmatos tinos estin*)—which, together with the female's menstrual material, either develops fully into a normal male or fails to develop fully and becomes "as it were, a deformed male," a female.[168] This failure to develop fully accounts for the female's defining deformity, her inability to concoct male seed, which Aristotle treats as the specific difference between male and female, explaining the lack of baldness in eunuchs as a result of their becoming female.[169] It also accounts for many other observable differences between the sexes. As imperfect men, women are by and large less rational than men, since rationality is what distinguishes humans from other animals.[170] Women are also said to be—

> more compassionate than man, more easily moved to tears . . . more jealous, more querulous, more apt to scold and to strike . . . more prone to despondency and less hopeful . . . more void of shame or self-respect, more false of speech, more deceptive, and of more retentive memory [i.e., less forgiving] . . . more wakeful, more shrinking, more difficult to rouse to action, and requires a smaller amount of nutriment.[171]

---

167. Plato, *Tim.* 50c–51b.
168. Aristotle, *GA* 730a30, 729a10–15, 765b10–15, 738b20–30, 737a25–30.
169. Aristotle, *GA* 784a6–12.
170. Aristotle, *Pol.* 1260a10–15.
171. Aristotle, *HA* 608b.

Such differences, says Aristotle, suit the woman to be ruled by the man, although not as the man rules his children and servants, for the woman is nearer to the man in virtue.[172]

Feminists have naturally found this view obnoxious and subjected it to much abuse, even caricaturing Aristotle's theory of generation as preformationism, whereby the male "deposits within the female a tiny homunculus for which the female serves as a vessel until this creature matures."[173] The reaction against such abuse has reached the other extreme, accommodating Aristotle to feminism by reducing the male's role in generation to merely that of "initiator of the motions that lead to birth," notwithstanding the many times Aristotle says the male does more than initiate.[174] Various other explanations have been offered as alternatives to the supposed "standard view" of the female as a teleological failure, but no consensus has been reached beyond the recognition that Aristotle's thinking on the subject was quite complex and not as disparaging as the female's role in generation as sometimes supposed. Suffice it to say here that Aristotle struggled to explain his knowledge of breeding on the basis of distinctions between form and matter, active and passive, mover and moved, associating males with the former and females with the latter. The result stressed the genetic role of males and the epigenetic role of females, with each contributing more or less equally to the new life.[175]

One consequence of this understanding of animal generation is that Aristotle cannot fit male and female into his system of categorization based on form (*aidos*) and family (*genos*). Aristotle reasoned that a thing might be recognized by many characteristics, but it is defined only by the form it shares with all others of its kind. The form says what the thing is,

172. Aristotle, *EN* 8.10.5; Aristotle, *Pol.* 1254b, 1259a35–b10, 1260a10–15.

173. Elshtain, *Public Man, Private Woman*, 3.

174. Besides plainly saying the male seed not only begins but also defines (*GA* 729a10–15, 729b20–25, 730a30, 730b15–20, 734b20–25, 738b20–30, 766b15), Aristotle also likens the male form and the female matter to a carpenter and his wood, a potter and his clay, the roundness of a ball and the wax of which it is made, medical treatment and the patient being healed, a craftsman's tools and the material with which he works (*GA* 729b15–30, 730b5–35). Aryeh Kosman, nevertheless, dismisses Aristotle's mentions of form as "exceptions," restricts the seed to the "principle of movement" (*archē kinēseōs*), and confines the female's "disability" (*vice* deformity) to her inability to concoct such seed. See Kosman, "Male and Female in Aristotle's *Generation of Animals*," 147–67.

175. In contrast, we today understand males and females to share the genetic role equally, except that the male's genetic contribution decides the sex of the embryo, with the female's epigenetic role having much less say over how the embryo develops.

as in the statement: Aristotle is a human being, an animal being, a living being, a material being, and a being. In this statement, each category of being is a form of the next category and the genus of the categories before it. But what if we said that Aristotle is *a man*, a human being, an animal being, and so forth? Is "man" or "woman" a form of human being? This question is never asked in Aristotle's *Categories*, but it is asked in his *Metaphysics* and answered negatively, with Aristotle arguing—briefly and unconvincingly—that male and female differ from each other neither in form (*eidos*) nor in substance (*ousia*) but only in matter (*hylē*) and in body (*sōma*).[176] This he says after having just said that "matter does not produce difference," at least not a difference of form, which prompts Giulia Sissa to complain:

> Dimorphism is preserved, but at the cost of having surreptitiously smuggled in a criterion from the realm of *eidos*. For what is form for Aristotle if not the form of a living body? What is a body, if not an organism defined by its anatomical and physiological structure, which is to say, by its form?[177]

Were we to speak of *species* instead of *form* or *eidos*, Aristotle might seem to make sense, but only because the modern definition of *species* requires reproductive capability, which is not required by Aristotle's definition of *eidos*. As Sissa says, "There is nothing in the concept of *eidos* that says stallion and mare, bull and cow, man and woman are not animals of different species."[178] Why, then, does Aristotle resist admitting that man and woman are different forms?

Aristotle gives us a clue in his final words on the subject: "Hence the same semen may, as the result of some modification [*pathon ti pathos*], become either female or male."[179] One must therefore refer to his *Generation of Animals* to learn that the failure of the form to develop fully accounts for the difference of male and female. This makes male and female "contraries" (*enantiotētes*) in the sense that formed and deformed are

---

176. Aristotle, *Meta.* 10.1058a.29–1058b.25. Aristotle allows that matter may produce difference but only between beings that are "other" in *eidos* on account of a difference of *logos*.

177. Sissa, "The Sexual Philosophies of Plato and Aristotle," 64. We might add that form also includes *telos* for Aristotle, but this would not settle Sissa's complaint, for the difference of male and female has its own obvious and essential *telos*, unlike bodily differences such as hair color.

178. Sissa, "The Sexual Philosophies of Plato and Aristotle," 63.

179. Aristotle, *Meta.* 10.1058b.23–24.

contrary. It would also make them separate species or forms if we were to reason according to Aristotle's *Categories* with the benefit of modern chromosomal science. But Aristotle knew nothing of chromosomes; he knew only of anatomical differences and behavioral differences, and while the former might suggest absolute contrariety and a difference of form, the latter, including effeminate men and mannish women, might suggest the opposite. Ignorant of the modern science of chromosomes and also, on account of his materialist assumptions, incredulous of both the Platonic concept of divine forms and the Stoic concept of seminal reason (*logos spermatikos*), Aristotle cannot clearly define male and female according to a specific difference—a difference that defines males and females as separate species within the genus of human being; he can only count the ways in which a particular male or female has failed to conform to the male ideal. In his ignorance, he arbitrarily selects a single "deformity"—the inability to concoct seed—to serve as his defining difference between male and female, but this expands the category of "female" to sterile men and boys, contrary to commonsense, so when arguing against male and female as separate categories (forms or species), Aristotle never mentions sterility, limits male and female to unnamed differences of matter and body, and then retreats into the obscurity of "some modification" that causes the male seed to develop fully or not.[180]

Thus, within his self-imposed system of categorization, and without a fuller and more accurate knowledge of sex differences, Aristotle's single-seed theory of generation forces him to classify all differences between males and females as merely accidental (*symbebēkos*) instead of essential because the human form is assumed to be essentially male and only accidentally female. As an accidental difference, male and female are more like a difference of skin color than like the essential difference of rationality distinguishing humans from other animals.

This would be the assumption of many generations of philosophers, who would be taught to think like Aristotle using Porphyry's third-century *Isagoge*, the standard introduction to Aristotle until the modern age. Maximus the Confessor would himself rely on what has come to be called "Porphyrian logic" to explain the divine Logos as the supreme category, the *summum genus*, the *Archetypos* of all creation.[181] And like Aristotle,

180. Aristotle, *Meta.* 10.1058b.23–24.

181. On Maximus's use of Porphyrian logic, see Tollefsen, *Christocentric Cosmology of St. Maximus the Confessor*, 64–69, 77–82; Törönen, *Union and Distinction in the Thought of St Maximus the Confessor*, 13–24, 87, 127–39.

Maximus would see the difference of male and female as essentially accidental and not definitive of human nature, as will be shown in chapter 4. Maximus might also have absorbed Aristotle's understanding of animal generation, which had become standard medical knowledge since its adoption by Galen in the second century, and which might have suggested to Maximus that human beings are not originally male or female but only become male or female accidentally while *in utero*.[182]

## After Aristotle

The four centuries following the death of Aristotle in 322 saw the evolution of Cyreniacs into Epicureans and Cynics into Stoics, the formalization of "Platonism" by the Old Academy, the degeneration of Platonism into the skepticism of the New Academy, and then the appearance in the first century before Christ of a more dogmatic and religious form of Platonism now known as Middle Platonism, as well as a revival of Pythagorean thinking in a more mystical and theistic form now known as Neopythagoreanism. Many philosophers later in these centuries adopted stricter standards of sexual ethics, following if not leading the general trend in their world.[183] Some taught that women should be educated in philosophy like men, though this did not mean a much changed role for women.[184] Two such philosophers also assumed a much higher regard for love and marriage than both their predecessors and their contemporaries.

---

182. On the influence of Aristotle on Galen's view of sexual distinction, see Allen, *The Concept of Woman*, 187–89.

183. Many social and political changes are thought to have contributed to these changes in philosophical regard for sexual ethics and marriage but are beyond the scope of this thesis. They include the migration of Greek men eastward under Alexander the Great and his successors; the turn toward romance in Greek theater with the appearance of New Comedy after the death of Alexander; the population crisis threatening the Greek homeland, noted by Polybius in the second century before Christ; increased participation of women in public life, including the rule of Ptolemaic queens such as Arsinoë II, Berenice II, and finally Cleopatra VII; Roman imitation of Greek romance in drama and Greek eroticism in poetry and sculpture; the Roman reaction in defense of republican virtue, social order, and higher birthrates, leading to radical reform of Roman marriage laws by Augustus; and the resulting enshrinement of family values as a lasting feature of Rome's imperial ideology. For an overview, see Skinner, *Sexuality in Greek and Roman Culture*, 148–239.

184. Despite early efforts to find feminists among the philosophers, further analysis has shown their feminism to have been greatly limited. See, for example, Nussbaum, "The Incomplete Feminism"; Blomquist, "Chryseïs and Clea, Eumetis and the Interlocutress," 173–90.

Among the Stoics, Musonius Rufus (d. 101) continued the process begun by Panaetius and the Middle Stoa of aligning Stoic virtues with civic virtues and the social order, in the interest of which he condemns sex within marriage solely for pleasure's sake and all sex outside of marriage, putting adultery on par with pederasty as an offence against nature.[185] Musonius names two reasons for men and women to marry: to make a life together and to produce children, but, he says, children alone are not reason enough for marriage for they can be gotten outside of marriage, as among beasts. His ideal marriage is not a baby factory but a "total symbiosis" of husband and wife, living together in perfect accord, "each striving to outdo the other in devotion."[186] Such a marriage he even recommends for philosophers, for no less than six reasons: (1) marriage is according to nature, (2) marriage is sanctioned by the gods, (3) the love of husbands and wives is the highest form of *philia*, (4) families are the building blocks of cities and the future of the race, (5) philosophers have the same duty as others and should set the example, and (6) the best philosophers are not hindered by marriage, in support of which he names Pythagoras, Socrates, and Crates.[187] The influence of Aristotle can be seen in Musonius's esteem for marital *philia*, but the Stoic concern for duty dominates his outlook, pushing both his marital ideal and his condemnation of sex outside marriage to un-Aristotelian extremes.

Among the Middle Platonists, Plutarch (d. 120), himself a happily married man, performs a similar service for the Platonist tradition, bringing its understanding of marriage up to date by assimilating the insights of Stoics and Aristotelians consistent with his understanding of Plato and rejecting those seen as inconsistent. In his dialogue *Amatorius*, the philosophy to be rejected is Epicureanism, specifically the Epicureans' selfish, utilitarian regard for marriage and their disdain for *erōs* in all forms. In making his case, Plutarch does what Plato does not, arguing at length for the superiority of heterosexual *erōs* over pederastic *erōs* as a path to virtue and philosophy. This has struck some modern readers as "anti-Platonic, almost anti-philosophical," in the words of D. A. Russell, but

185. Musonius, Fr. 12. For Musonius's place in Stoic tradition, see Bosman, "Utopia, Domestication and Special Status," 5–18.

186. Musonius, Fr. 13A. Fr. 13B concerns the best choice of a mate from the standpoint of Fr. 13A.

187. Bosman ("Utopia, Domestication and Special Status," 5–18) lists the same six reasons but in the order in which they appear in Musonius's Fr. 14, which is 6, 1, 3, 4, 2, 5.

such a judgment, as John Rist points out, depends on what one regards as the "correct" reading of Plato, and whereas modern readers judge Plato on the basis of his works, discriminating between his works and what Platonists later made of them, Middle Platonists like Plutarch revered the "divine Plato" as an oracle revealing and concealing mysteries that only a few will understand, always assuming consistency on his part, agreement on their part, and the continuing need of philosophers to reveal and conceal as the situation demanded.[188] In 120, when the *Amatorius* was written, the situation demanded a refutation of Epicureanism, which the *Amatorius* approaches indirectly by first attacking an easier target—the hedonism, selfishness, and misogyny of pederasts. The pederastic defense depended on the claim that the *erōs* of men for boys was purer and truer than that of men for women, against which Plutarch argues that husbands and wives are typically far more faithful and devoted to each other on account of their *erōs* being a higher, more natural form of the erotic "divine madness" of Plato's *Phaedrus*.[189] Two participants in the dialogue (one an Epicurean in another of Plutarch's dialogues) question this divine basis of *erōs*, beginning what Rist calls Act 2 of Plutarch's argument—a lengthy defense of theism against Epicurean atheism, which may be Plutarch's main reason for writing, though it appears that for Plutarch the two issues go hand in hand: The *erōs* of men and women is evidence of divinity, and divinity makes sense of their *erōs*.

Despite these defenses of marriage by Plutarch and Musonius, the general tendency of philosophers before and after them was to focus on the mind or the soul at the expense of the body and its difference of male and female. Musonius was not followed in his exalted estimation of marriage by even his own student, Epictetus, who contradicted his teacher in preferring the solitary Diogenes to the married Crates as the model of a true sage. Epictetus allowed marriage and children to lesser men but scorned them for philosophers:

> In the name of God, are those men greater benefactors to society who introduce into the world to occupy their own places two or three grunting children, or those who superintend as far as they can all mankind, and see what they do, how they live, what they attend to, what they neglect contrary to their duty?[190]

---

188. See Russell, *Plutarch*, 92; Rist, "Plutarch's *Amatorius*," 557–75.
189. Plato, *Phdr.* 244d–245a–c, 249d–e, 265a–b.
190. Epictetus, *Discourses*, 3.22.

Consistent with the modern popular perception of Stoics as unfeeling rationalists, Epictetus also urged rational detachment from all things that might trouble the mind, telling students to start small, with an earthen cup, and then proceed by steps to greater things, "to yourself, to your body, to the parts of your body, to your children, to your wife, to your brothers . . . that nothing give you pain when it is torn from you . . . for this is really freedom."[191]

Likewise, the family-friendly Middle Platonism of Plutarch gave way before long to the otherworldliness of Neoplatonism under the influence of Neopythagoreanism. The Pythagoreans had long been known for their mathematical metaphysics, strict code of sexual behavior, and ascetic lifestyle including vegetarianism. They were also reputed to have introduced among the Greeks the doctrine of metempsychosis, with its stark duality of soul and body, and the table of opposites listed by Aristotle as (1) Limit and the Unlimited, (2) Odd and Even, (3) Unity and Plurality, (4) Right and Left, (5) Male and Female, (6) Rest and Motion, (7) Straight and Crooked, (8) Light and Darkness, (9) Good and Evil, (10) Square and Oblong.[192] Plato, in his so-called *agrapha dogmata*, elaborated on the first opposition to posit the One and the Indefinite Dyad, understanding the former as the principle of unity and form, and the latter as the principle of plurality and diversity, called the "Great and Small," according to Aristotle.[193] Xenocrates, who succeeded Plato's nephew Speusippus as head of the Academy, posited a Monad (also termed Intellect) and a Dyad (also termed Multiplicity) and is alleged to have identified the Monad as male and the Father of all, and the Dyad as female, the Mother of the Gods, and the Soul of the Universe.[194] Much later, some Platonists and Neopythagoreans began dividing Plato's One in two, positing an even more transcendent One preceding the monad that acts upon the indefinite dyad.[195] This trend, begun by Eudorus of Alexandria of Alexandria in the first century before Christ, continued through Numenius of Apamea

191. Epictetus, *Discourses*, 4.1.

192. Aristotle, *Meta.* 986a.

193. Aristotle, *Meta.* 987b.

194. See Dillon, *The Roots of Platonism*, 17–18. As Dillon notes, Plutarch attests to Xenocrates's distinction of Monad and Dyad, but only the less reliable *Placita* of Aetius attests to their identification as male and female.

195. This is the standard view. The controversies over what Plato actually taught, how much he owed to the Pythagoreans, and how much the Neopythagoreans owed to Platonism need not bother us. For an overview, see Huffman, "Pythagoreanism."

in the second Christian century, reaching Plotinus of Alexandria in the next century, who posited the Neoplatonist trinity of the One, the Intellect, and the Soul.[196]

All along the way, the key Pythagorean oppositions of soul and body, mind and matter, unity and plurality, good and evil, survived to figure greatly in the vision of Plotinus. In the opening line of his *Life of Plotinus*, Porphyry describes his mentor as a man who "seemed ashamed of having a body." Plotinus himself declares matter ugly and evil in an unformed state.[197] Unity is the basis of all beauty and goodness; diversity is its opposite and therefore also ugly and evil. The soul itself is evil when in the body, which is necessarily individual and diverse.[198] The soul must therefore withdraw from the multiplicity of the body and the diversity of the sensible world to the simplicity of the soul and its contemplation of the One:

> Such is the life of the divinities; such is also that of divine and blessed men; detachment from all things here below, scorn of all earthly pleasures, and flight of the soul towards the Divinity that she shall see face to face (that is, "alone with the alone," as thought Numenius).[199]

Anything that reminds the soul of multiplicity, difference, or "unlikeness" is a hindrance to this flight of the soul, even self-consciousness because it arises from awareness of the difference of self and other.[200] "Withdraw within yourself," says Plotinus; cut away anything superfluous as a sculptor cuts away the stone hiding a statue, until "nothing foreign will anymore, by its admixture, alter the simplicity of your interior essence."[201]

The opposition of male and female also survives in Plotinus but is greatly minimized as merely metaphorical at the cosmic level and strictly biological at the human level, part of the diversity of human existence

---

196. Numenius is regularly identified as a Pythagorean, but Eudorus is sometimes a Pythagorean and sometimes a Platonist. Then as now, two terms often overlapped, as in the case of Philo of Alexandria.

197. Plotinus, *Ennead* 2.4. See also Rist, "Plotinus on Matter and Evil," 154–66.

198. Plotinus, *Ennead* 6.6.

199. Plotinus, *Ennead* 6.9.9, 94. Porphyry's edition of Plotinus's *Enneads* ends with these words.

200. Plotinus, *Ennead* 1.4.10.

201. Plotinus, *Ennead* 1.6.9, 32. Cf. 1.2.5, 141, where Plotinus discusses the purification of the soul, which is achieved when "recollecting herself from the various localities over which she had, as it were, spread herself, she retires within herself."

that must be chipped away in the sculpting process. Plotinus follows Plato closely on the significance of *erōs* and in his use of the two Aphrodites: Aphrodite Pandemos, patroness of marriage, and Aphrodite Ourania, who, says Plotinus, "does not preside over marriages, for the reason that there are none in heaven."[202] He then adds a distinctively Neoplatonist touch, identifying Ouranos, Kronos, and Aphrodite Ourania with the One, the Intellect, and the Soul, respectively. Implied in this correspondence is the common association of masculinity with intellect, form, activity, and generation and of femininity with emotion, matter, passivity, and receptivity.[203]

Plotinus's student, editor, and successor, Porphyry, pays barely more attention to male and female than does Plotinus but betrays his hostility toward the body when writing against the eating of meat, arguing that the mixture of contraries defiles the things mixed; that, "on this account, venereal connections are attended with defilement"; that intercourse without conception pollutes the body with foreign matter; and that intercourse leading to conception defiles a soul by investing it with a body. Summing up, he writes, "And, in short, all venery, and emissions of the seed in sleep, pollute, because the soul becomes mingled with the body, and is drawn down to pleasure."[204] The implication is that pleasure itself is evil because, as Porphyry writes elsewhere, "the life of the soul dies through pleasure, but through bitterness the soul resumes life."[205]

Late in life, Porphyry married Marcella, the widow of a close friend, not for love or desire but out of concern for her and her seven children. Only the first part of his *Letter to Marcella* has survived. In it, Porphyry tells Marcella, "Neither trouble yourself much whether you be male or female in body, nor look upon yourself as a woman, for I did not approach you as such. Flee all that is womanish in the soul, as though you had a man's body about you."[206] In these words, we find the prejudice against femininity common to all the philosophers, plus the disregard for sex as a component of personal identity. Porphyry leaves no doubt that he regards only the soul as the true self, also telling Marcella, "I am in reality not this person who can be touched or perceived by any of the senses, but

202. Plotinus, *Ennead* 3.5.1–2, 583. Cf. Plato, *Cra.* 396b–c; Plato, *Smp.* 180d–181c.

203. Plato had already associated Kronos with "pure intellect" in the *Cratylus*, 396b.

204. Porphyry, *On Abstinence from Animal Food*, 163–64.

205. Porphyry, *On the Cave of the Nymphs*, 24.

206. Porphyry, *Mar.* 58.

that which is farthest removed from the body, the colorless and formless essence which can by no means be touched by the hands, but is grasped by the mind alone."[207]

## Conclusion: Intellection vs. Relation

With Plotinus and Porphyry, we are well into the Christian age and cannot discount entirely the direct or indirect influence of Christianity upon Neoplatonism. After all, Plotinus was a generation younger than Origen, studied in Alexandria under the same teacher as did Origen, and inveighed against the same Gnostics as did Origen. Nevertheless, from Plato to Porphyry we see the same ideas at work. The dominant dichotomies are mind and matter, soul and body, unity and diversity, the impersonal One and the multi-personal many. The dichotomy of male and female is a minor concern. It is fitted into the larger scheme by the association of male with mind and female matter, but it is generally restricted to a biological difference of limited relevance—necessary for procreation and a factor in deciding who does what on account of the weakness of women, but bearing no greater significance ethically or ontologically. The inferiority of women—in body if not also in soul—is assumed by all and serves as the principal theoretical basis for the subjection of women to men, supported by the practical benefit of a division of labor.

Aristotle made the most of such practical thinking and stands almost alone among leading philosophers in founding his anthropology on the principle that "man is by nature a social being" inclined by nature to marriage first and society second. A wise man will have less need of society, but even he will benefit from good company because living alone is unnatural.[208] A main purpose of philosophy is to guide men in accepting, maintaining, forming, and strengthening social bonds in accordance with nature and reason so as to avoid isolation and enjoy right relations. Among relationships, marriage is most satisfying of man's need for companionship on account of its extreme intimacy, utility, and pleasure. Procreation is just one result of right relation and not the driving force behind the pairing desire. The distinction of male and female is therefore fundamentally relational. It exists for the purpose of bringing

---

207. Porphyry, *Mar.* 44.

208. Aristotle, *NE* 1.1097b.6, 10.1177b.4, 10.1178b.6, cf. *NE* 1.1099b.7–8, 10.1179a.1–5. See also Kraut, *Aristotle on the Human Good*, 6, 353.

people together and is defined in large part by how people live together. The sexes differ in nature and thus also in *aretai* (virtues, strengths); they therefore take different roles in society. They live as men *or* women so as to relate rightly to other men *and* women. The more family-friendly philosophy of the early Roman empire may have been influenced by such thinking.

In contrast, for Plato, man is a rational soul trapped in an irrational body that inhibits the soul's use of reason and obscures its vision of the good. The soul's goal is liberation from the body, which is achieved through philosophy, the practice of dying. Only when separated from the body can the soul recollect its forgotten knowledge of the good and achieve lasting happiness. Male and female is a difference only of the body. It matters in only three ways—as higher and lower levels of incarnation, as an introduction to beauty, and as a means of producing new bodies for other souls to inhabit. But producing new bodies is a significant distraction from the soul's attempts to apprehend true beauty and escape the body, so the virtuous soul is well advised to avoid marriage. Love, *erōs*, is a selfish desire to possess beauty, not a matter of relation based on personal identity. Its vulgar form is valued only as an incentive to procreation; its more enlightened form is valued only as an introduction to beauty serving to draw the soul upward from an emotional love for another person to an intellectual love for an impersonal reality. How men and women relate to each other is therefore of little relevance. Aside from some concern for procreation and feminine weakness, the sexes are to be treated the same.

The ranking of intellection over relation is also seen in the stages of progress in the Platonist ascent toward the divine. Plato's stages are levels of enlightenment—from least to most: conjecture (*eikasia*), belief (*pistis*), understanding (*dianoia*), and intellection (*noēsis*).[209] The soul progresses from knowledge of the beauty of a single person, to knowledge of the beauty of all persons, to knowledge of beauty of everything, to knowledge of the divine forms behind all beauty.[210] Plotinus adds a practical aspect at the beginning: First, the soul is purified by the practice of political virtues (*politikai aretai*); then it escapes sense-perception through the study of mathematics and philosophy; next, it learns to contemplate the *Nous* as the First Beauty; finally, it abandons contemplation and all awareness

---

209. Plato, *Rep.* 6.511d–e.
210. Plato, *Smp.* 180c, 210a–210e. Cf. Plato, *Leg.* 837c–d.

of self to experience ecstatic union with the One.[211] Porphyry also begins with a practical concern—mastering political virtues aimed at the Golden Mean, then "cathartic virtues" aimed at apathy through asceticism, then "contemplative virtues" of philosophy, and finally "paradigmatic virtues" yielding knowledge of the divine Forms.[212] In each case, the ultimate goal is an impersonal good; life with other persons is an elementary task that matters less and less as the soul approaches the impersonal.

Both of these philosophic traditions, the Platonic and the Aristotelian, share points of agreement with early Christian teaching on male and female, as diverse as it was, but only one, the Aristotelian, bears much resemblance to the Hebrew tradition, to which we will now turn.

---

211. Plotinus, *Enneads* 1.2.1, 1.3.3, 6.9.7–11.
212. Porphyry, *Sententiae* 34, 183–85.

# 3

# The Hebrew View of Male and Female

INSTEAD OF MIND AND matter, soul and body, intelligible and sensible, the dominant dichotomies of Hebrew Scripture are Creator and creation, God and man, Yahweh and Israel, and later Jew and Gentile. Male and female figure significantly as part of God's original created goodness, as the basis of social order, and as keys to God's promise of progeny and the prosperity of the people of Israel. They are also later used as metaphors for the relationship between God and Israel, with God cast as husband and father and Israel cast as bride and daughter, but they will not be treated as principles of non-animal existence. There will be no yin and yang, no Father Sky and Mother Earth, no cultic correlation between human and non-human fertility, no sex goddesses, and no temple prostitution—at least in the religion of the editors and translators of the Old Testament.

The religion of those Israelites who at times made more of male and female, as evident in Scripture, will not concern us because early Christians did not inherit that tradition; they inherited the edited tradition of the Old Testament text as handed down. That text became the basis of their understanding of male and female. They resorted to it quite frequently and often read it quite literally. The text itself is not entirely uniform in its treatment of male and female. Later books betray the influence of Hellenism on Jewish thinking, as do some later extra-biblical works. It is therefore worthwhile to summarize relevant aspects of the text itself to account for this change before taking up the later works and then the interpretations of the Old Testament by later Jews and Christians.

This chapter will go as far as Philo the Jew, founder of the very "Greek" Alexandrian tradition of biblical exegesis.

It is important to remember that our concern in this chapter is not with how ancient Hebrews really lived but with the written record of their living as received by early Christians. Much has been written lately from a feminist perspective speculating on a history supposedly hidden in the text of the Old Testament by its patriarchal writers and editors. Such speculations often provide alternative readings of the text very much at odds with traditional readings, but our traditional readings by and large come from early Christian readings, which are based on the text as written, edited, and interpreted by persons unaffected by modern feminist sensibilities and assumptions. This is not to deny all value to alternative readings but to say that while alternative readings may tell us more about what ancient Hebrews thought about male and female, they do not tell us much about what early Christians thought about what ancient Hebrews thought about male and female.

## Creation and Fall

The Book of Genesis gives us two very different but complementary accounts of creation—a so-called Priestly account (Gen 1:1—2:3) now thought to have been written in the fifth or sixth century before Christ, prefacing a so-called Yahwist account of much earlier origin (Gen 2:4–25). In contrast to the highly sexualized cosmogony of Greek mythology based on copulation and conflict, as well as to the Neoplatonist conception of successive stages of emanation from the impersonal One to the evil of unformed matter, both accounts of creation in Genesis begin with a transcendent but very personal God who speaks and acts, creating everything and everybody—but not sexually. Both also feature the distinction of male and female as an important part of God's "very good" creation.

In the first account, creation proceeds in an orderly fashion, step by step from nothing to formless matter to lands and seas that bring forth plant life, then sea life, and then land animals. All these things are declared "good," and then God creates man, saying, "Let us make man in our image, after our likeness, and let them have dominion" over all the earth (Gen 1:26). "So God created man in his own image; in the image of God created he him, male and female created he them" (Gen 1:27). Then God blessed them, commanded them to "be fruitful and multiply," and gave them dominion over the earth (Gen 1:28). God then surveys creation and finds it "very good" (Gen 1:31).

Gen 1:27 is the first mention of male and female in the Old Testament. It is repeated almost verbatim in Gen 5:1–2 to introduce the genealogy of Adam. In both instances, male and female are associated with the image of God, borne only by man. The commandment to "be fruitful and multiply" is also repeated, twice to Noah (Gen 9:1, 7), twice to Jacob (Gen 28:3; 35:11), once to Joseph (Gen 48:4), once to Ishmael (Gen 17:20), and once to the people of Israel (Lev 26:9). The "image of God" is mentioned just once more in Hebrew Scripture, in Gen 9:7 to condemn murder. Nowhere is the "image of God" defined, but the context of Gen 1:26–28 will suggest to some ancient Jews and Christians that it relates to dominion and perhaps also, in some way, to male and female, as we will see in chapter 5 of this book.

The second chapter of Genesis focuses on the creation of the first man "out of the dust of the ground," followed by the creation of the first woman from the first man. Everything is prepared for the man before the creation of the woman, but God then says, "It is not good that the man should be alone: I will make him an help meet for him" (2:18). So God causes the man to fall into a deep sleep and then takes one of the man's ribs from which he fashions the woman. When the man awakes, God brings the woman to him:

> 23And Adam said, This is now bone of my bone and flesh of my flesh: she shall be called Woman [*ishshah*], because she was taken out of man [*ish*]. 24Therefore shall a man leave his father and his mother, and shall cleave unto his wife and they shall be one flesh. 25And they were both naked, the man and his wife, and were not ashamed.

Already, in just the first two chapters of Genesis, we can see fundamental differences between the Hebrew and Greek views of male and female. The man and the woman share a common nature and an intimate connection on account of the man being the source of the woman. Both are made in the image of God and of the same flesh and bone. The stress is on their likeness, not their difference. The woman is created to be a helper better suited to the man than any other creature (Gen 2:21), but nothing is said about how she is to help the man or how she is better suited to help him beyond her sharing his flesh and bone. She is not a lesser being, neither an incomplete or deformed man as in Aristotle, nor a step down on the incarnational scale as in Plato. Her creation is a blessing and not a curse as it is in Hesiod.[1] The man and the woman are not yet opposed in any way. There is as yet no strife between them. They are created to cooperate with each other in subduing the earth and to cleave to each other so as to become "one flesh." They are not created as first men and then women, as in Hesiod, but as first one man and then one woman, establishing the singular correspondence of the sexes as the marital ideal.

Evil enters the narrative in the first verse of Genesis 3, immediately after the man meets the woman, with nothing said about their life before the appearance of the serpent, which is also a creature of God but apparently one already fallen. The serpent tempts the woman, first with a question, "Hath God said . . . ?," then with a lie, "Ye shall not surely die," and then with a truth, "Your eyes shall be opened, and ye shall be as gods, knowing good and evil" (Gen 3:1–5). It is worth noting that in the Hebrew, the Greek, and the English of the King James Version, the serpent's temptation is consistently plural: "*Ye* shall not surely die" and "*your* eyes shall be opened," instead of "*Thou* shalt not surely die" and "*thine* eyes shall be opened." Even the serpent treats the man and the woman as a unity, experiencing all things in common, and yet its tactic to subvert them is to approach only the woman, as if sin is essentially a disunity, the turning of one away from another. It is also worth noting that though the woman then sees "that the tree was good for food, and that it was pleasant to the eyes, and a tree to be desired to make one wise" (Gen 3:6), the serpent makes use of only the last aspect of the tree in its temptation: It appeals only to the woman's curiosity and pride in wanting to be like the gods, knowing good and evil. That is what turns her attention to the tree.

The woman eats of the fruit of the tree and then gives it to the man, who also eats of it. The quickness of the man's complicity, without any attempt at persuasion by the woman, is another indication of how close they are, as is the fact that it is only after both eat of the fruit that their eyes are opened and they notice their nakedness. In shame, they cover themselves with fig leaves and hide when they hear God "walking in the garden in the cool of the day" (Gen 3:8). God calls out to the man, who answers timidly, admitting his shame and fear. God then asks him if he has eaten from the forbidden tree. The man appears to blame the woman in saying she gave him the fruit, just as the woman appears to blame the serpent in saying it "beguiled" her (Gen 3:13), but an advocate speaking

---

1. Hesiod, *Th.* 600–610.

in their defense might argue, very reasonably, that both are only confessing what they have actually done: Both have acted at the instigation of another, following the lead of someone they were not created to follow. If this is part of their crime, they are obliged to confess it.

Upon hearing their confessions, God immediately curses the serpent to crawl on its belly, eat dust, and suffer the enmity of the woman and her seed. Then God says to the woman: "I will greatly multiply thy sorrow and thy conception; in sorrow thou shalt bring forth children; and thy desire shall be to thy husband, and he shall rule over thee" (Gen 3:16). The Hebrew word *teshuqah*, which appears as "desire" in the King James Version and most other English Bibles, is also sometimes translated as "longing" and is believed to derive from the verb *shuq*, meaning "to overflow," the basic sense being a stretching forth or reaching out like spreading water.[2] The noun *teshuqah* is used just three times in the Hebrew Bible: in Gen 3:16 to speak of the woman's desire for the man, in Song 7:10 to speak of a man's desire for a woman, and in Gen 4:7, which parallels Gen 3:16 and which has been variously translated to mean sin's desire for Cain or Abel's submission to Cain, along with Cain's mastery over either sin or Abel. The significance of Gen 4:7, whichever way the verse is understood, is that the desire or longing expressed by the Hebrew word *teshuqah* is not always sexual. It seems certainly sexual in Song 7:10 but certainly not sexual in Gen 4:7, which militates against a sexual reading of Gen 3:16, especially in view of the Septuagint's translation of *teshuqah* as *apostrophē*, which commonly means a change of course— turning back toward home or turning away from a trap—and rarely if ever refers to sexual desire.[3] It would seem that after turning toward the serpent by talking to it, believing it, and acting on its words, the woman must now turn back toward the man and hearken unto him in the same way, and this is the reason for the enmity decreed between the serpent and the woman.[4]

Having sentenced the serpent and the woman, God then sentences the man, prefacing his sentence with the words, "Because thou hast

---

2. See Brown, *Brown-Driver-Briggs*: http://biblehub.com/str/hebrew/8669.htm and http://biblehub.com/hebrew/7783.htm. The verb *shuq* is also used just three times in the Hebrew Bible: Ps 65:9; Joel 2:24; 3:13.

3. LSJ, 220.

4. This is how Philo of Alexandria understood *apostrophē* in Gen 3:16, reading it allegorically as a return of the outward senses to the control of the mind. See Philo, *QG* 1.49; Loader, *Philo, Josephus, and the Testaments on Sexuality*, 125.

hearkened unto the voice of thy wife, and hast eaten of the tree" (Gen 3:17). Here again is evidence that disobedience to the commandment to not eat of the tree is not the only fault at issue: The man has also taken the woman's lead, contrary to the order of creation. His sentence is thus:

> [17]cursed is the ground for thy sake; in sorrow shalt thou eat of it all the days of thy life; [18]Thorns also and thistles shall it bring forth to thee; and thou shalt eat the herb of the field; [19]In the sweat of thy face shalt thou eat bread, till thou return unto the ground; for out of it wast thou taken: for dust thou art, and unto dust shalt thou return.

Here again it seems the sentence passed is intended not just to punish the man for his transgression but to restore his right relation to the woman. Before the Fall, there is food in abundance with little effort needed to partake of it. God explicitly tells the man, before the creation of the woman, that he may "freely eat" of this abundance (Gen 2:16). After the creation of the woman, the man shows her what God has and has not provided for them to eat. She demonstrates her knowledge of this in her answer to the serpent. She also demonstrates her freedom to eat by partaking of the forbidden fruit. In the Fall, however, the woman dares to feed the man. Now, after the Fall, neither the man nor the woman may eat so freely, and the man must labor all his life to feed the woman.

Immediately after the man is sentenced, he names the woman "Life"—*Hawwah* in Hebrew, *Zoē* in the Greek Septuagint, *Eva* in the Latin Vulgate, and *Eve* in most English translations—"because she was the mother of all living" (Gen 3:20). This is the second time the man, Adam, has named the woman, the first being when he names her Woman, finishing his work of naming all the animals. It is also the first mention in the Bible of any distinguishing characteristic of the woman other than her being made from the man as his helper. It might seem odd for Adam to name Eve just at this time, having just been sentenced to a life of hard labor followed by the grave, but it is only after their eyes are opened and also after God decrees and foretells their future that their differences become apparent and their special roles are revealed.

The story of the Fall ends with God making Adam and Eve "coats of skins" to replace their fig leaves and then expelling them from the garden, lest they should eat of the Tree of Life and live forever in their fallen state (Gen 3:21–24). The text then says that Adam "knew" Eve and she conceived and bore a son, Cain. There is no hint of Adam's use of force, violence, or even persuasion to "know" Eve. Quite the contrary, Eve regards Cain as a blessing from God, saying, "I have gotten a man [*ish, anthrōpos*] from the Lord" (Gen 4:1).

At this point in the text, it is still not clear whether the man and the woman differ in any way that makes one naturally superior to the other. The woman has been "beguiled" by the serpent (Gen 3:13), which has suggested to many readers through the ages that she is naturally weaker than the man in terms of her rationality or sociality, either of which may make her more easily led or misled compared to the man. In that case, the decree or prophecy that "thy desire shall be to thy husband" (Gen 3:16) could be understood to speak of her weakness. But it may be that only the woman was beguiled because only the woman was tempted by the serpent, and that if the man had been tempted by the serpent, he also would have been beguiled, in which case her "desire" could be understood as the change of course suggested by the Greek of the Septuagint. Nothing so far in Genesis tells us which of these interpretations should be preferred.

It is also unclear, from just the first three chapters of Genesis, whether the woman's subjection to the man is a decree or a prophecy. God plainly says to the serpent, "I will put enmity between thee and the woman," and to the woman, "I will greatly multiply thy sorrow and thy conception" (Gen 3:14–16). He seems also to curse the ground to make life hard for the man (Gen 3:17–19). But he does not plainly say that he wills the man to rule over the woman. The text, by itself, could be understood either way or both ways, as the history of its interpretation demonstrates.

Much clearer in the biblical account of the Fall is the significance of a natural order of relation between the woman and the serpent, the man and the woman, and God and man, which is violated by the act of eating the forbidden fruit at the instigation of another, and which the sentences of God serve to restore. The wrong order is seen in the sequence of the temptation, which begins with the serpent, who misleads the woman, who misleads the man. The right order is seen in the sequence of God speaking first to the man, then to the woman, then to the serpent. It is also seen in God's sentencing of the three in reverse order: first the serpent, then the woman, then the man. This is just how a superior military commander would deal with different ranks in a mutiny, punishing the mutineers first to re-establish "good order and discipline" before relieving or reprimanding the officers whose poor leadership provoked the mutiny.

Sexual desire plays no certain part in the subsequent account of their fall. Sensuality *per se* plays only a very minor part. It is not part of the serpent's temptation of Eve (Gen 3:1–5), only a part of the fruit's appeal to Eve after she has turned her attention to it, when she notices that it is "pleasant to the eyes" (Gen 3:6). Sensuality is also not explicitly part of Eve's giving the fruit to Adam or his accepting the fruit from Eve; he appears to eat of the fruit solely because she offered it to him. Only after both eat do they notice their nakedness, but this sudden awareness leads not immediately to sexual desire and intercourse but to a felt need and effort to clothe themselves. Nakedness in the presence of others does normally produce feelings of self-consciousness and vulnerability unrelated to sexual desire. Adam himself says, "I was afraid because I was naked" (Gen 3:10), and it is only after he and Eve have left the garden that their new awareness of their bodies leads to carnal knowledge.

The unity of the man and the woman is confirmed throughout the account of their creation and fall. Only Eve speaks to the serpent, but that is the serpent's doing; it singles her out for temptation. Otherwise, the man and the woman act together at every step: They sin together, hide together, face God together, and leave the garden together. They do not quarrel or even question one another. They both appear to spread the blame for their sin—Adam to Eve (and God) and Eve to the serpent—but they do not contradict each other on any point of fact. In both their disobedience and their subsequent defensiveness they are united, as Adam himself testifies: "She gave me of the tree, and I did eat" (Gen 3:12). The dignity of the woman is confirmed throughout the account, despite her subjection to the man after the Fall. God does not speak only to the man; He speaks directly to both the man and the woman, questioning both before sentencing both. He does not question the serpent; He only curses it. He is not said to "curse" the man or the woman; he is only said to "curse" the serpent and the ground, which suggests that what he does to the man and the woman is not for their ill but for their good and therefore not truly a curse but at worst a consequence and at best a kind of blessing, a severe mercy.

## First Families

The history of the Hebrews as a distinct people begins with three generations of married couples that have served ever thereafter as models of marriage for both Christians and Jews: Abraham and Sarah, Isaac and Rebecca, Jacob and Rachel. All three couples are bound by affection and blood and share a common interest in progeny. The husbands are in charge but loving and yielding towards their wives, not domineering tyrants. The wives are dutiful and, although not always submissive, are never openly rebellious or contemptuous. There is no divorce among them or abuse by either husbands or wives. Their stories are familiar but worth reviewing for what they reveal about male and female in the Old Testament.

Abraham and Sarah start out as Abram and Sarai, half-siblings who twice conspire to hide the fact that they are also husband and wife so strangers will not murder Abram to take Sarai. Twice God foils their deception, forcing the strangers to return Sarai to Abram (Gen 12:11–20; 20:2–18). Four times God promises to make Abram the father of many (Gen 12:2; 13:16; 15:4; 16:10; 17:2), giving him the name *Abraham*, meaning "father of many." God also changes Sarai's name to *Sarah*, meaning "princess," securing her position in the household and recognizing her role as the mother of many. Yet the couple remain childless well into old age (Gen 17:5, 15). It seems not to have occurred to Abraham that he might take another wife by which to get an heir, but it does occur to Sarah, who urges Abraham to make her Egyptian handmaiden, Hagar, his concubine, which Abraham condescends to do, fathering Ishmael. Sarah soon regrets this and urges Abraham to get rid of Hagar and Ishmael, which Abraham again condescends to do, sending Hagar off into the desert, where she leaves her babe in the shade of a bush and sits down to die. But God has pity on Hagar and promises her that he will make Ishmael a great nation (Gen 16:10; 21:18). As promised by God, Sarah eventually bears a son, Isaac, and lives long enough to see him fully grown.[5] When she dies, Abraham weeps and mourns and buys a field with a cave in which to bury her (Gen 23). Sometime later, after Isaac's wedding to Rebecca, Abraham takes another wife, named Keturah, who bears him six sons. He is also said to have fathered sons by concubines,

---

5. Sarah laughs when she hears it said by God that she will conceive, saying, according to the Masoretic text, "After I am waxed old shall I have pleasure [*edna*], my lord being also old?" (Gen 18:12) It is unclear whether this refers to sexual pleasure or the joy of children. The word appears four more times in the Old Testament (2 Sam 1:24; Ps 36:8; Jer 51:34; Amos 1:5) without any hint of sexual pleasure, being also translated into English as "luxury," "dainty," and "delight." In the Septuagint, Gen 18:12 makes no mention of pleasure in any form, saying simply, "*oupō men moi gegonen eōs o de kurios mou presbuteros*," which Brenton, *Septuagint*, renders, "The thing has not yet happened to me even until now, and my lord is old." Likewise, the Orthodox Study Bible, based on the Septuagint, says, "I have not yet had a child until now, and my lord is old also."

but only Isaac is his heir; the others are given gifts and sent away before Abraham dies (Gen 25:1–6).

As the first of the Hebrew patriarchs, Abraham hardly seems patriarchal, at least as that word is used in feminist discourse. Sarah refers to Abraham as "my lord," but we see little evidence of his lordship (Gen 18:12). The couple act together to both please and displease God. She does as he bids in twice pretending to be his sister, and he does as she bids in twice dealing with Hagar. Sarah blames Abraham for Hagar's contempt for her, saying, "My wrong be upon thee" and "the Lord judge between me and thee"; Abraham does not defend himself and lets Sarah have her way with Hagar (Gen 16:5–6). God does not bless Abraham's intercourse with Hagar but also does not punish anyone for it. The same is true of Abraham's intercourse with his unnamed concubines and his second marriage to Keturah. Celibacy is never expected of Abraham; conjugal relations are.

Like father, like son: Isaac and Rebecca are also close. Rebecca is fair, kind, dutiful, modest, and Isaac's cousin. The story of her betrothal to Isaac is lengthy, all sixty-seven verses of Gen 24. Rebecca offers to water the camels of Abraham's servant, and this is the sign by which the servant knows she is God's choice to marry Isaac. She freely agrees to marry Isaac, and before meeting him she takes a veil to cover herself. Isaac is said to love Rebecca, and their wedding is said to console him for the loss of his mother. Later, the couple also pretend to be brother and sister, and God again intervenes to return wife to husband. Isaac prays and Rebecca conceives, bearing him twin sons, Jacob and Esau, who mirror Cain and Abel in that Esau is a hunter and Jacob is a mother's boy, "dwelling in tents" (Gen 25:27). Isaac favors Esau, but Rebecca favors Jacob and conspires with him to cheat Esau out of his father's blessing.

Fearing Esau's wrath, Jacob flees to his uncle Laban, falls in love with his daughter Rachel, and agrees to serve Laban for seven years to earn Rachel's hand in marriage, which "seemed unto him but a few days, for the love he had to her" (Gen 29:20). But Laban tricks Jacob into marrying Leah instead, so Jacob agrees to work another seven years for Rachel. In those years, seeing that Leah was less loved, God "opened her womb" and she bore Jacob four sons. Rachel pleads with Jacob to give her children "or else I die," and Jacob angrily tells her that God and not he has kept her childless (Gen 30:1–2). Rachel then gives him her handmaiden Bilhah, who bears Jacob two sons, and Leah retaliates by giving him her handmaiden Zilpah, who also bears him two sons. Leah herself bears Jacob two more sons and then a daughter, Dinah. At last, God opens Rachel's womb and she bears Jacob his eleventh son, Joseph, whom Jacob favors. Despite their rivalry, both Leah and Rachel side with their husband Jacob in his dispute with their father Laban, facilitating their escape and traveling with him back to the land of Canaan, where Jacob makes peace with Esau.

Jacob's approach to Esau is made without any assurance that Esau will forgive him. To soften Esau's heart, Jacob sends servants with herds and flocks of livestock across the river Jordan with instructions to offer them to Esau as gifts. He then sends all his other wealth across the river, including his wives and sons, staying behind alone for the night, still not knowing whether Esau will accept his gifts and welcome him home. This is the first supremely good thing anyone in the family does, and it is done on Jacob's own initiative, not commanded by God. Jacob has freely offered up everything he owns and loves for the sake of making peace with his brother. It is then that, while all alone the whole night, he wrestles with the angel of God and is given the name of Israel, "He who rivals God," by which God's elect will be known thereafter. Later at Bethel, God commands him, for the second time, to "be fruitful and multiply; a nation and a company of nations shall be of thee, and kings shall come out of thy loins" (Gen 35:11). But the only child of the flesh born to Jacob thereafter is Benjamin, whom Rachel bears before dying in childbirth.

There is a definite preference for monogamy in this history, seen in the divine favor shown to the husband's only or favorite wife and in the discord plaguing the women who share a man. But there is no punishment or even reprimand for polygyny or for widowers marrying again. God makes Ishmael the father of twelve princes and gives sons to Abraham's second wife and concubines. Jacob's sons by Bilhah and Zilpah are fully his sons, with the same standing as Leah's, although not quite Rachel's. Esau's two Hittite wives are "a grief of mind" to Isaac and Rebecca, but this is because they are foreigners, "daughters of Heth" (Gen 26:35; 27:46). Nothing else is said about them, but they are the reason Isaac sends Jacob to find a bride for himself among Rebecca's people.

## Gender Order and Disorder

As always everywhere for everyone, husbands and wives do not always get along in the Old Testament. Wives occasionally talk back to their husbands, as when Zipporah flings the foreskin of her son at Moses's feet and says, "Surely a bloody husband art thou to me!" (Exod 4:25), and when Tobit doubts that the kid his wife Anna has been given is actually a gift, and she reproaches him, saying, "Where are thine alms and thy righteous deeds?" (Tob 2:14). Rebecca tricks Isaac into blessing Jacob instead of Esau, yet he is not said to punish her for it and does as she wishes in telling his sons not to marry Canaanites (Gen 27). Rachel's pleas for children anger Jacob, but he does as she bids in taking her handmaid Bilhah, following Abraham's example with Hagar (Gen 30:1–4; 16:3–4). David and Michal give us the only certain example of a Hebrew husband and wife who come to hate each other: When she shames him for dancing nearly naked to celebrate the return of the Ark, he stops sleeping with her (2 Sam 6:16–23), but their relationship is obviously a casualty of David's conflict with Michal's father, King Saul.[6] Hosea's wife Gomer might appear as the worst example of an Israelite wife, but she is less a real wife than a literary device for the sake of "prophetic theater," as the marriage of Hosea and Gomer is a metaphorical dramatization of God's displeasure with the wayward house of Israel.[7] Samson's unnamed wife betrayed him to find out the answer to a riddle, but she was a Philistine (Judg 14:1–20). Delilah also betrayed Samson to his enemies, but she appears to have been not his wife but a harlot and perhaps also a Philistine (Judg 16).

None of these examples really challenges the gender order of the Old Testament, unless one sees that order as requiring absolute,

---

6. When David flees the palace, Saul marries Michal off to another man; David reclaims her after Saul's death, but their relationship never recovers. Some modern scholars see homosexuality in David's dancing and in his relationship with Jonathan, Michal's brother, but these possibilities do not appear in ancient commentaries and are considered anachronistic by other modern scholars. See Zehnder, "Observations on the Relationship between David and Jonathan," 127–74; Stansell, "David and His Friends," 115–31.

7. See Gruber, *Hosea*, 69–89, esp. 76–77, 88. Gruber provides a detailed analysis of Rabbinic commentary on Gomer, noting that the text does not in fact say Hosea married a prostitute or that Gomer was a prostitute, yet the "moral dilemma" of God ordering Hosea to marry a prostitute "has obsessed commentaries on the book of Hosea for several centuries." This may be true of Rabbinic literature and modern Christian literature, but it is not true of early Christian literature, which rarely mentions Gomer and stresses her redemption when it does. See Pentiuc, *Long-Suffering Love*, 28. H. W. Wolff suggests that Gomer's "whoredom" may only have been her participation in a Canaanite fertility rite, which may have included brief service as a temple prostitute. See Wolff, *Hosea*, 15.

unquestioning, uncomplaining subservience of wives to husbands, which the examples themselves and the Law of Moses give evidence against. The Law afforded women considerable protection and dignity, not always found in ancient times. The Decalogue required sons and daughters to honor both their fathers and their mothers (Exod 20:12; Deut 5:16). Women were protected from false charges of infidelity (Num 5:11–31; Deut 22:13–21). They were eligible to receive the patrimony of their father if he had no sons (Num 27:1–11). A man with two wives must favor the eldest son of his less favored wife even if the eldest son of his favorite wife is older (Deut 21:15–17). A man who seduces a woman before marrying her may never divorce her (Deut 22:28–29). A newly married man may not go to war or busy himself with business for one year, during which he is to remain at home "and shall cheer up his wife" (Deut 24:5). Women joined men in making music in the temple (1 Chr 25:5–6; Ezra 2:65; Neh 7:67), and when Ezra read the Law to the people after their return from Babylon, he read it to "both men and women, and all that could hear with understanding" (Neh 8:2).

The Law of Moses goes to great lengths to maintain the distinction of male and female, the natural order between them, and the subjection of the woman to the man on account of the Fall. It abominates disrespect for sexual distinction in apparel: "The woman shall not wear that which pertaineth unto a man, neither shall a man put on a woman's garment: for all that do so are abomination unto the Lord thy God" (Deut 22:5). It forbids men to trim their beards (Lev 19:27; 21:5). Only men may be priests. All men are required to offer a sacrifice to the Lord three times a year: at the feast of unleavened bread, the feast of weeks, and the feast of tabernacles (Exod 23:17; Deut 16:16). Women cannot go beyond the door of the tabernacle or their own court of the temple (Exod 38:8; 1 Sam 2:22). The vows of men and women are weighted differently: For ages twenty to sixty, men are valued at fifty shekels and women at thirty shekels; for age five to twenty, it is twenty for males and ten for females; for ages one month to five years, it is five and three; for ages over sixty, it is fifteen and ten (Lev 27:1–7). But those too poor to pay the set amount are to present themselves to a priest, who is to set an amount within their means (Lev 27:8), an indication, notes Hannah Harrington, that the different rates for males and females are based on an expectation of economic productivity, with men expected to pay more because they earn more.[8] Sex also determines the length of a mother's "uncleanness" after giving birth: A son means a mother is unclean for seven days and may not touch sacred things or come near the sanctuary for thirty-three days; a daughter means a mother is unclean for fourteen days and may not touch sacred things or come near the sanctuary for sixty-six days (Lev 12:2–6). The concern here is for ritual purity; the difference emphasizes the extra care women must take, because of menstruation, to avoid defiling holy things.[9]

The Law assumed the man's authority over the woman, per Gen 3:16. Husbands and fathers held the veto power over their wives' and daughters' oaths (Num 30:1–16), and the rule of women was considered a calamity: "As for my people, children are their oppressors, and women rule over them. O my people, they which lead thee cause thee to err, and destroy the way of thy paths" (Isa 3:12). This gender order is challenged three times in the Old Testament, however—twice by a woman and once by a man. In all three cases, the telling of the story supports the order.

In the first case, Moses's sister Miriam and brother Aaron challenge Moses's leadership because he has taken an Ethiopian wife. Miriam is barely known before this. As the only sister of Moses and Aaron mentioned in Scripture, she is presumed to have been the sister who was there when Pharaoh's daughter discovered the infant Moses (Exod 2:4–8; Num 26:59; 1 Chr 6:3). She is first mentioned by name in Exodus 15, where she is identified as a prophetess and sister of Aaron who leads the women in singing and dancing to celebrate the destruction of Pharaoh's army in the Red Sea (Exod 15:20–21). The next mention of Miriam is her complaint against Moses, in which she and Aaron say, "Hath the Lord indeed spoken only by Moses? Hath he not spoken also by us?" (Num 12:2). The

---

8. See Harrington, "Leviticus," 78.

9. See Harrington, "Leviticus," 76. Many feminists have written about how concern for ritual purity has been used against women, limiting their public role and contributing to their being viewed by men as a "dangerous Other." Women certainly do present a temptation to men, but men also present a temptation to women, and coitus made both men and women temporarily unclean in Mosaic law. Menstruation did limit the public role of Hebrew women, at least temporarily, but its greater significance is highly questionable. In her influential *Purity and Danger*, Mary Douglas held that ritual purity matters least when women are most oppressed and most when women rival men for power. She later came to see reverence for the tabernacle as driving the concern for ritual purity, even arguing that Leviticus and Numbers "never use the principle of ritual purity to separate classes or races, foreigners, or natives," since, "Everybody is liable to be defiled or defile." See Douglas, *Purity and Danger*, 142; Douglas, *In the Wilderness*, 25.

Lord, however, is angered by their impudence and summons the three of them to the tabernacle, where he declares Moses his chief prophet, the only one to whom he will speak not in dreams or visions but "mouth to mouth" (Num 12:8). When God departs, Miriam is struck with leprosy and turned "white as snow" (Num 12:10). Aaron pleads for her life to Moses, calling him "lord," and Moses beseeches God on her behalf. God relents, saying, "If her father had but spit in her face, should she not be ashamed seven days? Let her be shut out from the camp seven days, and after that let her be received in again" (Num 12:14). And so Miriam is shut out of the camp for seven days. The very next thing said about her, eight chapters later, is that she died and was buried, with no mention of honors or even mourning (Num 20:1).

Obviously, in the story as it is told, God was extremely displeased with Miriam. But not with Aaron. God does nothing to Aaron for challenging Moses. Aaron remains as Israel's first high priest and father of all of Israel's priests, continuing to play a very active role in guiding the people through the wilderness, for which he is mentioned thirty-seven more times before his death. His only punishment is the same as Moses's punishment for angrily striking the rock to get water at Meribah: Neither will live to enter the promised land. When Aaron dies atop Mount Hor, all the people of Israel are said to mourn for 30 days (Num 20:23–29). Nothing in the story explains this difference in treatment, except that it begins, "Miriam and Aaron . . ." (Num 12:1). Perhaps Miriam was the first to complain and incited Aaron to go along with her. And perhaps a woman again leading a man astray and challenging her divinely appointed head threatened to upset the natural and economical order. This is indeed the view of the second-century Irenaeus of Lyon, who says Miriam was punished and not Aaron because as a woman she was subjected to the man by both nature and the Law.[10]

The second case concerns the prophetess Deborah, but not in the way many readers would expect. The story lends itself easily to a feminist reading that presumes an oral tradition in which Deborah herself challenges the gender order, which the authors or editors of the Hebrew Bible have made less threatening by crafting the text of the story to minimize the threat posed by Deborah and maximize the shame of Barak. Plausible as that reading is, it is not how early Christians would have read the story. They would have read it as holy scripture, expecting the story to tell them

---

10. Irenaeus, Fr. 33, PG 7, 1245C (numbered as Fr. 32 in ANF 1:573).

right from wrong without speculating on the accuracy of the account or the motives of its authors and editors. The role of the two women in the story is now so often exaggerated that the story is worth a close look.[11]

The story begins with Deborah already a prophetess and a "judge," the only female judge in Scripture. The book of Judges covers a troubled time in Israelite history, when the people turned away from the Lord to serve Baal and Ashtaroth (Judg 2:8–13), and the only leaders in Israel were the few men and women of faith whom God raised up to "judge Israel." The calling of judge was not a formal office with specific rights and responsibilities. The lesser known judges (Tola, Jair, Ibzan, Elon, Abdon) seem to have been local clan leaders. Jephthah and Samson were great warriors. Samuel seems to have been simply a prophet. His single achievement as a leader is when he calls all of Israel together at Mizpeh for the purpose of prayer, after which "the Lord thundered with a great thunder" and the Philistines were defeated (1 Sam 7).

Deborah's story is similar to Samuel's. She dwelt under a palm tree between Ramah and Bethel "and the people of Israel came up to her for judgment" (Judg 4:5). Instead of calling all of Israel to her, she calls only Barak to tell him to gather ten thousand men to meet Sisera.[12] Barak tells Deborah, "If thou wilt go with me, then I will go, but if thou wilt not go with me, then I will not go." Deborah replies, "I will surely go with thee. Notwithstanding, the journey that thou takest shall not be for thine honor, for the Lord shall sell Sisera into the hand of a woman" (Judg 4:9). She goes with Barak because he will not go without her. The text says that "he went up with ten thousand men at his feet" and that "Deborah went up with him" (Judg 4:10). In other words, he was in command, leading his men to war; she was his spiritual guide. Her only act on the day of battle was to inspire him to act (Judg 4:14). He alone is said to have gone down the mountain with the army to meet Sisera; she is not said to have gone down and very likely stayed on the mountain to watch the battle (Judg 4:14). Barak wins the victory, but Sisera escapes and finds refuge in the tent of Jael, Heber's wife, who drives a tent peg through his temples while he sleeps. Jael then finds Barak to tell him the news. After the battle, Deborah and Barak sing a song of victory (Judg 5:1). The song bids her

---

11. For example, Anne Stewart lauds Deborah as a "wise and influential leader, a prophet, a poet, a judge, and a military commander." See Stewart, "Deborah, Jael, and Their Interpreters," 128–32.

12. Susan Niditch says Deborah "mobilizes the troops" before speaking to Barak, but the text does not support that. Cf. Judg 4:6–7 and Niditch, *Judges*, 60, 65.

to "awake, awake, utter a song"; it bids him to "arise, Barak, and lead thy captivity captive" (Judg 5:12). It lauds her as "a mother in Israel" (Judg 5:7), but it lauds him not at all. True to Deborah's prophecy, his honor goes instead to a woman, Jael, whom the song praises at length, beginning with the words, "Blessed above women shall Jael the wife of Heber the Kenite be, blessed shall she be above women in the tent" (Judg 5:24).

The story as told presents an obvious problem for both feminists and non-feminists. For feminists, the problem is how to understand Deborah's apparent rebuke of Barak, which appears to connect his refusal to go alone with his loss of honor to a woman. The solution offered by Susan Niditch and others is to deny the connection. Niditch says Barak was "wise to know that victory comes with the presence of God's favorite,"[13] that this "enhances [Deborah's] prestige as a woman warrior," and that her response, foretelling the honor going to a woman, merely "emphasizes a favorite theme of Judges and the Hebrew Bible concerning the victory of an unlikely hero." But this interpretation only makes sense if one assumes that there is no shame in a man submitting himself to the command of a woman and refusing to go to war without her. For those who assume there is, believing that God has subjected women to men and that war is properly a man's responsibility, the problem is how to explain the apparent exception of Barak submitting to Deborah.[14] The solution has long been to downplay Deborah and make excuses for Barak. The Septuagint itself adds a line of excuse to Barak's refusal to go alone, having him say, "For I know not the day on which the Lord prospers his messenger with me," though this hardly speaks well of him as a military leader, for when armies are already in the field, a competent commander knows when to fight.[15] The Septuagint also mentions Barak but not Deborah in 1 Samuel 12:11: "Then the Lord sent Jerub-Baal, Barak, Jephthah and Samuel, and he delivered you from the hands of your enemies all around you, so that you lived in safety" (NRSV).[16] Similarly, the Apostle Paul names Barak along with Gideon, Samson, Jephthah,

---

13. In support of this claim, Niditch, *Judges*, 65, cites 2 Kgs 2:12: "And Elisha saw it, and he cried, My father, my father, the chariot of Israel, and the horsemen thereof. And he saw him no more: and he took hold of his own clothes, and rent them in two pieces." Niditch takes this to mean, "Elijah is worth battalions."

14. Jael's murder of Sisera is not a problem for either perspective.

15. LXX Judg 4:8 in Brenton, *Septuagint*, 320.

16. The KJV follows the Hebrew text in naming "Bedan" instead of Barak in 1 Sam 12:11. Of this Bedan, nothing else is said except that he is the son of Ulam (1 Chr 7:17).

David, and Samuel, but not Deborah, among those "who through faith subdued kingdoms, wrought righteousness, obtained promises, stopped the mouths of lions, quenched the violence of fire, escaped the edge of the sword, out of weakness were made strong, waxed valiant in fight, turned to flight the armies of the aliens" (Heb 11:32–34). Deborah is presumably included in Paul's mention of "prophets" in Heb 11:32, but neither the Old nor the New Testament mentions her by name outside Judges 4 and 5. Some Rabbinic midrashim accuse Deborah of pride and say she lost the gift of prophecy on account of it. Some midrashim also depict Barak as less cowardly and more cooperative than subordinate, with one making Barak Deborah's husband to explain their cooperation.[17] Ambrose of Milan makes him Deborah's son to argue that wise women can raise sons to command armies. Ambrose also notes the lack of "manly justice" and "manly strength" that occasioned the Israelites' dependence on Deborah in the time of Judges. He praises Deborah, saying, "A widow, she governs the people; a widow, she leads armies; a widow, she chooses generals; a widow, she determines wars and orders triumphs," but he says this to deprive widows of the Greek excuse of feminine weakness in "the battle of faith and the victory of the Church," not to advocate that women be trained as soldiers or guardians, as in Plato's *Republic*.[18]

Of the third challenge to the gender order of the Old Testament, only this need be said: The only woman to ever actually rule over the Israelites was Jezebel's daughter, Athaliah, a "wicked woman" (2 Chr 24:7) who seized power in Judah in 841 BC after the death of her son, King Ahaziah, by murdering all possible claimants to the throne save one, Ahaziah's infant son Jehoash.[19] Six years later, the priest Jehoiada brought Jehoash to the temple and had him acclaimed king; the outraged Athaliah was then arrested and executed (2 Kgs 11:14–16; 2 Chr 23:12–15).

---

17. See Kadari, "Deborah 2."

18. See Ambrose, *Concerning Widows*, ch. 8, NPNF2 10:398–99.

19. Athaliah is rendered Gotholia in the Septuagint. She is said to have been the daughter of Ahab in 2 Kgs 8:18 and 2 Chr 21:6 and the daughter of Omri, Ahab's father, in 2 Kgs 8:26 and 2 Chr 22:2. Some have argued that she was Ahab's sister, but most commentaries have understood her to have been Omri's granddaughter. She is not said in scripture to be Jezebel's daughter, but Ahab is not said to have had any other wives.

## Sexual Order and Disorder

The first violent conflict in the Old Testament, between Cain and Abel, has nothing to do with sex, unless Abel's offering of animal flesh is more manly and therefore more pleasing to God than Cain's offering of vegetables. Sex also plays no part in the story of the Tower of Babel (Gen 11:1–9). There is a brief, strange tale of "sons of God" who saw that the "daughters of men" were fair, came down to them, and begat children by them, who became "giants . . . mighty men . . . men of renown" (Gen 6:4). It is then said that God saw the wickedness of men and decided to destroy both man and beast, which he does, sparing only Noah and his family and the beasts they take aboard the ark. Was this cross-breeding of angels and women the wickedness God saw, or sexual immorality generally? The text does not say. Noah is told to take pairs of male and female beasts aboard the ark. He and his sons also take their wives. Polygyny has already appeared, without God's blessing, in the days of Adam (Gen 4:19–25), but Noah and his sons each have only one wife, confirming the ideal of monogamy (Gen 7:13).

But if sexual immorality is only implicit in Genesis before the Flood, it becomes quite explicit after the Flood, first in the sin of Sodom. The story involves a patriarch only in God's consultation with Abraham before Sodom's destruction (Gen 18:16–33). Because his nephew Lot lives in Sodom, Abraham pleads with God not to destroy the entire city on account of the righteous who live there, but it is obvious that Abraham himself does not believe there are many righteous in Sodom. The required number of righteous to stay God's hand shrinks by steps from 50 to 10. Knowing there are not ten righteous men in Sodom, God sends two angels to bring Lot and his family out. When Lot takes the angels into his house, the men of Sodom appear at his door, demanding that he deliver the angels to them that the men might "know" them (Gen 19:5). Lot pleads with them not to persist in their wickedness, offering them his two virgin daughters instead, but the men are not dissuaded and threaten to do worse to Lot than to his visitors. The angels themselves intervene, striking the men blind to rescue Lot, then leading Lot and his wife and daughters out of the city before dawn, after which the city is destroyed by a hail of fire and brimstone. In all of ancient Hebrew literature, no city rivals Sodom and its sister city Gomorrah for extreme immorality.

Otherwise, sexual immorality hardly gets a mention before Jacob's return to Canaan. The text does not plainly say that Leah's daughter Dinah was defiled against her will (Gen 34:1–4), but it does plainly say that Jacob's eldest son Reuben lay with Bilhah, Jacob's concubine (Gen 35:22). Later, Jacob's son Judah lies with a woman he meets along the road, whom he believes to be a harlot but who turns out to be his widowed and childless daughter-in-law Tamar, who has tricked him into having sex with her because he has still not married her to another man who will give her children (Gen 38:14). Judah had at least sent Tamar his son Onan to "raise up seed" to her dead husband. Onan could have simply refused to do the deed; instead, he lies with Tamar but avoids impregnating her by spilling his seed upon the ground. This selfish act of enjoying his sister-in-law but preventing her from conceiving, presumably to avoid the responsibility of raising children to preserve his wicked brother Er's name, angers God, who strikes him dead just as he had struck Er dead (Gen 38:8–10). The act also earns Onan modern remembrance through the term *onanism*, which has been used to mean both contraception and masturbation.

Sexual immorality plays no part in the story of Jacob's favorite son Joseph, except in the failed attempts by Potiphar's wife to seduce him (Gen 39:6–20). It also plays no part in the story of Moses, except when Moses descends Mount Sinai to find the Israelites dancing naked about the golden calf (Exod 32:25). It seems to become a serious problem for the Israelites only when they return to Canaan after wandering in the wilderness. Even in the wilderness, Israelite men have shown a weakness for the daughters of Moab, taking them as wives and worshipping their god (Num 25). But only after the death of Joshua, when the Israelites are left leaderless, do we hear of them patronizing prostitutes, raping women, and collecting great numbers of wives and concubines. Gideon is said to have had enough wives and concubines to give him 70 sons (Judg 8:30–31). Jephthah is the son of a harlot (Judg 11:1). Samson gives his Gentile wife to a friend after she betrays him and later tries to take her back. Then after her death, he consorts with harlots, taking up with a woman who appears to be a harlot, who also betrays him (Judg 14–16).[20]

The worst example of sexual immorality after the Israelites return to Canaan is the rape and murder of the concubine of an unnamed Levite in an encounter similar to Lot's experience in Sodom. The Levite and his concubine have been offered a place to stay for the night by an old man

---

20. Samson is already a widower when he is said to visit a harlot (Judg 16:1). Delilah appears immediately thereafter. Samson is said to have "loved a woman" named Delilah, but she is never said to be "his woman," the Hebrew and Greek way of saying "his wife" (Judg 16:4).

in Gibeah, a city belonging to the tribe of Benjamin. During the night, the men of Gibeah beat on the door of the house demanding that the old man deliver the Levite to them "that we may know him" (Judg 19:22). The old man pleads with them not to demand the Levite and offers them his virginal daughter and the Levite's concubine, but the men persist in demanding the Levite. The Levite then gives them his concubine, whom the men rape and abuse all the night, leaving her to crawl back to the old man's door. In the morning, the Levite finds her dead on the doorstep. He then cuts her body into twelve pieces, which he sends to the twelve tribes of Israel (Judg 19:30). A long and bloody civil war ensues between the Benjamites and the other tribes of Israel, who at last prevail. But to save the tribe of Benjamin from extinction, the victors give the surviving Benjamites women taken by force from the Israelites who did not fight the Benjamites; they also allow the Benjamites to kidnap women from the people of Shiloh during a feast of the Lord (Judg 21:6–23).

The immorality does not end, however, for later it is said that the lawless sons of Eli the priest "lay with the women that assembled at the door of the tabernacle of the congregation" (1 Sam 2:22).[21] Even David, God's anointed, sends Uriah the Hittite to his death in battle so he can claim Uriah's widow, Bathsheba, whom he has seen bathing on her rooftop (2 Sam 11). David repents, but his house is not cleansed. His son Amnon tries to seduce and then rapes his own sister, another Tamar, for which he is later murdered by Absalom, another of David's sons (2 Sam 13). Solomon, David's son by Bathsheba, is said to have "loved many strange women" among his seven hundred wives and three hundred concubines, who are said to have "turned away his heart" in his old age (1 Kgs 11:1–3).

The Law of Moses appears to forbid a king appointed by God to take more than one wife, "that his heart turn not away" (Deut 17:17), but it does not explicitly condemn polygyny for other men and seems even to require it for men whose brothers have died childless for the purpose of raising up seed to them (Deut 25:5). The Law also does not explicitly condemn masturbation, despite the penalty paid by Onan; there is only a requirement that if any seed goes out of a man, he shall wash himself completely and be unclean until the evening, also washing anything on which the seed falls (Lev 15:16–17).

The Law does explicitly condemn many other sex acts, however. Adultery, prostitution, sodomy, bestiality, and incest are all abominated.

---

21. This aspect of their lawlessness is not mentioned in the Septuagint's parallel verse: 1 Kingdoms 2:22.

Adultery and coveting thy neighbor's wife are condemned in the Decalogue (Exod 20:14, 17; Deut 5:18, 21). Death is decreed for rape (Deut 22:25), adultery (Lev 20:10; Deut 22:22–24; cf. Exod 20:14; Lev 18:20;Deut 15:18), homosexuality (Lev 20:13; cf. Lev 18:22; Deut 23:17), bestiality (Exod 22:19; Lev 20:15–16; cf. Lev 11:43-44, 18:23; Deut 27:21), and incest (Lev 20:12, 14, 20–21; cf. Deut 22:30; 25:22–23). A bride who is discovered not to be a virgin is to be stoned (Deut 22:20–21). A priest's daughter who defiles herself by fornication is to be burned (Lev 21:9). Neither men nor women may practice prostitution, and money made from prostitution may not be used to pay a vow (Deut 23:17–18; cf. Lev 19:29). Quite a few verses in Leviticus say who may not "uncover the nakedness" of whom, possibly to curb wanton nakedness such as exhibited by the Israelites while Moses was on Mount Sinai (Exod 32:25) but also possibly to guard against incest, as most such prohibitions involve family members (Lev 18:6–18; 20:17–21).[22] Priests are held to a higher standard, being forbidden to marry women who are no longer virgins for any reason (Lev 21:7, 9, 13–14). They are also required to wear linen breeches fully covering their loins (Exod 28:42).

Women receive some leniency in the Law. The betrothed female slave who lies with another man is only to be scourged instead of put to death because, being a slave, she is not considered to be fully in control of herself (Lev 19:20). A man found lying with an unbetrothed virgin must marry her and pay her father fifty shekels and can never divorce her (Deut 22:28–29; cf. Exod 22:16). The penalty for prostitution is merely exclusion from the religious community, but a prostitute can give up prostitution and still marry an Israelite who is not a priest, and at least one prostitute, Rahab, is counted among the righteous in Israel for helping deliver Jericho to the Israelites (Josh 2:1–25; Ps 87:4; 89:10; cf. Heb 11:31; Jas 2:25). Incest is severely condemned in the Law, but childless women who have resorted to incest by trickery so as to conceive, as did Tamar with Judah and Lot's daughters with Lot (Gen 19:31–38), are not punished in Genesis as Onan was. Judah even declares that Tamar has been more righteous than he (Gen 38:26). In the Law, it is better for a man to have two wives than for a widow to remain childless. Thus, as

---

22. We know that the words "uncover the nakedness" are not merely a euphemism for sexual intercourse because Leviticus speaks unmistakably of sexual intercourse as "lying with," and several verses (Lev 20:11, 17, 18, 20) mention both "lying with" and "uncovering the nakedness" as clearly separate actions.

noted above, a man is obliged to wed his brother's widow as a duty owed to both him and her (Deut 25:5).

The overwhelming majority of references to "whoring" or "whoredom" in Hebrew Scripture refer not to women selling sex but to Israelites turning away from the God of Abraham. Often the whoredom we hear about is Israelite men making wives of foreign women and worshipping their gods (Num 25; Judg 3; Ezra 10). Sexual immorality is just one of many possible results of this turning away. Child sacrifice is another, which is also abominated in the Law (Lev 18:21, 20:2–5; cf. 2 Kgs 23:10; Jer 32:35; LXX Amos 5:26). To avoid all such immoralities, intermarriage between Israelites and foreigners is forbidden, except between Israelite men and foreign women among a defeated enemy, who presumably pose much less of a threat (Num 31:15–18; Deut 7:3–4, 21:10–14). The Law allows men to divorce their wives for indecency (Deut 24:1), but the only time we hear of any women actually being divorced is after the return from Babylon, when Ezra persuades the people to recommit themselves to God by swearing a covenant to put away their "strange wives" (Ezra 10). It seems that in the Law it is also better for a man to have two wives than for a man to divorce one wife to marry another, as the practice of polygyny seems to have kept divorce to a minimum.

The Old Testament has little to say about sexual temptation either as a passion or as a pleasure. Accounts of sexual sins are often stated as simple matters of fact without elaboration. We are told, for example, only that Bathsheba was beautiful and what David did after seeing her bathing; we are not told how he felt at any time during his seduction of Bathsheba or his scheming against Uriah. Only when God sends Nathan to accuse David does David show any emotion, becoming angry when hearing the accusation before knowing who is being accused, and then weeping and fasting while his son by Bathsheba lies dying. His behavior toward Bathsheba and Uriah appears as a serious ethical lapse but not a passionate loss of self-control. There is no inner struggle between conscience and concupiscence; he simply forgets about God and thinks only of himself. David himself sees his failure as a religious apostasy, saying he has "sinned against the Lord" (2 Sam 12:13).

Such an approach to recounting incidents of sexual sin avoids making the story itself a source of temptation. The attraction of the sin is minimized. The excuse of a conflicted human nature torn between soul and body is disallowed. The focus is squarely on the divine-human relationship being violated and the gravity of the consequences. The general sense from such incidents and from all else in Hebrew Scripture is that sex is serious business but not inherently problematic, much less inherently sinful or shameful, even among the ascetics of Qumran. There, says William Loader:

> The primary concern appears to be right time, right place, and right order—based on a fairly carefully worked out understanding of each. Within these parameters of assumed rightness, however alien to contemporary valuing of human rights and equality, sexuality was seen as unproblematic, and more than that, as belonging to the blessings of creation.[23]

Within these limits, sex is morally blameless, psychologically uncomplicated, and not especially dangerous so long as one keeps faith with God. Sex is resistible, but one must have a reason to resist it. Fear of God is that reason. That is what distinguishes the righteous from the wicked—those who do "that which is right in the eyes of the Lord" (Deut 13:18; cf. 1 Kgs 11:33; 14:8; 15:5, 11; 22:43; 2 Chr 14:2) from those who do "whatsoever is right in his own eyes" (Deut 12:8; cf. Judg 17:6; 21:25; Prov 12:15; 21:2).

Hebrew Scripture condemns many sex acts as abominations that defile, pollute, or profane persons, places, or things (e.g., Gen 49:4; Lev 18; 21:7, 9, 14–15). Virgins are said several times to be "humbled" by rape or seduction (Gen 34:2; Deut 21:14; 22:24, 29; Judg 19:24). Dinah, the daughter of Jacob, is said to be both "humbled" and "defiled" by her rape or seduction by the Canaanite Shechem (Gen 34:2, 5, 13, 27). But no Israelite bride is said in Scripture to have been "humbled" or "defiled" on her wedding night, and though lawful marital relations are said to make both husband and wife temporarily "unclean" (Lev 15:16–18), the stronger terms for defilement applied to sexual sins (*chalal* in Hebrew, *bebēloō* and *miainō* in the Septuagint) are not applied to lawful sexual relations with either wives or concubines. Thus modern Old Testament scholars commonly distinguish between ritual defilement and moral defilement: The former is a matter of nature remedied by washing and waiting; the latter is a matter of sin requiring atonement or exile.[24] This distinction is stronger in the Septuagint than in Hebrew texts because the Hebrew uses *tāmē* for both ritual and moral uncleanness, whereas the Septuagint consistently uses *miainō* for defilement resulting from sexual sins and *akathartos* for the temporary uncleanness resulting from lawful sexual relations.

---

23. Loader, *The Dead Sea Scrolls on Sexuality*, 390.
24. See Klawans, "Idolatry, Incest, and Impurity."

Hebrew scriptures make no mention of a custom comparable to Rome's Vestal Virgins or of any woman taking a vow of virginity. The Nazarite vow of Numbers 6 did not require celibacy, and the only person named as a Nazarite in the Old Testament was Samson, who was not celibate. Samuel also did not remain celibate, despite his pious upbringing, presumably as a Nazarite (1 Sam 1:11; 8:1; 1 Chr. 6:28). Moses, the greatest of Old Testament prophets, married a Midianite (Zipporah) and also possibly, based on Num 12:1, an Ethiopian (Tharbis, according to Josephus).[25] Isaiah was already a prophet when he begat his son Mahershalalhashbaz by his wife "the prophetess" (Isa 8:3). Hosea also begat two sons and a daughter as a prophet, if we take him literally (Hos 1). The prophetesses Deborah and Huldah were married (Judg 4:4; 2 Kgs 22:14). The only prophet who is said not to have married is Jeremiah, but the reason for Jeremiah's celibacy is explained in Scripture as having nothing to do with avoiding sexual passion or keeping himself undefiled; it was to spare him the great grief to be experienced by others in Judah's impending downfall, so as to preserve his independence as a prophet (Jer 16:1–7). Of the other prophets, no mention is made of their being married or unmarried.[26] Marriage does not seem to have been an issue for prophets or for any other holy men or women.

Abstinence from sexual relations was expected at certain times, as when Moses, before he ascends Mount Sinai to receive the Ten Commandments, tells the Israelites, "Be ready against the third day; come not at your wives" (Exod 19:15). Likewise, Abimelech says that David's hungry henchmen may eat the showbread "provided they have kept themselves from women" (1 Sam 21:4). Coitus made both the man and the woman unclean until the following evening, and coitus during menstruation made a man unclean for seven days (Lev 15:16–18, 24). In later literature, these strictures were extended to forbid copulation during menstruation and pregnancy, on the sabbath, and possibly also on high holy days.[27]

---

25. Josephus, *AJ* 2.10. Many modern exegetes believe Moses married only once and that the mention of his taking a Cushite (Ethiopian) wife (Num 12:1) is a reference to Zipporah's dark skin, but Josephus writes that Moses married an Ethiopian princess named Tharbis before he fled Pharaoh's court to live in the land of Midian, where he married Zipporah, the daughter of a Midian priest named Reuel (Exod 2:15–21) and Jethro (Exod 3:1).

26. A later Christian tradition assumes Elijah never married, but this is not stated in Scripture.

27. Jub 50:8; *Damascus Document*, CD 11.5, 12.4. See Loader, *Dead Sea Scrolls on Sexuality*, 365–66.

But for most Jews the procreative imperative to "be fruitful and multiply" was so strong that they never held celibacy in high regard and had no tradition of perpetual virginity until the Hellenistic period. Childlessness was seen as a curse for both men and women. To die a virgin was an especially terrible misfortune for a maiden. Jephthah's daughter asks him for two months in which to wander up and down the mountains bewailing her doomed virginity with her fellow maidens before his vow is fulfilled, and thereafter the daughters of Israel mourned her for four days each year (Judg 11:37–40). Several late works promise abundant offspring as the future reward for the faithful, including the *Wisdom of Solomon, 1 Enoch, 2 Baruch,* the *Damascus Document,* and Qumran's *Treatise of the Two Spirits* and the *Community Rule*.[28] Three of these texts—*1 Enoch, 2 Baruch,* and the *Community Rule*—seem to see no incongruity between continued breeding and angelic life. *1 Enoch* says the righteous "will live until they beget thousands," "shine like the stars," and know joy "like that of the angels in heaven."[29] *2 Baruch* promises the obedient "shall be made like unto the angels" and also that there will be childbirth without pain.[30] The *Community Rule* promises "length of days and fruitful offspring . . . and a crown of glory with majestic raiment in eternal light."[31] It appears that to the Jews of the last few centuries before the birth of Christ, sex was not always inconsistent with angelic perfection, neither was it always inconsistent with prelapsarian innocence, for *Jubilees* even speaks of sex before the Fall, retelling Genesis 2 to say that Adam "knew" Eve immediately after her creation and before declaring her "bone of my bones and flesh of my flesh."[32]

## Hebrew Hellenism

The Jewish reaction to Greek sexual culture brought by the conquest of Judaea by Alexander the Great in 332 is marked by both imitation and

---

28. Wis 3:13; 1 En 10:17–18; 2 Bar 73:7; *Damascus Document,* CD 2.11b–12.a; *Two Spirits,* 1QS/IQ28 4.6b–8, 4Q257 5.4–5. Loader writes, "Abundant offspring was a common theme [in late Hebrew literature]. . . . Most depictions of the glorious righteous [in the next life] go hand and hand, as we have seen, with promises of abundant offspring." See Loader, *Making Sense of Sex,* 98–99.

29. 1 En 10:17–18; 104:2–3.

30. 2 Bar 51:9–10; 73:7.

31. 1QS/IQ28 4.6b–8, See Loader, *Making Sense of Sex,* 98.

32. Jub 3:6.

resistance. The Book of Proverbs, for example, contains quite a few verses warning of sinful or foolish women. Nearly half of them (nine of twenty-two) appear in the first nine of chapters, which are thought to be the last of the book's six sections written, possibly during the Hellenistic period.[33] No verse of Proverbs speaks ill of all women, however. The first book of the Bible to do that is Ecclesiastes. Traditionally assigned to Solomon as a work of his old age, Ecclesiastes is now widely believed to have been written after the Jews returned from Babylon in 450 and possibly in the early Hellenistic period, between 330 and 180. The evidence for the later date is the book's pessimistic reflection on wisdom and worldliness and the skepticism, nihilism, and Epicureanism of Hellenistic philosophy.[34] The following passage from chapter 7 is one example:

> [23]All this have I proved by wisdom: I said, I will be wise; but it was far from me. [24]That which is far off, and exceeding deep, who can find it out? [25]I applied mine heart to know, and to search, and to seek out wisdom, and the reason of things, and to know the wickedness of folly, even of foolishness and madness: [26]And I find more bitter than death the woman, whose heart is snares and nets, and her hands as bands: whoso pleaseth God shall escape from her; but the sinner shall be taken by her. [27]Behold, this have I found, saith the preacher, counting one by one, to find out the account: [28]Which yet my soul seeketh, but I find not: one man among a thousand have I found; but a woman among all those have I not found. [29]Lo, this only have I found, that God hath made man upright; but they have sought out many inventions.

Here we have a Socratic acknowledgement of one's own ignorance (v. 23), followed by a Platonic recognition of the elusiveness of wisdom that is "far off and exceeding deep" and accessible to only a few (vv. 24 and 28), followed by what could be a typically Greek expression of misogyny disdaining women as both ruinous temptations and lesser intellects (vv. 25–29). Many commentaries, ancient and modern, have found other ways to read verses 26 and 29. Verse 26 has been read three ways, to mean

---

33. Ten proverbs warn of the dangers of "strange [i.e., foreign] women": Prov 2:16; 5:3; 5:20; 6:24; 7:5; 20:16; 22:14; 23:27; 23:33; 27:13. Six warn of loose or foolish women: Prov 6:26; 6:32; 7:10; 9:13; 30:20; 30:23. As mentioned earlier, five lament the burden of contentious wives: Prov 21:9; 21:19; 25:24; 27:15–16. One warns, "Give not thy strength unto women, nor thy ways to that which destroyeth kings" (Prov 31:3). On the dating of Proverbs, see Alter, *The Wisdom Books*, 183–84.

34. See Bartholomew, *Ecclesiastes*, 25–38.

all women, some women, or a particular woman.[35] "Some women" is the most common reading, but even then the indictment of some women as "more bitter than death" expresses a rather extreme view of the danger women present to men. Verse 29 has often been understood to refer to mankind generally, thus the *New English Bible* has the Ecclesiast say, "God, when he made man, made him straightforward, but man invents endless subtleties of his own." Verses 27 and 28 are more problematic for two reasons: They are arguably impossible to translate in a way favorable to women, and they provide the only context linking verses 26 and 29. Even feminists are therefore inclined toward a misogynistic reading of the passage. Tikva Frymer-Kensky, for example, translates verse 26 as, "Now I find woman more bitter than death; she is all traps, her hands are fetters and her heart is snares."[36] The Ecclesiast does have one good thing to say about women: "Live joyfully with the wife whom thou lovest all the days of the life of thy vanity, which he hath given thee under the sun, all the days of thy vanity: for that is thy portion in this life, and in thy labor which thou takest under the sun" (Eccl 9:9).

There is less uncertainty about the misogyny of an even later text, the Wisdom of Joshua ben Sirach, also known as the Wisdom of Sirach and as Ecclesiasticus. Written not long before 175, after a century and a half of Greek rule, the Wisdom of Sirach bears many similarities to the Book of Proverbs, mixing warnings about sinful women with praise of virtuous women.[37] Both also personify wisdom as a woman, although in its erotic imagery the Wisdom of Sirach sounds more like the Song of Songs, another book thought to date from the Hellenistic period.[38] In Prov 9:1–6,

---

35. "All women" is indicated by the insertion of a comma between "woman" and "whose," which makes the phrase beginning with "whose" a nonrestrictive relative clause in the King James Version and the Orthodox Jewish Bible; the Authorized Version and most other English translations omit the comma. Both restrictive and nonrestrictive readings are offered as possibilities by *The Expanded Bible*. Wycliffe particularized the verse so that is says, "I found a woman bitterer than death, the which is the snare of hunters, and her heart is a net, and her hands are bonds."

36. Frymer-Kensky, *In the Wake of the Goddesses*, 205–6.

37. See Skehan and Di Lella, *The Wisdom of Ben Sirach*, 9.

38. Some scholars still defend an early dating of the Song of Songs, traditionally ascribed to Solomon and often called the Song of Solomon, but many believe it was written well after Solomon's time, possibly as late as the third century. Patrick Hunt concludes that "the dating problem is unlikely to be resolved even though the preponderance of cumulative evidence in 20th c. scholarship supports later rather than earlier dating for this book despite recent pendulum swings backward." See Hunt, *Poetry in the Song of Songs*, 8.

Wisdom is a woman building a house, preparing a meal, and inviting the simple to eat her bread and drink her wine, whereas in Sirach the wise man is invited to plough and sow Wisdom's fields and drive a tent peg into the wall of her house (Sir 6:19; 14:24; cf. 4:15; 14:23). Nevertheless, amid the many verses warning of sinful women are several that seem to speak ill of all women in very Greek ways: "Give me any plague, but the plague of the heart: and any wickedness, but the wickedness of a woman" (Sir 25:13). "All wickedness is but little to the wickedness of a woman: let the portion of a sinner fall upon her" (Sir 25:19). "Of the woman came the beginning of sin, and through her we all die" (Sir 25:24). "Behold not every body's beauty, and sit not in the midst of women, for from garments cometh a moth, and from women wickedness" (Sir 42:12–13).

It also seems that under Greek influence Jews were hard pressed, just as the Greeks were, to maintain their traditional sexual morality. Thus, the Wisdom of Sirach prescribes the separation of men and women: A wise man must stay away from women not of his own family (Sir 9:9); he must build a "hedge" around his wife for her protection as he would for his gold and silver (Sir 36:24–25; cf. 28:24); he must keep his daughters under thumb, for if allowed too much liberty she will befriend strangers and "open her quiver against every arrow" (Sir 26:10–12). Pseudo-Phocylides offers similar advice around the time of Christ's birth: "Guard a virgin in closely shut chambers, and let her not be seen before the house until her wedding day. The beauty of children is hard for parents to protect."[39] He also condemns both male and female homosexuality and advises parents not to make their boys look too pretty by braiding their hair, lest they attract predators.[40] The Jewish books of the *Sibylline Oracles* repeatedly condemn pederasty; Pseudo-Aristeas condemns male prostitution, likening it to incest; and *2 Enoch* (10:3, 34:1–2) explicitly abominates anal intercourse among males of all ages.[41] The book of *Jubilees*, from the second century before Christ, condemns naked athletics, and the so-called *War Scroll* (1QM), one of the original

---

39. Pseudo-Phocylides, *Sentences*, 215–17, quoted in Loader, *Making Sense of Sex*, 35.

40. Pseudo-Phocylides, *Sentences*, 3 and 190–92, quoted in Loader, *Making Sense of Sex*, 133.

41. The *Sibylline Oracles* are not to be confused with Rome's much older Sibylline Books. Books 1 and 2 of the *Oracles* were written by Christians, while books 3, 4, and 5 were written by Alexandrian Jews from the second century before Christ to the second century of the Christian era. Pseudo-Aristeas is from the second century BC, and 2 Enoch from the first century AD. See Loader, *Making Sense of Sex,* 132–33.

seven Dead Sea Scrolls discovered at Qumran in 1947, bans nakedness in camp.[42] The *Damascus Document* explains the history of mankind and the Jews as a series of repeated failures to avoid sexual wrongdoing, beginning with the "Watchers" who lay with the daughters of men in Gen 6:5, the story that also begins *1 Enoch*, another late work.[43] The *Damascus Document* includes a long list of sexual transgressions; it also extends the ban on cross-dressing in Deut 22:5 to both outer and under garments.[44]

## Philo of Alexandria

The *Damascus Document* also seems to some to speak of two distinct categories of Jews living in "perfect holiness": those who marry and have children yet live piously in camps, separated from the immorality of the city, and those who remain entirely celibate yet are blessed with spiritual progeny for a "thousand generations."[45] Somehow word of these celibates seems to have gotten to Pliny the Elder (d. 79), who mentions a sect of Jews he calls *Esseni* who do not marry or raise children yet have survived for "thousands of generations" (*saeculorum milia*).[46] Philo of Alexandria, writing earlier in the same century, says the Essenes are "all full-grown men, and even already declining towards old age, such as are no longer carried away by the impetuosity of their bodily passions," leaving open the possibility that these men once had wives and had long ago fulfilled their responsibility to the race by begetting children.[47] Later, he explains

---

42. The War Scroll is also known as *The War of the Sons of Light Against the Sons of Darkness*. See Loader, *Making Sense of Sex*, 92.

43. See Loader, *The Dead Sea Scrolls on Sexuality*, 91–186; Loader, *Making Sense of Sex*, 98–107.

44. See Loader, *The Dead Sea Scrolls on Sexuality*, 132.

45. The assurance that those who abide in perfect holiness "shall live for a thousand generations" appears in both extant versions of the *Damascus Document*, CD–A 7.5b–6a and CD–B 19.1–2. For a reading supporting two orders, one celibate and one not, see Qimron, "Celibacy in the Dead Sea Scrolls and the Two Kinds of Sectarians," 287–94. See also Loader, *The Dead Sea Scrolls on Sexuality*, 128–31; Loader, *Making Sense of Sex*, 94.

46. Pliny the Elder, *Natural History* 5.29. Popular report of the Essenes seems to have turned the *Damascus Document*'s promise of a "thousand generations" into a history of the Essenes' survival for "thousands of generations."

47. Philo, *Hypothetica* 11.3, 745. See also Loader, *Dead Sea Scrolls on Sexuality*, 370. Loader (*Dead Sea Scrolls on Sexuality*, 375–76) notes that this is supported by archeological data from the cemetery at Qumran, which gives evidence of a mostly male population with few women and no children.

the Essenes' celibacy as a practical measure to preserve the peace of the community, "because woman is a selfish creature and one addicted to jealousy in an immoderate degree, and terribly calculated to agitate and overturn the natural inclinations of a man, and to mislead him by her continual tricks."[48] Elsewhere he expresses a rather Peripatetic but also commonly Greek view of the inferiority of women, writing, "for the minds of women are, in some degree, weaker than those of men, and not so well able to comprehend a thing which is appreciable only by the intellect, without any aid of objects addressed the outward senses."[49]

Philo speaks more approvingly of women when telling of another sect of pious Jews whom he calls *Therapeutae* (feminine, *Therapeutrides*), who live as solitary contemplatives avoiding all but absolutely necessary demands of the body so as to dedicate themselves solely to the pursuit wisdom through the study of Hebrew Scripture, philosophy, allegory, and worship. He strongly implies that these celibates are also mostly mature men, saying they have given up wives and children, although the women, he says, are "mostly aged virgins" who are

> indifferent to the pleasures of the body, desiring not a mortal but an immortal offspring, which the soul that is attached to God is alone able to produce by itself and from itself, the Father having sown in it rays of light appreciable only by the intellect, by means of which it will be able to perceive the doctrine of wisdom.[50]

This is the first appearance of perpetual virginity as a way of life for Jews, and it is so out of step with mainstream Judaism before, during, and after Philo's time that some modern scholars have judged it incredible. Joan Taylor doubts Philo's characterization of the *Therapeutrides* as "mostly aged virgins," arguing that this is just his way of making female philosophers appear less threatening.[51] Troels Engberg-Pedersen goes further, making a case for Philo's account of the *Therapeutae* (male and female) as merely a "philosopher's dream" meant to advance his vision of contemplative Judaism.[52] Mary Ann Beavis makes a brief contrary case that

48. Philo, *Hypothetica* 11.14, 746. See also Loader, *Philo, Josephus, and the Testaments on Sexuality*, 108.

49. Philo, *Legat.* 319.

50. Philo, *De vita contemplativa*, 68, 704. Eusebius (*Ecc. Hist.* 2.17) treats these "aged virgins" as proof that the *Therapeutae* were Jewish Christians.

51. Taylor, "Virgin Mothers," 37–63.

52. Engberg-Pedersen, "Philo's *De Vita Contemplativa* as a Philosopher's Dream," 40–64.

there is nothing necessarily implausible in Philo's account, given what we know of Philo and his class of educated Jews in first-century Alexandria, but she also draws an interesting parallel between Philo's *Therapeutae* and the fictional Heliopolitans in a utopian novel attributed to a Greek merchant named Iambulus, excerpted by Diodorus Siculus in his *Bibliotheca Historica*, written a century before Philo's time. Beavis's parallel builds on Doron Mendels's parallel of the Heliopolitans and the Essenes, but whereas Mendels argues that the story of the Heliopolitans inspired the Essenes to create their community, Beavis argues that Philo's account of the *Therapeutae* was crafted to showcase elite Jews as real-world Heliopolitans.[53]

Philo's own Hellenism is readily evident in his many references to Plato and his many Platonizing allegorizations of Hebrew Scripture, with occasional borrowings of Stoic, Pythagorean, and Aristotelian ideas.[54] He is today classed as a Middle Platonist, but Philo himself names the Pythagoreans the "most sacred sect," and Clement of Alexandria twice labels him a Pythagorean, perhaps to avoid prejudicing Christians against him by calling him a Jew or a Platonist, which, in the latter case, would have associated him, in popular opinion, with the supposed immorality of Plato's *Symposium* and *Republic*.[55] But an equally obvious reason argued by David Runia is Clement's recognition of Philo's less Platonist and more Pythagorean fascination with numbers, ascetic inclination, and tragic view of *erōs*, associating it with man's fall into sensual pleasure.[56] Runia elsewhere writes, "Philo's connection of *erōs* with physical pleasure and the descent into wickedness represents a severer view than we find in Plato. Indeed, when looked at in detail, Philo's attitude to sexuality bears little resemblance to that of Plato."[57]

---

53. See Beavis, "Philo's Therapeutai," 30–42; Mendels, "Hellenistic Utopia and the Essenes," 207–22.

54. For a brief survey of Philo's use of Plato and occasional use of others, see Sterling, "Philo's Hellenistic and Hellenistic Jewish Sources," 93–97.

55. Philo, *Quod*, 2; Clement of Alexandria, *Strom*. 1.72.4, 1.152.2. Similarly, the second-century Pythagorean Numenius of Apamea has been suspected of being a Jew, but see Edwards, "Atticizing Moses?" 64–75. John Chrysostom gives evidence of Plato's infamy among Christians in his Homily 5 on Titus (see chapter 5).

56. See Runia, "Why Does Clement of Alexandria Call Philo 'The Pythagorean'?" 1–22. Eusebius (*Ecc. Hist.* 2.4) also notes Philo's enthusiasm for both Plato and Pythagoras, but he may have been relying upon Clement in the matter.

57. Runia, *On the Creation of the Cosmos according to Moses*, 355. Also Dillon, *The Middle Platonists*, 139–83.

Philo was the first to divide the creation of man into two separate acts, the first in Gen 1:27 creating the idea of man made in the "image of God," the second in Gen 2 creating individual men and women with earthly bodies. He writes:

> And very beautifully after he had called the whole race [*genos*] "man," did he distinguish between the sexes, saying, that "they were created male and female"; although all the individuals of the race had not yet assumed their distinctive form [*eidē*]; since the extreme species [*ta proschestata tōn eidōn*] are contained in the genus, and are beheld, as in a mirror, by those who are able to discern acutely.[58]

Here we see that Philo does not balk, as Aristotle does, at defining the sexes as different forms or species of the same genus, with no in-between, God having also ordained different roles for each sex (domestic for women, political for men) and a difference of dress so that there be no mannish women or effeminate men.[59] There is, says Philo, "no greater impiety" than to confuse the male and the female.[60] Yet there is also, he says, a "vast difference" between embodied men and women and the human genus of Gen 1:27, for "man, made according to the image of God, was an idea, or a genus, or a seal, perceptible only by the intellect, incorporeal, neither male nor female, imperishable by nature."[61]

Philo is often openly dismissive of literal readings of Scripture, saying, for instance, of the creation of Eve (Gen 2:21–22), "The literal statement conveyed in these words is a fabulous one, for how can anyone believe that a woman was made of a rib of a man, or, in short, that any human being was made out of another?"[62] He freely allegorizes Gen 2 to recast Adam and Eve as higher and lower aspects of the soul, "For in

---

58. Philo, *Opif.* 76. See also Baer, *Philo's Use of the Categories of Male and Female*, 34; Loader, *Philo*, 12–13.

59. Philo, *Virt.* 20–21.

60. Philo, *Spec.* 3.180.

61. Philo, *Opif.* 134. Daniel Boyarin writes that Philo's "first Adam" of Gen 1:27 is a "spiritual androgyne," both male and female, whereas the "carnal Adam" of Gen 2 is either "ungendered or male" before the creation of Eve. He concludes, "Bodily gender is thus twice displaced from the origins of 'man.'" See Boyarin, *Carnal Israel*, 37, cf. 78–79. Loader, however, argues that Philo's understanding of Gen 1:27 "excludes any notion of androgyny, for it reduces male and female here to potential or pattern within a genus" (Loader, *Philo*, 12). The latter makes more sense and is supported by Harrison, "The Allegorization of Gender," 520–34.

62. Philo, *Legum* 2.19.

human beings the mind occupies the rank of the man, and the sensations that of the woman."[63] Likewise, in Gen 3, the serpent symbolizes pleasure, Eve symbolizes the senses, Adam symbolizes the mind, and their "coats of skins" symbolize the body.[64] These associations would seem to exclude sexual desire as the cause of the Fall, but Philo is not bound by his own allegories (few allegorists are) and speaks plainly elsewhere of Adam and Eve meeting for the first time, embracing, and desiring intercourse

> with a view to the generation of a being similar to themselves. And this desire caused likewise pleasure to their bodies, which is the beginning of iniquities and transgressions, and it is owning to this that men have exchanged their previously immortal and happy existence for one which is mortal and full of misfortune.[65]

Philo expresses this rather negative view of sexual relations in many ways. He sees sexual intercourse as only for procreation, even condemning sex with sterile or post-menopausal women as a "licentious pleasure" reducing man to the level of "pigs and goats," and judging marriage to women no longer young a violation of nature.[66] He also points out that whereas Adam is said to "know" Eve, the most virtuous men in Hebrew Scripture—Abraham, Isaac, Jacob, and Moses—are never said to "know" any woman, explaining that the woman is a symbol of the physical senses and that knowledge consists in alienation from the body and its senses, but also excusing his married patriarchs from knowing their own wives by casting their wives as symbols of virtue, which a virtuous man would seek to know.[67] Moses was Philo's favorite, "the greatest and most perfect man that ever lived," whom Philo depicts as an ascetic master in total control of his desires, never eating anything unnecessary and copulating only to beget legitimate children.[68] Philo is the first to claim that Moses gave up conjugal intercourse before beginning his prophetic ministry, saying:

63. Philo, *Opif.* 165.

64. See Philo, *Opif.* 134, 157–58; Philo, *Legum* 22–75; Philo, QG 1.31, 1.37, 1.47, 1.53. Also Loader, *Philo*, 66–76.

65. Philo, *Opif.* 152.

66. Philo, *De specialibus legibus* 3.34–36; Philo, QG 1.27. Philo's single concession is to men who have unknowingly married sterile women. See Loader, *Philo*, 202–3. Gaca (*The Making of Fornication*, 205–7) attributes Philo's "procreationist" limitation on sexual intercourse to Pythagorean influence.

67. Philo, *De cherubim* 40–41. See Loader, *Philo*, 136.

68. Philo, *Mos.* 1.1, 1.28, 2.192. See Loader, *Philo*, 100–101, 180–83; Satlow, "Philo on Human Perfection," 500–519.

> [I]t was necessary for him to purify not only his soul but also his body, so that it should be connected with and defiled by no passion, but should be pure from everything which is of a mortal nature, from all meat and drink, and from all connection with women. And this last thing, indeed, he had despised for a long time, and almost from the first moment that he began to prophesy and to feel a divine inspiration, thinking that it was proper that he should at all times be ready to give his whole attention to the commands of God.[69]

Philo is still enough of a Jew to see the distinction of male and female as a natural good ordained by God, to condone conjugal relations whenever there is at least the possibility of conception, to condemn those sex acts proscribed by Jewish Law, and to envision a future reward of long life with abundant offspring for those who obey the Law, per Exodus 23:26. Yet in relating this promise of a long, happy, prosperous, and prolific afterlife, Philo makes no mention of the pleasure of sex or of the joy of married life, speaking only of the joy of offspring. He also foresees an end to this afterlife, writing of human existence as a series of steps up a ladder that "will eventually arrive at the last of all, that which is near to death, or rather to immortality," leaving open the possibility of a sexless eternity after all of the faithful have obtained the always important promise of progeny.[70]

## Conclusion: Carnal Israel

The resistance to sexual renunciation in early rabbinical literature gives evidence of the attraction of sexual renunciation among Hellenized Jews and of the fundamental difference between the popular Hebrew understanding of male and female and that of the philosophers.[71] As Daniel Boyarin writes, the Rabbis saw man not as a soul trapped in a body but as a body animated by a soul.[72] Human existence was essentially corporeal and therefore also sexual. The asceticism of philosophers and Christians

---

69. Philo, *Mos.*, 2.68–69, 497. Cf. Loader, *Philo*, 101; Koltun-Fromm, *Hermeneutics of Holiness*, 179.

70. On the afterlife, see Philo, *De praemiis et poenis* 108–10, 674.

71. Boyarin (*Carnal Israel*, 136) writes: "Extravagant praise of the married state, which occurs over and over in rabbinic texts, is a marker not of how happily married the Rabbis were but of how much pressure against marrying there was in their world."

72. Boyarin, *Carnal Israel*, 35.

made little sense inasmuch as it denied the body for the sake of the soul. Steven Fraade writes that the Rabbis preferred "a milder and more symbolic form of self-denial."[73] Eliezer Diamond writes their asceticism was "instrumental" rather than "essential."[74] Paul Heger goes even further to argue that what Fraade, Diamond, and others see as asceticism in the rabbinic literature is not asceticism at all, as commonly understood, but merely the application of the "rabbinic preventative principle of אמש 'perhaps'—that is, prohibiting a permitted act because it may lead inadvertently to performing a prohibited act."[75]

When the subject is sex, however, there is greater agreement, both among modern scholars and among the Rabbis. "Everyone was expected to marry, have sex, and have children, and people who refused to do so were hyperbolically stigmatized as murderers and blasphemers," Boyarin writes, citing Tosfeta Yevamot 8:7 and Babylonian Talmud Yevamot 63b.[76] This insistence on marriage set Jews apart from Christians and was used by both Jews and Christians to accuse the other. The "Persian sage" Aphrahat, actually a Syriac Christian, gives us the Jewish view of Christian celibacy when he writes of a Jew who tells a Christian that he is "impure" because he does not marry and claims that Jews are holy and better because they do.[77] Augustine of Hippo provides a Christian rejoinder when he writes that Jews fail to grasp the meaning of 1 Cor 10:18 ("Behold Israel according to the flesh . . .") "and as a result they prove themselves indisputably carnal."[78]

The Rabbis' enthusiasm for procreation produces some rather strange readings of Hebrew Scripture. Genesis Rabba says that Adam and Eve had sex before the Fall and that this taught the animals how to copulate—a reversal, as Brown and Boyarin both note, of the earlier belief that Adam and Eve learned to copulate from the animals.[79] The same text says the serpent saw Adam and Eve having sex, was inflamed with lust for Eve, and had sex with her when Adam fell asleep, so the fault that caused the Fall was not sensuality per se but illicit sensuality,

---

73. Fraade, "Ascetical Aspects of Ancient Judaism," 272.
74. Diamond, *Holy Men and Hunger Artists*, 12.
75. See Heger, *Women in the Bible, Qumran and Early Rabbinic Literature*, 252.
76. Boyarin, *Carnal Israel*, 35.
77. Aphrahat, *Demonstrations* 18.12/841.3–9.
78. Augustine, *Tractatus adversus Judaeos* 7.9, quoted by Boyarin, *Carnal Israel*, 1.
79. Brown, *The Body and Society*, 94n43; Boyarin, *Carnal Israel*, 83.

specifically adultery and bestiality. Serious as these crimes are, the Rabbis avoid heaping too much blame on Eve, seeing her as naturally sexual and a victim of deceit.[80] They also go lightly on Miriam in several fanciful readings of her challenge against Moses that also demonstrate the high value they placed on marital intercourse.[81] In each telling, Miriam learns that Moses is not sleeping with Zipporah, his wife, and enlists Aaron in the cause of holding Moses to account for his dereliction of duty. She is therefore credited with diligence in ensuring obedience to the commandment to "be fruitful and multiply" and faulted only for failing to appreciate Moses's exceptional standing among prophets. Some modern commentators have understood these midrashim to condone at least temporary marital celibacy for religious reasons, but Boyarin argues persuasively that the Rabbis' sympathies are with Miriam and that when forced to confront the accepted tradition, first found in Philo, that Moses remained celibate during his prophetic ministry, they dealt with it in such a way as to neutralize its endorsement of celibacy, honoring Miriam for her faithfulness to the rule and making Moses an exception to it.[82]

The Rabbis were also keen to insist strictly on sexual distinction in both dress and demeanor and to assign men and women different religious obligations, excluding women from synagogue worship and from the study of the Torah. The Middle Ages would see the appearance of Jewish mysticism, possibly influenced by Neoplatonism, with an unknowable source of all being from which emanate presences perceived as masculine or feminine. Gen 1:27 will then be interpreted as indicating man's resemblance to these divine emanations, which husbands and wives are said to unite by sexual intercourse.[83] These developments are beyond the scope of this thesis, but they show the increasing importance of male and female in Jewish thinking.

Early Christians did not pay much attention to the writings of the Rabbis. Their authoritative guide to the religion of the Jews was the Hebrew Scriptures, mainly as translated by the Septuagint, which they read much the way Christians today read it, as the revelation of a transcendent deity of masculine aspect, who made man both in his own image and male and female, who commanded man to live as male and female, but

---

80. Some midrashim do blame Eve for the Fall, but just as many blame Adam, says Boyarin, *Carnal Israel*, 84.

81. See Meir, "Miriam: Midrash and Aggadah."

82. Boyarin, *Carnal Israel*, 159–65.

83. See Frankiel, *The Voice of Sarah*, 82–83.

who nevertheless transcended male and female by being, in the words of Tikva Frymer-Kensky, "not imagined below the waist."[84]

---

84. Frymer-Kensky, *In the Wake of the Goddesses*, 188.

# 4

# The Greek Christian View of Male and Female

CHRISTIANITY WORKED A RADICAL change in the sexuality of the ancient world—the first "sexual revolution" in Western history. This change owed much to fundamental differences between Christians and others on several nonsexual issues. Christians believed strongly in free will and in eternal rewards for those who choose good over evil. They saw this life as a brief preliminary to a glorious eternity in which the saved would live like angels. They also believed they were called to preach the Gospel to all the world and to be their brothers' keepers. This combination of characteristics made Christians less erotic (in the common modern sense of the word) than both pagans and Jews in that they cared less for procreation and more for natural limits to sexual behavior and for demonstrating the power of Christian faith by permanent celibacy and total dedication to God. Daniel Garrison's characterization of Christianity as "virulently anerotic" is thus not without a basis in fact, especially in view of the militance of Christian emperors in reforming public morality, principally by outlawing sexual slavery, pedophilia, and homosexuality.[1]

Yet the anerotic tendency in early Christianity owed much to the anerotic tendency in Greek philosophy and the intellectual climate of the Greco-Roman world. The philosophers' belief in the inherent impurity of matter and in the contamination and entrapment of the soul by the body underlay the Gnostic challenge to orthodox Christianity as well as the continuing Encratite tendencies of many otherwise orthodox Christians.

---

1. See Harper, *From Shame to Sin*, 15–16, 141–58.

Such tendencies were controversial among Christians as early as the apostolic era and continued to cause trouble for centuries afterward. The controversy was contained to some degree by the ecumenical anathematization of Encratism and Origenism, but Encratite and Origenist ideas continued to flourish in carefully expurgated forms to become almost mainstream thinking, particularly in monastic circles, contributing to the convergence of Neoplatonism and Christianity in speculative theorists such as Maximus the Confessor, who viewed sexual distinction as a temporary "division" to be "driven out" of human nature such that men and women would be no longer men and women but merely human beings.

This chapter will trace the influence of Greek thinking on Christian thinking about male and female, beginning with those passages of the New Testament seen as supporting the Greek view. This is not to suggest that these passages of Holy Scripture are themselves evidence of Greek influence; rather, it is to acknowledge up front those passages of Holy Scripture on which early Christians based their more Greek opinions. The chapter will then trace the evolution of the Greek Christian view from the early Encratites and Gnostics to Maximus the Confessor in the seventh century. The next chapter will then examine the other side of coin, surveying Christian teaching and practice preserving and affirming a more Hebrew view of male and female during the same centuries.

## New Testament Support for the Greek View

Significant differences between Hebrew and Christian views of male and female are immediately apparent in Christian scripture. Besides the celibate examples of Christ himself and John the Baptist, there are the words of Christ in four passages of the Synoptic Gospels. Christ tells the Sadducees that "in the resurrection they neither marry, nor are given in marriage, but are as the angels of God in heaven" (Matt 22:30; cf. Mark 12:25; Luke 20:34–36). He also tells his disciples that "there be eunuchs which have made themselves eunuchs for the kingdom of heaven's sake" (Matt 19:11–12). Together, these passages express a high regard and arguable preference for celibacy as well as the expectation expressed in all three Synoptic Gospels that there will be no marriage in heaven, contrary to the common Hebrew preference for marriage in this life and expectation of marriage and offspring in the next.

## The Greek Christian View of Male and Female

Beyond the Gospels, there is the celibate example of the Apostle Paul, who expresses an undeniable preference for celibacy in 1 Corinthians 7, where he says, "it is good for a man not to touch a woman" (v. 1), it is better not to marry (v. 38), virgins who marry shall have "trouble in the flesh" (v. 28), virgins can care more for the Lord and be "holy in both body and in spirit" (vv. 32–34), widows would be happier not marrying again (v. 40), and he would prefer that "all men were even as I myself, but every man hath his proper gift of God" (vv. 7–8) and therefore virgins, widows, and men may marry without sinning if celibacy is too hard for them (vv. 2, 9).

Next there are the Apostle's comments on the resurrection in 1 Corinthians 15, in which he distinguishes our corrupt earthly bodies from the incorrupt heavenly bodies of the resurrection. The first he calls *sōma psychikon*; the second, *sōma pneumatikon*. English translations commonly render the first as the "natural" or "physical" body and the second as the "spiritual" body, but this is potentially misleading in that it suggests that the latter is unnatural and nonmaterial, whereas the contrast intended is between a body animated only by a soul, with its passions, and a body made incorruptible by the spirit. The Apostle makes this plain in the next verse, when he says, "The first man Adam was made a living soul [*psychēn zōsan*]; the last Adam was made a quickening spirit [*pneuma zōopoioun*]." (v. 45) Nevertheless, the contrast is heightened by the Apostle's analogy of the *sōma psychikon* to a grain of wheat, by his saying "that flesh and blood cannot inherit the kingdom of God" (v. 50), and by his mention elsewhere of "our vile body" vs. Christ's "glorious body" (Phil 3:21).

Then there are the Apostle's words to the Galatians, without precedent in Hebrew Scripture: "There is neither Jew nor Greek, there is neither bond nor free, there is neither male nor female: for ye are all one in Christ Jesus" (Gal 3:28). More will be said of this verse in the next chapter when we consider how it was commonly understood. For now, it is enough to note what will be shown in this chapter—that some made sense of the verse's inclusion of the natural distinction of male and female by understanding them allegorically, associating male and female with anger and desire, in the Greek fashion, while others read the verse literally to speak of an ultimate end of sexual distinction, when either women would become men or all would become merely human.

Finally, as far as the New Testament is concerned, there is the vision in the Apocalypse or Revelation of the Apostle John of a chorus of

144,000 men with the Father's name written on their foreheads, singing a song only they have learned:

> These are they which were not defiled [*ouk emolunthēsan*] with women; for they are virgins. These are they which follow the Lamb whithersoever he goeth. These were redeemed from among men, being the firstfruits unto God and to the Lamb. And in their mouths was found no guile: for they are without fault before the throne of God. (Rev 14:4–5)

Here again is another striking difference between Christian and Hebrew thinking. Nowhere in the Old Testament are men termed virgins or are virgins accorded any special religious status, yet here verse 4 speaks of men who are "not defiled" by women, as if sexual intercourse, even within marriage, were somehow unholy and permanently degrading for men and presumably also for women.

Many second-century Christian texts attest to this new regard for virginity. The *First Apology* of Justin Martyr boasts that "many, both men and women, who have been Christ's disciples from childhood, remain pure at the age of sixty or seventy years."[2] The second-century Infancy Gospel of James (also known as the *Protevangelium of James*) assigns seven "undefiled virgins" the task of making a veil for the temple, a provision without precedent in the Old Testament.[3] The *Acts of Paul and Thecla* tells of Thecla jilting her fiancé after hearing the Apostle preach on virginity. Thecla's story is first attested in the late second century, when Tertullian denounced it as spurious and impious on account of Thecla's carrying on like a man and outshining Paul, yet her story was widely circulated by early Christians and imitated by both later martyrs and later hagiographers.[4]

Not surprisingly, with this higher regard for virginity came also a greater concern for the danger of sexual temptation, evident in the *Testaments of the Twelve Patriarchs*, an early Christian work in its extant form, arguably based in part on Jewish material such as the *Aramaic Levi*

---

2. Justin Martyr, *First Apology* 15, 167.

3. The book also tells of Joseph being accused of defiling Mary, having "married her by stealth," but the taking of a virgin before marriage always constituted a defilement.

4. Noting the paucity of icons of the Virgin before the sixth century, Averil Cameron writes, "As a female figure of Christian devotion one might say that [Mary] was outranked by Thekla, the virginal heroine of the late second-century Acts of Paul and Thekla." See Cameron, "The Early Cult of the Virgin." Tertullian denounces *The Acts of Paul and Thecla* as spurious in *On Baptism* 17.

*Document* found at Qumran.⁵ Sex is a recurring theme of the *Testaments*, which inveigh, often at length, against the sins of adultery, homosexuality, and incest. Marriage is sanctioned in the Pauline way as preferable to immorality, but the language used is often more extreme than we find in canonical Hebrew or Christian Scripture. The *Testament of Simeon* terms sexual immorality "the mother of all evil" on the basis of Gen 6:5, as dramatized in the *Book of the Watchers* of *1 Enoch*.⁶ The *Testament of Reuben* alludes to the same story, blaming women for seducing the Watchers. It also plainly says that women are "evil" [*ponērai*] and are "overcome by the spirit of sexual immorality more than men."⁷ The *Testament of Benjamin* says, "He who has a pure mind in love [*agapē*] does not look at a woman wantonly [*eis porneian*]; for he has no defilement in his heart, because the spirit of God rests upon him."⁸ The *Testament of Issachar* declares Rachel more pious than Leah because Rachel "despised intercourse with a man and has chosen continency [*egkrateian*]"; it goes on to say she had sex only for the sake of having children.⁹

## Early Encratism

A handful of early, obscure Christian sects—Agapetae, Borborites, Carpocratians, and Nicolaitans—used Christian freedom as an excuse for sexual indulgence, but the far greater threat to early Christian orthodoxy came from the opposite extreme—from the many more popular sectarians who not only chose *egkrateia*, like Rachel in the *Testaments*, but also preached against marriage and childbearing along with meat-eating and wine-bibbing, thus earning the label of "Encratites" from Irenaeus of Lyon.¹⁰

Encratism was, as Eric Fuchs says, more an attitude than a philosophy, or, as Kyle Harper says, "less a coherent movement than a recurrent tendency," variously justified.¹¹ The Encratism of Marcion of Sinope was

---

5. For a discussion of the *Testaments* origins, see Loader, *Philo*, 368–71.

6. *T. Sim.* 5:3, in Loader, *Philo, Josephus, and the Testaments on Sexuality*, 391.

7. *T. Reub.* 5:1–7, in Loader, *Philo, Josephus, and the Testaments on Sexuality*, 384–88.

8. *T. Ben.* 8:2, in Loader, *Philo, Josephus, and the Testaments on Sexuality*, 426. Loader scrupulously translates *porneia* as "sexual immorality" (see 368n1) and thus renders *eis porneian* in *T. Ben.* 8:2 as "with a view to sexual immorality."

9. *T. Iss.* 2:1–3, in Loader, *Philo, Josephus, and the Testaments on Sexuality*, 412.

10. See Irenaeus, *Adv. Haer.* 1.28.

11. Fuchs, *Sexual Desire and Love*, 88; Harper, *From Shame to Sin*, 106.

based on a cosmic dualism pitting a tyrannical creator god of the Old Testament against a loving savior god of the New Testament: The former divided man between male and female and between Jew and Gentile, commanding the sexes and his chosen to "be fruitful and multiply"; the latter abolished all of the old commandments and divisions, along with marriage and the fleshly relationships it created. In contrast, Tatian the Syrian, said to have been a follower of Justin Martyr with ideas similar to the Gnostic Valentinus of Alexandria, adopted a more Platonic cosmology, stressing freedom from the flesh and despising marriage as an invention of the devil.[12] Both men drew large followings, especially in the East. Marcionites virtually monopolized the name "Christian" in Mesopotamia and Persia up until the end of the sixth century, and Tatian's *Diatessaron* was for many years the standard Gospel book in Syria.[13]

David Hunter distinguishes between radical Encratites, who condemned coitus as evil and therefore forbade marriage, and moderate Encratites, who disdained coitus as shameful but allowed it within marriage as a concession to weakness.[14] Traits shared by both included (a) ruthless rigorism based on extreme confidence in free will, which left no excuse for not choosing the better way;[15] (b) anti-material spiritualism disdaining the body, blamed on Greek philosophy by anti-Encratites such as Irenaeus of Lyon, Hippolytus of Rome, and Clement of Alexandria;[16] and

12. See Irenaeus, *Adv. Haer.* 1.28; Clement of Alexandria, *Strom.* 3.12.81. A much weaker dualism appears in Plutarch (*On Isis and Osiris*, 369E), who writes of two "antithetic powers," one an evil power that must be kept in order by the Demiurge. Later in the second century, Numenius extends such thinking to the human soul, positing, in Dillon's words, a "lower, irrational soul derive[d] from the evil, material Soul of the cosmos." Dillon comments, "It would appear, after all, that there is a degree of dualism in the air of the second century CE." See Dillon, *The Roots of Platonism*, 28–34.

13. On the Marcionite presence in the East, see Brown, *The Body and Society*, 87–90.

14. See Hunter, *Marriage, Celibacy, and Heresy in Ancient Christianity*, 115. The differentiation of moderate and radical Encratites is Hunter's; the identification of the traits shared by them is mine but is supported by Hunter. Similarly, Andrew Guffey identifies four possible motives for Encratism: Hellenistic moral philosophy, demonology, social demarcation, and Pythagorean ethics. See Guffey, "Motivations for Encratite Practices in Early Christian Literature," 515–49.

15. For example, Tertullian, classed as a moderate Encratite by Hunter, writes, "When you do what God merely wills and despise what God preferentially wills, your choice is more offensive than meritorious. You are, in part, guilty of sin." Tertullian, *Exhortation to Chastity*, 3.4–5, quoted in Hunter, *Marriage, Celibacy, and Heresy*, 117.

16. Irenaeus, *Adv. Haer.* 2.14; Hippolytus, *Refutation of All Heresies*, 5.1; Clement of Alexandria, *Strom.* 3.3.21, 3.13.93.

(c) eschatological impatience based on the belief that since the kingdom has already come, Christians are now to live as angels.[17]

A fourth trait more common among radical Encratites was the association of male and female with division and death, which, as we have seen, was not a part of Hebrew thinking but was very much a part of Greek thinking, evident in virtually every aspect of Greek culture—mythology, cosmology, sociology, and politics.[18] As expressed in many Encratite scriptures, Christ overcomes division and death by ending marriage and making women male, doing away with both sexual distinction and sexual relations. This seems to have been the theme of the *Gospel of the Egyptians*, an early second-century (if not late first-century) work surviving only in excerpts, most of them provided by Clement of Alexandria as evidence against Encratism. Among the excerpts, we find it said that "the Savior himself said: I came to destroy the works of the female," and "Salome asked the Lord: 'How long shall death sway?' He answered, 'as long as you women bear children.'"[19] In the words of a later Gnostic text found at Nag Hammadi, Egypt, in 1945, "[O]ut of the earth the primal pleasure blossomed. The woman followed earth. And marriage followed woman. Birth followed marriage. Dissolution followed birth."[20]

The end of male and female is also a recurring theme of the *Gospel of Thomas*, also found at Nag Hammadi. In it, Peter says to Jesus, "Let Mary leave us, for women are not worthy of life," and Jesus answers, "I myself shall lead her in order to make her male, so that she too may become a living spirit resembling you males. For every woman who will make herself male will enter the kingdom of heaven."[21] The book also says:

---

17. For example, Cyprian of Carthage, who was greatly influenced by Tertullian and is also classed as a moderate Encratite by Hunter, writes, "The glory of the resurrection you already have in this world; you pass through the world without the pollution of the world; while you remain chaste and virgins, you are equal to the angels of God." Cyprian, *The Dress of Virgins*, 22, quoted in Hunter, *Marriage, Celibacy, and Heresy*, 121.

18. *Erōs* leads inevitably to *thanatos*, in the words of Gilles Quispel, "The Study of Encratism, 343.

19. Clement of Alexandria, *Strom.* 3.6.45, 3.9.63–64. Clement's "Gospel of the Egyptians" is not to be confused with the *Coptic Gospel of the Egyptians* found at Nag Hammadi, which is a Gnostic work also known as the *Holy Book of the Great Invisible Spirit*.

20. *On the Origin of the World* 109, 178.

21. *Gospel of Thomas* 114, 138.

> They said to him, "Shall we then, as children, enter the kingdom?" Jesus said to them, "When you make the two one, and when you make the inside like the outside and the outside like the inside, and the above like the below, and when you make the male and the female one and the same, so that the male not be male nor the female female; and when you fashion eyes in the place of an eye, and a hand in place of a hand, and a foot in place of a foot, and a likeness in place of a likeness; then will you enter the kingdom."[22]

A similar passage appears in the second-century pseudepigraphic work known as 2 Clement, with the added explanation, "And by the male with the female, neither male nor female, he meaneth this; that a brother seeing a sister should have no thought of her as a female, and that a sister seeing a brother should not have any thought of him as a male."[23] The Gospel of Thomas also says:

> His disciples said, "When will you become revealed to us and when shall we see you?" Jesus said, "When you disrobe without being ashamed and take up your garments and place them under your feet like little children and tread on them, then will you see the son of the living one, and you will not be afraid."[24]

This saying is also quoted by Clement of Alexandria, slightly altered: "When Salome asked when she would know the answer to her questions, the Lord said, 'When you trample on the robe of shame, and when the two shall be one, and the male with the female, and there is neither male nor female.'"[25] Clement attributes the saying to the *Gospel of the Egyptians* as well as to Julius Cassianus, whom Clement names the originator of Docetism, saying he was a former Valentinian whose teaching was closer to Tatian's. Of Cassianus, Clement writes that "this worthy fellow thinks in the Platonic fashion," believing that souls preexist bodies and "become female by desire" and that the "coats of skins" fashioned by God for Adam and Eve after the Fall (Gen 3:21) were human bodies.[26] In the last belief, Cassianus followed Philo of Alexandria and many Jewish and

---

22. *Gospel of Thomas* 22, 129.
23. *2 Clem* 12:5.
24. *Gospel of Thomas* 37, 130.
25. Clement of Alexandria, *Strom.* 3.13.92, translated by Chadwick, *Alexandrian Christianity*, 83.
26. Clement of Alexandria, *Strom.* 3.12.93, 3.14.95.

Christian Gnostics.²⁷ The metaphor of the body as the clothing of the soul is a Greek commonplace, attributed to philosophers from Empedocles in the fifth century before Christ to Porphyry in the third century of the Christian era.²⁸

Yet Clement also sometimes thinks in the Platonic fashion, as when he allegorizes Gal 3:28 to counter Cassianus by saying that he "seems to me not to know that it refers to wrath in speaking of the male impulse and desire in speaking of the female."²⁹ The association of anger and desire with male and female is another Greek commonplace, seen in the character of Ares and Aphrodite. Philo makes the association explicit when borrowing Plato's analogy of the soul to a chariot in the *Phaedrus*.³⁰

## The Valentinian Gnosis

Many Gnostic sects inclined toward Encratism, in theory if not always in practice. Definitions of Gnosticism have been disputed, but most scholars still find the label useful in identifying sects that stressed the importance of secret knowledge (*gnōsis*) of the spirit world, which is beyond human experience and revealed through an elaborate cosmological myth. The influence of Greek and specifically Platonist thinking is obvious.³¹ The Gnostic view of reality was essentially Plato's Allegory of the Cave in book seven of *The Republic*, a portion of which (from book nine, 588A–589B) was in the cache of Gnostic texts found at Nag Hammadi. Gnostics typically saw human beings in the Platonic manner as souls trapped in bodies, yet their regard for the body ranged from hostility to indifference. On one hand, the body was a source of suffering and deceit. Sexuality in particular was associated with violence and ignorance, a demonic invention originating as rape in the prison of the material world. This is the view of *The Apocryphon of John*, a second-century Sethian text, found at Nag Hammadi.³² On the other hand, a true Gnostic, in possession of the

27. Philo, *QG* 1.53. See also Chadwick, *Alexandrian Christianity*, 85n9.

28. Empedocles, Fr. 126; Porphyry, *Abst.* 1.31.

29. Clement of Alexandria, *Strom.* 3.13.93, translated by Chadwick, *Alexandrian Christianity*, 83–84.

30. Philo, *Agri.*, 73, cf. Philo, *Migr.*, 66; Plato, *Phdr.* 246a–254e.

31. On Greek influence upon Gnosticism, see Broek, *Gnostic Religion in Antiquity*, 206–9; Löhr, "Christian Gnostics and Greek Philosophy in the Second Century," 349–77.

32. See Brakke, *The Gnostics*, 67–68.

divine gnosis, had no reason to fear the body and therefore less reason to fight it. Theoretically, he could indulge in sexual relations without forgetting what he knew. This is the view of the third-century Gnostic *Gospel of Philip*, also found at Nag Hammadi, which advises, "Fear not the flesh nor love it. If you fear it, it will gain mastery over you. If you love it, it will swallow and paralyze you."[33] Thus it is not surprising that Gnostics were often suspected and sometimes accused of sexual immorality, as in the case of the second-century Valentinian heresiarch Marcus, who seduced the wife of a deacon in the diocese of Irenaeus of Lyon.[34]

Clement of Alexandria credits the Valentinians with publicly defending marriage and childbearing.[35] Irenaeus quotes Ptolemy, a Valentinian in Rome, saying, "Whoever has been in the world and has not loved a woman in such a way as to unite himself with her is not from the Truth and will not attain to the Truth."[36] Theodotus, a Valentinian in Asia Minor, defended the bearing of children as necessary "until the previously reckoned seed be brought forth."[37] This follows from the Valentinians' elaborate metaphysics based on fifteen successive emanations of aeons, in pairs called *syzygies* ("yokings"), consisting of higher and lower powers termed "male" and "female," which together constitute the fullness (*pleroma*) of divinity, from which Sophia ("Wisdom"), the female aeon of the last syzygy, departed on account of her ignorance and impatience, scattering seeds of spirit (*pneuma*) throughout the material world; Christ was sent into the world to harvest the mature spirits and thereby reunite Sophia with the Pleroma.[38] Marriage imitates this reunion, overcoming the division of male and female in soul and body, though not in spirit, while also providing bodies in which the scattered spiritual seeds may mature.

Even so, as Peter Brown cautions, it is difficult to tell with certainty what any Gnostic truly thought about marriage or sexual relations. Gnostic texts concentrate heavily on a particular spiritual gnosis with little attention to earthly ethics, and given the Gnostics' fundamentally Platonist

33. *Gospel of Philip* 66, 149.
34. Irenaeus, *Adv. Haer.* 1.13.3. See also Brown, *The Body and Society*, 110–11.
35. Clement of Alexandria, *Strom.* 3.1.1.
36. Irenaeus, *Adv. Haer.* 1.6.4.
37. Clement of Alexandria, *Excerpta ex Theodoto*, 67.
38. Clement of Alexandria, *Excerpta ex Theodoto*, 67:4–5. In Western Valentinianism, Sophia splits in two, one half remaining in the Pleroma and the other half falling out of it. The "fallen Sophia" (*katō Sophia*) was also called *Achamōth*.

perspective on reality, there is always some uncertainty as to whether what is written is secret knowledge or "noble lie." The Valentinians were more Platonist and also more public and popular than other Gnostic sects. Valentinus himself was a well-educated, charismatic Alexandrian who earned such esteem in Rome that he was once considered a candidate for pope.[39] He divided people into three classes: *pneumatikoi*, who possessed the divine gnosis, which ensured their salvation; *somatikoi*, who lived an entirely material life and were therefore predestined for damnation; and *psychikoi*, who were in between, capable of perceiving some truths intellectually but lacking an experience of spiritual reality. Valentinians disagreed among themselves on whether the *psychikoi* could be saved. The Western or Italian branch of Ptolemy and Heracleon was more open to the possibility and also more interested in mainstreaming Valentinianism within the catholic Church.[40] It is therefore possible that marriage was held forth publicly as acceptable, at least for *psychikoi* and *somatikoi*, but still considered beneath the dignity of *pneumatikoi*. Brown suspects that it was tolerated among the Valentinians as a means of "guttering out" the "fire of sexual desire" in an early stage of the spirit's transcendence of soul and body.[41]

The Valentinian restoration of spiritual reality was effected through a process of baptism, anointing, a eucharistic meal called a "wedding-feast" by Theodotus, a sacrament of redemption involving prayers for the ascent of the soul to the heavenly realm, and finally a sacrament known as the "bridal chamber," in which the fully formed Gnostic was finally filled with light and united with an angelic bridegroom.[42] The third-century *Gospel of Philip* contrasts "marriage of defilement" and the "undefiled marriage" of the "bridal chamber"—the former earthly, the latter angelic. The earthly marriage is consummated at night, whereas the angelic marriage is consummated in the daytime: "It is not fleshly but pure. It belongs not to desire but to the will. It belongs not to the darkness or the night but to the day and the light."[43] The ultimate "bridal chamber" was a strictly spiritual union occurring at the end of the world, admitting Gnostic spirits to the divine Pleroma after they have shed both their bodies and their

---

39. Brown lauds Valentinus as "one of the greatest spiritual guides" in Rome in the second century. See Brown, *The Body and Society*, 105.

40. See Quispel, "Origen and the Valentinian Gnosis," 33–34.

41. Brown, *The Body and Society*, 114–17.

42. Irenaeus, *Adv. Haer.* 1:7:1, 1:13:3, 1:13:6, 1:21:5.

43. *Gospel of Philip* 82, 158.

souls, as well as their sex. Thus, despite the Valentinians' endorsement of marriage, their erotic vision of salvation made the union of husband and wife a shameful, brutish parody of the union of higher and lower spirits.

## Origen on the Body

Origen (c. 184–253) was a native of Egypt who moved to Alexandria after his father's martyrdom. Though fiercely Christian, he studied under Ammonius Saccas, who is suspected of having been a Neopythagorean and who also taught Plotinus (203–70), another native of Egypt.[44] Through Ammonius, Origen was introduced to the Neopythagorean Numenius of Apamea, the Stoic Chrysippus, the Peripatetic Alexander of Aphrodisias, and the Middle Platonists Albinus, Antiochus of Ascalon, and Eudorus of Alexandria. He saw himself as spoiling the "learning of the world" to furnish the Church as the Israelites spoiled the Egyptians to furnish their tabernacle, and he advised the young Gregory Thaumaturgus to do the same, studying philosophy, geometry, and astronomy "as may be helpful for the interpretation of the Holy Scriptures" and seeking "the hidden sense which is present in most passages of the divine Scriptures," thus prompting modern scholars to suspect him of Pythagorean influence.[45] He was well versed in Valentinian thought through his study of Heracleon and, we will argue, incorporated aspects of the Valentinian vision into his own.[46] He does not appear to have been greatly influenced by Clement of Alexandria, his elder among catechists in Alexandria, whom he occasionally references but never names, but he does appear to have been greatly influenced by Philo of Alexandria, demonstrating his familiarity with at least half of Philo's works and imitating his allegorical approach to Scripture, often innovatively, with less respect for "this gross and visible body of ours" and little concern for procreation in this life or the next.[47]

Whereas Clement of Alexandria mounted one of the strongest anti-Encratite defenses of marriage and childbearing in early Christian history, of which more will be said in the next chapter, Origen embedded

---

44. See Grant, "Early Alexandrian Christianity," 133–44, esp. 139.

45. Origen, *Letter to Gregory*. See also Grant, "Early Alexandrian Christianity," 140.

46. Norman Russell counts forty-eight references to Heracleon's commentary on the Gospel of John in Origen's own commentary on John. See Russell, *The Doctrine of Deification*, 96n30. See also Berglund, "Origen's Vacillating Stances," 541–69.

47. Origen, *Prin.* Prologue. See Runia, "Philo of Alexandria," 171.

in Christian thinking the Gnostic and Encratite goal of eliminating male and female to achieve perfect oneness in Christ, per Gal 3:28.[48] He was the first to argue that Christ was born of a virgin to keep from being contaminated by sexual intercourse.[49] He allowed marriage on account of weakness per 1 Cor 7 but considered sexual relations shameful, believing that even married couples are defiled by sexual relations and saying couples ought not pray in the same room where they have sex.[50] He seems to quote the contemporaneous *Gospel of Philip* when he writes that "every marriage takes place in darkness . . . but the marriage of Christ, when he takes to himself the Church, occurs in the light."[51] Or perhaps the *Gospel of Philip* is quoting him.

Eusebius of Caesarea reports that while still a young man but already a popular catechist, Origen took to heart Matt 19:12 on those "which have made themselves eunuchs for the kingdom of heaven's sake"—and did just that.[52] (He may also have had in mind Matt 18:8–9 and Mark 9:47: "if thine eye offend thee, pluck it out . . .") As an apologist for Origen schooled by his successors in Caesarea, Eusebius attributes the act to youthful zeal and treats it as evidence of his great piety.[53] Peter Brown emphasizes the radicality of the act: Origen viewed human sexuality as a "passing phase . . . a dispensable adjunct of the personality that played no role in defining the essence of the human spirit." By having himself castrated, he had not just asserted rational control over his body to eliminate a nagging desire; he had "opted out of being male" to become a "walking lesson in the basic indeterminacy of the body."[54]

---

48. See, for example, Origen's use of Gal 3:28 in his *Commentary on the Song of Songs*, 3.9.

49. Origen, *Homilies on Leviticus*, 12.4.1–2, cf. 8.3.5. See Hunter, *Marriage, Celibacy, and Heresy*, 184–85.

50. Origen, *Com.Matt* 17.35; Fr. 29 on 1 Cor; Oration 31.4; Oration 2.2.

51. Origen, Fr. 39 on 1 Cor, quoted by Hunter, *Marriage, Celibacy, and Heresy*, 127. This similarity between Origen and Valentianism is noted by Brown, *The Body and Society*, 174.

52. See Eusebius, *Ecc. Hist.* 6.8. The story is doubted by Chadwick, *Early Christian Thought and the Classical Tradition*, 67, but accepted by Brown, *The Body and Society*, 168n44, and Crouzel, *Origen*, 9n32.

53. Self-castration is forbidden by canons 22, 23, and 24 of the so-called 85 Canons of the Holy Apostles. On Eusebius's treatment of Origen, see Grant, "Early Alexandrian Christianity"; Rogers, "Origen in the Likeness of Philo," 1–13.

54. Brown, *The Body and Society*, 168–69.

Controversy still rages over what Origen did and did not teach about the nature of man. A crucial text, Origen's thirteen-volume commentary on just the first four chapters of Genesis, exists only in fragments, many of the them preserved by his detractors.[55] For most of another crucial text, his *Peri Archōn*, we are dependent on the often paraphrastic Latin translation of Rufinus, entitled *De Principiis*, whose faithfulness to the Greek original has been doubted since its publication. The relevant comments attributed to Origen in that and other works are not easily reconciled, even when fragments are excluded. In Rufinus's *De Principiis*, Origen writes that only God is absolutely incorporeal, so all creatures must have some sort of material existence; he also likens rational beings (*logika*) and their material bodies to the Father, Son, and Holy Spirit to say that there is no before and after between them: They cannot exist without each other.[56] Elsewhere, Origen follows Philo in dividing the making of man into two acts, but whereas Philo took Gen 1:27 to speak of both creations sequentially, first of the genus "man" and then of particular men and women, Origen understands the verse as speaking only of the "inner man" who is "made" (*epoiēsen*) "in the image of God" (Gen 1:27) and is therefore "invisible, incorporeal, incorruptible and immortal," as opposed to the visible, corporeal, corruptible and mortal "outer man" which is "formed" (*eplasen*) "of the dust of the earth" (Gen 2:7), and that the two verses are therefore "not even said about the same persons."[57] He allegorizes the mention of "male and female" in Gen 1:27 to deny that male and female have anything to do with the "inner man" or the "image of God."[58] He also allegorizes the "coats of skins" in Gen 3:21, calling them "vestments of unhappiness," saying they symbolize mortality, and linking the verse to Plato's image in the *Phaedrus* of the soul losing its wings and

---

55. For an accounting of the fragments, see Heine, "Testimonia and Fragments," 122–42.

56. Origen, *Prin.* 2.2.1–2, 2.3.3.

57. Origen, *HomGen* 1.13; Origen, *Dial. Her.* 154–55; Origen, *ComMatt* 14.16–17; Origen, *ComRom* 7.4; Origen, *ConCel* 4.37, quoting Ps 119:73: "His hands have made and fashioned me."

58. In his first homily on Genesis (*HomGen* 1.14–15), Origen allows that "male and female" may be understood literally as "perhaps" foretelling the creation of the woman or "perhaps" expressing the harmony of creation, also seen in the pairings of heaven and earth and sun and moon, but the allegorical understanding he then offers, without a qualifying "perhaps," makes "male and female" mean the higher and lower parts of the "inner man"—the "male" spirit and the "female" soul—and it is this understanding he repeats in his *Commentary on Matthew* (*ComMatt* 14.16–17).

falling into an earthly body.[59] He describes the human body as light and luminous before the Fall, thick and heavy since the Fall, and shining like the sun and moon as the spiritual body of "the sons of the resurrection," but the difference between these three conditions is not entirely clear.[60] He appears to take quite literally the Apostle Paul's words that "flesh and blood cannot inherit the kingdom of God" (1 Cor 15:50), disparaging as poorly educated or feebleminded those who believe our future body will be much like our present body, and writing that "what at first was flesh (formed) out of earthly soil, and was afterwards dissolved by death and reduced to dust and ashes . . . will be again raised from the earth" to become a spiritual body—but he does not call what is raised "flesh," for the flesh does dissolve, leaving only, he says, a seed, per 1 Cor 15:38 ("But God giveth it a body as it hath pleased him, and to every seed his own body"), which seed would seem to be the "inner man" in a very different body, despite assurances to the contrary.[61]

We are therefore left to wonder whether the diversity of male and female will survive this transition from body to body and to suspect that Origen believed that it would not, but on the subject of bodies before and after death, Origen is rather vague. Henri Crouzel, an advocate for Origen, suspects that he is deliberately vague about the body because he "does not want to embarrass his hearers by going into his hypothesis of pre-existence."[62] But Origen had good reason to be vague about the body for another reason. When the oldest extant attack on Origen was made, in the early fourth century by Methodius of Olympus (+311), the complaint against him concentrated on both his allegorization of the "coats of skins" and its relation to the bodily resurrection, which directly threatened popular Christian belief about the resurrection of Christ as well as what Christians could expect of their own resurrection.[63] Whenever writing about the body, Origen stressed the dissimilarity of our present body with what came before and what will come after, giving Christians inclined to read their Scriptures more literally good reason to wonder

---

59. Origen, *HomLev* 6.2.7; Origen, *ConCel* 4.40; Plato, *Phdr* 246c.
60. Origen, *Prin.* 2.2.2, 2.9.6, 2.10.2.
61. Origen, *Prin.* 2.10.3, 3.6.5–7, ANF 4, 294 and 346–48.
62. Crouzel, *Origen*, 94. Origen himself commends Plato's use of myth to hide plain truth from the *hoi polloi*, mentioning the "coats of skins" as an instance of such concealment. See Origen, *ConCel* 4.39–40.
63. Methodius's *Discourse on the Resurrection* leads off with the issue of the "coats of skins" (1.2) and returns to it repeatedly throughout the work.

how human Origen's resurrected body would be, whether it would still be the body of a man or a woman, whether it would still be flesh and blood, and whether it would be less a resurrected body than a wholly new body imaginable only as light, assumed by an upwardly migrating soul. Methodius voices this objection when he mocks Origen by asking whether the resurrected body will be "spherical, polygonal, cubical, or pyramidal"—words that, with Origen's treatment of celestial spheres (sun, moon, and stars) as rational beings, inspired the condemnation of those who believe the dead will rise as spheres in both the fifth anathema of the emperor Justinian in 543 and the tenth anathema issued by the Fifth Ecumenical Council (II Constantinople) in 553.[64]

## Origen on the Soul

Origen's view of the body was a major and even the ultimate issue for Epiphanius of Salamis and Theophilus of Alexandria in the late fourth and early fifth centuries.[65] But his view of the body derived from his view of the soul, which took shape amid his engagement with Valentinianism. In his determination to defend the goodness of God against the Valentinian belief that some souls were created for damnation, Origen argued that "in the beginning" God created all rational beings at the same time and in the same way, each as an equal intellect (*nous*) sharing all the same knowledge, "made equal and alike, because there was in Himself no reason for producing variety and diversity."[66] But, having nothing to do but contemplate God, each intellect became complacent, cooling in its ardor for God to become a soul—called *psychē* ("soul") on account of being *psychros* ("cold"), an etymology found among Platonists and adopted by Origen.[67] This cooling to greater and lesser degrees, for which the souls

---

64. Methodius, *Discourse on the Resurrection*, 3.2.10; Origen, *On Prayer*, 20.

65. Clark, *The Origenist Controversy*, 121. See also 116, where Clark writes that Theophilus's later attacks on Origenism "centered squarely on the status of the body" and that his shift toward greater emphasis on the body "parallels the narrowing concern of Epiphanius's attack."

66. Origen, *Prin.* 2.9.1, 2.9.6, ANF 4, 291–92.

67. Origen, *Prin.* 2.8.3–4. Philo similarly writes of the souls of reptiles as having suffered from "satiety of divine things" and "descended to that mortal and evil district, the earth" (*Her.* 49[240]) as well as of the souls of men descending to three levels of earthly existence (*Som.* 1.22[138–40]), mirroring Diotima's three levels of souls in Plato's *Symposium* (209c).

themselves are responsible, caused them to descend to different levels of material existence, as God deemed appropriate, and this descent "is the cause of the diversity among rational creatures, deriving its origin not from the will or judgment of the Creator, but from the freedom of the individual will."[68] Finally, Origen speculates on the consummation of all things, reasoning that "when things have begun to hasten to that consummation that all may be one, as the Father is one with the Son [cf. John 17:11, 22], it may be understood as a rational inference, that where all are one, there will no longer be any diversity."[69]

The difficulty of squaring this fall of rational beings into souls and then bodies, or what most scholars still call the "preexistence of souls," with the biblical accounts of creation and fall scandalized early Christians and still divides scholars. Henri Crouzel laments that Origen did teach the preexistence of souls, which he blames on Origen's Platonism, and cites Procopius of Gaza in support of the view that Origen read Gen 2:7 as meaning man's original, preexistent, ethereal body and read the "coats of skins" in Gen 3:21 as man's fallen flesh, but Crouzel himself resists reading preexistence any further into Gen 1–3, viewing the double creation as "logically distinct" but "chronologically simultaneous."[70] Caroline Bammel admits the difficulty of reading preexistence into Genesis and prefers to focus on Origen's (and Didymus the Blind's) allegorical relation of "male and female" and Adam and Eve to Christ and the Church, yet she concludes that the easiest way to systematize Origen's scattered comments on creation and fall is to think in terms of "two falls" instead of a "double creation": a general fall of rational beings into the bodies "fashioned" for them, per Gen 2, and then a fall of the same beings subjecting their bodies to corruption and death, per Gen 3.[71]

Two falls would mean four bodies—one before the first fall, one after first fall, one after the second fall, and one after the resurrection—but only if we assume that God alone is absolutely incorporeal, as claimed in Rufinus's translation of *Peri Archōn*.[72] Peter Martens doubts Rufinus's faithfulness on this point to argue, in his words, "the regnant position,

---

68. Origen, *ConCel*, 1.32, 4.40; Origen, *Prin*. 2.9.6, 3.6.4; Origen, *Prin*. 2.9.6, ANF 4, 292.

69. Origen, *Prin*. 3.6.4.

70. Crouzel, *Origen*, 90–94, 206–7.

71. See Bammel, "Adam in Origen," 62–141. Also Harl, "La préexistence des âmes," 244–46.

72. Origen, *Prin*. 2.2.2, 2.3.3.

that humans were originally unembodied souls or minds, and that their first abode, sometimes called *paradise* in Origen's writings, was heavenly and incorporeal."[73] According to Martens, Origen viewed both accounts of creation in Genesis mainly as allegories of the same fall of preexistent souls into present bodies, showing little patience for literal readings and taking every opportunity in his many works to correlate the many pairs that appear in Gen 1–3 (heaven and earth, male and female, Adam and Eve, the two trees, and what is "made" and what is "fashioned," including the "coats of skins") with the distinctions of intelligible and sensible, soul and body, mind and matter, "inner man" and "outer man," the pre-eternal Christ and the pre-existent Church)—all to offer a scripturally based version of preexistence in opposition to similar but more fanciful Gnostic claims of preexistence based on the same Scriptures.[74]

Benjamin Blosser also ascribes preexistence to Origen, noting that Origen never expressly denies the fall of souls into bodies when mentioning the subject and repeatedly suggests that some men are born good or bad on account of earlier events.[75] Similarly, Mark Scott all but assumes that Origen taught the fall of souls into bodies, but whereas Blosser declares Origen a "bona fide Middle Platonist" for his fall of incorporeal *logika*, Scott stresses the scriptural basis of Origen's preexistence and the difference between it and the Platonist version.[76]

Mark Edwards goes further to deny both Platonism and preexistence in Origen, declaring the latter an ancient "calumny" unsupported by Origen's extant works and arguing that "except in a vestigial form that is not heretical, Origen never embraced this doctrine, either as an hypothesis or as an edifying myth."[77] Edwards insists that none of the passages that can be trusted as Origen's and that are commonly thought to speak of preexistence certainly express a fall of human souls on account of some preincarnate fault.[78] Like Crouzel, he understands Origen's "double creation"

---

73. See Martens, "Response to Edwards," 186–200, esp. 187. On his and others' doubts about Origen's qualification of incorporeality, see Martens's "Embodiment, Heresy and the Hellenization of Christianity," 594–620, esp. 611n61 and 614n73.

74. See Martens, "Origen's Doctrine of Pre-Existence," 516–49.

75. See Blosser, *Become Like the Angels*, 159, 171–74, 195–96. Passages cited by Blosser and others on "anterior causes" for innate predispositions include *Prin.* 3.1.21, 3.3.5. 3.2.3, 2.8.3, *ComJn* 2.24–25, and *ConCel* 1.32, 4.40.

76. See Scott, *Journey Back to God*, 53–79.

77. Edwards, *Origen against Plato*, 89.

78. Edwards, *Origen against Plato*, 89; Edwards, "Origen in Paradise," 163–85; Edwards, "Origen's Platonism," 20–38, 34.

as logical rather than chronological, occurring simultaneously or very nearly simultaneously and thus allowing for at most an "instantaneous pre-existence in the hand of God before embodiment."[79] Edwards argues that, for Origen, the first embodiment of humans souls per Gen 2 was not of flesh and blood, thus bringing Origen closer to Philo in associating the "coats of skins" of Gen 3:21 with the bodies we now bear, which differ from our original bodies by their mortality and, hints Origen, by their inclusion of organs suited for survival outside Paradise but serving no purpose in it.[80]

Edwards's reading of Origen on the body closely matches that of Procopius of Gaza and helps explain why many early Christians found Origen objectionable, as Methodius, Theophilus of Alexandria, Epiphanius, and Jerome all accused Origen of identifying the "coats of skins" with our present bodies and thus impugning both marriage and resurrection.[81]

## Origen and Valentinianism

Panayiotis Tzamalikos also exonerates Origen on the preexistence of souls and, in doing so, inadvertently sheds light on another problematic aspect of Origen's cosmology. Reading Origen in the light of later Origenists such as Gregory of Nyssa and Maximus the Confessor, Tzamalikos distinguishes between the making of plans called *logoi* (reasons, principles) and the making of creatures according to the plans.[82] The *logoi* exist only in the Logos, who is the *archē* of creation, which is why Origen says that Gen 1:1 refers not to the temporal creation of heaven and earth, but to their source in Christ.[83] Martens also emphasizes this reading of Gen 1:1, but whereas Martens understands Origen's first creation "before all things" to be "the creation of the world of rational creatures prior to the corporeal creation," Tzamalikos stresses Origen's first creation as merely an act of God "*in* his wisdom," saying of Gen 1, "It was the reasons

---

79. Edwards, *Origen against Plato*, 160.

80. Edwards, "Origen in Paradise," 165, 179–81. The hint is found in Fr. 121 of Origen's *Commentary on Genesis* 22, in which Origen asks how all our present body's members can perform their proper function if Paradise is, as he says, a "divine place." See also Heine, "Testimonia and Fragments," 122–42, 140; Jacobsen, "Genesis 1–3 as Source for the Anthropology of Origen," 213–32.

81. See Clark, *The Origenist Controversy*, 86–98, 113–20, 135–38.

82. Tzamalikos, *Origen*, 44.

83. Origen, *HomGen* 1.1.

[*logoi*] of the world that constitute what was created."[84] And yet these *logoi* are not just ideas or forms in the mind of God; they have a life of sorts, but not a life of their own, only a life in Christ. Tzamalikos is rather vague about the next step, calling it the "most delicate tenet" of Origen's theology and an apparent paradox that Origen himself "did not wish to elaborate on": Somehow, some "one" falls out of Christ, and this begins an evolutionary process of creation of individual beings.[85] "It is only then that actual creation comes into existence," writes Tzamalikos.[86] "Thus personal creaturely life starts only with existence of the actual creation. For only then do personal beings begin to exist as individuals; it is only then that they acquire a life of their own."[87] In other words, souls cannot be said to fall into bodies because they do not exist until their time to be created with bodies according to the *logoi* still in Christ.

We have therefore a sequence of three "realities," according to Tzamalikos: preeternal God, creation in Christ (*logoi*), and creation from Christ (persons and things), the last of which will be returned to Christ in the apocatastasis, "that God may be all in all" (1 Cor 15:28).[88] Only in the apocatastasis will the original unity of God and creation be reestablished. Until then, creation will be marred by multiplicity, schism, division, and disagreement, all of which Origen sees as "signs of wickedness." Tzamalikos writes, "This conviction is so strong that these characteristics are established as a guideline for exegesis: whenever these notions are found in Scripture, they should be interpreted as denotations of evil and the relevant passages should be interpreted accordingly."[89]

Much of this will be appear later in Gregory of Nyssa, Evagrius Ponticus, and Maximus the Confessor—so much that one wonders whether it is Tzamalikos reading Origen or Tzamalikos reading Origenism into Origen. Ilaria Ramelli follows Tzamalikos on key points and sees Gregory and Evagrius as quite close to Origen on the subject of preexistence.[90]

---

84. Martens, "Origen's Doctrine of Preexistence," 526; Tzamalikos, *Origen*, 47, 72.

85. Tzamalikos, *Origen*, 66, 74–78. Tzamalikos writes, ""Whenever Origen speaks of the Fall, he refers to it as a fall of 'one' that has 'moulted' [*pterorruēsas*] and, therefore, fell from the 'bliss.'" Tzamalikos, *Origen*, 76.

86. Tzamalikos, *Origen*, 71, 78, citing Origen, *ComJn* 19.20.

87. Tzamalikos, *Origen*, 81–82.

88. Tzamalikos, *Origen*, 70–71.

89. Tzamalikos, *Origen*, 79, citing Origen, *Prin*. 6.6.2, 2.1.3, 3.5.4, 3.6.3, 3.6.8, and *selPs*. 117. See also Tzamalikos, *Origen*, 55, 83.

90. Ramelli, "'Preexistence of Souls'?" 167–226.

Other scholars, not reading Origen quite the way Tzamalikos does, see similarities between Origen and contemporary Platonism. Whereas Aristotle associated diversity with form, saying matter does not produce diversity, Origen thinks more like a Platonist or Pythagorean, associating diversity with matter, without which "variety and diversity" cannot exist.[91] Other similarities include the foundational distinction between intelligible and sensible; the view of divinity as simplicity and diversity as always a step away from divinity; the corollary that the more beings are like God, the more they are the same, because reason and virtue are the same for all; the identification of the human person with the rational soul trapped in a body rather than a union of soul and body; the notion of spiritual progress as an intellectual ascent of the soul from the body; and the unrestrained use of allegory to interpret foundational texts as supporting of their systems.

Tzamalikos himself sees a likeness to Valentinianism, saying the Valentinian doctrine of creation as it appears in the *Tripartite Tractate* found at Nag Hammadi "seems to stand close to that of Origen." He notes two similarities (free will and benevolent creation) and one difference (no change in God as a result of creation in Origen).[92] Many more similarities set Origen and Valentinus apart from other Christians, including a fall of heavenly spirits as the beginning of the process of material creation; a process of redemption by which fallen spirits are freed from material creation and returned to their original unity with God; the characterization of creation as a casting down (*katabolē*) into a material world; the trichotomy of spirit, soul, and body in which the spirit is the original God-like component and the soul and body are merely results of the spirit's fall; a radical transformation of human being in its material descent and spiritual ascent; and the Platonic eroticization of spirituality, seen in the Valentinian notion of the "bridal chamber" and Origen's equation of *erōs* and *agapē* in his reading of the Song of Songs as expressing love, not between God and Israel (as among Jews) or between Christ and the Church (as among Christians before and after Origen), but between God and the soul.[93]

91. Aristotle, *Meta.* 10.1058b; Origen, *Prin.* 2.1.4, 2.3.3.

92. Tzamalikos, *Origen*, 63–64.

93. Brown notes the similarity between the erotic aspects of Origen's and the Valentinian spirituality, suspecting the influence of the latter on the former. See Brown, *The Body and Society*, 171–74. See also Crouzel, *Origen*, 121–26; Boersma, "Nuptial Reading," 227–58. For more on other similarities, see Daniélou, *Origen*, 191–94;

Of special interest, on account of its limitation to Origen and the Valentinians, is that the process of creation and redemption begins with a freely willed fall away from divinity by spiritual beings, creating a division among spiritual beings that necessitates the creation of the material world. Among Neoplatonists, beings come into existence as emanations of the One, existence proceeding by necessity through successive emanations; for Valentinus and for Origen, the One creates spirits, spirits fall, and the result is the material world impregnated with fallen spirits.[94]

Crouzel denies this similarity, claiming that the Valentinian fall of spirits from the divine Pleroma was the result of Sophia's "irrepressible desire" and not an act of free will and that "free will plays practically no part in the Valentinian gnōsis as events unfold."[95] Quispel, however, shows that free will was indeed responsible for the fall of spirits in the Western Valentinianism of Heracleon, as evidenced by the *Tripartite Tractate*, which Heracleon himself may have written.[96] This text differs from other Valentinian teaching in treating the creation of the world as less accidental than providential inasmuch as the material world functions as a net to catch falling spirits so as to keep them from falling further, which is also true of Origen's system. More importantly, the *Tripartite Tractate* speaks of the Father willing the autonomy or free will (*autexousion*) of the aeons, even knowing that one would fall, saying, "For the free will which was begotten with the Totalities [i.e., the Pleroma] was a cause for this one to do what he desired, with no one to restrain him."[97] The "he" and "him" here is the "offspring of wisdom" identified by other Valentinians as Sophia but whom the *Tripartite Tractate* calls Logos, saying that he only "became weak like a female" when he suffered a division (from the stress of attempting more than he could manage) and part of him fell out of the Pleroma.

---

Quispel, "Origen and the Valentinian Gnosis," 36–42; Markschies, "Gnostics," 103–6; Broek, *Studies in Gnosticism and Alexandrian Christianity*, 129–30.

94. Early on, Plotinus imitated Valentinus in attributing the creation of the world to the World Soul's impatient audacity (*tolma*), but in late life he attributed creation to the World Soul's unrestrained love (*erōs*) for the beauty of the Intellect. Cf. Plotinus, *Enneads* 4.7.13(18), 4.8.4, 5.1.1, 6.6.1, and 3.5.3. See Quispel, "Origen and the Valentinian Gnosis," 37; Borodai, "Plotinus's Critique of Gnosticism," 66–83; Bradshaw, *Aristotle East and West*, 82–83.

95. Crouzel, *Origen*, 217.

96. Quispel, "Origen and the Valentinian Gnosis," 35.

97. *Tripartite Tractate*, 75, 72.

It is possible that Origen derived his freely willed fall of spirits from non-Valentinian sources. The concept of "cosmic sympathy," positing an original order and unity of the cosmos, had been introduced before the time of Christ by the Stoic Posidonius of Apamea. Free will entered Middle Platonism about the same time through Antiochus of Ascalon, from whom Origen borrows to counter Valentinus's predestinationism.[98] Free will also appears in Philo of Alexandria and was a main plank of Christian apologetics in the second and third centuries, but only in Origen and the *Tripartite Tractate* is free will the cause of a cosmic fall beginning a process of creation and redemption.

It is also quite possible that Origen got his idea of a freely willed fall of incorporeal beings resulting in the material creation from Heracleon, his elder by at least a generation.[99] We know that Origen was well acquainted with Heracleon's version of Valentinianism, for in his *Commentary on John* Origen references Heracleon's lost commentary on the same gospel 48 times.[100] We also know that Origen rarely credited anyone for his ideas and often disrespected those from whom he borrowed, including Heracleon.[101] This is a difference between Origen and Clement of Alexandria, who often honored the philosophers but made less use of them. Origen was especially hard on Plato, yet his own debt to Plato was so great that he was labelled a Platonist by both Christians like Eusebius of Caesarea and pagans like Porphyry.[102]

---

98. Quispel, "Origen and the Valentinian Gnosis," 37–38; Trigg, *Origen*, 67–68, 72–73. Trigg says Origen used Antiochus of Ascalon's argument for the soul's free will against Valentinus's predestinationism.

99. Quispel writes, "It may even be that Origen took this idea from Heracleon. For if the idea of free will was widespread in Hellenistic and Christian circles, the specific view that the worldprocess is due to the free decision of one spiritual being in the beyond cannot be attested elsewhere than in Origen and the *Tractatus tripartitus* of the Codex Jung. Here evil is no longer a by-product of evolution, but due to a contingent decision of a spiritual being." See Quispel, "Origen and the Valentinian Gnosis," 39.

100. See Russell, *The Doctrine of Deification*, 96n30; Trigg, *Origen*, 45.

101. Daniélou provides several examples where Origen follows Heracleon in his anagogical approach to Scripture, which "enables him to claim that the whole of his theological system can be found in Scripture. . . . His exegesis ceases to be the Church's at this point and becomes no more than the discovery of his own ideas in Scripture." See Daniélou, *Origen*, 191–94.

102. Eusebius, *Ecc. Hist.* 6.19. See also Chadwick, *The Early Church*, 100–101. It would be easy to psychologize Origen's conflicted regard for pagan philosophy. The son of a martyr, he needed to prove that his father was right and did not die in vain, but the only way he could prove that was to show how philosophically correct

With that in mind, along with the similarities already noted, we have good reason to believe that Valentinianism did contribute significantly to Origen's imagination and that his vision of a cosmic process of descent and ascent is essentially a stage in the evolution of the Valentinian vision.[103] The basis of the vision remains the same: Man is not a union of soul and body made both in the image of God and male and female (per Gen 1:27); he is instead a sexless spirit made in the image of God but burdened with a male or female body that prevents the spirit from enjoying its original unity with God. The function of the myths is also the same: Both the myth of the aeons and the myth of preexistent spirits are meant to solve the same problem created by the attempts of Valentinus and Origen to combine Christian and Platonist presuppositions about human nature: How can godlike rational beings come to be separated from God and burdened with bodies in all their unfortunate diversity? The first myth blames impatient desire for God on the part of one aeon; the second blames boredom with God among all preexistent spirits. The transition from the first to the second is managed by Heracleon's modification of the first myth to make free will the cause of the fall, which inadvertently obviates the drama of Sophia once the preexistence of all spirits is assumed. Thus, despite the many aspects of Valentinianism that Origen does not adopt, his vision remains fundamentally Valentinian and another expression of the "wild Platonism" of his era.[104]

## The Cappadocians

Less than a century after Origen's death in 253, a bishop of Sebastea in Cappadocia named Eustathius inspired an ascetic movement that included vows of celibacy, abandonment of marriages and of masters, and women dressing and cutting their hair like men—all condemned by the Council of Gangra sometime before 341. Basil of Caesarea addressed his first extant epistle to this Eustathius, addressing him as "the philosopher." Basil's first experience of ascetic life was likely under Eustathius's influence. He also read Origen and collaborated with Gregory of Nazianzus in the compilation of passages from Origen published later as the *Philocalia*.

---

Christianity was without crediting the religiously incorrect philosophers he used to validate Christianity.

103. See Russell, *The Doctrine of Deification*, 96.
104. Brown, *The Body and Society*, 172–74.

## The Greek Christian View of Male and Female

Neither Basil nor Gregory had much to say about male and female, but both followed Origen in their use of Gal 3:28. In his commentary on Ps 144, Basil writes:

> No longer is there the danger of slipping into sin. For, there is neither rebellion of the flesh, nor cooperation of a woman in sin. Therefore, there is no male and female in the resurrection, but there is one certain life and it is of one kind, since those dwelling in the country of the living are pleasing of their Lord.[105]

Likewise, Gregory, in his eulogy for his brother Caesarius, melds Gal 3:28 with Col 3:11 to write:

> This is a great mystery planned for us by God . . . that we might all become one in Christ, who became perfectly in all of us all that he himself is, that we might no longer be male and female, barbarian, Scythian, slave or free (which are identifying marks of the flesh), but might bear in ourselves only the form of God.[106]

Evagrius Ponticus, Gregory's student and later deacon, also had little to say about male and female, but much of what he did say on human nature followed Origen and Valentinus in its sequence of descent, ascent, and reunion: In the beginning, the intellect fell away from God to become a soul and then fell further to become a body; in the end, the reverse will happen: the three will reunite in their ascent toward God and be returned to perfect unity as mere intellect.[107] In the unexpurgated Syriac version of his *Kephalaia gnostika* (S2), he writes: "The final judgment will not show the transformation of bodies, but it will reveal their elimination."[108] "Just as colors, shapes, and numbers pass away together with mortal bodies, likewise matter also is eliminated together with the four elements."[109] "There will be only bare/naked intellects who

---

105. Basil, *Homily 22 on Ps 114* (PG 29 492C), in *Exegetical Homilies*, 357.

106. Gregory of Nazianzus, *Oration 46*, 7.23 (PG 35 785C), quoted by Harrison, "Male and Female in Cappadocian Theology," 459.

107. Evagrius Ponticus, *Letter to Melania*, 26–30.

108. Evagrius Ponticus, *KG* 2.77, 135. The authenticity of S2 is doubted by Gabriel Bunge and Augustine Casiday but accepted by Ramelli, Brian Daley, and many others. For a historical review of scholarly opinion on Evagrius, see DelCogliano, "The Quest for Evagrius of Pontus," 387–401. For a critique of Casiday's arguments, see Rivas, "The Two Versions of Evagrius Ponticus' *Kephalaia gnostika*," 485–92.

109. Evagrius Ponticus, *KG* 1.29, 29.

continually satiate themselves from its impossibility to satiate."[110] All diversity according to merit will be overcome through successive aeons of moral improvement, so that in the end there will be only perfect unity and equality, with "no leaders, nor (others) submitted to leaders, but all of them will be gods."[111] Such speculations are now generally agreed to lie behind the anathemas against Origenism promulgated by the emperor Justinian in 543 and the Fifth Ecumenical Council (II Constantinople) in 553. They may also have contributed to the first great Origenist controversy, which broke out soon after Evagrius's death in 399.[112]

Although made a reader by Basil and made a deacon by Gregory of Nazianzus, Evagrius has come to be seen as closer personally and intellectually to Basil's younger brother, Gregory of Nyssa, who was nearer Evagrius in age, also in Constantinople for the council in 381, also in Palestine shortly thereafter, and also more inclined than Basil or Gregory of Nazianzus to philosophic speculation along Origenist lines.[113] Both Evagrius and Gregory of Nyssa credited women as significant influences in their lives (his sister, Macrina the Younger, for Gregory; Melania the Elder for Evagrius), and both also held opinions later condemned as Origenist.[114] Like Evagrius, Origen, and Valentinus, Gregory of Nyssa saw salvation as a radically transformative ascent from this world to the next—in the words of Hans Boersma, echoing Gregory's *On the Soul and the Resurrection,* "an anagogical transposition that will allow us to leave behind all of the diastemic characteristics of the mortal body, including gender, sexuality, childbearing, maturation, nourishment, bodily functions, disease, bodily passions, and death."[115]

In his speculations on human nature and spirituality, Gregory corrects some of Origen's more unorthodox ideas but also adds several complications of his own. He explicitly rejects the preexistence and

---

110. Evagrius Ponticus, *KG* 1.65, 64.

111. Evagrius Ponticus, *KG* 4.51, 227. Cf. Evagrius Ponticus, *KG* 2.75 and 6.75, with Ramelli, *Evagrius's Kephalaia Gnostika,* 134, 363–64.

112. See Clark, *The Origenist Controversy,* 117.

113. Ramelli writes, "[Julia] Konstantinovsky is right to remark that Evagrius's ideas are not very similar to those of 'the Cappadocians,' though in fact they prove to be not very similar to those of Basil (and, to some extent, Nazianzen), but they are quite similar to those of Nyssen (for instance, in metaphysics and eschatology)." Ramelli, "Evagrius and Gregory," 129.

114. See Corrigan, *Evagrius and Gregory,* 1.

115. Boersma, *Embodiment and Virtue in Gregory of Nyssa,* 87.

*The Greek Christian View of Male and Female* 127

transmigration of souls as "fabulous doctrines of the heathens," not mentioning Origen by name but attributing such notions to "some of those before our time who have dealt with the question of 'principles'"—a sly reference to Origen's *Peri Archōn* (*On Principles*).[116] He defends the bodily resurrection, arguing that God creates souls and bodies at the same time, that both are dependent upon the other for what they are meant to be, and that soul and body will be brought back together in the resurrection, which will return man to his original state of being.[117] He even honors the body as an expression of the godlike dignity of the human being, saying that it is "adapted for royalty" inasmuch as it stands upright with its intellectual, sensory, and communicative organs at top and its strictly animal digestive and genital organs below.[118] Man, he says, is the mean between the extremes of divine and brutish, not a soul trapped in a body but a composite being of both soul and body spanning the divide between the rational and the irrational, the incorporeal and the merely corporeal.[119] In that sense, Gregory's regard for the body is less negative, less Platonist, and more conventionally Christian than that of Origen and the Valentinians.

On the other hand, Gregory's thinking is firmly founded in the fundamental Platonic oppositions of intelligible and sensible, spiritual and material, immutable and mutable. Following Philo and Origen, he freely allegorizes Scripture to fit his philosophy, ignoring his brother Basil's warnings about allegory.[120] He also follows Origen in his essentially angelic view of human nature, his idealization of virginity, his low regard for marriage, his contrast between the "coats of skins" we now wear and the "holy bodies" we will put on in the resurrection, his Platonic eroticization of love between God and the soul, and his expectation of a final apocatastasis returning creation to God and man to his original state of angelic innocence.[121]

---

116. Gregory of Nyssa, *HO* 28, 419–20.

117. Gregory of Nyssa, *HO* 29–30. See also Boersma, *Embodiment and Virtue in Gregory of Nyssa*, 87–116.

118. Gregory of Nyssa, *HO* 4.1, 8.1–2.

119. Gregory of Nyssa, *HO* 16.9.

120. See Basil, *Hexaemeron*, 9.

121. Gregory writes: "Now the resurrection promises us nothing else than the restoration of the fallen to their ancient state. . . . If then the life of those restored is closely related to that of the angels, it is clear that the life before the transgression was a kind of angelic life, and hence also our return to the ancient condition of our life

Gregory offers his own version of a double creation based on Gen 1:27, coming closer to Philo than to Origen but investing it with much greater significance than did either Philo or Origen.[122] According to Gregory, the words "in the image of God created He him" refer to the creation of universal human nature modeled on the "Archetype," which is Jesus Christ, whereas the words "male and female created He them" refer to the distinction of male and female added to human nature for the sake of survival in man's fallen state. Gregory is characteristically vague about what constitutes human nature, but he is quite emphatic that our universal nature bearing the image of God, on account of its creation after the Archetype, does not include the differentiation of male and female, which "has no reference to the Divine Archetype," being "a thing which is alien from our conceptions of God" and "a departure from the Prototype, for 'in Christ,' as the apostle says, 'there is neither male nor female.'"[123]

The abandonment of male and female seems to be the veiled meaning of Gregory's *On the Making of Man*. Midway through the work, just before setting forth his version of the double creation, Gregory warns us that he will not "set forth that which occurs to our mind authoritatively, but will place it in the form of a theoretical speculation before our kindly hearers."[124] He then begins the exercise, belaboring the identification of human nature with the image of God as well as the exclusion of male and female from the image. He claims that since there are angels in abundance, there must be angelic ways to reproduce without the bestial binding of male to female—as if God did not make enough angels in the beginning and cannot make more of them whenever he pleases. This notion that sexual intercourse was not necessary for reproduction

---

is compared to the angels." Gregory of Nyssa, *HO* 17.2, 407. See Zachhuber, *Human Nature in Gregory of Nyssa*, 165. For Gregory's use of "coats of skins," see Boersma, *Embodiment and Virtue in Gregory of Nyssa*, 87–92, 100–101. For his eroticization of divine love, see Boersma, *Embodiment and Virtue in Gregory of Nyssa*, 113–15.

122. Origen's second creation was the fall of sexless souls into earthly bodies; Philo's was the creation of the form of man followed by the creation of individual men and women. Gregory likewise writes of the creation of the "image of God" followed by the creation of Adam "from the earth." See Gregory of Nyssa, *HO* 16.7-8, 22.3-4. For a brief comparison of different versions of double creation, see Thunberg, *Microcosm and Mediator*, 147–49.

123. Gregory of Nyssa, *HO* 16.14, 406; 16.7-8, 405. Cf. Gregory of Nyssa, *HO* 22.3-4. Gregory does not clearly distinguish "Archetype" and "Prototype" and appears to use them interchangeably.

124. Gregory of Nyssa, *HO* 16.15, 406.

first appears a generation earlier in a brief comment by yet another Alexandrian, Athanasius the Great, who writes in his commentary on Ps 50/51:5 that God intended man to reproduce by some other means, "But the transgression of the commandment introduced marriage on account of the lawless act of Adam."[125] The notion may have originated as a result of attempts to correct Origen on the preexistence of souls while retaining Origen's disdain for human sexuality as an animal aspect of bodily existence, which begged the question of why God would have created man "male and female" to "be fruitful and multiply" like beasts. Gregory's answer is that God did not give us an angelic means of reproduction because he foreknew that man would prefer the bestial to the angelic after his fall. He writes:

> He Who brought all things into being and fashioned Man as a whole by His own will to the Divine image, did not wait to see the number of souls made up to its proper fulness by the gradual additions of those coming after; but while looking upon the nature of man in its entirety and fulness by exercise of His foreknowledge . . . in order that the multitude of human souls might not be cut short by its fall from that mode by which the angels were increased and multiplied—for this reason, I say, He formed for our nature that contrivance for increase which befits those who had fallen into sin, implanting in mankind, instead of the angelic majesty of nature, that animal and irrational mode by which they now succeed one another.[126]

Gregory goes on to stress the unity of mankind based on a "universal nature," saying, "Man, then, was made in the image of God; that is, the universal nature, the thing like God; not part of the whole, but all the fulness of the nature together was so made by omnipotent wisdom."[127] In another work, *On Not Three Gods*, Gregory argues that just as there is just one God but three divine Persons, there is just one man and therefore to speak of "many men" is a "customary abuse of language" tantamount to speaking of "many human natures."[128] He makes the same point in *On the Making of Man*, saying, "For this reason the whole race was spoken of as one man. . . . Our whole nature, then, extending from the first to the last,

---

125. Gregory of Nyssa, *Commentary on the Psalms* (Ps 50:5), PG 27 240C, translation by Trenham, *Marriage and Virginity according to John Chrysostom*, 69.
126. Gregory of Nyssa, *HO* 17.4, 407.
127. Gregory of Nyssa, *HO* 22.4, 411.
128. Gregory of Nyssa, *On Not Three Gods*, 332.

is, so to say, one image of Him Who is; but the distinction of kind in male and female was added to His work last, as I suppose, for the reason [of reproduction]."[129] The picture painted not precisely but impressionistically is of a fully formed, godlike nature that is all that humans truly are, to which is attached an animal attribute serving no purpose except for reproduction in the fallen state.

This picture is so dark that some scholars have attempted esoteric readings of Gregory's works that brighten things up, heeding Gregory's warning that he does not mean to be straightforward and concluding that in praising virginity he is actually justifying marriage and that in opposing angelic and bestial means of reproduction he is actually defending our bestial means as angelic when employed in a rational manner.[130] But Gregory has hardly anything good to say about marriage, which he elsewhere names "the primal root of all striving after vanities," at best a distraction from excellence and contemplation, at worst a deceitful calamity of pain-causing pleasure.[131] "So many-sided, then, so strangely different are the ills with which marriage supplies the world," he moans.[132] Even at its best, beneath all its pleasures, "the fire of an inevitable pain is smouldering."[133]

*On the Making of Man* is therefore much easier to read esoterically as advancing an idea for which Origen had already been attacked—that men and women will not be men and women in the next life. When writing esoterically, one does not begin or end with one's reason for writing; one buries that reason safely in the middle, which lazy readers will never reach, using what goes before to throw some readers off the scent and condition others to think uncritically, and using what comes after to calm and distract while still slyly confirming one's conclusions.[134] This is what Gregory does in *On the Making of Man*. He spends the first half of the work (fifteen of thirty chapters) laying the groundwork with humdrum

---

129. Gregory of Nyssa, HO 16.18, 406.

130. See, for example, Behr, "The Rational Animal," 224; Behr, "Marriage and Asceticism," 24–50, esp. 39–49; also Hart, "Reconciliation of Body and Soul," 450–78; Hart, "Gregory of Nyssa's Ironic Praise of the Celibate Life," 1–19. For refutations, see Boersma, *Embodiment and Virtue in Gregory of Nyssa*, 100–108; Smith, "The Body of Paradise and the Body of the Resurrection," 207–28.

131. Gregory of Nyssa, *Virg.* 7, 352; 4, 349.

132. Gregory of Nyssa, *Virg.* 3, 348.

133. Gregory of Nyssa, *Virg.* 3, 345.

134. See Melzer, *Philosophy Between the Lines*, 287–324, esp. 321–22.

## The Greek Christian View of Male and Female 131

Platonic contrasts of mind and matter, soul and body, rational and irrational, so that when the division of male and female is first mentioned at the work's mid-point, chapter 16, it stands out as a problematic complication rather than as a normal, natural, enduring dimension of human existence.[135] After discoursing pointedly but also obscurely on the problem, he walks the reader away from this difficulty before the implications become obvious, distracting him with digressions that supplement his main point and prove his orthodoxy on related issues.[136] Finally, in his long last chapter, he gives us a lengthy examination of the human body—its brain, heart, liver, lungs, sinews, bowels, etc.—with only passing reference to unnamed organs "adapted with a view toward succession of descendants," thus dialing down the sexual aspects of even our bodies to the barest minimum.[137] Then, in the end, he employs Plotinus's metaphor of the sculptor chiseling away extraneous marble to reveal the perfect form inside, just before telling us that our passionate, bestial means of reproduction has obscured the image of God in us so we must "put away childish things" (1 Cor 13:11), "put off the old man" (Col 3:9), and "put on the new, which is renewed after the image of Him that created him" (Col 3:10). His final words are: "Now may we all return to that Divine grace in which God at the first created man, when He said, 'Let us make man in our image and likeness,' to Whom be glory and might for ever and ever. Amen."[138]

Clearly for Gregory, the return he intends is to the first creation without the second. This is his reason for writing. This is the dangerous idea he does not want to lead with or plainly state, lest he be accused of Origenism. The "making of man" in his title is not the story of Adam and Eve, whom he barely mentions, but the creation of a sexless ideal of divine humanity and then the realization of that sexless ideal in the resurrection. Everything in between is merely the process by which the Archetype

---

135. Melzer, *Philosophy Between the Lines*, 297–98, explains that esoteric writing typically begins as literal writing and only turns esoteric when a warning is given and a problem is introduced, which happens in chapter 16 of *On the Making of Man*. First, Gregory warns us he will not speak straightforwardly, then he introduces a contrast quite unlike those preceding.

136. This is when Gregory denies the preexistence and transmigration of souls while also using Origen's arguments for the transformation of human existence from seed to plant and for the complete reconstitution of the body in the resurrection, without crediting Origen.

137. Gregory of Nyssa, *HO* 30.30, 422.

138. Gregory of Nyssa, *HO* 30.30, 427.

"brings man to perfection by a certain method and sequence."[139] In the end, we become angels, just as in Origen—angels with bodies of some sort, but not bodies subject to passion because they are no longer male or female. This is the significance Gregory assigns to Gal 3:28 in his homilies on the Song of Songs, in which he writes that "when we all become one in Christ, we put off the signs of this difference along with the whole of old humanity."[140] This is also how Gregory speaks of his sister, Macrina the Younger, wondering, "if, that is, we may call her a 'woman,' for I do not know if it is appropriate to apply a name drawn from nature to one who has risen above nature."[141] Later, he writes that on her deathbed, "I suspected that she had transcended the common nature . . . [for she] seemed no longer to be a part of human realities. Instead it was as if an angel had providentially assumed human form."[142]

## Ambrose and Augustine

Origen's influence was not restricted to the East, for even before his works were translated into Latin, some educated Romans were reading them, along with more recent works of the philosophers and the Cappadocians. Ambrose of Milan (+397) was a well-educated Christian of the senatorial class who had already begun a successful career in public service and been elected bishop of Milan before accepting baptism to take up the post. His catechist, advisor as bishop, and hand-picked successor was Simplicianus, who had shepherded the Neoplatonist philosopher Marius Victorinus into the Church and who would later do the same for the young Augustine. Ambrose knew Greek, read Origen, Philo, Plato, Plotinus, Porphyry, and the Cappadocian Fathers, and borrowed from them often. He was not a system-builder like Origen or a philosophical mystic like Gregory of Nyssa but an activist bishop like Basil of Caesarea, intent on defending the purity of the Church against heretical challenges. In that effort, he made wide use of intellectual resources, freely plagiarizing Plotinus, Cicero, and other classical authors when it suited his

---

139. Gregory of Nyssa, *HO* 30.30, 426.
140. Gregory of Nyssa, *Homily 7*, 225.
141. Gregory of Nyssa, *Life of Saint Macrina*, 21.
142. Gregory of Nyssa, *Life of Saint Macrina*, 40.

purposes and often following Philo and Origen in his allegorical exegesis of Scripture.[143]

Ambrose modeled his *Hexameron* on Basil's unfinished *Hexaemeron*, but, as Alexander Pierce has recently shown, he sometimes combines Basil's reading of Gen 1 with Origen's and also sometimes prefers Origen's, prompting Jerome to accuse him of using Basil, along with Hippolytus, as cover for Origen.[144] Origen took "beginning" (*archē*) in Gen 1:1 to mean Christ; Basil considers this interpretation but rejects it, taking "beginning" to mean the creation of the sensible cosmos in space and time; Ambrose, however, takes "beginning" to mean both Christ and the creation of sensible cosmos, thus to deny the philosophers' belief in uncreated matter.[145] Basil furthermore uses the image of a spinning top to speak of creation as a single act, but Ambrose uses "heaven" and "the firmament" to make Origen's distinction between "made" (*epoiēsen*) and "formed" (*eplasen*).[146] Ambrose ends his *Hexameron* as Basil did, after the creation of man in the image of God but before any mention of male and female, thus also avoiding the double creation in Philo, Origen, and Gregory of Nyssa. But whereas Basil defers discussion of the image of God for a later homily, never written, Ambrose argues that the soul alone bears the image of God and is the very essence of man such that "the soul is called *homo* in Latin and *anthrōpos* in Greek."[147] He also details the body from head to toe, saying that it "excels all things in grace and beauty" as the "royal palace" of the soul.[148] Even the genitals receive a brief mention of their purpose "for the function and satisfaction of procreation."[149] Yet in many other works, Ambrose sets the soul and the body at odds in typically Platonist language: The body is the prison, the fetters, and the enemy of the soul; "Therefore death is in every way a good, because it separates elements in conflict," i.e., soul and body; the soul is called "black" in Song 1:5 because it has been "darkened by her union with the body"; the soul is "enveloped in the thick substance of the body and covered over by stains

---

143. For example, see Boersma, "'Let Us Flee to the Fatherland,'" 771–81.

144. Jerome (*Letter 84*, 179) writes, "Recently also Ambrose appropriated his [Origen's] *Six Days' Work*, but in such a way that it expressed the views of Hippolytus and Basil rather than Origen." See Pierce, "Reconsidering Ambrose's Reception," 414–44.

145. See Pierce, "Reconsidering Ambrose's Reception," 435–37.

146. See Pierce, "Reconsidering Ambrose's Reception," 438–40.

147. Ambrose, *Hexameron*, 9.46, 259.

148. Ambrose, *Hexameron*, 9.54, 9.68, 268, 278.

149. Ambrose, *Hexameron*, 9.73, 281.

and pollutions of the flesh"; thus "weighed down by its perishable body, the soul hardly knows herself."[150]

In *On Paradise*, Ambrose follows Philo in allegorizing the temptation of Eve: "The serpent is a type of the pleasures of the body. The woman stands for our senses and the man, for our minds. Pleasure stirs the senses, which, in turn, have their effect on the mind. Pleasure, therefore, is the primary source of sin."[151] In a letter to the church of Vercellae warning them against Jovinian, who taught the equality of marriage and virginity, Ambrose asks rhetorically, "How then can pleasure recall us to paradise, seeing that it alone deprived us of it?"[152] Virginity was a favorite theme for Ambrose. He wrote five treatises on the topic, championing the perpetual virginity of Mary, holding her and other virgins up as models of the Church, and sometimes treating the choice of marriage as a choice against God, asking, "Are they, then, who are allowed to choose a man not allowed to choose God?"[153]

Ambrose also followed Origen in linking the Virgin Birth to sexual intercourse and sexual intercourse to Original Sin, writing that the Holy Spirit "poured untainted seed" into the Virgin's womb and thus Christ "received a stainless body, which not only no sins polluted, but which neither the generation nor the conception had been stained by any admixture of defilement."[154] Peter Brown writes that "Ambrose's thought on virginity could be summed up in one word: *integritas*. This meant the precious ability to keep what was one's own untarnished by alien intrusion."[155] Brown then quotes two lines from different works by Ambrose: "For in what does the chastity of a virgin consist, but in an integrity unexposed to taint from the outside?"[156] "And indeed, when a girl is de-

---

150. Ambrose, *Death as a Good* (*De Bono Mortuis*), 2.5, 4.14–15, 11.49, in *Seven Exegetical Works*, 72–73, 80, 106; Ambrose, *On Isaac, or the Soul*, 4.13, in *Seven Exegetical Works*, 19; Ambrose, *On Virginity* 15.95, 47. See Boersma, "Nuptial Reading," 227–58.

151. Ambrose, *On Paradise* 15.73, FC 42, 351–52.

152. Ambrose, *Letter* 63.14, 459.

153. Ambrose, *Concerning Virgins* 1.11.58, 372.

154. Ambrose, *Expositio evangelii secundum Lucan* 2.55–57, in Hunter, *Marriage*, 199–200; Ambrose, *On Repentance* 1.3.13, 331. Cf. Ambrose, *Hexameron* 5.67; Ambrose, *Letter* 63.22.

155. Brown, *The Body and Society*, 354.

156. Ambrose, *Concerning Virgins*, 1.5.21, in Brown, *The Body and Society*, 354.

flowered by the customary process of marriage, she loses what is her own, when something else comes to mix with her."[157]

Tertullian linked marriage and fornication on the basis of the concupiscence and "commixture of the flesh" common to both,[158] as also did Porphyry, as seen above, in language even closer to Ambrose's, speaking specifically of the pleasure, mixture, and defilement of sexual intercourse, saying that the mixture of contraries defiles the things mixed, that "on this account, venereal connections are attended with defilement," and that, "in short, all venery, and emissions of the seed in sleep, pollute, because the soul becomes mingled with the body, and is drawn down to pleasure," in which the soul dies.[159] Ambrose follows both Tertullian and Porphyry in extending the Greco-Roman sense of sexual shame to the marriage bed without actually condemning marriage. Here Kyle Harper's contrast between the pagan sense of shame and the Christian understanding of sin is helpful. Among the Greeks and Romans, a virgin raped or a male penetrated by another male suffered a loss of honor even as an innocent victim.[160] For Ambrose, the lawfully wedded Christian bride does not sin in submitting to her husband on her wedding night but nevertheless suffers a permanent degradation in her condition, being forever "scarred" by carnal knowledge.[161]

Other passages of Ambrose's could be quoted sounding much less like Tertullian, denying that in honoring virginity he is dishonoring marriage, but between Ambrose and Porphyry there is rarely any dissonance on sexuality, especially when Ambrose is urging men and women to choose God by forsaking sex. The effect of such preaching on Augustine was to convince him to submit to permanent celibacy before accepting baptism. But, as Brown notes, the same preaching had the opposite effect

---

157. Ambrose, *Exhortation to Virginity*, 6.35, in Brown, *The Body and Society*, 354.

158. Tertullian, *Exhortation to Chastity* 12, PL 2 925A; ANF 4, 55.

159. Porphyry, *On Abstinence from Animal Food*, 163–64; Porphyry, *On the Cave of the Nymphs*, 24.

160. See Harper, *From Shame to Sin*, 5–7.

161. Ambrose refers to the "scar" of sexuality and to Christ as "unscarred" by sexual origin and sexual impulses in *Expositio evangelii secundam Lucam* 5.24 and 10.125, respectively. Brown attributes Ambrose's regard for virginity to the influence of Origen in *The Body and Society*, 350–51. This is quite likely, but the influence of Porphyry is also evident, although unremarked by Brown.

on Augustine's friend Verecundus, who was already married and therefore refused baptism because he could not submit to celibacy.[162]

By his own account, Augustine's conversion to continence had been difficult. He had taken a concubine and begun reading Cicero at the same early age, nineteen, and had struggled ever since with conflicting desires for sex and for the philosophic ideal of indifference to physical pleasure. He was, in his own words, a "miserable young man, supremely miserable even in the very outset of my youth," whose prayer was, "Grant me chastity and continency, but not yet."[163] It had been possible for him to keep his concubine as a Manichee with the secondary status of *auditor*, but after joining a circle of Christian Neoplatonists in Milan, reading Plotinus and Porphyry, and hearing Ambrose preach, Augustine was greatly shamed by the example of Christians who had done what he had not—forsaken sex to serve God.[164] He was also convinced that he could enter the Church only as either a married man or a divorced man who could never remarry, since, for a Christian, leaving one woman for another would constitute adultery.[165] Unwilling to marry his concubine, he gave her up and sent her home to Africa.[166]

The power of sex over Augustine and his determination to resist it is most evident the year after his conversion, in which he writes:

> I have decided that nothing is so much to be shunned as sexual relations, for I feel that nothing so much casts down the mind of man from its citadel as do the blandishments of women and that physical contact without which a wife cannot be possessed.[167]

He would grant that a wise man who marries is "to be admired, but not, therefore, to be imitated," saying of himself, "I now neither seek nor

---

162. Augustine, *Confessions* 9.3.5. See also Brown, *The Body and Society*, 350.

163. Augustine, *Confessions* 8.7.17.

164. He writes, "the more ardently I loved those whose healthful affections I heard tell of, that they had given up themselves wholly to Thee to be cured, the more did I abhor myself when compared with them." Augustine, *Confessions* 8.7.17. On the influence of Plotinus and Porphyry on Augustine, see Brown, *Augustine of Hippo*, 88–114, 168–69.

165. This is the understanding Augustine states explicitly in *On the Good of Marriage* 5.5 and *Sermon* 392.2.2. See also Brown, *The Body and Society*, 393.

166. Augustine never names his concubine, possibly to spare her embarrassment. He does, however, sometimes mention their son, Adeodatus, who remained with him.

167. Augustine, *Soliloquies*, 1.10.417.

desire anything whatever of this sort. It is with horror and loathing that I even remember it."[168]

Yet, from his own experience, Augustine understood the joys of married life as well as the difficulty of celibacy, and this tempered his regard for both marriage and monasticism. Later, as a bishop, he defended marriage as a model of Christian concord, stressing the harmony of husband and wife over the purpose of procreation.[169] He warned consecrated virgins not to look down on wives, reminding them that continence is a gift not given to everyone, to be greatly valued but not as setting the virgin over the wife, for virginity was no guarantee of holiness.[170] Wives like Crispina of Theveste could also win the martyr's crown, a far greater glory than virginity, for, as Augustine pointed out, the faithful pray *to* martyrs but *for* deceased virgins.[171] Augustine did not insist on clerical celibacy or welcome wandering monks into his diocese, neither did he urge celibacy on lay men and women, taking to task a married woman for assuming a monastic habit and pressing celibacy on her husband.[172]

As a recent convert, under the indirect influence of Origen via Ambrose, Augustine attempted an allegorical, anti-Manichean reading of Genesis in which Adam and Eve represented higher and lower parts of human nature.[173] Later, he would disavow this notion and give Genesis a more literal reading.[174] He followed Philo of Alexandria in distinguishing between the creation of man in potentiality in Gen 1 and the creation of man in actuality in Gen 2, but he differed from Philo in understanding the first creation as including the distinction of male and female, holding that human nature was "complete in both sexes."[175] He reasoned that God made Eve to help Adam have children and that if this were not so,

168. Augustine, *Soliloquies*, 1.10.417.

169. See Fuchs, *Sexual Desire and Love*, 116–17.

170. The word "gift" appears more than twice as often on average in Augustine's *On Virginity* as in Gregory of Nyssa's *On Virginity*.

171. Augustine, *On Virginity*, 44–46. See also Brown, *The Body and Society*, 397–98.

172. Augustine, *Letter 262*. See also Brown, *The Body and Society*, 397–401.

173. See Augustine, *De Genesi contra Manichaeos*, 2.11–12. On the influence of Origen on Augustine, see Teske, "Origen and St. Augustine's First Commentaries on Genesis," 179–85; Ramelli, "Origen in Augustine," 280–307; Pârvan, "Genesis 1–3," 56–92.

174. His disavowal of male and female as representing different parts of the same person is in *The City of God*, 14.121. His more literal commentary on Genesis is *De Genesi ad litteram*, or *The Literal Meaning of Genesis*.

175. Augustine, *On the Trinity*, 12.7.10.

God would have made Adam a brother instead of a wife, yet he did not reduce procreation to a survival mechanism needed only after the Fall, as Gregory of Nyssa did.[176] Augustine saw sex as fully natural and procreation as always intended, even venturing that the primal pair would have enjoyed sexual intercourse innocently in Paradise had they not fallen.[177] He furthermore defended the persistence of male and female in the resurrection, arguing, against the belief that women would become men, that "the sex of woman is not a vice, but nature," that "the female members shall remain, adapted not to the old uses but to a new beauty," and that "He, then, who created both sexes will restore both." He even followed Tertullian and Jerome in arguing that Christ indicates the persistence of male and female when he says the resurrected "neither marry nor are given in marriage" (Matt 22:30; cf. Mark 12:25; Luke 20:35), since those words presuppose the resurrection of men and women.[178]

Late in life, however, Augustine's view of sexuality hardened in the course of his campaign against Pelagianism, with long-lasting consequences for Western Christianity. Pelagius preached an extremely optimistic estimation of man's natural ability to live without sin, owing much to Origen's anti-deterministic emphasis on free will and Stoic confidence in human willpower.[179] Pelagius believed that God had made man both good and strong and had shown him the way to live through the Law, the Prophets, the Incarnation, and the Church; man had only to hear and obey, having no excuse for not obeying. Such views were welcomed at the time by many ascetics, but they struck Augustine, Jerome, and others as presumptuous and unmerciful—a step back toward obedience to law as the way to salvation.[180]

---

176. Augustine, *The Literal Meaning of Genesis*, 9.5.

177. Augustine, *City of God*, 14.24. The notion that Adam and Eve could have had intercourse in Paradise is not found among Church Fathers before Augustine, although some Fathers such as Irenaeus of Lyon and Theophilus of Antioch did see Adam and Eve as not yet adults before the Fall and treat their sexual relationship afterwards, beginning with Gen 4:1, as a matter of merely growing up rather than the final act of the Fall, as it appears in Gregory of Nyssa. See Irenaeus, *Adv. Haer.* 4.38.3; Theophilus, *To Autolycus* 2.25; Gregory of Nyssa, *Virg.* 12.

178. See Augustine, *City of God*, 22.17, 495–96. Cf. Tertullian, *On the Resurrection of the Flesh*, 36; Jerome, *Letter 108 to Eustochium*, 23.

179. See Evans, *Pelagius*, 43–65.

180. On the connection between Origenism and Pelagianism, see Evans, *Pelagius*, 6–25, Clark, *The Origenist Controversy*, 194–244.

In opposition, Augustine stressed the absolute necessity of grace on account of Original Sin, which so corrupted human nature that sin was unavoidable. Sexuality was implicated in two ways: First, sexual intercourse was the means by which Original Sin was transmitted to each new soul as a congenital disease, so that babes are born sinful and must therefore be baptized as soon as possible, lest they die and be damned;[181] second, lust of the flesh (*concupiscentia carnis*) was prima-facie evidence of Original Sin, which burdened human beings with uncontrollable desires that made living without sinning impossible. In Augustine's mind, fallen man could not help but feel a desire for sex that defied reason in that its object was merely pleasure and not procreation, the only legitimate purpose of sex. That is why, he writes, Adam and Eve were suddenly ashamed at their nakedness after the Fall; their bodies were already stirred involuntarily by illicit lust.[182]

Some modern critics have seen the influence of Platonism and Stoicism in Augustine's view of Adam, who functions not just as a prototype but as an archetype, the *rationes seminales* of human being, such that all after him are extensions of his person and therefore stand condemned with him even before assuming their own "proper life" (*vita propria*).[183] But Augustine's Pelagian nemesis, Julian of Eclanum, saw another source of trouble, never tiring of tagging Augustine as a Manichee for his insistence on man's sinful nature, which to Julian's mind made the devil man's co-creator and impugned marriage itself as sinful. Had Augustine not preached that Christian couples must "descend with a certain sadness" to the task of begetting children on account of their complicity in Adam's sin?[184] And were they not also propagating sin by begetting sinners? Julian defended sexual desire as a physiological phenomenon of no great concern, a natural desire like many others, needing only to be tamed by ascetic discipline, in or out of marriage.[185] Augustine, however, moralized

---

181. See Augustine, *On the Holy Trinity*, 13.12; Augustine, *On Marriage and Concupiscence 2*, 50 (29). Cf. Ambrose in *Death as a Good* 11.49 and *On Repentance* 1.3.13.

182. See Augustine, *Literal Meaning of Genesis*, 11.32.42; Augustine, *On Marriage and Concupiscence* 2, 52 (30). See also Brown, *The Body and Society*, 416–17.

183. See, for example, Phipps, "The Heresiarch," 132; Clark, *The Origenist Controversy*, 232–34.

184. Augustine, *Sermon 51.15.25*, quoted in Brown, *The Body and Society*, 426.

185. Brown, *The Body and Society*, 412–14. Brown notes that many Eastern Christians shared this opinion, of which more will be said in the next chapter. See also Clark, *The Origenist Controversy*, 244n426.

sexual desire beyond all other desires, setting it, as Brown says, "irremovably at the centre of the human person," such that thereafter the Christian West was "washed by a dark current of sexual shame."[186]

## Maximus the Confessor

Maximus the Confessor tells us he was born about 580, but the place of his birth is now disputed. His tenth-century Greek hagiography has him born to patrician parents in Constantinople and receiving a first-rate education before assuming a top position in the imperial palace at an early age, but his seventh-century Syriac anti-hagiography has him born to a Persian slave girl in Palestine and entering an Origenist monastery in the Judean desert while still a boy. Many scholars still trust the hagiographic tradition, but some now argue that the Syriac version better explains Maximus's eastern associations and early interest in Origenism.[187] More is known about his later years, when his main interest was defending the Chalcedonian definition of the two natures of Christ. Much of the final third of his long life was spent in Carthage and Rome, where he guided the decisions of the Lateran Synod of 649. Quotations from Augustine were used at the time to back up the synod's decisions, but in his own works Maximus never mentions Augustine by name and does not appear to have been greatly influenced by him.[188] His own ideas were well formed by that time and owed much to eastern thinkers, both pagan and Christian. He knew of Aristotle's system of categorization through Porphyry's *Isagoge* and used it in his approach to unity and diversity.[189] Three of Maximus's main influences—Gregory of Nyssa, Evagrius Ponticus, and the sixth-century writer now known as Pseudo-Dionysius—put Maximus well within the allegorizing, Platonizing, Alexandrian tradition begun by Philo, introduced among Christians by Valentinus, and embedded in Christian thinking by Origen. Much has been said already about Gregory and Evagrius; something must now be said about Pseudo-Dionysius, both for how his thinking does and does not contribute to

---

186. Brown, *The Body and Society*, 422, 426–27.

187. See, for example, Jankowiak and Booth, "A New Date-List of the Works of Maximus the Confessor," 19–83.

188. See Börjesson, "Augustine on the Will," 212–34.

189. One minor terminological difference is that Aristotle's "accidental" difference is in Porphyry an "individual" difference and in Maximus a "hypostatic" difference. See Törönen, *Union and Distinction*, 13–24.

## The Greek Christian View of Male and Female 141

Maximus's vision and for how his concept of *hierarchy* will bear upon on the conclusions offered in the last chapter.

Nothing is known about Pseudo-Dionysius except that he (or she) borrowed heavily from the works of the Neoplatonist Proclus and hid the identities of himself and his source by assuming the persona of Dionysius the Areopagite, the first-century Athenian evangelized by the Apostle Paul (Acts 17:34). The inauthenticity of his works was already suspected when we first here of him in the early sixth century but was only established in the modern age. Even today scholars dispute whether he was a Christian making the best use of pagan philosophy or a pagan sneaking Neoplatonism into Christianity.[190] Ernesto Sergio Mainoldi has recently outlined an intriguing argument for Dionysius as a convert from Neoplatonism named Hegias writing in the early sixth century with three main aims in support of the emperor Justinian's imperial theology: (1) polemicizing against pagan philosophy by establishing a much earlier Christian precedent for key Neoplatonist insights, (2) bridging the divide between Monophysites and Dyophysites with a carefully worded Christology acceptable to both sides, and (3) supplanting the influence of Origen by replacing his (and Evagrius's) fluid ontology of rational beings with fixed ranks of beings.[191] This theory helps explain key differences between Pseudo-Dionysius and Maximus the Confessor.

Dionysius coined the word *hierarchy*, but his conception of it is basically Proclean, and his works betray the elitism, secrecy, and disingenuousness of which Pythagoreans, Platonists, Gnostics, and Origenists were sometimes accused. The contrast between the gnostic few and the agnostic many is fundamental to his vision inasmuch as his hierarchies are based on inequality of illumination and godlikeness.[192] The transmission of illumination from greaters to lessers is strictly ordered and dependent upon intermediaries: God deals directly with the first order of angels and indirectly with all the rest.[193] Likewise, hierarchs work through priests

---

190. For a recent example of the latter thesis, see Lankila, "The Corpus Areopagiticum as a Crypto-Pagan Project," 14–40.

191. See Mainoldi, "Why Dionysius the Areopagite?" 425–40.

192. Pseudo-Dionysius, *CH* 3, PG 3, 164D; Pseudo-Dionysius, *Letter 8 to Demophilus*, PG 3, 1092B. Also Perl, *Theophany*, 65–81.

193. Pseudo-Dionysius, *EH* 537C, 372D–373A, 505A–B. Dionysius devotes an entire chapter of his *Celestial Hierarchy* (300B–308B) to arguing that it must have been a low-ranking angel and not a seraph who visited Isaiah, even though Isaiah 6:6 says it was seraph.

and deacons, with the laity kept safely at a distance; one of the benefits of the order of deacons, say Dionysius, is that it "keeps priests from contact with the profane."[194] Dionysius repeatedly disparages the *hoi polloi* for their benightedness, often when exhorting his reader to secrecy.[195] He also rhapsodizes on the *hierourgia* of the "godlike hierarch" (*theoeidēs hierarchēs*) who alone contemplates awesome mysteries while common folk content themselves with "symbols."[196] Christ's repeated warnings about the first being last and the last being first are never mentioned by Pseudo-Dionysius.[197] Neither is the Apostle Paul's exhortation, "in lowliness of mind let each esteem other better than themselves" (Phil 2:3).

Maximus favorably names, quotes, or alludes to Pseudo-Dionysius at least 40 times, always assuming him to have been the first-century Dionysius.[198] Maximos Constas writes that the Confessor "derived his fundamental philosophical framework" from Pseudo-Dionysius, but Constas also writes of the Confessor's "tacit rejection" of Pseudo-Dionysius's conception of *hierarchy*, noting that Maximus regularly uses the more general term *thesis* in place of *hierarchy*, which he never uses except to mention Pseudo-Dionysius's *Ecclesiastical Hierarchy*.[199] Maximus also reverses Pseudo-Dionysius's Neoplatonist sequence of remaining (*monē*), procession (*proodos*), and return (*epistrophē*), which begins with an original unity followed by a fall into material diversity. Instead, Maximus begins with creation *ex nihilo* followed by evolutionary movement toward an "ever-moving rest" of perfect unity in diversity, a sequence also expressed in Maximus's distinction of being, well-being, and eternal being, which extends Pseudo-Dionysius's distinction of being and well-being.[200] The result is a reversion to an open-ended anthropology more like Origen's than like Pseudo-Dionysius's.

---

194. Pseudo-Dionysius, *EH* 473D–476B, 508B.

195. See, for example, Pseudo-Dionysius, *MT* 1000A; Pseudo-Dionysius, *CH* 140B, 145C; Pseudo-Dionysius, *EH* 372A, 376C, 473D–476B. Cf. Proclus, *Commentary on Parmenides*, 5.1024; also Evagrius Ponticus, *Letter to Melania*, 17.

196. Pseudo-Dionysius, *EH* 428A.

197. Matt 18:3; 19:30; 20:16; Mark 9:35; 10:31, 42–45; Luke 13:30; 22:24–26.

198. See Andia, "Pseudo-Dionysius the Areopagite," 177.

199. See Constas, "Maximus the Confessor," 1–12.

200. Maximus, *Amb.* 7.2. See Andia, "Pseudo-Dionysius the Areopagite," 181–82; Andreopoulos, "Eschatology in Maximus the Confessor," 328; Loudovikos, *A Eucharistic Ontology*, 76–84.

Maximus also adapts much of Evagrius's ascetic psychology and imitates his aphoristic approach to writing, offering his insights in brief, often unrelated "chapters" collected into groups called "centuries." He rarely borrows anything from anyone without amending it in some way and argues at length against many Origenist notions such as the fall of souls into bodies, consistently defending the body as a fundamental component of human nature.[201] Even so, the opposition of soul and body, intelligible and sensible, and the discontinuity of human existence dominate Maximus's anthropology, in which this life is but a temporary mean between the extremes of God's original intent and man's divinization in Christ, which Maximus illustrates by quoting carefully pared parts of Gen 1:26, Gen 1:27, and Gal 3:28:

> An "extreme" is: *And God said, Let us make man according to our image and likeness.* A "mean" is: *And God made man, male and female He made them.* Again, an "extreme" is: *In Christ Jesus there is neither male nor female.*[202]

Our next life, he says, will be "completely free from the constituent properties of this present life, which is marred by corruption" and will not consist "in the breathing of air, or in the flow of blood from the liver, but in the fact that God will be wholly participated by whole human beings."[203] Again: "The end bears no resemblance at all to the intermediate state, since [then] it would be no end ... [and] since the end of the saved is God, in the highest end nothing from the intermediate state will be co-envisioned [*syntheōroumenon*] with those who have come to be saved."[204]

According to Maximus, the fundamental fault of fallen man—the "mother of the vices" and "beginning of all passions"—is self-love (*philautia*), defined as "the impassioned, unreasonable affection for one's body," a focus originating with Philo and emphasized by Evagrius.[205] In

---

201. Maximus, *Thal.* Q42.13–20.

202. Maximus, *Amb.* 67.10, 297. This passage may be the only place Maximus quotes Gen 1:27 on "male and female" as well as the only place he credits God with having made man male and female.

203. Maximus, *Amb.* 7.26, 113.

204. Maximus, *Theo.* 1.69, 83. Cf. Maximus, *Theo.* 1.70, 83–84.

205. Maximus, *Char.* 3.8. Cf. Maximus, *Thal.* Prologue, 1.1.3. Plato also points a finger at self-love (*eautou philia*; *Laws* 5, 731d–732a), but the prominence of sensuality as the basis of self-love begins with Philo and culminates with Evagrius. Thunberg (*Microcosm and Mediator*, 232–47) contrasts this "Eastern" view with the "Western," Augustinian view focusing on pride, although some Eastern Fathers before Augustine

no uncertain terms, Maximus writes that God made man to enjoy only the intelligible pleasures of the soul, excluding from human nature the capacity for sensible pleasure, but "at the same moment that he was brought into being," man turned away from the intelligible things of God toward the sensible things of the world and "came to know pleasure activated contrary to nature."[206] Afterwards, God added pain and death to man's experience to limit pleasure's hold on man.

Maximus follows Origen in holding the unnatural pleasure of sexual reproduction (*gennesis*) responsible for the sinful condition of all mankind, with the exception of the Savior, who was conceived without it.[207] The saying of the Psalmist that "in sin did my mother conceive me" (Ps 50/51:5), says Maximus, "signifies that Eve, the mother of us all, first conceived sin by becoming wanton with pleasure."[208] Marriage and corruption are both consequences of sin and not originally intended by God.[209] Maximus does not condemn marriage (*gamos*), but neither does he say much in its favor, only that if we say marriage is evil (*kakos*), we must also say that the "natural law of creation" is evil and implicate God in the creation of evil.[210] Curiously, Maximus makes this point only syllogistically, never plainly declaring marriage good, never actually saying that it is not evil. And even if marriage is not evil, its consummation is nevertheless beastly and inhuman, a sign and source of corruption, which is why Hans Urs von Balthasar calls marriage, for Maximus, "a sacrament of sin."[211] Doru Costache exaggerates when he writes that Maximus sees "married life as a pathway to holiness equal to the monastic way" and that, according to Maximus, "Moses achieved perfection whilst enjoying the fullness of married life"—after quoting Maximus saying only that Moses was not "prevented by marriage from becoming someone who yearns for the divine glory."[212] Elsewhere Maximus writes, "[B]ut let each of us, according

---

also emphasized Eve's pride in hearkening to the serpent, as will be shown in the next chapter.

206. Maximus, *Thal.* Q61.2. Cf. Maximus, *Thal.* Intro 1.2.13 and Q1.2; Maximus, *Amb.* 42.7.

207. Maximus, *Amb.* 31.2; Maximus, *Thal.* Q61.5; Maximus, *Commentary on Our Father*, 4.

208. Maximus, *QD* I, 3, 142.

209. Maximus, *QD* I, 3, 141.

210. Maximus, *Amb.* 42.24.

211. Balthasar, *Cosmic Liturgy*, 199.

212. See Maximus, *Amb.* 10.31a.5, PG 90 1161D; Costache, "Gender, Marriage,

to his ability, rank, and the grace of the Spirit that has been given to him, partake of the divine Word in conformity with the meaning of each of His parts," with those who come closest to the Word remaining "perfectly undefiled."[213]

As marriage begins our life of sin, so our life in Christ begins by forsaking it. In *Ambiguum* 41, Maximus counts five "divisions" created by the Fall: created nature and uncreated nature, the intelligible and the sensible, heaven and earth, paradise and the inhabited world, and finally male and female. Man was meant to heal these divisions by first

> completely shaking off [*ektinaxamenos*] from nature, by means of a supremely dispassionate condition of divine virtue, the property [*idiotēta*] of male and female, which in no way was linked to the original principle [*logon*] of the divine plan concerning human generation, so that he might be shown forth as and become solely a human being [*anthrōpon monon*] according to the divine plan, not divided by the designation of male and female (according to the principle [*logon*] by which he formerly came into being), nor divided into the parts that now appear around him, thanks to the perfect union, as I said, with his own principle, according to which he exists.[214]

"Then," says Maximus, man will "unite" paradise with the inhabited world, heaven with the earth, the intelligible with the sensible, and created nature with uncreated nature such that he will live as the angels live now, not limited in his movement or experience by these "divisions," as he is in his fallen state. Christ himself "unites" the first four divisions by his incarnation, but he does not "unite" male and female. That word Maximus uses only of the other divisions. Instead, in becoming man, Christ

> drove out [*exōthoumenos*] from nature the difference and division into male and female, a difference, as I have said, which He in no way needed in order to become man, and without which existence would perhaps have been possible. There is no need

---

and Holiness," 352, 358, and 357. Costache's reading of *Amb.* 10 is perhaps influenced by Constas's English translation, which has Maximus saying, "the mysteries of marriage and celibacy stand equally next to the Word" (in the persons of Moses and Elijah at the Transfiguration). But Constas's Greek text does not say "equally": "*ta kata ton gamon kai tēn agamian mystēria para tō Logō einai.*" See Maximus, *On Difficulties*, 1:260–61. Cf. Louth's translation of the same passage, with no indication of equality, in *Maximus the Confessor*, 130.

213. Maximus, *Amb.* 48.4 and 48.6, 217 and 219–21.
214. Maximus, *Amb.* 41.3, 105–7.

for this division to last perpetually, for *in Christ Jesus*, says the divine apostle, *there is neither male nor female*.²¹⁵

Note the use of Gal 3:28, understood quite literally to include not just "division" (*diairesis*) but also "difference" (*diaphora*).²¹⁶ Christ drove that out, too. But Maximus is still not finished with his eradication of male and female. He continues in the same work with the same emphasis:

> Thus He united, first of all, ourselves in Himself through removal [*aphaireseōs*] of the difference between male and female, and instead of men and women, in whom this mode of division is especially evident, He showed us as properly and truly to be simply human beings [*anthrōpous monon*], thoroughly formed according to Him, bearing His image intact and completely unadulterated, touched in no way by any marks of corruption.²¹⁷

Thus, in *Ambiguum* 41, the very "difference" and "property" of male and female—not just their "division"—are said to be unintended, unnecessary, an adulteration, and a mark of corruption. They may also be said to be unnatural on account of being not according to the "original principle of the divine plan concerning human generation."²¹⁸ If they were part of the original principle or *logos* of human nature, they could not be "shaken off" or otherwise "innovated," for, says Maximus in *Ambiguum* 42, "when a principle is innovated it effectively results in the destruction of the nature."²¹⁹ Thus, male and female can only be "natural" according to a nonoriginal principle of fallen human nature, which Christ destroys and replaces with the sexless nature originally intended.²²⁰ Such is the significance Maximus repeatedly attaches to Gal 3:28, always ignoring the context and literal meaning of the verse, which does not exclude marriage or sexual distinction, to advance his eschatological vision of

---

215. Maximus, *Amb.* 41.7, 111. Emphasis added.

216. Maximus uses the word *diaphora* to mean a difference of nature or substance, which is a matter of *logos* and not *tropos*. Difference is therefore a matter of *what* something is, whereas division is a matter of the *way* things are. See Thunberg, *Microcosm and Mediator*, 51–57.

217. Maximus, *Amb.* 41.9, 115. The words "especially evident" may refer to Aristotle's observation (*HA* 9.608b.4–8) that sexual dimorphism is most evident in higher forms of life, man being the highest.

218. Maximus, *Amb.* 41.3, 105.

219. Maximus, *Amb.* 42.26, 173.

220. Maximus, *Amb.* 41.3, 107.

freedom from "the characteristics [*sēmeia*] and the passions of a nature subject to corruption and generation."[221]

## Maximus, Gregory, and Aristotle

Much of the foregoing is foreshadowed by Gregory of Nyssa. Gregory excludes "male and female" from the Archetype and its image in humanity, saying that it was later affixed to human nature for the time-limited purpose of procreation. Gregory understands marriage (*gamos*) in the Greek way as all about bestial breeding, naming it the last stage of man's departure from God, when Adam "knew" Eve after the Fall (Gen 4:1), and therefore "the first thing to be left" in our return to God.[222] Gregory speculates that human reproduction could have occurred asexually, by some angelic means, had man not fallen, saying God gave man the beastly means of reproduction because he knew that sinful man would prefer it.[223] Gregory blames pain on pleasure and the passions on the Fall, seeing them signified by the "coats of skins" in Gen 3:21; Maximus actually says he learned this from Gregory.[224] Gregory writes that the "signs" (*sēmeia*) of sexual distinction will disappear in the resurrection.[225] He also writes that being made in the image of God means man's participation in all of God's goodness, of which the pre-eminent goodness is "freedom from bondage to any natural power," suggesting the open-ended ontology found in Maximus, who begins *Ambiguum* 41 with a quotation of Gregory of Nazianzus saying "natures are innovated" when God becomes man, and who speculates in *Ambiguum* 7 that in the end the "wholly chaste and faithful" will be "completely free from the constituent properties of this present life, which is marred by corruption."[226]

Maximus's personal touches are his concept of means and extremes, his limitation of man's pre-fall capacity for pleasure to intelligible pleasures only, his instantaneous fall of soul and body as soon as they are created, and his vehement insistence that not just marriage and sexual

---

221. Maximus, *Commentary on the Our Father*, 110. Cf. Maximus, *Char.* 2.30.

222. Gregory of Nyssa, *Virg.* 12, 358.

223. Gregory of Nyssa, *HO* 17.4.

224. Gregory of Nyssa, *Virg.* 12.2, 18.25; Gregory of Nyssa, *An et res*, 3. Maximus, *Thal.* 1.2.

225. Gregory of Nyssa, *Homily 7 on the Song of Songs*, 224–25.

226. Gregory of Nyssa, *HO* 16.10–11. Gregory of Nazianzus, *Oration* 39.13. Maximus, *Amb.* 7.26, 113.

reproduction but "male and female" were not intended by God from the beginning and must be done away with. Taken together, these doctrines make historical readings of Gen 1–3 impossible, and, not surprisingly, Maximus shows little interest in them. He does not follow Gen 1 in calling God's making man male and female "very good," or make much of Eve's creation from Adam in Gen 2, or anywhere mention of the "coats of skins" of Gen 3.[227] Maximus also does not follow Gregory of Nyssa in saying God preveniently added male and female to human nature before the Fall (Gregory's version of "double creation").[228] Instead, Maximus associates male and female only with fallen human nature, the mean between the extremes of divine intent and eschatological end, declaring male and female an unintended consequence of man's instantaneous fall.[229] Gregory imagines man returning to his original, passionless state of soul and body, vaguely hinting at what might happen to male and female; Maximus envisions no such return, only progress from the fallen mean marred by male and female, begun by shaking off male and female.

With his mean and extremes, instantaneous fall, and pre-fall lack of capacity for physical pleasure, Maximus leaves man with no experience of the body before his fall. Any existence man might have had before his fall is merely intentional in God and theoretical for us, conceived but never realized. It is as if God made man to fall without somehow intending him to fall, and as if God made man male and female without somehow intending him to be male and female.

How can God do what He does not intend? Or rather, what was Maximus thinking when reading and writing (at least once) that God made man male and female while also thinking and writing (many times) that male and female were not intended by God?

He might have been thinking of Aristotle. As we have seen, neither Aristotle's system of categorization nor his theory of human generation provide a clear and certain basis for the differentiation of male and female. In his system of categorization, male and female are just

---

227. Thunberg writes that the closest Maximus comes to commenting on "coats of skins" is when he argues, in *Amb.* 45, that Adam before the Fall was not naked in having no body but in not needing protection for his body. See Thunberg, *Microcosm and Mediator*, 153–54.

228. This is also Thunberg's conclusion, *Microcosm and Mediator*, 151–53.

229. Others who see male and female as a result of the fall include Thunberg, *Microcosm and Mediator*, 373; Mitralexis, "Rethinking the Problem of Sexual Difference in *Ambiguum* 41," 373–86.

"accidental" possibilities within a species, neither of which is found in all members of the species and therefore definitive of the species, and in his theory of human generation, the seed develops as more or less male or female as an accidental result of nourishment *in utero*, just as after birth the child continues to develop as more or less male or female as an accidental result of nurture and culture. Such thinking on both categorization and human generation was conventional wisdom in Maximus's day, and it all fits easily with Maximus's distinction of *logos* and *tropos*, if one assumes, as Maximus did, that the difference of male and female is solely a matter of *tropos*, the particular way each person expresses human nature, which can be good or bad, "according to nature" (*kata physin*) or "contrary to nature" (*para physin*).[230] In Maximus's version of Aristotle's system of categorization, male and female are "hypostatic" possibilities for each member of the human race, which as merely possibilities are not definitive of human nature, and in Maximus's anthropology, man begins as neither male and female according to the *logos* of human nature and only assumes the *tropos* of male or female as an individual, hypostatic response to the fallen world.[231]

Thus, by following Aristotle, Maximus could reason that just as God endowed canine nature with the potential of diversity among dogs without intending any to become wolves, so God endowed human nature with the potential of diversity in man without intending any to become male or female. Unfortunately for Maximus, just as modern science testifies against Aristotle's theory of human generation, both Holy Scripture and Holy Tradition testify against Maximus's theory of human genesis, as will be shown in the next chapter.

## Conclusion: The Ascent of Alexandrian Anthropology

With Maximus, we have reached the acme of Greek influence on Christian thinking on male and female. Before moving on, let us briefly trace the trajectory of that influence.

---

230. A hypostatic *tropos* can also be "above nature" (*hyper physin*) but only by grace. Dionysios Skliris explores this possibility with regard to gender in "The Ontology of Mode," as does Doru Costache in "Living Above Gender," without reaching the same conclusions or my conclusions.

231. An obvious difference is that whereas Aristotle assumed male to be the norm, Maximus assumed neuter to be the human norm, following Gregory of Nyssa in not regarding female as inferior to male.

From the very beginning, the early Church attracted converts whose view of male and female was shaped less by Hebrew scripture and tradition than by Greek philosophy and culture. Their imagination was basically dualistic, pitting the soul against the body. They viewed male and female as an unfortunate division of human nature having only to do with the body, believing that souls are sexless but female bodies are weaker than male bodies. Without the benefit of modern medicine, they suffered greatly in the body and turned to otherworldly religions and philosophies for relief from the body's weaknesses and temptations. They therefore tended toward Encratism, despising marriage along with meat-eating and wine-bibbing and seeking salvation through ascetic denial of the body.

Educated converts brought their learning with them, including the philosophers' disdain for the body and for marriage and their resort to allegory to claim divine inspiration for the myths and scriptures used to support their philosophies. Some concocted their own myths and scriptures with more to say about the burden of the body and the mysterious world of souls than was handed down by the Apostles. These were the first Gnostics, of which the most influential was Valentinus of Alexandria, whose mystic vision mixed Christianity and Platonism, with a fall of the soul into the body and a bodiless afterlife of sexless souls.

At the same time, educated Christians, called to defend the Gospel of Christ against both Gnosticism and paganism, naturally made what use they could of the philosophy of their day, including the Platonist or Pythagorean allegorizations of Hebrew Scripture by Philo of Alexandria. Chief among these apologists was Origen, whose education in philosophy, reading of Philo, and dialogue with Valentinians like Heracleon shaped his vision of the descent and ascent of souls, including extreme discontinuity between earthly bodies and heavenly bodies, which caused Origen to be accused of denying the resurrection of the body. His prodigious genius inspired generations of educated, intellectual Christians, whose education was still basically classical and whose restless intellects were not satisfied with literal readings of the Old and New Testaments. The controversy surrounding Origen muted speculation on male and female for many years, explaining Gregory of Nyssa's cautious, even cryptic peroration on the "making of man" just before the first great Origenist controversy. Maximus the Confessor's much plainer, bolder speculations came two centuries later, well after the second great Origenist controversy, and were informed not just by Gregory but also by the outright

### The Greek Christian View of Male and Female 151

Origenism of Evagrius Ponticus and the Christianized Neoplatonism of Pseudo-Dionysius.

Maximus's heroism as a champion of Chalcedonian orthodoxy caused him to be widely read and often followed, but his bolder speculations about "shaking off" male and female were honored with silence. Many Church Fathers before and after him, including John of Damascus, also taught that mating was not meant for man before the Fall and that God could have provided another means of reproduction had man not fallen, but Maximus's "shaking off" was not included in the Damascene's *Exact Exposition of the Orthodox Faith*, an authoritative summary of patristic teaching written in the early eighth century.[232] The first indication of that notion's survival appears in the *Periphyseon* of John Scotus Eriugena, the ninth-century Neoplatonist who translated many of Maximus's works, along with those of Pseudo-Dionysius and Gregory of Nyssa. Eriugena read Maximus quite literally, explaining, while discoursing on Maximus's *Ambiguum 41*, that the disciples sometimes failed to recognize the risen Christ because "it was not in the bodily sex but simply in man that He rose from the dead."[233]

No consensus exists among modern scholars on what Maximus meant by the "shaking off" of male and female. Many read him less literally, avoiding Maximus's own words and ignoring the extremity of what he says about male and female compared to what he says about the other divisions. Adam Cooper, for example, writes of the "reunion" and "reconciliation" of male and female in Maximus, which, he says, does not include the elimination of physical differences and is "primarily a matter of knowledge and will . . . of recognizing the single human nature common to all."[234] Dionysios Skliris also sees a way in which male and female may survive in the eschaton, but only as part of a person's historical narrative, a remnant of one's personal *tropos* of existence, like the stigmata of martyrs. Otherwise:

---

232. John of Damascus staunchly defends the resurrection of the body, "not meaning change into another form (God forbid!), but rather the change from corruption into incorruption." See John of Damascus, *Exact Exposition of the Orthodox Faith* 4.27, 101.

233. Eriugena, *De Divisione Naturae*, II (PL 122, 537D–538A), 138. The work was condemned by Pope Honorius III in 1224 and by Pope Gregory XIII in 1585. It was published as *De Divisione Naturae* after its rediscovery at Oxford in 1681.

234. Cooper, *The Body in St. Maximus the Confessor*, 222. Others who minimize the effect of Maximus's "shaking off" include Thunberg, *Microcosm and Mediator*, 185, 374–81; Blowers, *Maximus the Confessor*, 221; Costache, "Gender, Marriage, and Holiness," 366.

> The fact that the genders do not belong to the *logos* of humanity entails a rejection of heteronormativity. There is not one single anthropological norm which would include the dyad of the genders, namely the male and the female. This paves the way for an *apophaticism of gender and of the unchartered human body*.[235]

Thus, in the postmodern debate between "essentialists" and "constructivists," Maximus sides with the latter: Male and female is a sinful construction of fallen man, not an essential aspect of human nature.

Finally, it must be said that while Maximus is often said to have refuted Origen's Platonist dualism of soul and body, it is more accurate to say that he has merely corrected it by eliminating the preexistence of the soul without the body. Origen's fall of the soul into the body is preserved by Maximus in man's original insensibility to the pleasures of the body and his unnatural turn toward the sensible the instant he is created, which leaves man with no experience of the body before his fall, just as in Origen. Maximus's instantaneous fall toward the sensible is more like Origen's fall into the body than like the "very good" creation of man as male and female in Gen 1 and 2 followed by the experience of creation in its goodness by the man and the woman before their fall in Gen 3. Of those chapters, Maximus, Gregory of Nyssa, Evagrius Ponticus, and most other Origenists have little to say, and what they do say is highly selective and allegorical, often ignoring the distinctive roles of Adam and Eve in the story and misrepresenting the serpent's temptation of Eve, which makes no mention of the sensual pleasure of eating.[236]

When Origenists do address the creation of man in Holy Scripture, their first concern is to undo the connection of "male and female" to the "image of God" in Gen 1:27. There are three obvious reasons why they would want to do so: (1) They wish to distinguish the Christian God from the sexually promiscuous gods and goddesses of the Greeks; (2) they equate femininity with weakness, as Gregory of Nazianzus does when he writes that Christ was born male as "the stronger for the strong" (Christ for Adam) and "chiefly because there is in Him nothing feminine, nothing unmanly"; and (3) they have founded their understanding of human nature on the anti-sexual philosophy of the Greeks, which cannot make

---

235. Skliris, "The Ontology of Mode," 57–58. Emphasis original.

236. As noted in chapter 3, the serpent only speaks to Eve of knowledge and equality (Gen 3:4–5), and only then does she notice that the fruit is pleasant to look at and good for food (Gen 3:6).

sense of male and female except as a means of reproduction.[237] For these reasons, Gregory of Nyssa writes that the distinction of male and female is "alien to our conception of God."[238]

And yet Scripture does connect the creation of man in the image of God with the creation of man as male and female. Then it says God blesses them, commands them to be fruitful and multiply, surveys all that He has created, and declares everything "very good" (Gen 1:28). Let us now see how the early Church preserved this more Hebrew, more scriptural view of male and female despite the speculations of some sainted Fathers.

---

237. Gregory of Nazianzus, *Second Oration on Easter*, 13, 427.
238. Gregory of Nyssa, *On the Making of Man*, 16, 405.

# 5

# The Hebrew Christian View of Male and Female

WE HAVE SEEN HOW Greek influence on Christian thinking about male and female began with common Greek assumptions about sex added to Christian expectations of an imminent eschaton in which the saved would "neither marry or be given in marriage." The combination of these assumptions and expectations inspired extreme asceticism, Gnostic fantasies of the spirit world, and philosophic speculations on the nature of the soul and the body. Such speculations quickly proved controversial among Christians and required successive stages of correction before they could be safely shared and widely accepted. The boldest speculations by Evagrius Ponticus and Maximus the Confessor on the eventual disappearance of the distinction of male and female were never widely accepted and remain controversial to this day, despite the latter's unquestioned status as a champion of orthodox Christology.

Now we will hear from the other side, examining evidence of a much higher, more Hebrew regard for male and female in the teaching and practice of the early Church. This evidence comes in many forms from many sources, including several of the same Church Fathers mentioned in the preceding chapter such as Basil of Caesarea, Gregory of Nazianzus, Ambrose, Jerome, Augustine, and even Origen, who despite their Alexandrian assumptions about the limited purpose of male and female nevertheless assigned considerable practical and pastoral importance to maintaining the distinction. We shall also hear from several Fathers who differed from the Alexandrians on the key issue of the image of God, seeing the image not just in the spiritual or intellectual virtues of the soul but also in ordered relations between persons, with one person acting as the head, the source, the creator even, of other persons.

Our primary sources will be more diverse in terms of both authors and genre, including fewer books but more sermons and canons, the latter promulgated by bishops meeting in council and therefore carrying more weight in terms of orthodoxy. None of these sources gives evidence of having been written esoterically or pseudonymously. Though in some cases the author is not known, in no case does it appear that the author assumed a false name to hide his or her identity. Neither does it appear that any of the representatives of a more Hebrew view of male and female expected his public comments on the subject to cause scandal. All seem to have expected that most Christians would agree with them, even though in some cases opinion turned against them.

Other differences between the more speculative Fathers of the previous chapter and the more mainstream Fathers of this chapter include the extent to which the latter based their teaching on Holy Scripture and the consistency of their more literal reading of Scripture over time. The New Testament had more to say in support of the Hebrew view of male and female than the handful of verses used by theorists to support the Greek view. With more spelled out in Scripture, the Hebrew view saw much less change through the centuries. It was from the start more popular and less controversial than the Greek view and therefore required much less modification to conform to the Christian consensus. Much more was written against the Encratites and Origenists than against Jovinian and Vigilantius, the only early Christians of significance who went too far in defending marriage in the view of most early Christians.

This chapter will therefore not proceed chronologically as the preceding chapter did. It will instead use key passages of the New Testament to demonstrate how early Christians understood them, citing and summarizing the teachings of Church Fathers on both marriage and the gender order. Then it will briefly consider the impact of the growing veneration of the Virgin Mary on the perceptions of male and female among Christians of late antiquity.

## "What God hath joined together"

The preceding chapter showed that a significant difference between the Hebrew view and the Christian view is immediately apparent in the New Testament's endorsement of celibacy (1 Cor 7:1), virginity (Rev 14:4), and a marriageless afterlife (Matt 22:30). This section will show that significant difference between the Hebrew view and the Christian view is also immediately apparent in the New Testament's prohibition of divorce except for reason of adultery (Matt 19:9; cf. Mark 10:11; Luke 16:18), but whereas the first difference on celibacy and virginity makes less of marriage and of male and female, the second difference on divorce makes much more of marriage and of male and female, shifting the basis of both from the need for progeny to the relation of the man and the woman as head and body.

In Matt 19:3–9, before Jesus tells his disciples that some men make themselves eunuchs "for the kingdom of heaven's sake," he answers the Pharisees' question about divorce, saying:

> "Have ye not read that he which made them at the beginning made them male and female, and said, 'For this cause shall a man leave father and mother, and shall cleave to his wife: and they twain shall be one flesh'? Wherefore they are no more twain, but one flesh. What therefore God hath joined together, let not man put asunder." (Matt 19:4–6)

With these words, Christ confirms the sanctity of the marriage bond, for which God himself is responsible, using the very words of Gen 1:27 and 2:24 without any hint that a husband and wife becoming "one flesh" is somehow sinful, unfortunate, unnatural, or beastly. The parallel passage in Mark 10:2–12 is almost identical. Christ also seems to bless marriage at the wedding feast in Cana of Galilee, where he performs the first miracle of his earthly ministry by turning water into wine (John 2:1–11). He speaks against divorce in two more passages, Matt 5:31–32 and Luke 16:18, and the Apostle Paul follows suit in 1 Cor 7:10–11, saying, "yet not I, but the Lord" forbids divorce among believers.

There is therefore a difference between the Old and New Testaments on divorce, but it is a difference that makes marriage *more* meaningful to Christians than it was to the Hebrews. As we have seen in chapter 3, the ancient Israelites saw marriage as part of a normal course of life enabling men and women to satisfy natural desires for sexual congress, companionship, and progeny. Little in that understanding stood in the way of divorce, which the Law of Moses allowed and sometimes required for several reasons short of adultery.[1] The Christian view in evidence in the New Testament is both significantly similar and significantly different from the Hebrew view. It still treats marriage as normal and natural for the same reasons, but it adds a spiritual dimension that makes marriage normal but not necessary on one hand and yet deeply theological on the other hand.

The theological aspect of marriage is set forth most obviously in Ephesians 5, where the Apostle draws an analogy between husbands and wives and Christ and the Church, saying, "For the husband is the head of the wife, even as Christ is the head of the church: and he is the savior of the body" (v. 23). Wives are therefore to submit to their husbands "as unto the Lord" (vv. 22, 24, 33), and husbands are to love their wives "as their own bodies" and "even as Christ also loved the church, and gave himself for it" (vv. 25–30). There is, in this passage, no mention of procreation, but Gen 2:24 is again quoted: "For this cause shall a man leave his father and mother, and shall be joined unto his wife, and they two shall be one flesh" (v. 31). This time, however, Paul tells us he is speaking of "a great mystery . . . concerning Christ and the church" (v. 32). The great mystery would seem to be, at least in part, the Son leaving the Father to become man in the Incarnation, and then, through the Holy Eucharist, becoming "one flesh" with those who partake—a meaning more obvious when one considers that what Latin Christians called a *sacramentum*, Greek Christians called a *mystērion*. In speaking of the "mystery" of Christ and the Church, Paul is speaking of the sacrament of Holy Communion to analogize Christ's self-giving love for the Church and a husband's self-giving love for his wife.

Christ himself makes this new dimension to marriage possible through his incarnate example, in which God the Son assumes our flesh and bone to give his life for us. Before his coming, the Hebrews had yet no direct experience of a self-giving God. Their God gave gifts, as many gods do, but not his own life. Their vision of marriage and of Israel as the beloved bride of the Song of Songs was therefore incomplete. Still to be

---

1. By the time of Christ, the vagueness of the Hebrew words *erwāt dābār* in Deut 24:1, which the Septuagint renders *aschēmon pragma*, had led to widely varying rabbinic opinions on permissible grounds for divorce, from adultery only to finding a fairer face. Christ himself presupposes the Law's greater lenience on account of the "hardness of your hearts" (Matt 19:8; Mark 10:5). See Neudecker, "Marriage and Divorce," 262–86.

revealed was the extent of the bridegroom's love, which Christ revealed in his sacrificial love for the Church. In the light of Christ, as explained by Paul, the marriage of a man and a woman is an image and a type—a realization, on a small scale, of the loving, self-giving, head-and-body unity Christ has come to create, which divorce destroys.

Elsewhere, Paul affirms the good of marriage without making too much of it. He claims the right (not exercised) "to lead about a sister, a wife, as well as other apostles, and as the brethren of the Lord, and Cephas" (1 Cor 9:5). He recommends celibacy because it frees one to serve God more, without the cares of married life (1 Cor 7:1, 7–8, 26–28, 32–35, 40), but he also recommends marriage for most people as a defense against sin (1 Cor 7:2, 5, 9), declaring marriage "honorable" and the marriage bed "undefiled" (Heb 13:4), saying that those who marry do not sin (1 Cor 7:28), recognizing that "every man hath his proper gift of God" (1 Cor 7:7, 17), and even relating childbearing to salvation not as an inhibitor but as an enabler, a way for the female sex to undo its part in the Fall (1 Tim 2:15).[2] He does not limit sexual relations within marriage to the purpose of procreation, explicitly advising married couples to have relations as needed to avoid temptation (1 Cor 7:3–5). Neither does he require celibacy of anyone but the unmarried. He advises that bishops and deacons be "men of one woman"—words forbidding second marriages (and keeping both a wife and a concubine) but also suggesting marriage as the norm even for bishops (1 Tim 3:2, 12). He also warns strongly against those who will later forbid marriage and the eating of meat, "which God hath created to be received with thanksgiving by them which believe and know the truth" (1 Tim 4:1–3).

In sum, for Paul, Christian marriage is not merely a means of obtaining legitimate offspring, as it was for the Greeks, or a means of perpetuating one's memory or one's flesh through sons and daughters, as it was the Hebrews, or merely a means of avoiding temptation, as it was for some Christians. Neither is it the "courtly love" of the age of chivalry, nor the idolizing indulgence of the Romantics, nor the self-actualizing "companionate marriage" of the twentieth century. Instead, Christian marriage in Paul is a natural, normal, blameless, and blessed (but neither necessary nor best) choice of life for an intimately ordered relationship based on loving self-giving by the "head" and humble service by the "body," as exemplified by Christ and the Church.

2. This is how John Chrysostom understands 1 Tim 2:15. See his *Homily 9 on 1 Timothy*.

## "The head of every man is Christ"

Paul also draws a relational analogy of the man and the woman in 1 Cor 11:2–16, not to Christ and the Church but to Christ and the man and then to God and Christ, saying, "But I would have you know, that the head of every man is Christ, and the head of the woman is the man, and the head of Christ is God" (1 Cor 11:3). This begins a brief discourse in support of the Christian custom of women but not men covering their heads when they pray or prophesy. The custom appears to have been uniquely Christian. Corinth was re-founded as a Roman colony in the first century before Christ, and Roman men and women habitually covered their heads when they prayed. Greek men and women adopted this practice under Roman rule, and Jewish men and women may have done the same. Nothing in Hebrew Scripture related head-coverings to the image of God in any way or prohibited men from covering their heads in prayer. On the contrary, the Law required high priests to wear a turban (*mitznefet*; LXX *kidaris*) when in the tabernacle or temple (Exod 28:4, 36–41; 29:6, 29–31; Lev 9:9; 16:4), and eventually head-coverings (prayer shawls, skullcaps) became obligatory for all men.[3] Nevertheless, it is possible that in Paul's time Jewish men were not yet in the habit of covering their heads in prayer and that Christian men followed Jewish men in this, but that Christian women assumed the habit of covering their heads in prayer on account of the public nature of Christian worship, with men and women worshipping together in church, and that Paul or the other Apostles divined a reason for this custom of men praying bareheaded while women remained covered, so as to encourage it.

Many unfounded assumptions are now often made about 1 Cor 11:2–16. To undo them, we should note what the controversial passage does not say before considering what it does say. First, nothing in the passage limits its meaning to husbands and wives. The Greek words used, *anēr* and *gynē*, do often mean husband and wife, but there is no mention of marriage in the passage, which appeals instead to nature as the basis of the difference in coverings and hairstyles. Latin translations of the passage therefore avoided restricting the passage to husbands and wives by using *maritus* and *uxor* for *anēr* and *gynē*. Only in the twentieth century did some popular English translations introduce *husband* and *wife* to the passage.[4]

---

3. See Oster, "When Men Wore Veils to Worship," 481–505.

4. The first seems to have been the Revised Standard Version in 1946. The English

Second, there is no mention of the setting of the prayer or prophecy. Many modern exegetes assume that Paul is speaking here of public prayer and prophecy, which brings the passage into conflict with a later passage in the same epistle, 1 Cor 14:34–35, in which Paul emphatically forbids women to speak in church. The supposed conflict is variously resolved, often by dismissing 1 Cor 14:34–35 as an interpolation, sometimes by arguing that 1 Cor 14:34–35 refers not to women generally but to wives or even only to the wives of prophets. No such understanding appears among Church Fathers, for good reason: Paul does not take up the subject of public worship in 1 Corinthians until 1 Cor 11:17, after his discourse on head-covering, and when he does turn to the issue of public worship, he clearly indicates his change of subject, saying:

> Now in this that I declare unto you I praise you not, that ye come together not for the better, but for the worse. For first of all, when ye come together in the church, I hear that there be divisions among you; and I partly believe it. (1 Cor 11:17–18)

The words "Now in this that I declare unto you *I praise you not*" parallel the words that preface his discourse on head-covering: "Now *I praise you*, brethren, that ye remember me in all things, and keep the traditions, as I delivered them to you" (1 Cor 11:2). So first he praises the Corinthians for their faithfulness to tradition, adding an explanation for head-covering without actually accusing them of not keeping that particular tradition, then he faults the Corinthians for what they do in church, saying that the first fault he finds "when ye come together" is divisions among them. There is therefore no necessary conflict between 1 Cor 11:2–16 and 1 Cor 14:34–35, and when Montanists used the former passage to justify women prophesying in public, other Christians used the private prophecies of the Virgin Mary and her cousin Elizabeth (Luke 1:41–55) to refute them.[5]

Third, there is nothing in the passage that references the Fall in any way—no mention of Eve's deception, disobedience, or curse. Instead, the Apostle bases his argument on the sexes' natural relation per Gen 2. The woman was created "for the man" (v. 9) and is therefore "of the man" (v.

---

Revised Version (1881), American Standard Bible (1901), Douay-Rheims-based Confraternity Bible (1941), New American Standard Bible (1963), and New International Version (1978) say only *man* and *woman*.

5. Roger Gryson provides examples from Didymus the Blind's *On the Trinity* and from an anonymous fourth-century dialogue found in the Escorial Library. See Gryson, *The Ministry of Women*, 75–77.

8, 12) and "neither without the man in the Lord" (v. 11); the man was not created "for the woman" (v. 9) and therefore is not "of the woman" (v. 8), but he is "by the woman" (v. 12) and not "without the woman . . . in the Lord" (v. 11). The man dishonors "his head" when he prays or prophesies with his head covered because he is "the image and glory of God," but the woman dishonors "her head" when she prays or prophesies without covering her head because she is "the glory of the man" (vv. 4–7). Paul supports this with an appeal to commonsense and what seems natural, saying nature itself teaches that it is shameful for a man to wear his hair long like a woman's, whereas it is shameful for her to cut her hair short like a man's, for her hair is a "glory to her" and "given to her as a covering" (vv. 13–15). Finally, he says, the churches of God have no other custom (v. 16).

Church Fathers quoted 1 Cor 11:2–16 quite often to justify this universal custom, which remained common among Christians until the mid-twentieth century, when hats fell out of fashion for both men and women. No Father disputes the custom or wonders much about the words that trouble many Christians today. Minor differences of interpretation do appear among the Fathers. Clement of Alexandria understood "head" (*kephalē*) in the passage to mean "ruling power."[6] Cyril of Alexandria understood it as "archetypal beauty" and thus the source of shared being.[7] Theodoret of Cyrus understood it to mean "source," using 1 Cor 11 to argue for the divinity of the Son based on the Father being the source of the Son.[8] This is also the sense of *kephalē* in Col 2:19 and Eph 4:15, which speak of the head (Christ) as the source of the body (the Church). The word *kephalē* did more often mean "source" prior to the Christian era. The Septuagint, for example, uses *kephalē* interchangeably with *archē* ("beginning") to translate the Hebrew word *rōsh*, meaning both "head" and "beginning," as in *Rōsh Hashanah* ("head of the year"), in the "heads" or "headwaters" of Genesis 2:10, and in the phrase "head of the corner" (cornerstone) in Ps 117:22 (also Matt 21:42; Mark 12:10; Luke 20:17; Acts 4:11; 1 Pet 2:7).[9] Modern scholars have debated which

---

6. Clement of Alexandria, *Strom.* 4.8, 420.

7. Cyril of Alexandria, *Commentary on 1 Corinthians 11*, 879–82.

8. Theodoret of Cyrus, *Commentary on the Letters of St. Paul*, PG 82, 309–14.

9. In Isaiah 9:15, the Septuagint even uses *archē* to explain *kephalē* in the previous verse. See Bedale, "The Meaning of *kephalē* in the Pauline Epistles," 211–15. Bedale (213) writes, "If this virtual equation of κεφαλή and ἀρχή be conceded a new and illuminating interpretation of several Pauline passages becomes possible." This chapter and the last chapter will offer just that.

meaning is more appropriate, "source" or "ruling power," but no Church Father understood one to exclude the other, and indeed the word *archē* could also mean either.[10]

Cyril of Alexandria extends Paul's wording of 1 Cor 11:7 to say that "in a way the female is ordered after him in honor and glory" on account of her being "the likeness of the man and the image of the image, and the glory of the glory," bearing the image of God "through the man, because the nature of the woman differs in some small way."[11] Theodoret of Cyrus concurs, calling the woman "the image of the image."[12] We have seen in the preceding chapter how those who followed Origen (Gregory of Nyssa, Maximus the Confessor) identified the image of God with the rational soul, which is neither male nor female. Other Fathers, however, viewed the image of God rather differently. Theodoret sees the image of God not only in man's soul but also in his creativity—his building of "houses, walls, cities, harbors, ships," etc. He notes the difference that God sometimes creates things from nothing, whereas man always creates things from other things, "Yet creating even in this fashion, the human being to some extent imitates the Creator as an image its archetype."[13] Clement of Alexandria, Origen's predecessor, says that in obeying the commandment to "be fruitful and multiply" (Gen 1:28), "the human being becomes the image of God, by cooperating in the creation of another human being."[14] This makes the image relational—a matter of one person being the source of another. The Fathers of the Antiochene school, including John Chrysostom, Ephrem the Syrian, and Theodoret of Cyrus, also saw the image as relational, identifying the image of God with dominion (*archē*), per Gen 1:26: "Let us make man in our image, after our likeness, and let them have dominion [LXX, *archete*]."[15] In this view, the woman is the image of God toward creation but not toward the man, whereas the man is the image of God toward the woman and creation. Augustine takes a similar view

---

10. For a detailed analysis of the controversy attending Paul's use of *kephalē*, see Grudem, "The Meaning of the Word *Kephalē* ('Head')," 425–68.

11. Cyril of Alexandria, *Commentary on 1 Corinthians 11*, PG 74, 881–84.

12. Theodoret of Cyrus, *Commentary on 1 Corinthians 11*, PG 82, 309–14.

13. Theodoret of Cyrus, *Questions on Genesis*, 1.20, 53–54.

14. Clement of Alexandria, *Paed.* 2.10.83, quoted in Ford, *Women and Men in the Early Church*, 30n84. Cf. Clement of Alexandria, *Strom.* 3.9.66.

15. John Chrysostom, *Homily on Genesis 2.8*, *Homily 7 on the Statues*, and *Homily 26 on 1 Cor*; Theodoret of Cyrus, *Questions on Genesis*, 1.20, and *Commentary on 1 Cor 11*; Ephrem the Syrian, *Commentary on Genesis 1*.

when commenting on 1 Cor 11:7, saying the woman bears the image of God but only in association with the man, whereas the man bears it always.[16] The Apostle Paul himself seems to indicate a relational view of the image of God when he says that the man is "image and glory of God" and the woman is the "glory of the man" without mentioning the image.

The only other part of 1 Cor 11:2–16 understood variously by early Christians was verse 10: "For this cause ought the woman to have power [*exousia*] on her head because of the angels." Tertullian linked this mention of angels to Gen 6:2–4, which tells of the "sons of God" taking the "daughters of men" as wives and begetting children who "became mighty men which were of old, men of renown"; virgins should therefore stay covered so as not to tempt the angels.[17] Others including John Chrysostom, Cyril of Alexandria, and Theodoret of Cyrus understood Paul to mean that a woman praying or prophesying bareheaded offends the angels by her insolence, her covering being a symbol of her subjection.[18] If one understands head-covering as a symbol of subjection, verse 10 could be understood to refer to the consequences of the Fall, but it need not, depending upon how one understands subjection, whether it is natural or merely economical, of which possibilities more will be said later in this chapter and the next.

## "For Adam was first formed, then Eve"

The Apostle Paul's words to the Ephesians about husbands and wives are epitomized in the so-called "household codes" of three other New Testament epistles. To the Colossians, Paul writes, "Wives, submit yourselves unto your own husbands, as it is fit in the Lord. Husbands, love your wives, and be not bitter against them" (Col 3:18–19). To Titus, he writes that older women are to teach younger women "to be sober, to love their husbands, to love their children, to be discreet, chaste, keepers at home, good, obedient to their own husbands, that the word of God be not blasphemed" (Titus 2:4–5). Likewise, the Apostle bids wives to follow the example of "holy women" of the Old Testament, that their husbands may be won over by their "chaste conversation coupled with fear," saying,

---

16. Augustine, *On the Trinity*, 12.7, 158–60.

17. Tertullian, *On the Veiling of Virgins*, 7–8, 11; Tertullian, *On Prayer*, 22.

18. John Chrysostom, *Homily 26 on 1 Corinthians*; Cyril of Alexandria, *Commentary on 1 Corinthians 11*; Theodoret of Cyrus, *Commentary on 1 Corinthians 11*.

"Even as Sara obeyed Abraham, calling him lord, whose daughters ye are, as long as ye do well" (1 Pet 3:6).

Other New Testament passages speak of the woman's subjection more generally, also referencing the Church's Hebrew inheritance, without limiting subjection to wives. To the Corinthians, Paul writes that women are not permitted to speak in church, even to ask questions, because "they are commanded to be under obedience, as also saith the law" (1 Cor 14:34–35). To Timothy, he says that women are to "learn in silence with all subjection," adding that they may not teach (*didaskein*) or boss (*authentein*) men on account of both creation and fall: "For Adam was first formed, then Eve. And Adam was not deceived, but the woman being deceived was in the transgression" (1 Tim 2:13–14).

Early Church authorities often quote 1 Cor 14 and 1 Tim 2 together and without comment. Cyprian of Carthage quotes them as his precept 46 on the silence and subjection of women.[19] Basil of Caesarea quotes them in support of Rule 73 of his *Moralia*: "That women should keep silence in the church, but be zealous at home to inquire about the manner of pleasing God."[20] Cyril of Jerusalem quotes them to instruct male candidates for baptism to read aloud or pray aloud together while waiting in church, but to prescribe silence for female candidates, who are to wait "either singing or reading quietly, so that their lips speak, but others' ears catch not the sound."[21] Canon 70 of the Quinisext Council in 692 quotes the same passages to say that women are not permitted to speak during the Divine Liturgy. Epiphanius of Salamis quotes 1 Cor 11:8, 1 Tim 2:12, and 1 Tim 2:14 along with Gen 3:16 to quickly condemn the Quintillianists, of whom he says, "They have women bishops, presbyters, and the rest; they say that none of this makes any difference because 'in Christ Jesus there is neither male nor female.'"[22]

Genesis 2 and 3 are often cited by Church Fathers to show that the woman's subjection is a matter of both nature and law, as Irenaeus of Lyon does to explain that Miriam but not Aaron was punished for opposing Moses "because the woman was the more culpable, since both nature and the law place the woman in a subordinate condition to the man."[23]

19. Cyprian of Carthage, *Treatise 11*, 546.
20. Basil, *Ascetical Works*, 190–91.
21. Cyril of Jerusalem, *Procatechesis*, 4.
22. Epiphanius, *Panarion*, 2.4.29/49, 2.22.
23. Irenaeus, Fr. 32 in ANF, 573, but Fr. 33 in PG 7, 1245C.

On the Apostle Paul's mention of the law in 1 Cor 14:34, John Chrysostom says, "And where doth the law say this? 'Thy desire shall be to thy husband, and he shall rule over thee'" (Gen 3:16).[24] Some Fathers do at times speak of Gen 3:16 as a prediction of future tyranny, as Augustine does to distinguish the "bond of love" to which Eve was subject before the Fall from the "condition similar to that of slavery" she was later to suffer.[25] But Augustine elsewhere says of Gen 3:16 that "we are to understand that the husband is to rule his wife as the soul rules the flesh," and, as with 1 Cor 11:3, there is no necessary conflict between the two readings, and no argument among the Fathers that one excludes the other.[26]

John Chrysostom often makes a point of the equality the woman enjoyed before the Fall. He imagines Adam recognizing that Eve is "of his kind, with the same properties as himself, of equal esteem, in no way inferior to him."[27] He imagines God saying to Eve, "In the beginning I created you equal in esteem to your husband, and my intention was that in everything you would share with him as an equal, and as I entrusted control of everything to your husband, so did I to you; but you abused your equality of status."[28] Chrysostom explains: "The woman, you see, had dreams of equality with God and hastened to taste the fruit."[29] He voices Eve's curse as follows:

> Because you abandoned your equal, who was sharer with you in the same nature and for whom you were created, and you chose to enter into conversation with that evil creature the serpent, and to take the advice he had to give, accordingly I now subject you to him in the future and designate him as your master for you to recognize his lordship, and since you did not know how to rule, learn well how to be ruled.[30]

Ephrem the Syrian summarizes Eve's actions similarly:

> She hastened to eat before her husband that she might become head over her head, that she might become the one to give command to that one by whom she was to be commanded, and that

24. John Chrysostom, *Homily 37 on 1 Corinthians*, 222.
25. Augustine, *The Literal Meaning of Genesis*, 11.37.50, 2, 171.
26. Augustine, *City of God*, 15.7, 289.
27. John Chrysostom, *Homily 15 on Genesis*, 197–202.
28. John Chrysostom, *Homily 17 on Genesis*, 230–42.
29. John Chrysostom, *Homily 16 on Genesis*, 208–16.
30. John Chrysostom, *Homily 17 on Genesis*, 230–42.

she might be older in divinity than the one who was older than she in humanity.[31]

And yet, for Chrysostom, the equality that existed before the Fall did not exclude a kind of order in which the man was even then the head, and thus he blames Adam for abdicating his position:

> After all, you are head of your wife, and she has been created for your sake; but you have inverted the proper order: not only have you failed to keep her on the straight and narrow but you have been dragged down with her, and whereas the rest of the body should follow the head, the contrary has in fact occurred, the head following the rest of the body, turning things upside down.[32]

Note here the concern of both Chrysostom and Ephrem for the relational aspect of the Fall, focusing not on the physical attraction of the forbidden fruit, but on the misorientation of Eve toward the serpent and of Adam toward Eve, which upends their natural relation with each other and God. Similarly, Augustine sees pride as the source of Eve's fall, saying of the serpent's words to Eve:

> How could these words persuade the woman that it was a good and useful thing that had been forbidden by God if there was not already in her heart a love of her own independence and a proud presumption on self which through that temptation was destined to be found out and cast down?[33]

Chrysostom speaks of order and equality existing simultaneously even after the Fall, likening the man and the woman to the Father and the Son, as Paul does in 1 Cor 11:3:

> For what if the wife be under subjection to us? It is as a wife, as free, as equal in honor. And the Son also, though He did become obedient to the Father, it was as the Son of God, it was as God. For as the obedience of the Son to the Father is greater than we find in men towards the authors of their being, so also His liberty is greater.[34]

Elsewhere, discoursing on Phil 2:5–8, Chrysostom again draws an analogy between the Son's "becoming obedient" and the wife's subjection to

---

31. Ephrem the Syrian, *Commentary on Genesis*, 113.
32. John Chrysostom, *Homily 17 on Genesis*, 230–42.
33. Augustine, *The Literal Meaning of Genesis*, 11.30.39, 162.
34. John Chrysostom, *Homily 26 on 1 Corinthians*, 150.

her husband, characterizing marriage as a "state in which there is equality and liberty, since in that the subjection is but slight."[35]

Three times the Apostle Paul refers to Genesis when speaking of men and women (1 Cor 11:2–16; 14:34–35; 1 Tim 2:12–14), so it is hardly surprising that Church Fathers also base their understanding of the man and the woman on Genesis. The fashioning of the woman from the man served as their starting point, establishing the sexes' common, equal human nature but also an order of precedence analogous to that of the Father and the Son. Hippolytus of Rome gives the order of baptism as children, men, and then women.[36] Likewise, the fourth-century *Apostolic Constitutions* specifies the communion of all honored men before any honored women: bishop, presbyters, deacons, subdeacons, readers, chanters, and ascetics, "then of the women: the deaconesses, and the virgins, and the widows; then the children; and then all the people in order [i.e., men, then women]."[37] Reversing the order made sense only in peculiar instances such as this one cited by Jerome:

> Let us see what they find. "Mary and Joseph" [Luke 2:16]. If she were truly wife, it would be improper to say, they found the wife and the husband; but the Gospel named the woman first, then the man. What does Holy Writ say? "They found Mary and Joseph": they found Mary, the mother, and Joseph, the guardian.[38]

This precedence was not limited to marriage or to the Church, but applied generally to all society. Chrysostom even applies it to children, "according to their age and sex since among the children the female doth not possess equal sway."[39]

At the same time, there is added to the natural order a lawful subjection decreed by God on account of the Fall. "For with us indeed the woman is reasonably subjected to the man, since equality of honor causeth contention," says Chrysostom.[40] This is the first of many lawful subjections instituted for our own good, as Chrysostom says elsewhere: "And from the beginning He made one sovereignty only, setting the man over the woman. But after that our race ran headlong into extreme disorder,

---

35. John Chrysostom, *Homily 6 on Philippians*, 209.
36. Hippolytus, *Apostolic Tradition*, 104–5.
37. *Apostolic Constitutions*, 490.
38. Jerome, *Homily 88 on the Nativity*, 224.
39. John Chrysostom, *Homily 34 on 1 Corinthians*, 204.
40. John Chrysostom, *Homily 26 on 1 Corinthians*, 150.

He appointed other sovereignties also, those of Masters, and those of Governors, and this too for love's sake."[41]

## "There is neither male nor female"

The words "male and female" occur just three times in the New Testament, twice when Christ speaks of man's creation as "male and female" (Matt 19:4; Mark 10:6) and once when the Apostle Paul makes his case for justification by faith and not works of the Law to the Galatians, saying:

> For ye are all the children of God by faith in Christ Jesus. For as many of you as have been baptized into Christ have put on Christ. There is neither Jew nor Greek, there is neither bond nor free, there is neither male nor female [*ouk eni arsen kai thēlu*], for ye are all one in Christ Jesus. And if ye be Christ's, then are ye Abraham's seed, and heirs according to the promise. (Gal 3:26–29)

Paul says something similar about unity in Christ in two other epistles, but without including "male and female." Writing to the Corinthians in defense of the distribution of diverse gifts to members of the Church, he says, "For by one Spirit are we all baptized into one body—whether we be Jews or Gentiles, whether we be bond or free—and have been all made to drink into one Spirit. For the body is not one member, but many" (1 Cor 12:13–14). He then likens the Church to the human body to argue that not all are apostles, not all are prophets, not all are teachers, etc., but all are still members of the Body of Christ. Then, in exhorting the Colossians to "set your affection on things above, not on things on the earth" (Col 3:2), Paul writes:

> Lie not to one another, seeing that ye have put off the old man with his deeds, and have put on the new man, which is renewed in knowledge after the image of him that created him, where there is neither Greek nor Jew, circumcision nor uncircumcision, Barbarian, Scythian, bond nor free, but Christ is all and in all. Put on therefore, as the elect of God, holy and beloved, bowels of mercies, kindness, humbleness of mind, meekness, long-suffering, forbearing one another and forgiving one another. (Col 3:9–13)

---

41. John Chrysostom, *Homily 34 on 1 Corinthians*, 205.

The subject of these three passages is therefore very different: It is faith in Gal 3, gifts in 1 Cor 12, and virtue in Col 3. Yet only in Galatians does Paul mention male and female. We hardly need wonder why Paul does not mention male and female in 1 Cor 12. In Gal 3, his point is that faith in Christ makes all who are baptized in Christ "heirs of the promise," regardless of race, sex, or legal standing, but in 1 Cor 12 his point is that all who are baptized in Christ have different gifts with different callings, regardless of race and legal standing but not regardless of sex, as the Apostle's comments in 1 Cor 11:2–16 and 14:34–35 make plain.

What about Col 3? Why would the Apostle add circumcision and uncircumcision as well as Barbarian and Scythian to his longest list of categories but exclude male and female, when the subject of Colossians 3 is vices versus virtues, which are the same for both sexes?

The answer may lie in when the epistles were written. Galatians and 1 Corinthians are commonly thought to be early epistles, with the former preceding the latter by a few years. Colossians, however, mentions Paul's imprisonment (Col 4:18) in Rome or Caesarea and is therefore thought to be a much later epistle.[42] It makes sense, then, that having first told the Galatians how sex does not matter and then told the Corinthians how sex does matter, Paul excluded sex from his lesson to the Colossians on vices and virtues, not because of any moral difference between the sexes, but because including the important natural difference of male and female among unimportant accidental differences such as ethnicity, legal standing, or physical condition (circumcised or uncircumcised) might have given the Colossians the wrong idea.[43]

We have already seen how some early Christians did get the wrong idea, using Gal 3:28 to condemn marriage, as did the Encratites mentioned by Clement of Alexandria, or to ordain women, as did the Quintillianists mentioned by Epiphanius.[44] We have also seen how some Church Fathers, understanding male and female only in the Greek way as all about what we now call "sex," leaned heavily on Gal 3:28 to advance an eschatological vision of a resurrection without either sexual desire or sexual distinction.[45]

---

42. For a discussion of both dating and authorship, see Pascuzzi, "Reconsidering the Authorship of Colossians," 223–46.

43. For a similar analysis, see Martin, "The Covenant of Circumcision," 111–25.

44. Clement of Alexandria, *Strom.* 3.13.93; Epiphanius, *Panarion*, 2.4.29/49, 21–23.

45. See Harrison, "Male and Female in Cappadocian Theology," 441–71.

Few Fathers, however, make so much of Gal 3:28. Some do take Gal 3:28 to be a "reference to concupiscence of carnal sex," in the words of Augustine.[46] "And, indeed," says Jerome, "when chastity is observed between man and woman, it begins to be true that there is neither male nor female."[47] Thus Athanasius relates Gal 3:28 to Matt 22:30 on there being no marrying in the resurrection.[48] Thus also John Chrysostom quotes Gal 3:28 to shame men and women of his own day for needing to be screened off from each other in church, saying the men and women of old were more pious and needed no screens, for they were neither male nor female in Christ Jesus.[49]

But more often Gal 3:28 was cited simply to stress unity in Christ irrespective of nonspiritual differences, a meaning much closer to the context of the verse. In one instance, Clement of Alexandria allegorizes "male and female" in Gal 3:28 to correct the Encratite interpretation of Julius Cassianus, as we have seen, but in two other instances Clement uses the verse to teach that the Church is not divided by piety or illumination, with those who marry and beget children classed as less pious or less enlightened.[50] In many similar citations by Church Fathers, "male and female" receives little or no attention. For Hilary of Poitiers (+367), the issue of importance is the sacrament of Holy Baptism, which is how "these are one amid so great diversities of race, condition, [and] sex."[51]

Often the reason for citing Gal 3:28 is to include women in the promise of Gal 3:29 ("And if ye be Christ's, then are ye Abraham's seed, and heirs according to the promise") and in the grace that deprives them of any excuse on account of female weakness. Women are "fellow-heirs of grace with us," says Augustine.[52] They, too, will call upon the name of the Lord in the end times, says Chrysostom.[53] They, too, will contend in the spiritual arena, he says:

---

46. Augustine, *On the Works of Monks*, 523.
47. Justin Martyr, *First Apology*, 1.29, 497–98.
48. Athanasius, *Against the Arians*, 2.69.
49. John Chrysostom, *Homily 73 on Matt*, 3.
50. Clement of Alexandria, *Strom.* 3.13.93; *Exhortation to the Heathens* 11; *Paed.* 1.6.
51. Hilary of Poitiers, *On the Trinity*, 139–40.
52. Augustine, *On the Trinity*, 160. Cf. Augustine, *Reply to Faustus*, 317.
53. John Chrysostom, *Homily 5 on Acts*, 34.

## The Hebrew Christian View of Male and Female 171

> Neither do men alone disrobe [as a wrestler before a match], in order that the women may not take refuge in the weakness of their nature, and seem to have a plausible excuse, nor have women only quitted themselves like men, lest the race of men be put to shame; but on this side and on that many are proclaimed conquerors, and are crowned, in order that thou mayest learn by means of the exploits themselves that in Christ Jesus neither male nor female, neither sex, nor weakness of body, nor age, nor any such thing could be a hindrance to those who run in the course of religion.[54]

Chrysostom also cites Gal 3:28 to show how close husbands and wives are, there being no spiritual difference between them.[55] Likewise, Jerome cites Gal 3:28 to console a widow for the loss of her husband, praising her husband for treating her as a spiritual equal while also assuring her that the verse does not mean she and her husband will be no longer woman and man in the resurrection, contrary to "that heresy [Origenism] which holds out great but vague promises only that it may take away hopes which are at once modest and certain."[56]

Several mentions of Gal 3:28 are merely corrections of abuses of the verse by those who make too much of it, as when Augustine warns of ascetics who look down on married people and use Gal 3:28 to avoid work expected of men or women, and when Hippolytus of Rome accuses a Gnostic sect of abusing the verse to claim that the "Perfect Man" is "neither male nor female, but a new creature, a new man, a hermaphrodite."[57]

Many mentions of Gal 3:28 follow Paul's example in 1 Cor 12 and Col 3 by omitting "male and female." Chrysostom omits male and female from his use of Gal 3:28 at least four times.[58] Even in his Homily 3 on Galatians 3, he quotes Gal 3:28 in full but does not comment on male and female, saying that all who are baptized share "one form and one mould, even Christ's" and then conspicuously omitting male or female when he says, "He that was Greek, or Jew, or bond-man yesterday, carries

---

54. John Chrysostom, *Eulogy on Ignatius*, 135. Cf. John Chrysostom, *Homily 30 on Romans*, 550.

55. John Chrysostom, *Homily 20 on Ephesians*, 143.

56. Jerome, *Letter 75 to Theodora*, 155–56.

57. Augustine, *On the Works of Monks*, 523; Hippolytus, *Refutation of All Heresies* 5.2, 49.

58. John Chrysostom, *Homily 12 on 1 Corinthians, Homily 40 on 1 Corinthians, Homily 12 on Colossians*, and *Homily 1 on Philemon*. In these, Chrysostom's focus is on slave or free.

about with him the form, not of an Angel or Archangel, but of the Lord of all."[59] Here Chrysostom's omission of "male and female," coupled with his emphasis on our semblance to the incarnate Christ over our semblance to the angels, seems almost to deny the Alexandrian understanding of Gal 3:28.

No Apostolic Father (i.e., those who knew the Apostles personally) quotes Gal 3:28 at all, except in the longer, spurious version of Ignatius of Antioch's epistle to the Philadelphians (*Phld.* 4), which also omits "male and female," and no Father at all, not even Maximus the Confessor, uses Gal 3:28 to argue against the apostolic limitations on the participation of women in church. How could they, when the Apostle credited with Gal 3:28 was also credited with the several verses requiring the silence, veiling, and subjection of women?[60]

The Church's dogmatic understanding of the relevance of Gal 3:28 in this life is clearly seen in its administration of the sacraments: The Church confined the relevance of male and female to the sacraments of Holy Matrimony and Holy Ordination, making no distinction on the basis of sex or any other natural, conditional, or cultural difference in the sacraments by which people were added to the Body of Christ—Holy Baptism, Holy Anointing (Chrismation), and Holy Communion.

As for the next life, the fierce, persistent, and successful resistance to Origenist teaching on the afterlife indicates that most Christians did not understand Gal 3:28 to mean the eventual disappearance of sexual distinction. Many spoke out publicly in defense of the continuance of male and female, including Augustine, Jerome, Tertullian, and Pseudo-Justin, with Jerome saying, "What the Lord promises to us is not the nature of angels but their mode of life and their bliss."[61] Many others argued the same implicitly, stressing fleshly continuity between this life and the next against the Origenist stress on discontinuity. Some such as Chrysostom and Jerome even seem to have held out the hope that husbands and wives would not only remain men and women but also continue to enjoy each

---

59. John Chrysostom, *Homily 3 on Galatians*, 30.

60. Gregory of Nyssa comes the closest to challenging the Apostle when he gives his reason for writing his *Life of Saint Macrina*, saying that "she who had raised herself through philosophy to the highest limit of human virtue should not pass along this way veiled and in silence." Gregory of Nyssa, *Life of Saint Macrina*, 21.

61. Augustine, *Letter 108 to Eustochium*, 208. See also Augustine, *City of God*, 22.17; Tertullian, *On the Resurrection of the Flesh*; Pseudo-Justin, *On the Resurrection*, 2–3.

other's company.⁶² Only denying that men and women would remain men and women ignited controversy, and though the Church, in the Fifth Ecumenical Council (II Constantinople), and the state, in the anathemas of Justinian, stopped short of explicitly declaring the continuance of male and female, the condemnations of both came down only on those suspected of denying it.

## The Good of Marriage

With the aforementioned passages of New Testament scripture as a foundation, mainstream Christian teaching on male and female changed very little over time. The most significant and perhaps surprising change was the growing popularity of the Apostle Paul's better way of virginity, and yet the earliest indications of this are not exhortations to attempt the better way but warnings against boasting about it. Calling continence a gift from God, Clement of Rome writes, "Let him that is pure in the flesh not grow proud of it, and boast, knowing that it was another who bestowed on him the gift of continence."⁶³ Likewise, Ignatius of Antioch writes to Polycarp of Smyrna, "If anyone can continue in a state of purity, to the honor of Him who is Lord of the flesh, let him so remain without boasting. If he begins to boast, he is undone."⁶⁴

Many early Christian texts approve of marriage. Ignatius advises men and women to marry with the consent of their bishop, "that their marriage may be according to God, and not after their own lust."⁶⁵ The *Epistle to Diognetus* reports that Christians "marry, as do all [others]; they beget children; but they do not destroy their offspring. They have a common table, but not a common bed. They are in the flesh, but they do not live after the flesh."⁶⁶ The *Shepherd of Hermas* warns against coveting another's wife, saying, "But if you always remember your own wife, you will never sin."⁶⁷ Canon 6 of the Holy Apostles forbids clergy to put away their wives on account of asceticism, and canon 51 condemns clergy

---

62. See John Chrysostom, *Homily 20 on Ephesians*, quoted below, and Jerome, *Letter 75 to Theodora*, quoted above.

63. *1 Clem* 38, in ANF 1, 15.

64. *Epistle to Polycarp* 5, in ANF 1, 95.

65. *Epistle to Polycarp* 5, in ANF 1, 95.

66. *Epistle to Diognetus* 5, in ANF 1, 26–27.

67. *The Shepherd of Hermas* 2.4.5, in ANF 2, 21.

who disdain marriage, "forgetting that [in Genesis] 'all things were very good,' and that 'God made man male and female.'"[68] In the late second century, Theophilus of Antioch explains that God made the woman from the man, rather than from the earth, for the sake of mutual affection, noting that men put their wives before their parents and siblings, "So that often, for the sake of their wives, some submit even to death."[69] His contemporary in the West, Irenaeus of Lyon, is credited with having named and defined Encratism as a heresy, and although Irenaeus does not waste many words condemning it, the threat might have been real enough to have secured the inclusion of the so-called Pastoral Epistles in the New Testament canon.[70]

Perhaps in the late second century Encratism was more of a threat in the East than in the West. That would explain Clement of Alexandria's lengthy defense of marriage in book three of his *Stromata*. Educated in much the same way as Origen, a generation earlier than Origen, Clement makes many standard Greek assumptions about the nature and purpose of sexual distinction, limiting its nature to the body and its purpose to procreation.[71] We even find in Clement the Gnostic and Encratite idea that sexual desire is a divisive force that must be overcome. Commenting on the absence of marriage in heaven (Matt 22:30), he writes, "There the rewards of this social and holy life, which is based on conjugal union, are laid up, not for male and female, but for man [*anthrōpos*], the sexual desire which divides humanity being removed."[72] This, says Clement, is the reason both the man and the woman bear the common name *anthrōpos* and also, as children, the common name *paidarion*.

Yet Clement is unequivocal about the positive value of marriage, saying there is as much difference between marriage and fornication as between God and the devil.[73] He considers marriage and celibacy

---

68. Apostolic Canons, ANF 7, 500, 503. These canons were handed down through book 8 of the fourth-century *Apostolic Constitutions* but were believed to be more ancient and possibly apostolic. They were later endorsed by canon 2 of the Quinisext Council in 692.

69. Theophilus of Antioch, *To Autolycus* 2.28, in ANF 2, 105.

70. See Hunter, *Marriage, Celibacy, and Heresy*, 96, 101–15.

71. E.g., Clement of Alexandria, *Paed.* 1.4, 2.10; *Strom.* 2.19, 3.4.37, 3.7.57, 3.11.71, 3.12.82.

72. Clement of Alexandria, *Paed.* 1.4, 211.

73. Clement of Alexandria, *Strom.* 3.12.84.

*The Hebrew Christian View of Male and Female* 175

"different forms of service and ministry to the Lord."[74] He says that "the human being becomes the image of God, by cooperating in the creation of another human being."[75] He explains Christ's words about no marrying in heaven (Matt 22:30; Mark 12:25; Luke 20:34–36) as relevant only to the age to come.[76] He argues Christ did not marry because he did not need to, having the Church as his bride and believers as his children.[77] He points to patriarchs and prophets of the Old Testament and to the Apostles Peter and Philip as examples of holy men who were married.[78] He says good husbands make good clergymen, citing the Apostle Paul's comments on bishops and deacons being the "husband of one wife" (1 Tim 3:2–12).[79] He considers celibates "in most respects untried," saying:

> And true manhood is shown not in the choice of a celibate life; on the contrary, the prize in the contest of men is won by him who has trained himself by the discharge of the duties of husband and father and by the supervision of a household, regardless of pleasure and pain—by him, I say, who in the midst of his solicitude for his family shows himself inseparable from the love of God and rises superior to every temptation which assails him through children and wife and servants and possessions.[80]

Clement sees the family as a little church in which "two or three are gathered in my name" (Matt 18:20).[81] He rarely mentions virgins or virginity and even notes, with apparent approval, that some people esteem widows more than virgins because widows know better what comforts and pleasures they have forsaken.[82] He writes that "there is nothing meritorious about abstinence from marriage unless it arises from love to God [*sic*],"

---

74. Clement of Alexandria, *Strom.* 3.12.79.

75. Clement of Alexandria, *Paed.* 2.10.83, quoted in Ford, *Women and Men in the Early Church*, 30n84. Cf. Clement of Alexandria *Strom.* 3.9.66.

76. Clement of Alexandria, *Strom.* 3.12.87.

77. Clement of Alexandria, *Strom.* 3.6.49.

78. Clement of Alexandria, *Strom.* 3.6.52.

79. Clement of Alexandria, *Strom.* 3.12.79, 3.12.89.

80. Clement of Alexandria, *Strom.* 7.12.70, in Chadwick, *Alexandrian Christianity*, 138.

81. Clement of Alexandria, *Strom.* 3.10.68.

82. Clement of Alexandria, *Strom.* 3.16.101. The higher status of widows compared to virgins is seen in two early church orders: the *Apostolic Tradition,* attributed to Hippolytus and believed to reflect the practice of the church in Rome in the third century, and the *Testamentum Domini*, a fifth-century Syrian work.

and that "even the seed of the sanctified is holy."[83] He distinguishes between modesty (*aidōs*) and shame (*aischunē*) to say that there is nothing shameful about the genitals, for only evil (*kakia*) is shameful.[84] His stress throughout is on temperance, not purity, and he is clear that temperance does not mean absolute abstinence, for the temperate man "does not abstain from everything" but "is self-controlled on such things as he thinks fit."[85]

Peter Brown sees Clement as the voice of the "silent majority" of married Christians, whose defense of marriage was "soon drowned" by more monastic voices.[86] David Hunter, however, notes that Clement, along with Irenaeus and others, succeeded in establishing a new and lasting limit to Christian asceticism, securing the acceptance of marriage and the condemnation of those who forbade it.[87] Ironically, this achievement freed Christianity to make more of monasticism without destroying marriage, by offering two honorable options: "safe sex" and "safe asceticism," so to speak.

Thus, a century later, Methodius of Olympus (+311), Origen's first major critic, would begin his lengthy dialogue in praise of virginity with high praise of marriage. In *The Banquet of the Ten Virgins*, written in imitation of Plato's *Symposium*, Methodius speaks through the virgin Theophila, who begins her apology for marriage saying that God's work of creation is still ongoing and will continue until the predestined number of people is reached, "But at present man must cooperate in the forming of the image of God, while the world exists and is still being formed; for it is said, 'Increase and multiply.'"[88] Theophila likens sexual intercourse not to the raging of wild horses but to the creation of Eve, saying the man "falls into a kind of trance, softened and subdued by the pleasures of generation as by sleep, so that again something drawn from his flesh and from his bones is, as I said, fashioned into another man," and this act of creation results not from sinful, selfish desire but from

---

83. Clement of Alexandria, *Strom.* 3.6.51, 3.6.46, in Chadwick, *Alexandrian Christianity*, 64, 62.

84. Clement of Alexandria, *Paed.* 2.6.52, 251. See Trenham, *Marriage and Virginity*, 48.

85. Clement of Alexandria, *Strom.* 3.16.101.

86. Brown, *The Body and Society*, 138.

87. Hunter, *Marriage, Celibacy, and Heresy*, 113.

88. Methodius of Olympus, *Banquet* 2.1, 313.

"the harmony of the bodies being disturbed in the embraces of love."[89] She notes that perpetual virginity—"being a eunuch for the sake of the kingdom of heaven"—is a gift not given to all, then ends by saying that the Church is "adorned and crowned not only with the flowers of virginity, but also with those of child-bearing and of continence."[90] All the other virgins respond with applause. How different is the dismal indictment of marriage that begins Gregory of Nyssa's *On Virginity*, which blasts marriage as "the predisposing cause" of all error![91]

John Chrysostom also spoke quite highly of marriage, going beyond the practical purpose of procreation to stress marriage as a "type of the Church," a "mystery of love," a relation of head and body, which are "not two bodies" but one, "For there is a certain love deeply seated in our nature, which imperceptibly to ourselves knits together these bodies of ours."[92] Chrysostom is unashamed to speak of sexual intercourse and chides his audience for their embarrassment, saying, "Why art thou ashamed of the honorable, why blusheth thou at the undefiled?"[93] He describes the physical union of man and wife is an act of self-giving and thanks-giving:

> And how become they one flesh? As if thou shouldest take away the purest part of gold, and mingle it with other gold; so in truth here also the woman as it were, receiving the richest part fused by pleasure, nourisheth it and cherisheth it, and withal contributing her own share, restoreth it back a Man. And the child is a sort of bridge, so that the three become one flesh, the child connecting, on either side, each to other.[94]

There is no relation closer than that of man and wife, he says, "if they be joined together as they should be," which is why Adam prophesied that the man and the woman would not merely dwell together but cleave to each other, "thus showing the closeness of the union, and the fervent

---

89. Methodius of Olympus, *Banquet* 2.2, 314.

90. Methodius of Olympus, *Banquet* 2.7, 316.

91. Gregory of Nyssa, *On Virginity*, 4, 349.

92. John Chrysostom, *Homily 12 on Colossians*, 318; John Chrysostom, *Homily 20 on Ephesians*, 144–46.

93. John Chrysostom, *Homily 12 on Colossians*, 319. Cf. Heb 13:4.

94. John Chrysostom, *Homily 12 on Colossians*, 319.

love."[95] Man's creation as male and female is thus a divine demonstration of unity in diversity:

> What do we learn from this? That great is the power of union. The wise counsel of God at the beginning divided the one into two: and being desirous of showing that even after division it remaineth still one, He suffered not that the one should be of itself enough for procreation.[96]

Chrysostom also notes that inasmuch as the home is a "little church," the faithful management of the home by husband and wife will prepare them for greater things, saying, "Thus it is possible for us by becoming good husbands and wives, to surpass all others."[97] He even suggests that the bond of marriage continues on into the next life, saying, "For our time here is brief and fleeting. But if we shall be counted worthy by having pleased God to so exchange this life for that one, then shall we ever be both with Christ and with each other, with more abundant pleasure."[98] It is hard to imagine Gregory of Nyssa or Maximus the Confessor saying the same.

## The Challenge of Virginity

Chrysostom also praised virginity with equal if not exceeding enthusiasm, and from the third century onward that option did receive more rhetorical support from both Eastern and Western Fathers, no doubt at least partly because, as Gregory of Nyssa admits, the marriage option needed less support, having human instinct to "plead sufficiently on its behalf."[99] It should also be remembered that the intent of many homilies and treatises on celibacy and virginity was not to encourage men and women to become monks and nuns but to encourage monks and nuns to keep their vows, at a time when taking vows of perpetual celibacy was a fashionable thing to do for zealous young converts in the fourth and fifth centuries. The same is true of many popular hagiographies, especially

---

95. John Chrysostom, *Homily 20 on Ephesians*, 143, 148.
96. John Chrysostom, *Homily 12 on Colossians*, 318.
97. John Chrysostom, *Homily 20 on Ephesians*, 148.
98. John Chrysostom, *Homily 20 on Ephesians*, 151. See also Tertullian, *On Monogamy*, 10.
99. Gregory of Nyssa, *On Virginity*, 8, 352. For a thorough survey of Chrysostom's preaching on virginity and monasticism, see Trenham, *Marriage and Virginity*, 132–47.

those Kyle Harper calls "anti-romances" because they tell a story not of lovers who resist temptation to remain true to each other, but of individual men and women who resist sexual temptation to remain true to Christ.[100] Those who failed when tempted sexually—whether monks or nuns, married or unmarried—testified against the power of faith in Christ to free men and women from the demands of the flesh. Virginity therefore had a very public symbolic value far beyond the spiritual benefit to the virgin. In a sense, it took the place of circumcision for the Jews as an act of faith initiating and symbolizing separation from the world and total commitment to God.[101]

Nevertheless, patristic preaching and popular piety did sometimes go too far. The fourth century saw the emergence of monasticism of various kinds, including the kind inspired by the extreme Origenism represented by Evagrius Ponticus. The Church had to contend against several extreme ascetic sects—Eustathians in the East, Priscillianists in the West, and Manichaeans all over.[102] Peter Brown suggests that the movement toward clerical celibacy in the West was in part an attempt to create a "middle party" of reasonably continent clerics "between the shrill ascetics and the new men of power, grossly stained by the world."[103] But the reason for clerical celibacy given by fourth-century exponents including Pope Siricius, Ambrose of Milan, and Ambrosiaster was that clerical duties required clerics to be always ritually pure, "undefiled by any marital intercourse" (*nec ullo coniugali coitu violandum*), in Ambrose's words.[104] By the end of the fourth century, the Western Church had also added a new rite, the *velatio virginis*, modeled on the Roman wedding ceremony, by which avowed virgins were publicly made "brides of Christ." The rite encouraged young women to choose virginity over marriage by adding earthly honor and eternal reward to the benefits of longer life (no risk of death in childbirth) and freedom from conjugal subjection.

Faced with such changes, the "silent majority" was not always silent. "Our religion has invented a new dogma against nature," complained

---

100. See Harper, *From Shame to Sin*, 206–36.

101. Lampe attests to this, providing scores of examples of *parthenia* meaning not physical virginity but spiritual virginity or human perfection. See Lampe, *A Patristic Greek Lexicon*, 1034.

102. See Hunter, *Marriage, Celibacy, and Heresy*, 130–46.

103. Brown, *Body and Society*, 358, quoted with approval by Hunter, *Marriage, Celibacy, and Heresy*, 218.

104. Ambrose, *On the Duties of the Clergy*, 1.249, 261.

Jovinian, a celibate ascetic who nevertheless objected to ranking Christians by marital status and elevating teen-age girls who had merely sworn to remain virgins above wives and widows who had proven their faithfulness through years of serving husbands and raising children.[105] Jovinian attracted a large following in Rome by arguing that baptism bestowed no benefit on virgins greater than that bestowed on wives and widows and therefore marriage and virginity were of equal merit among Christians in both this world and the next. He was not opposed to celibacy and remained a celibate all his life, but he was accused of causing monks and virgins to marry and was condemned by synods at Rome and Milan in 393.

By appearing to contradict the Apostle Paul on the better way of virginity, Jovinian went too far, but Jerome also went too far in attacking Jovinian. His treatise *Against Jovinian* horrified even Jerome's friends and Jovinian's critics with its denigration of marriage and women, prompting accusations of heresy against Jerome, an apology from Jerome, and a rebuttal from the unknown author of a dialogue entitled *Consultations of Zaccheus and Apollonius*, which defended both the goodness of marriage and the betterness of virginity, making many of Jovinian's arguments while also countering many of Jerome's.[106] Augustine did much the same in his *On the Good of Marriage* and *On Holy Virginity*, written ten years after Jovinian's condemnation but with Jerome's *Against Jovinian* in mind.[107] The result of the Jovinian controversy, as Hunter shows, was to establish the better way as dogma while also confirming Encratism as heresy.

The Church in the East seems not to have noticed the Jovinian controversy. No Eastern Council condemned him, and no Eastern Father was moved to mount a defense of marriage amid the rise of monasticism. The valuing of virginity over marriage seems to have been assumed in the East from at least the third century onward. The good of marriage appears to have been doubted by Origenists but not publicly denied by them. Many Orthodox scholars such as Josiah Trenham and David Ford believe the ancient Christian East viewed marriage more positively than the ancient Christian West. Non-Orthodox scholars have tended to see more

---

105. Hunter, *Marriage, Celibacy, and Heresy*, 1.

106. Hunter, *Marriage, Celibacy, and Heresy*, 250–58.

107. Augustine notes his reasons for writing these works in his *Retractationes* 2.22. See Hunter, *Marriage, Celibacy, and Heresy*, 5, 269–84.

similarity, paying more attention to the Eastern Fathers of the previous chapter and to other Eastern works that exalt virginity over marriage.[108]

The issue cannot be settled here, but two facts are worth noting. The first fact is that the West was still reading Tertullian's denigrations of marriage in Latin while the East was still reading Clement of Alexandria's defense of marriage in Greek. These two men were poles apart in temperament and on marriage and influenced their respective linguistic communities in very different ways, seen in Jerome's use of Tertullian in attacking Jovinian and in Chrysostom's many echoes of Clement, as when he likens the family to the Church and when he tells his audience not to be ashamed of what is honorable and undefiled. The second fact, which should not surprise us in view of the first, is that the West did begin to require celibacy of bishops, priests, and deacons in the fourth century, possibly as early as the Council of Elvira in 306 but certainly by the end of the century, as attested by the letters of Pope Damasus I (+384) and Pope Siricius (+399), which also attest to the unpopularity of the requirement among Western clerics.[109] The East, however, never required celibacy of priests and deacons and only came to require it of bishops in the sixth century by imperial edict (Justinian's Novella 6).[110] It would seem, then, that the East did not consider marital intercourse quite so defiling, however much they might have valued virginity.

The East did see more and more eunuchs becoming bishops toward the end of the period under examination, but this trend followed the secular trend of employing eunuchs to oversee the imperial household, begun presumably in the reign of the Persianizing pagan emperor Diocletian (286–305).[111] Most palace eunuchs were imported from abroad because Roman law, repeatedly affirmed by both pagan and Christian emperors, outlawed involuntary castration and the sale of Roman-born eunuchs, but in later centuries some Byzantine parents had their own sons

---

108. Peter Brown, for example, paints the darkest pictures possible of Methodius of Olympus and John Chrysostom in his chapters on them in *The Body and Society*, although he does slightly lighten his characterization of Chrysostom to later paint an even darker picture of Augustine. See Brown, *The Body and Society*, 414.

109. Hunter provides citations for and against the authenticity of these letters in *Marriage, Celibacy, and Heresy*, 214.

110. Cf. Canons 6, 13, and 48 of the Quinisext Council in 692. Canon 48 confirms Novella 6.

111. See Guilland, "Les Eunuques dans l'Empire Byzantin," 197–38.

castrated to improve their chances for employment in the palace.[112] Early Church canons permitted ordination of men who had been castrated for medical reasons or against their will, but not ordination of those who had been castrated voluntarily.[113] The mention in Matt 19:12 of those "which have made themselves eunuchs for the kingdom of heaven's sake" was understood as to speak of celibacy, not castration, with John Chrysostom declaring that those who castrate themselves are "venturing on the deed of murderers and giving occasion to them that slander God's creation. . . . For to cut off our members hath been from the beginning a work of demoniacal agency and satanic devise."[114]

Kathryn Ringrose has argued that the social standing of eunuchs improved over the centuries to the point where they were generally accepted as a "third gender" with its own distinctive style in dress and demeanor. It is certainly true that many Byzantines did see eunuchs as somewhat angelic, believing them (inaccurately) to be free of sexual desire. It seems also true that eunuchs influenced Byzantine depictions of angels as beardless androgynes, despite the witness of Scripture, in which angels appear often as men and once as women (Zech 5:9). Greek thinking would have contributed to this view of angels and eunuchs, but Hebrew thinking is still much in evidence throughout Byzantine history, and although many Byzantines thought eunuchs chaste and angelic, many others thought of them as monstrous deformities subject to all kinds of vices.[115] Shaun Tougher argues that Ringrose's theory rests heavily on Theophylact of Ochrid's eleventh-century tract *In Defense of Eunuchs*, but Theophylact wrote this defense as a kindness to his brother, who was himself a eunuch distressed by the hostility eunuchs experienced in his own day, which

---

112. Legislation against eunuchs began with the pagan emperors Domitian (81–97), Nerva (96–98), and Hadrian (117–38) and continued with the Christian emperors Constantine the Great (306–37), Leo I (457–74), Justinian I (527–65), and Leo VI (886–912). See Guilland, "Les Eunuques dans l'Empire Byzantin," 197–203.

113. See Apostolic Canons 21 and 22 and Canon 1 of the First Ecumenical Council (I Nicaea) in 325.

114. John Chrysostom, *Homily 62 on Matthew*, 384.

115. In apparent anger, Basil of Caesarea describes the heretic Simplicia's eunuchs as "neither woman nor man, lustful, envious, ill-bribed, passionate, effeminate, slaves of the belly, made for gold, ruthless, grumbling about their dinner, inconstant, stingy, greedy, insatiable, savage, jealous. What more can I say? At their very birth they were condemned to the knife. How can their mind be right when their feet are awry? They are chaste because of the knife, and it is no credit to them. They are lecherous to no purpose, of their own natural vileness." Basil, *Letter 115 to Simplicia*, 191.

testifies against much improvement in public opinion of eunuchs.[116] Tougher also notes that there was no special attire for eunuchs, only their uniforms of office, which non-eunuchs in the same offices also wore. And what need had eunuchs of special attire? They were already recognizable by their beardlessness, which is generally believed to have inspired the fashion of beards among Byzantine men: They did not want to be mistaken for eunuchs. Contempt for eunuchs as a class was often expressed both early and late in Byzantine history, with eunuchs commonly criticized as effeminate, either on account of castration or for having been "raised in the shade" of the gynaeceum.[117] Yet eunuchs always dressed as men and took the roles of men, including leading roles in the government, the Church, and sometimes the military. Even when serving in the gynaeceum, eunuchs substituted not for women but for unmutilated men, the principal advantage of eunuchs being that they could not impregnate wives or daughters. What Byzantine eunuchs thought of themselves is not in evidence, but it hardly seems likely they thought of themselves not as men but as something wholly other.

## Distinction, Relation, Separation

Eunuchs aside, Eastern and Western Christians hardly differed at all on male and female in the centuries under examination. Both insisted on distinctly different roles for men and women in the Church and in the world. Both also condemned effeminacy in men and mannishness in women. The Old Testament's abomination of cross-dressing (Deut 22:5) and the Apostle Paul's requirement of long hair and covered heads for women and short hair and bare heads for men (1 Cor 11:2–16) remained in force. Justin Martyr, writing around 150, berates the Greeks for various impieties, including the sexual ambiguity of their gods:

> And I say nothing of the masculine character of Minerva, nor of the feminine nature of Bacchus. . . . What seemliness is there in a woman's girding herself with armor, or in a man's decorating himself with cymbals, and garlands, and female attire, and accompanied by a herd of bacchanalian women?[118]

---

116. See Tougher, *The Eunuch in Byzantine History and Society*, 96–118, esp. 108–9.
117. See Tougher, *The Eunuch in Byzantine History and Society*, 103.
118. Justin Martyr, *Discourse to the Greeks*, 271–72.

Clement of Alexandria disparages the Athenians for "forgetting their manhood" and wearing long, fancy robes fit for women. He would have men and women dress very plainly, but he recommends softer clothes and shoes for women and bare feet for men except soldiers.[119] He also requires men to be bearded and women to be "entirely covered" whenever not at home. The beard, he says, "lends the face dignity and paternal terror," whereas a clean-shaven face is disgraceful, as are "twisted locks" and "womanish ringlets" on a man.[120] Likewise, the third-century *Didascalia Apostolorum* and the fourth-century *Apostolic Constitutions* also forbid men to "unnaturally change the form of a man" by shaving their beards or wearing long hair or fancy hairdos.[121] Both works also require women to cover their heads in public.[122]

In the mid-fourth century, the Council of Gangra in Asia Minor condemned the Eustathians for despising marriage and encouraging women to live like men. Canon 13 condemns cross-dressing by women. Canon 17 condemns women cutting their hair, "which God gave her as the reminder of her subjection."[123] Gangra is among the local councils endorsed by the Quinisext Council in 692, which also condemns cross-dressing common at feasts of the pagan gods Bacchus and Pan. Canon 62 decrees "that no man from this time forth shall be dressed as a woman, nor any woman in the garb suitable to men."[124]

Strict sexual distinction supported an almost as strict division of labor according to natural differences between men and women. The sexes were said to share a common human nature but also different mental and physical abilities not limited to their reproductive roles.[125] "As man is considered to be more skillful in public duties, so woman is esteemed to be more adaptable to domestic ministrations," says Ambrose.[126] Clement of Alexandria says that "we do not train our women like Amazons to manliness in war, since we wish the men even to be peaceable."[127] He therefore recommends the gymnasium for boys but different diversions

---

119. Clement of Alexandria, *Paed.* 2.11, 2.12.
120. Clement of Alexandria, *Paed.* 3.11–12.
121. *Didascalia Apostolorum*, 2; *Apostolic Constitutions*, 1.2.
122. *Didascalia Apostolorum*, 3; *Apostolic Constitutions*, 1.3.
123. Gangra 17, in NPNF2 14, 99.
124. Gangra 62, in NPNF2 14, 393.
125. Cf. Clement of Alexandria, *Strom.* 4.8, 419–20.
126. Ambrose, *On Paradise*, 329.
127. Clement of Alexandria, *Strom.* 4.8.

for girls, consistent with their domestic duties.[128] In a day when many more daily necessities were manufactured at home, women were seen as possessing special skills that suited them to tasks contributing crucially to the wellbeing of all. "For it is God Himself who gave to woman-kind skill in woven work," says Chrysostom, who rejects woven work for men, saying, "Woe be to covetousness, which suffers not this difference to appear! For the general effeminacy hath gone so far as to introduce our men to the looms, and put shuttles into their hands, and the woof, and threads."[129] Chrysostom does not disparage women's work, however. Instead, he holds it up as equal to the work of men, saying a wife's work is such "that in spiritual things only wilt thou be able to surpass her."[130]

Besides the practical matter of different abilities, we find throughout early Christian teaching a concern for natural order and an association of gender disorder with sexual immorality, as above in Justin Martyr and here in Chrysostom, when, railing against Greek philosophy with Plato's *Republic* and *Symposium* in mind, he links women warriors with homosexuality as ultimate depravities:

> O ye subverters of all decency, who use men as if they were women, and lead out women to war as if they were men! This is the work of the devil, to subvert and confound all things, to overlap the boundaries that have been appointed from the beginning, and remove those which God has set to nature. For God assigned to woman the care of the house only, to the man the conduct of public affairs. But you reduce the head to the feet, and raise the feet to the head. You suffer women to bear arms, and are not ashamed.[131]

Thus, the segregation of men and women in church, like head-coverings for women, served two related purposes: the practical purpose of eliminating occasions for temptation and the pedagogical purpose of instilling in the faithful the proper regard for male and female. We have already heard Chrysostom bearing witness to the screens that separated the sexes in the church of his day.[132] The third-century *Apostolic Tradition*, the third-century

---

128. Clement of Alexandria, *Paed.* 3.10.

129. John Chrysostom, *Homily 34 on 1 Corinthians*, 205. Cf. John Chrysostom, *Homily 34 on 1 Corinthians*, 205.

130. John Chrysostom, *Homily 5 on 2 Thessalonians*, 397. Cf. John Chrysostom, *Homily 8 on 2 Timothy*, 505.

131. John Chrysostom, *Homily 5 on Titus*, 539.

132. John Chrysostom, *Homily 73 on Matthew*, 3.

*Didascalia Apostolorum*, and the fourth-century *Apostolic Constitutions* all separate men and women in church, as does Cyril of Jerusalem, who warns of the danger of temptation while also pointing out that the animals entering the Ark did so with their own kind.[133]

Silence was seen as an especially feminine form of piety, for the rule of silence is often repeated in the briefest summaries of behavior appropriate for women such as those already mentioned by Cyprian, Basil, Cyril of Alexandria, and the Quinisext Council. John Chrysostom says, "To such a degree should women be silent that they are not allowed to speak not only about worldly matters, but not even about spiritual things, in the church. This is order, this is modesty, this will adorn her more than any garments."[134] Ambrose recommends silence for virgins:

> I should prefer, therefore, that conversation should rather be wanting to a virgin, than abound. For if women are bidden to keep silence in churches, even about divine things, and to ask their husbands at home, what do we think should be the caution of virgins, in whom modesty adorns their age, and silence commends their modesty?[135]

Likewise, Basil, writing about female monastics, says that "in women's life more and greater modesty is required, as regards the virtues of poverty and quiet and obedience and sisterly love."[136] Gregory of Nazianzus praises both his sister and his mother for their silence. Of his mother, Nonna, he writes that "in the holy assemblies, or places, her voice was never to be heard except in the necessary responses of the service."[137] Of his sister, Gorgonia, he says, "Who had a fuller knowledge of the things of God, both from the Divine oracles, and from her own understanding? But who was less ready to speak, confining herself within the due limits of women?"[138] Jerome credits Marcella of Rome with the same modesty, saying that "when she answered questions she gave her own opinion not

---

133. Hippolytus, *Apostolic Tradition*, 18; *Didascalia Apostolorum*, 12; *Apostolic Constitutions*, 2.7; Cyril of Jerusalem, *Procatechesis*, 14.
134. John Chrysostom, *Homily 9 on 1 Timothy*, 435.
135. Ambrose, *On Virgins*, 382–83.
136. Basil, *Sermon 70*, 143–44.
137. Gregory of Nazianzus, *Oration on Nonna*, 257.
138. Gregory of Nazianzus, *Oration on Gorgonia*, 241.

as her own but as from me or someone else ... [so] she would not seem to inflict a wrong upon the male sex."[139]

Women sang in church as members of the congregation and sometimes also as separate choirs.[140] Ambrose writes, "The Apostle commands women to be silent in the church, but they may sing the psalms; this is fitting for every age and for both sexes."[141] Nuns also acted as readers and chanters in convents, but we have no record of women receiving the "priestly tonsure" required by Canon 33 of the Quinisext Council to be ranked among the clergy as readers or chanters, and it is only among heretics that we hear of women taking leading roles in the singing of cathedral or parish churches.[142] In the late fourth century, we hear calls for women not to sing in church. This is sometimes a complaint from monks against the showiness of singing in city churches, but it appears also at times to be a complaint not against women singing among the people but against women singing as readers or chanters.[143] Jerome seems to mean the latter when he relates singing to both reading and teaching in an attack on the Pelagians:

> Who does not know that women should sing the praises of the Lord—in their own chambers, far removed from the meetings of men and the assemblies of the multitude? But you permit what is not permissible, namely, that they do what should be performed by them secretly and without any witnesses as though they were lawfully constituted teachers.[144]

The connection between singing and teaching is more obvious when one considers that Scripture readings were chanted in church and known traditionally in English as "lessons" (from the Latin *lectio*, "a reading").

The prohibition on women teaching men was not absolute. Commenting on Acts 18:26, which says that Priscilla, with her husband

---

139. Jerome, *Letter 127*, 255–56.

140. See Quasten, *Music & Worship*, 79.

141. Ambrose, *Enarratio in Psalmum 1*, PL 14, 925A, quoted by Quasten, *Music & Worship*, 78.

142. The four Byzantine nuns are remembered for their hymnography: Kassia, Theodosia, and Thekla of the ninth century and Palaiologina of the fourteenth century. See Topping, *Sacred Songs*, 29–42.

143. For the monastic objection to the theatricality of church singing, see, e.g., Isidore of Pelusium, *Letter 1.90*, PG 78, 243–46. Also Quasten, *Music & Worship*, 81.

144. *Dialogus Adversus Pelagianos*, PL 23, 519A-B, in Quasten, *Music & Worship*, 82.

Aquila, taught Apollos, Chrysostom says 1 Tim 2:12 "concerns teaching from the pulpit and giving speeches in public, which belongs to priestly duties. But he does not forbid exhorting and advising in private."[145] As for public teaching, he says the matter is so plain that only the impious would question it, saying, "For, tell me, while Paul was teaching, or Peter, or those saints of old, had it been right that a woman should intrude into the office? Whereas we have gone on till we have come so debased, that it is worthy of question, why women are not teachers."[146]

Irenaeus of Lyon is sometimes cited in support of women prophesying in church, based on his mention of "men and women in the Church prophesying" (*viros et mulieres in Ecclesia prophetantes*), but these words are part of an argument against Montanism, and Irenaeus's point is not that both men and women prophesied *in church*, but that the gift of prophecy was already given to the Church at Pentecost, so Montanists sin against the Holy Spirit by claiming a "new outpouring" of the Spirit.[147] The setting of the prophesying is irrelevant to Irenaeus's argument and therefore not specified.

Likewise, Theodoret of Cyrus quotes Joel 2:28 ("I shall pour out my spirit upon all flesh, and your sons and your daughters will prophesy") to explain 1 Cor 14:34, saying, "Since, however, not only men but also women enjoyed grace . . . [Paul] had to regulate for the latter as well: 'Let your women keep silent in the churches.'"[148] The unknown Latin author of a fourth-century anti-Montanist dialogue also saw no conflict between 1 Cor 11 and 1 Cor 14, saying:

> We do not reject the prophesies of women. Blessed Mary prophesied when she said: "Henceforth all generations shall call me blessed." And as you yourself say, Philip had daughters who prophesied, and Mary, the sister of Aaron, prophesied. But we do not permit women to speak in the assemblies, nor to have authority over men.[149]

---

145. John Chrysostom, *Homily 1 on "Salute Priscilla and Aquila"* in Gryson, *The Ministry of Women*, 81–82. Cf. John Chrysostom, *Homily 31 on Romans*, 554; John Chrysostom, *Homily 9 on 1 Timothy*, 435–37; John Chrysostom, *Homily 4 on Titus*, 531–32; John Chrysostom, *Homily on 13 on Ephesians*, 116–17; John Chrysostom, *Homily 5 on 2 Thessalonians*, 397.

146. John Chrysostom, *Homily on 13 on Ephesians*, 116–17.

147. Irenaeus, *Adv. Haer.* 3.11, PG 7, 891A.

148. Theodoret of Cyrus, *Commentary on 1 Corinthians*, PG 82 347A, 1:223.

149. See Gryson, *The Ministry of Women*, 76.

The *Didascalia Apostolorum* and the *Apostolic Constitutions* also cite examples from the New and Old Testaments to say that women may teach or prophesy privately but not publicly.[150] Origen, commenting on Titus 2:3–4, is a bit more restrictive, "Certainly, women should also 'teach what is good,' but men should not sit and listen to a woman, as if there were no men capable of communicating the word of God." Of women teaching in an assembly, he says, "clearly this abuse is denounced as improper—an abuse for which the entire assembly is responsible."[151]

## Last Adam, New Eve

Just as there were sects that denied the good of marriage, there were sects that defied distinct roles for men and women—Montanists first and foremost, but also Collyridians and Quintillianists.[152] The Christian mainstream, however, remained firmly committed to traditional sex roles that were not doubted to be apostolic. Tertullian is the only Christian writer of note who, in his Montanist years, wrote in favor women prophesying in public, yet he also gives an example of a Montanist prophetess who would receive her revelations while in church but wait until afterwards to relate them to others privately.[153]

The gradual disappearance of deaconesses is sometimes assumed to have been part of a sexist shift in Christian thinking away from the egalitarianism of the apostolic era. Yet there is little evidence that the Church experienced such a shift. On the contrary, the Church consistently resisted challenges within and without to become more sexually egalitarian, both from heretical sects that featured women prominently in their leadership and worship and from assertive women rulers and aristocrats who often involved themselves in church matters more than Church leaders thought appropriate.[154] If anything, the Church experienced a shift in the opposite direction—toward a more egalitarian regard

---

150. *Didascalia Apostolorum*, 15, 132–38; *Apostolic Constitutions*, 3.1, 427–29.
151. Origen, Fr. 74 on 1 Corinthians, in Gryson, *The Ministry of Women*, 28–29.
152. Epiphanius, *Panarion*, 21–23, 620–29.
153. Tertullian, *On the Soul*, 188. Cf. Tertullian, *Against Marcion*, 445–46.
154. Of women rulers, there were very few. In the Byzantine Empire's 1,129 years (324–1453), women ruled as regents for about thirty-nine years and in their own right, without emperor-husbands, for just seven. See Ostrogorsky, *History of the Byzantine State*, 540.

for male and female denying neither their differences nor their order, but exalting both sexes as equally divine in their properly distinct relation.

Appreciation of this mystery began slowly. In the first century, the Apostle Paul wrote of Christ as the "last Adam" (1 Cor 15:45), saying, "The first man is of the earth, earthy; the second man is the Lord from heaven" (1 Cor 15:47). In the second century, Justin Martyr and Irenaeus of Lyon did the same for the Virgin Mary, establishing her as the "New Eve" in Christian thinking. Irenaeus writes:

> And if the former did disobey God, yet the latter was persuaded to be obedient to God, in order that the Virgin Mary might become the advocate of the virgin Eve. And thus, as the human race fell into bondage to death by means of a virgin, so is it rescued by a virgin; virginal disobedience having been balanced in the opposite scale by virginal obedience.[155]

Toward the middle of the same century, the Protevangelium of James appeared, a pseudepigraphic work originating or incorporating many Marian traditions.[156] The Church was slow to make use of the work, however, and for many years it seems the Virgin was out-shone by other female saints whose martyrdoms people had actually witnessed or whose tales were entertainingly told. Noting the paucity of icons of the Virgin Mary before the sixth century, Averil Cameron writes, "As a female figure of Christian devotion one might say that she was outranked by Thekla, the virginal heroine of the late second-century Acts of Paul and Thekla."[157] At the end of the fourth century, John Chrysostom could still speak publicly about Mary's impatience, incomprehension, and "superfluous vanity" without causing controversy.[158] But from the fifth century onward, the Church experienced a dramatic feminization of popular piety exalting Mary as the *Theotokos* ("Birth-giver of God") and making words such as Chrysostom's seem impious if not heretical.

That this trend was seen by some as a threat to the natural order is evident in the confrontation between the heresiarch Nestorius and the empress Pulcheria days after Nestorius was installed as archbishop of

---

155. Irenaeus, *Adv. Haer.* 5.19.1, 547, replacing "patroness" with "advocate" for *advocata*. Cf. Irenaeus, *Adv. Haer.* 3.22.4, and Justin Martyr, *Dialogue with Trypho*, 100.

156. Also known as the Infancy Gospel of James, it is first mentioned in the third century by Origen, *Commentary on Matthew*, 10.17.

157. See Cameron, "The Early Cult of the Virgin."

158. John Chrysostom, *Homily 44 on Matthew*, 279. Cf. John Chrysostom, *Homily 21 on John*, 74–75.

Constantinople in 428. Pulcheria was an avowed virgin devoted to the Theotokos and the first woman to rule as regent over the Roman Empire, on behalf of her younger brother, Theodosius II. Her regency lasted just two years (414–16), but she continued to influence Theodosius until his death in 450. As empress, Pulcheria was in the habit of communing in the altar with the emperor and the clergy, but when Nestorius saw her enter the altar for the first time, he barred her way, telling her that "only priests may walk here." Pulcheria is said to have replied, "Why? Have I not given birth to God?" Nestorius is said to have answered, "You? You have given birth to Satan!"[159] The incident raises the possibility that Nestorius's objection to the title *Theotokos* was in part a reaction to nascent feminism inspired by the veneration of the Virgin. Thereafter Nestorius gave more evidence of his disdain for women, excluding them from late night vigils and limiting their participation in other services, while Pulcheria plotted against him, making an issue of his refusal to honor Mary as the *Theotokos*.[160] In the end, Nestorius was condemned by the Third Ecumenical Council (Ephesus) in 431 and then deposed by Theodosius.

The Council of Ephesus inaugurated a new era of reflection on Mary's role in the Incarnation. Homilists and melodists turned to legendary and apocryphal works such as the Protevangelium of James for material with which to dedicate new churches and celebrate new feasts.[161] Before Pulcheria's death in 453, Constantinople had added two new Marian feasts and three new Marian churches, having had just one of each before Ephesus.[162] Jerusalem added three more Marian feasts in the sixth century (Nativity of the Theotokos, Entry into the Temple, and Dormition) and two more in the seventh (Annunciation and Conception of the Theotokos). Constantinople would add another in the ninth (Protection of the Theotokos) to celebrate the Virgin's deliverance of Constantinople from the besieging Slavs in 910.[163]

Yet the flourishing of the Virgin's cult did not fulfill Nestorius's fears of feminism. Little changed in relations between men and women

---

159. On the encounter between Pulcheria and Nestorius, see Holum, *Theodosian Empresses*, 152–55; Constas, "Weaving the Body of God," 173–74.

160. See Holum, *Theodosian Empresses*, 152.

161. The feast of the Dormition is based on several legends in circulation since the fourth century. See Limberis, "The Council of Ephesos," 321–40.

162. See Holum, *Theodosian Empresses*, 142–45; Limberis, "The Council of Ephesos," 321–22; Cunningham, "All-Holy Infant," 129, 136.

163. See Wybrew, *Orthodox Feasts of Jesus Christ and the Virgin Mary*, 16–22.

in the centuries that followed, and what did change was not a triumph for feminism, for the rise of the Theotokos coincided with the decline of the female diaconate, suggesting the possibility that the former contributed to the latter, not by changing the gender order but by challenging it, thereby obliging Church Fathers to exercise more care in maintaining apostolic limits.[164]

A more obvious and more profound effect of the rise of the Theotokos was to concentrate Christian attention on the virtues of motherhood and virginity. This was the focus of Proclus of Constantinople in a provocative sermon preached in Nestorius's presence in 428, on the Virgin's original memorial feast-day, December 26, about which Proclus declared, "The mystery it celebrates is the boast of the whole race of women and the glory of the feminine, on her account who was at once mother and maiden."[165] The veneration of Mary as the Theotokos was justified at Ephesus by the divinity of Christ in the womb, but the popular appeal of the Theotokos before and after Ephesus was as an ever-loving, never-judging, wonder-working *übermutter* who keeps her children safe and intercedes on their behalf before her son, the judge. That is how she appears in the earliest known hymn to the Theotokos, dating from the third or fourth century: "Beneath thy compassion, we take refuge, O Theotokos: Despise not our supplications in adversities: but deliver us from perils, O only pure, only blessed one."[166]

Thus, instead of overthrowing gender stereotypes, the veneration of the Theotokos reinforced them by glorifying feminine humanity in the role of virgin and mother, thereby redeeming the daughters of Eve from the reproach of all misogynists. From thenceforth, orthodox Christians would worship with always two images before them, two distinct models of divine humanity, one male and one female, the Last Adam and the New Eve—not sexual partners, not husband and wife, but man and woman as they are meant ultimately to be.

---

164. On the disappearance of deaconesses, see Martimort, *Deaconesses*; Mitchell, *The Disappearing Deaconess*.

165. *Acta conciliorum oecumenicorum*, 1.1.1, 103, in Holum, *Theodosian Empresses*, 155.

166. On the dating of the hymn, see O'Carroll, *Theotokos*, 336.

## Conclusion: Continuity and Consensus

Between the more mainstream Fathers of this chapter and the more speculative Fathers of the preceding chapter was a fundamental difference of vision: Whereas the latter treated male and female extremely narrowly and negatively as a strictly bodily difference valued only as an embarrassing means of reproduction, the former took a much broader view, seeing more to male and female than marriage and more to marriage than reproduction. They therefore dealt not just with the issue of the relative value of celibacy versus marriage but also with the issue of gender order in the family, in the Church, and in the world, about which the leading theorists of the preceding chapter had little or nothing to say.

The mainstream view of marriage and sexual distinction made both *more* meaningful to Christians than they were to both the Hebrews and the Greeks. Mainstream Christians viewed marriage as a "great mystery"—a small-scale realization of the self-giving and thanks-giving head-and-body unity of Christ and the Church, meaningful for that reason and not just as a means of reproduction. They viewed the man and the woman as similar and equal on account of the woman being made from the man, but also different in important ways and ordered on account of both their creation and their fall. Many viewed the "image of God" as a matter of relation, with the man taking the God-like roles of source and lord toward the woman but both the man and the woman taking the same roles toward children and the world. They viewed the Fall as a matter of mis-relation on account of pride, not desire for physical pleasure, paying closer attention to the text of Genesis 2 and 3 than did the speculators. They likewise read Gal 3:28 in context, as a comment on what both men and women share in Christ, without absolutizing its mention of male and female. They reinforced distinctly different roles for men and women in the Church and in the world, condemning the blurring of male and female in the strongest possible terms and obliging men and women to behave as either men or women even in private prayer, either baring their heads as men or covering their heads as women. They balanced the value of virginity as an expression of spiritual purity with the good of marriage as a type of church. They also balanced the economic order subjecting the woman to the man with the eschatological goal of divinized humanity that is still distinctly male or female, as exemplified by Christ and the Theotokos. To the Apostle Paul's analogy of Christ to Adam, the Fathers added the analogy of the Virgin Mary to Eve, setting icons of the Theotokos alongside icons of Christ, holding up for veneration two distinct models of humanity—not consciously to reinforce the gender order but unconsciously expressing and reinforcing the Christian ideals of man and woman.

This view was not, as we have seen, the only Christian view of male and female, but it was the dominant Christian view, the view that could be preached publicly without controversy, and the more appealing view to both Christians and non-Christians. It certainly did not meet present standards of gender equality and was of course diametrically opposed to today's rebellion against the binary of male and female, but it was more reasonable, more equitable, and more humane than the culture it replaced (addicted as that culture was to sexual slavery and pedophilia), as well as more biblical, more traditional, and more natural than the antisexual philosophy of the Greeks and their Christian imitators.

# 6

# "That They May Be One, Even as We Are One"

THE FOREGOING CONTRAST OF Greek and Hebrew thinking about male and female has demonstrated two very different approaches to righteousness—the Greek approach concentrating on personal perfection and enlightenment aimed at union with God, and the Hebrew approach aimed at relating rightly to others as couples, as families, as a religious community, and as children of God. Early Christians preached both approaches with differing degrees of emphasis and sometimes tension. Both may be said to be required by the two "Great Commandments" named by Christ as summing up the Law and the Prophets: "Thou shalt love the Lord thy God with all thy heart, and with all thy soul, and with all thy mind," and "Thou shalt love thy neighbor as thyself" (Matt 22:37–39; cf. Lev 19:18; Deut 6:5; Mark 12:30–31; Luke 10:27; also Rom 13:9; Gal 5:14; Jas 2:8).

This last chapter will critique the impact of each approach to righteousness on Christian thinking about male and female, demonstrating the difficulty of reconciling the two views before offering a theological basis for male and female that challenges a key assumption of the Greek Christian view—that male and female have no part in the image of God—by relating male and female to a particularly divine form of love, the self-giving love of the Father for the Son and of Christ for the Church, to which Christians are also called by the "new commandment" given by Christ to His disciples at the Last Supper: "That ye love one another, as I have loved you" (John 15:12, cf. 13:34; 15:17).

## The Greek Way

The Church's Greek inheritance focused early Christians much more on the first Great Commandment. Aristotle saw man as a social being inclined by nature to both marriage and politics, but most philosophers after Aristotle (Stoics, Epicureans, Neopythagoreans, and Neoplatonists) imagined man as more of a solitary being whose main aim was escape from suffering. The Neoplatonist escape was an ascent of the soul from diverse, changeable, sensible matter toward the perfectly unitary and purely intelligible source of all being. The practice of social virtues was just the first step in this ascent: One learned to live with others before progressing to the study of arts and sciences and then of philosophy in preparation for ultimate enlightenment, conceived as an ecstatic experience of the divine. Intellect mattered more than relation in this ascent, which only superior intellects could achieve. Other people often hindered the philosopher's progress by involving him in the swirling diversity of the material world. They were distractions, temptations, and often enemies—ignorant prisoners of the cave who resisted enlightenment because it threatened the only world they knew. For their own good, philosophers therefore resorted to secrecy, deception, and detachment. They were elitists in principle, believing themselves wiser than others and dealing differently with the knowing few and the unknowing many. Humility was not a philosophic virtue, neither did the philosophers have much to say about loving one's neighbor, much less loving one's spouse. The love that concerned them most was not the self-giving *agapē* of Christ's Great Commandments (and Ephesians 5) but the selfish *erōs* of Plato, understood as a passionate desire to possess beauty, either the intelligible beauty of things above or the merely sensible beauty of things below. The pleasure of the latter was to be avoided as a pull in the wrong direction. The passion of *erōs* for other persons was also to be avoided as unnecessary, irrational, disturbing, embarrassing, dangerous, and, when consummated, defiling. It was therefore a passion "from which good men are free."[1]

Such thinking entered Christian thought very early. We first hear of it in the Apostle Paul's warning that "in the latter times some shall depart from the faith, giving heed to seducing spirits, and doctrines of devils... forbidding to marry and commanding to abstain from meats" (1 Tim 4:1–3). The Encratites of the second century fulfilled the Apostle's

---

1. D.L. 7.113, summarizing the Stoic view of *erōs*.

prophecy, despising marriage and preaching an end to male and female, or at least an end to female. In the same century, Valentinus of Alexandria introduced among Christians the Platonic vision of the descent and ascent of souls to and from the material world. The Valentinian vision included a claim of secret knowledge, a spiritual elite of the knowing few, a process of creation and redemption aimed at returning souls to their original unity, and an explicitly erotic notion of spiritual ascent. Origen of Alexandria contended against Valentinianism but on the basis of the same basic vision, inspired also by the Platonism of fellow Alexandrians Philo and Ammonius Saccas, the former of which pioneered the allegorical approach to Hebrew Scripture in imitation of the Platonist approach to Greek myth.

Origen's own speculations and allegorizations proved both influential and controversial, inspiring the extreme Origenism of Evagrius Ponticus as well as the moderate Origenism of Gregory of Nyssa. A recurring complaint against Origenists was that they taught an end to male and female in the resurrection, which seemed to deny the resurrection of the body. Evagrius was accused and condemned for such teaching; Gregory escaped condemnation by insisting on bodily resurrection and obscuring the full significance of his beliefs about male and female. Nevertheless, the two shared the same basic conception of salvation as a radically transformative process maximizing the discontinuity of the human condition from creation to redemption and minimizing the significance of the body relative to the soul. For Evagrius, this meant the fall of the soul into the body and the eventual elimination of the body and all personal differences in the apocatastasis, when all things would return to their original unity; for Gregory, it meant the fall of the body into the beastly, unnatural condition of "coats of skins," followed by an angelic afterlife in a body but without the "signs" of male and female or the passions caused by them.

Maximus the Confessor capped the development of such thinking with a fuller correction of the Origenist scheme, further minimizing the body by denying the soul any blameless experience of the body before its instantaneous fall and by denying the body any definite relevance in the resurrection, when the redeemed would supposedly be as unbounded by human nature as the resurrected Christ. On the matter of male and female, he followed Gregory very closely but with a bolder declaration of the necessity of abandoning the "division" and "difference" of male and female as the first step in reuniting Creator and creation.

To be sure, Christian contributors to this long-standing tradition of Alexandrian Platonism had more to say about loving one's neighbor than their pagan counterparts, but they typically emphasized a generic love for others without distinction as a practice of Christian virtue. Maximus has the most to say about love, but he frequently stresses equality of love for one's neighbors without distinction or special attachment.[2] He writes:

> He who is perfect in love and has attained the summit of detachment knows no difference between "mine and thine," between faithful and unfaithful, between slave and freeman, or indeed between male and female. Having risen above the tyranny of the passions and looking to nature, one in all men, he considers all equally and is disposed equally toward all. For in Him there is neither Greek nor Jew, neither male nor female, neither slave nor freeman, but everything and in all things Christ.[3]

Here, in writing of perfect love and the summit of dispassion, Maximus would seem to speak of a far-off end state in which human beings (if they could still be called that) are not merely most angelic but most Godlike. A similar end is also the aim of Neoplatonism, and for both Christians and Neoplatonists this end is not simply bestowed on us by God but is achieved by us through contemplation and ascetic labor, which must include practicing and mastering the loving of all equally if that is our goal.

Yet, unless love means merely a vague wish of good for others, we are doomed to fail at the task of loving all equally. For if love also means doing actual good to others, then we, as finite beings, cannot love all others equally; we can only love *some* others, the particular others God has brought our way, and we can only love them within the limits of our encounter with them. The greater our experience of others, the more we will be able to love them, not just in quantity but also in quality. For the greater our experience is of others, the more we will be able to love them not as generic human beings but as the beautifully unique creatures they truly are.

Yet, of love for particular human beings—for the actual men and women who are in flesh and blood our neighbors, including parents, spouses, and children—Maximus had little or nothing to say, so focused was he on a theoretical love for all.

---

2. See Sherwood, *Maximus the Confessor*, 93, 238n398. Sherwood identifies seven instances in which Maximus insists on equality in his *Four Centuries on Charity*: 1.17, 1.24, 1.25, 1.61, 1.71, 2.10, 2.30.

3. Maximus, *Char.* 2.30, 158.

## The Hebrew Way

Compared to this Greek approach to righteousness leaning heavily on the first Great Commandment, the Hebrew approach to righteousness was more balanced. Both commandments come from Hebrew Scripture (the first from Deut 6:5, the second from Lev 19:18), and the whole history of the Hebrew people is a history of dual concern for oneness with both God and each other. The precedence of the first Great Commandment is dramatically established very early by Abraham's aborted sacrifice of Isaac, in which Abraham demonstrates his willingness to put God before his own flesh and blood. Afterwards, several other pivotal events in Hebrew history demonstrate the importance of neighborly love, including Jacob humbly making peace with his brother Esau, for which God gave him the name *Israel* ("He who rivals God"), and then Joseph generously forgiving his brothers for their betrayal and blessing their descendants as the twelve tribes of Israel.

The Israelites struggled to keep both commandments, at times forsaking God and each other and later often making more of their relation by blood than their relation in faith. This was clearly demonstrated by the chief priests and Pharisees when they decided that for the sake of the nation this Jesus must die (John 11:47–53), a decision later ratified by the mob in their choice of a known villain, Barabbas, over the innocent Christ. Christ himself preaches plainly against such tribal ethics in his parable of the Good Samaritan (Luke 10:25–37), expanding the definition of "neighbor" in Lev 19:18 to all men, at least all men one is given an opportunity to love.

Having noted Maximus's emphasis on loving all equally, we ought now ask: What if the man left for dead along the way had been the Samaritan's own son? Would the Samaritan have been a loving father doing for his own son only what he did for the stranger? Hardly. God and nature both ordain that fathers take greater responsibility for their own sons than for someone else's, doing more for them, which means loving them more.

Such love by itself does not make man less Godlike. Does the Father not love the Son more than He loves us? Does Christ not love His mother more than He loves us? Only in the absence of a higher love for God does the love of sons, of tribes, of "me and mine," become selfish and idolatrous. Fortunately for the Hebrews, they had both Great Commandments epitomizing their law and prophets, which all together gave them what the Greeks did not have—a well-defined social concept, including a firm code of sexual ethics, grounded in their experience of God. Their relationship with God defined and supported their relationships with each other.

After love for God, the love most often in view in Hebrew Scripture is the love not of husbands and wives but of parents for their children. Marriage was largely taken for granted as natural and good, but children were the most longed-for gift from God, the capstone of a good life, the source of their fathers' and mothers' greatest joy or greatest grief. With the coming of Christ, the love of fathers and mothers for their children took on even greater meaning, with the names Father and Son signifying the supreme love of God for God; with the love of God for us demonstrated by the Father's giving of His Only-begotten Son; with the Son teaching us to pray to the Father as "Our Father"; and with us responding gratefully to the Father as His adopted sons, in imitation of the Son's humble obedience to the Father.

The coming of Christ also revealed the fuller meaning of marriage by the Apostle Paul's analogy of the man and the woman both to Christ and the Church (Eph 5) and to the Father and the Son (1 Cor 11). Each of these relationships is based on one party being the source of the other party: The Son comes from the Father, the Church comes from Christ, and the woman comes from the man in the Hebrew account of creation. That account connects the image of God with the distinction of male and female, crediting God with creation of both the image and the distinction at the same time and then declaring His whole work of creation "very good." Hebrew Scripture preserved this sense of the goodness of creation and of male and female, along with clear parameters for how the man and the woman were to relate to each other in sexually distinct ways.

The Hebrews were also always strongly communal. Their personal identity was closely tied to their corporate identity as "children of Israel." They kept faith with God and each other by regular rituals, both individual and corporate. They understood the second Great Commandment as an obligation to aid other children of Israel and created communities of their own, anchored by synagogues, wherever they went. Much more could be said about the importance of community to the Hebrews. The point here is that the Hebrew path of righteousness was not the philosopher's selfish, solitary, ascetic, intellectual escape from the body and ascent to the One, in which other people were incidental distractions if sometimes also teachers and pupils; it was a life decently lived always in the body as well as always with and for other people sharing a kinship of faith and blood.

The early Church, heeding the nearly equal emphasis of the Gospels on both Great Commandments, continued in this tradition, replicating the community of the Old Covenant in the community of the New Covenant. The children of the "New Israel" were more open to outsiders, stressing relation by faith much more than relation by blood, but they also theologized marriage and made parenthood their model for priesthood without sexualizing God or divinizing coitus. The Church also valued solitary asceticism and offered monasticism as an alternative to marriage. It held the former to be theoretically superior as a greater dedication to God, but communal spirituality always took precedence over individual asceticism. All need not forsake marriage and family to be saved, but all must live as parts of the Body, communing regularly together, respecting the bonds of marriage and family relationships, and submitting to one another in the sexually distinct manner prescribed by the Apostles.

## Remaining Differences

Still, it must be admitted that the Church of the first seven centuries was of two minds on male and female. Some Church Fathers took a more Greek Christian view, minimizing the good of marriage as well as the significance of sexual distinction, identifying both with our sinful condition and therefore believing that both would be left behind in the grave. Other Church Fathers took a more Hebrew Christian view, seeing more love than lust in marriage and assuming sexual distinction to be fundamental to human existence, part of the goodness of creation that endures even in the afterlife. The Greek view was controversial and was therefore developed cautiously and sometimes surreptitiously, mainly in monastic circles, receiving its plainest expression from Maximus the Confessor; the Hebrew view was more evident all along in Scripture and tradition and therefore less controversial as well as less developed theoretically on account of the Church's trust in Scripture, tradition, common experience, and commonsense to maintain sexual sanity and social order.

Can the two be reconciled?

Alfred Kentigern Siewers has argued that there is really no conflict between them, that Maximus the Confessor provides a positive valuation of marriage and sexual distinction as a necessary though temporary "mean" between the "extremes" of archetypal intention and eschatological perfection.[4] The problem with this mean-between-extremes argument is that it begs the question of what "male and female" means in Maximus. Is it just sexuality in the sense of passionate attraction and intercourse driven by desire for pleasure and progeny? Or is it also the passionate "complications, prejudices, and discriminations" supposed by Doru Costache? In others words, is "male and female" merely sex, or is it also gender, such that its "shaking off" means the "liberation of humankind from the tyranny of gender categories"?[5]

If "male and female" is the latter, then it is hard to see how the Greek Christian and Hebrew Christian views can be reconciled. The Hebrew Christian view obliges us to practice living as either male or female all our lives. Its understanding of right and wrong, of beauty and abomination, are based in part on the natural goodness of sexual distinction. Respecting that goodness requires us, quite literally, to discriminate between male and female—to recognize the difference and base our behavior on it. "Shaking off" this understanding, after the experience of consciously practicing it all our lives, would require us to forget much of what we have learned about who we are individually and corporately, which happens to be, not surprisingly, the expectation of Plotinus, who says the soul forgets its experience of the body once it has escaped the body.[6] If we are not to forget, then we must unlearn, but unlearning requires time. It is a process. When would the process begin? What is this life for, if not to learn now what we will need to know later? If "male and female" means more in Maximus than sexuality, if it means what is now called "gender," then it makes no sense for us to continue practicing gender; we must begin now the practice of shaking it off.

If, on the other hand, "male and female" means only passionate attraction and intercourse, then, at the very least, we must say that Maximus's understanding of male and female is extremely narrow—too narrow to explain the broad range of observable sex differences, many of which have no direct relation to sexuality; too narrow to justify the gender order of the early Church, with its subjection of women and insistence on

---

4. Siewers uses Maximus to defend traditional marriage by arguing against "sexual identitism," claiming that Christianity allows two modes of life: "being and becoming a man or a woman in marriage or a celibate virgin monastic." See Siewers, "Mystagogical, Cosmological, and Counter-Cultural," 353–94, esp. 368–69.

5. Costache, "Mapping Reality," 287.

6. Plotinus, *Enneads* 4.3.31–4.4.2.

differentiation in appearance and behavior; too narrow even to justify his own claim that in the next life men and women will be no longer men and women but "merely human beings [*anthrōpous monon*]," for if the passion of sex is all that is shaken off, then resurrected human beings will remain not just recognizably male or female but fundamentally male and female in every cell of their bodies—still very different beings.[7] The only way Maximus can claim that men and women will no longer be men and women is if all surviving sex differences no longer matter in any way, but in that case we are back to denying the relevance of gender and to shaking it off as a necessary first act in the reuniting of Creator and creation.[8]

It would seem, then, that the Greek Christian and Hebrew Christian views on male and female are irreconcilable, differing as they do on a fundamental aspect of human nature that is significantly definitive of personal identity in the only life we know and therefore relevant to both this world and the next. One holds that male and female is a temporary imposition on human nature solely for the purpose of procreation, having nothing to do with the image of God and therefore impeding the process of *theosis*, whereby human beings realize their calling to become more and more like God; the other abominates the blurring of male and female, believing human nature to be complete in two sexes, both bearing the image of God, each expressing the image in its own way as God intended and declared "very good."

But how valid is the key Greek Christian assumption that male and female have nothing to do with the image of God? The evidence already provided from Scripture and the Fathers gives us reason to wonder, as both clearly link male and female to the plurality of Persons in the Trinity, giving us a basis for a relational understanding of both the image of God and male and female, which the rest of this chapter will demonstrate.

---

7. Maximus, *Amb.* 41, 9.

8. Thus, commenting on the "one who is perfect in love" in Maximus's *Chapters on Love* (2.30), Archimandrite Aimilianos of Simonopetra writes: "That you are male or female is mere information to such a person; it is not something that conditions the way his being responds and relates to the world, because he is no longer seeing the world through the filter of his passions." See Aimilianos of Simonopetra, *The Mystical Marriage*, 176.

## The Image of God

The first scriptural mention of male and female appears in Gen 1:27: "So God created man in his own image, in the image of God created he him; male and female created he them." This verse, and its reprise in Gen 5:1–2, could be read as a Hebrew parallelism, a poetic way of saying the same thing twice. Parallelisms abound in the Psalms: "Purge me with hyssop and I shall be clean: Wash me and I shall be whiter than snow" (Ps 50/51:7). Read in such a way, Gen 1:27 and 5:1–2 would indicate a relation between the image of God and the distinction of male and female. Indeed, the animals created before man are not said to be distinguished by sex in Gen 1. Only when a creature is made in the image of God does the distinction male and female enter the picture.

The Apostle Paul draws two analogies between God and the sexes based on headship: The man is the "head" of the woman as God is the "head" of Christ (1 Cor 11:3) and as Christ is the "head" of the Church (Eph 5:23). He also relates the first analogy to the image of God, saying the man is the "image and glory of God" and the woman is the "glory of the man" (1 Cor 11:7). We have seen in chapter 5 how John Chrysostom, Ephrem the Syrian, Clement of Alexandria, Theodoret of Cyrus, and others of the Antiochene school related headship and the image of God to dominion, per Gen 1:26–28.[9] We have also seen how Cyril of Alexandria, Theodoret of Cyrus, and Clement of Alexandria, related headship and image to source of being, with Clement saying, "the human being becomes the image of God, by cooperating in the creation of another human being," and Cyril and Theodoret saying the woman takes her being from the man as the Son takes his being from the Father.[10]

Yet the Fathers of the Church all avoided describing God as male and female—some because they identified the image of God with the sexless soul, some because they associated femininity with weakness, but all because their conception of God did not extend, in Tikva Frymer-Kensky's words, "below the waist."[11] Describing God as male and female would have projected too much humanity on God, sexualizing divinity in a Gnostic or pagan way. Some modern scholars have been more daring,

---

9. See McLeod, *The Image of God in the Antiochene Tradition*, 205–49.

10. Cyril of Alexandria, *Commentary on 1 Corinthians 11*, 879–82; Theodoret, *Commentary on 1 Corinthians 11*, 309–14; Clement of Alexandria, *Paed.* 2.10.83, quoted in Ford, *Women and Men in the Early Church*, 30n84.

11. Frymer-Kensky, *In the Wake of Goddesses*, 188.

associating the sexes in one way or another with one or more Persons of the Trinity, as noted in chapter 1, but these attempts have not won general acceptance, satisfying neither feminists, because they tend still to subordinate the female to the male, nor traditionalists, because they stray too far from the traditional Christian conception of God.

Yet there is a way to relate male and female to God that is more respectful of tradition, more illuminating of personal relationships (both sexual and nonsexual), and more supportive of the spiritual equality of the sexes. This better way, instead of starting with man and projecting stereotypically male and female characteristics on God, would start with God and search the Scriptures and the Fathers for what they say about the Father, Son, and Holy Spirit, before considering how the man and the woman might "image" them.

The Gospels tell us very little about the Holy Spirit but quite a lot about the Father and the Son. Many things said of one are also said of the other. They are both said to know the other (John 10:15) and dwell in the other (John 10:38; 14:10–11, 20; 17:21) as one (John 10:30; 17:21). Each is said to reveal the other: The Father acknowledges the Son at his baptism (Matt 3:17; 17:5; Mark 1:11; Luke 3:22; cf. 2 Pet 1:17); the Son reveals the Father through his words and deeds (Matt 11:27; Luke 10:22; John 1:18; 14:9). Each is said to honor and glorify the other: The Father honors (John 8:54; 2 Pet 1:17) and glorifies (John 17:1, 5, 24; Acts 3:13; cf. 2 Pet 1:17) the Son; the Son honors (John 8:49) and glorifies (John 17:1, 4; cf. 14:13) the Father. Both are said to love the other, but, significantly, the Father is said to love the Son eleven times (Matt 3:17; 17:5; Mark 1:11; 9:7; Luke 3:22; 9:35; John 3:35; 5:20; 10:17; 15:9; 17:24; cf. 2 Pet 1:17), whereas the Son said to love the Father just once (John 14:31), which is consistent with the Old Testament pattern of parents and husbands being said more often to love children or wives than *vice versa*.[12] Both the Father and the Son are said to send the Holy Spirit: The Father is said to send Holy Spirit in Son's name (John 14:26), while the Son is said to send the Holy Spirit from the Father (John 15:26).

---

12. Susan Ackerman observes that Michal, David's wife, is the only woman said to love a man in the Bible (1 Sam 18:20) and that most persons said to love others are the dominant person in the relationship, i.e., fathers, mothers, or husbands (four of them: Isaac in Gen 24:67, Jacob in Gen 29:18, Samson in Judg 16:4, and Elkanah in 1 Sam 1:5). Ackerman therefore suggests that Michal saw herself as outranking David on account of her being Saul's daughter. This would also hold true for Jonathan, Saul's son and heir, who is said to love David (1 Sam 18:1–3; 20:17; 23:17). See Ackerman, "The Personal is Political," 437–58.

Many other things are said of one but not the other. Here is a brief comparison from the Scriptures of what one does to or for the other that the other does not do in return:

- The Father gives (Matt 11:27; 20:23; Luke 10:22; John 3:16, 35; 5:22, 26–27, 36; 6:37, 39; 13:3; 17:2, 4, 8–9, 11; 18:11), knows (Mark 13:32), shows (John 5:19–20, 30, 35; 16:13), teaches (John 8:28), sends (John 5:23–24, 30, 35–37; 6:38–39, 44, 57; 8:16, 18, 42; 12:44–45, 49; 14:26; 17:18, 23, 25; 20:21; 1 John 4:14), commands (John 10:18; 12:49–50; 14:31; 15:10), empowers (Luke 22:29; John 5:19–22), sanctifies (John 10:36), and exalts (Phil 2:9) the Son.
- The Son thanks the Father (Matt 11:25; Luke 10:21; John 11:41), comes from the Father (John 16:27–28), humbles himself and becomes obedient to the Father (Phil 2:8), does the will and works of the Father (Matt 26:39, 42; Mark 14:36; Luke 22:42; John 5:17, 30, 36; 10:25, 32, 37; 14:10–12), pleases (Luke 3:22; John 8:39), petitions (Matt 26:39, 42, 53; Mark 14:36; John 12:27; 14:16; 16:26; 17:11), confesses the Father as "greater than I" (John 14:28; cf. 10:29), and returns to the Father (John 13:1, 14:12, 28; 16:16–17, 28; 17:11, 13; 20:17).

The contrast between the Father and the Son is quite clear: The Father is said many times to be loving and giving, and the Son is said many times to be thankful and obedient. Not once in Holy Scripture is the Father said to thank the Son, and not once in Holy Scripture is the Son said to give anything to the Father *except thanks*. This defines their relationship more clearly than anything else: The Father gives to the Son all that he has, even his very being; the Son in return gives thanks to the Father, showing his thanks by doing the Father's will.

In the Gospel of John, the Father is the source of both the Son and the Holy Spirit. All that they do begins with him; all that they say they hear first from him. Christ tells the Apostles, "The Son can do nothing of himself, but what he seeth the Father do: for what things soever he doeth, these also doeth the Son likewise. For the Father loveth the Son, and showeth him all things that himself doeth" (John 5:19–20). And, "I can of my own self do nothing; as I hear, I judge: and my judgment is just; because I seek not my own will, but the will of the Father which hath sent me" (John 5:30). The same applies to the Holy Spirit, "for he shall not speak of himself; but whatsoever he shall hear, that shall he speak" (John 16:13). In the words of John of Damascus:

> All then that the Son and the Spirit have is from the Father, even their very being, and unless the Father is, neither the Son nor the Spirit is. And unless the Father possesses a certain attribute, neither the Son nor the Spirit possesses it.[13]

The Son and Holy Spirit share the Father's very essence (*ousia*), from which, says Gregory of Nazianzus, "flows both the equality and the being of equals."[14] The three are thus each free, equal, fully God, and perfectly one not despite but *because of* the Father being the source of the Son and the Holy Spirit.

## Archy Versus Hierarchy

At this point, it would help to put a name to the peculiar kind of relationship we have just described—a relationship that is both ordered and equal based on one person being the self-giving source of a thanks-giving other.

As noted in chapter 1, John Zizioulas—without distinguishing relations on the basis of self-giving and thanks-giving, as I have here—has defended the *monarchy* of the Father based on the Father being the *monē archē* of the Son. But Zizioulas's use of *monarchy* and *hierarchy* does not match patristic usage or current popular understanding. Patristic ascription of *monarchia* to the Trinity expressed, not relations within the Trinity, but the oneness of the Trinity in support of the equality of the Son to the Father. Thus Gregory of Nazianzus contrasts the "polyarchy" and "anarchy" of the pagan pantheon with the "monarchy" of the Christian Godhead, which is "a monarchy not limited to one Person."[15] Furthermore, as currently used, the term *monarchy* carries considerable baggage. Its political use implies inequality and to some even tyranny, while its theological use suggests the heresies of subordinationism (denying the equality of the Son and Holy Spirit) or monarchianism (denying that there are actually three persons within the Godhead). Zizioulas's use of the term *hierarchy* is even more problematic because inequality and subordination are the very basis of *hierarchy* as originally conceived by

---

13. John of Damascus, *Exact Exposition of the Orthodox Faith*, 9.
14. Gregory of Nazianzus, *Oration on Holy Baptism*, 375.
15. Gregory of Nazianzus, *Third Theological Oration*, 301.

Pseudo-Dionysius, who defined *hierarchy* as a "sacred order and science and operation" for the purification, illumination, and perfection of the less godlike by the more godlike.[16] All hierarchical relation is therefore a matter of mediation between highers and lowers. For this reason, Pseudo-Dionysius does not describe the Trinity as a hierarchy, as doing so would constitute subordinationism and betray a patently Neoplatonic conception of God.

Pseudo-Dionysius also does not describe relations within the family or between the sexes as hierarchical. He explains hierarchy among humans the same way he explains hierarchy among angels, even though humans relate to other humans in ways angels do not relate to other angels. Unlike angels, humans sometimes relate to each other causally: They reproduce. This is a major difference between the Neoplatonist hierarchy of Proclus and the Christian hierarchy of Dionysius. The activity of the Dionysian hierarchy is not causative; its angels neither create as God does nor reproduce as humans do.[17] Dionysius, however, has nothing to say about this difference. He treats man as merely a fallen, flesh-bearing angel.

Dionysius does, however, acknowledge the causative nature of relations within the Trinity, writing that the Father is the "source" (*pēgē*) and "cause" (*aitia*) of the Son and the Spirit and that the names *Father*, *Son*, and *Holy Spirit* are not interchangeable, for "the Father is not a Son nor is the Son a Father."[18] He also quotes Scripture to argue that "the entire wholeness [of divinity] is participated in by each of those who participate in it; none participates in only a part."[19] And among them, "there is distinction in unity, and there is unity in distinction."[20] Furthermore, "Each of the divine persons continues to possess his own praiseworthy

---

16. Pseudo-Dionysius, *CH*, 3.1, PG 3 164D, trans. by Parker. Cf. Pseudo-Dionysius, *Letter 8 to Demophilus*, 2, PG 3 1092B.

17. Bradshaw (*Aristotle East and West*, 186) writes, "The hierarchy of Proclus, like its predecessor in Plotinus, is concerned with how things come into being. . . . The Dionysian hierarchies, by contrast, are concerned not with how thing come into being but with purification, illumination, and perfection." Eric Perl disagrees, saying that in Proclus, "Illumination is production, and in both Dionysius and his Neoplatonist forbears it is at once direct and hierarchically mediated." See Perl, *Theophany*, 74. Nevertheless, Dionysius himself nowhere equates illumination and production.

18. Pseudo-Dionysius, *DN* 2, PG 3 641D, 645B.

19. John 10:30; 16:15; 17:10; Pseudo-Dionysius, *DN* 2, PG 3 637B–C, 641B, 644A. Luibheid's translation.

20. Pseudo-Dionysius, *DN* 2, PG 3 641B. Luibheid's translation.

characteristics, so that one has here examples of unions and of differentiations in the inexpressible unity and subsistence of God."[21]

Thus, Dionysius himself provides us a model for loving unions of distinct yet equal persons who share the same nature equally on account of one being the source of the others, yet who relate to one another in distinct ways. But he cannot call it *hierarchy*, and neither can we without confusion. We can, however, call it *archy* on account of the identification of the Father as the *Archē* of both the Son and the Holy Spirit—the "principle" of their being, indeed, their very "beginning."

Defending the equal divinity of the Son amidst the fourth-century Eunomian controversy, Gregory of Nazianzus confessed his fear of referring to the Father as the *Archē* of the Son and Holy Spirit, saying:

> I should like to call the Father the greater because from Him flows both the Equality and the Being of Equals (this will be granted on all hands), but I am afraid to use the word Origin [*Archē*], lest I should make Him the Origin of Inferiors, and thus insult Him by precedencies of honor. For the lowering of those Who are from Him is no glory to the Source.[22]

Nevertheless, Gregory himself elsewhere acknowledged the Father as the *Archē achronos* ("Eternal Principle") whom Christ came to represent.[23] Some modern theologians resist naming the Father as the *archē* of the Son, but many ancient theologians did just that, including Gregory of Nyssa, Methodius of Olympus, Epiphanius of Salamis, John of Damascus, Eusebius of Caesarea, and the Alexandrians Athanasius, Cyril, Dionysius, and Origen.[24] Some of the aforesaid might be fairly accused of subordinationism, but John of Damascus, speaking for the patristic consensus in the eighth century, is quite clear that the *archic* relation of the Father to the Son does not make the Son unequal to the Father:

> But if we say that the Father is the origin [*archē*] of the Son and greater than the Son, we do not suggest any precedence in time or superiority in nature of the Father over the Son (for through

---

21. Pseudo-Dionysius, *DN* 2, PG 3 641D. Luibheid's translation.

22. Gregory of Nazianzus, *Oration on Holy Baptism*, 375–76.

23. Gregory of Nazianzus, *Second Oration on Easter*, 433. See also Gregory's *Oration 20.7*.

24. See Lampe, *A Patristic Greek Lexicon*, 235, for more names and complete citations.

His agency He made the ages) or superiority in any other respect save causation.[25]

Likewise, in the fourteenth century, the great Orthodox theologian Gregory Palamas writes, "The Father is called Father only in relation to His Son [i.e., not in relation to the Spirit]. In relation to both the Son and Spirit, He is called *Archē*, even as He is called *Archē* in relation to the creation."[26]

It is true that the word *archē* also often meant "dominion" or "rule," becoming almost indistinguishable from other words for rule, like *kratos*. Thus our modern political vocabulary, borrowed largely from the Greeks, mixes words like *monarchy* and *oligarchy* with *democracy* and *aristocracy*. Yet the basic sense of *archē* is "beginning," while the basic sense of *kratos* is "force." *Kratos* is in fact a cognate of the English word *hard*, its Epic and Ionic form being *kartos*.[27] The difference between *archē* and *kratos* can be seen throughout Greek history. In Modern Greek, *to kratos* means "the State." In the Byzantine era, the people of Constantinople were divided into factions or *dēmoi* known as the Blues and the Greens, each headed by a civil leader called a *dēmarchos*, who was responsible for public works, and a military leader called a *dēmokratōr*, who was responsible for civil defense. At a higher level, the Church was headed by a *patriarchēs*, and the empire by an *autokratōr*, with only the latter bearing the sword. At the highest level, the concepts of *archē* and *kratos* were united in one person, Jesus Christ, Archpriest and Pantocrator.[28]

Thus, with *archē*, in contrast to *kratos*, we have at least a theoretical basis for ordered relations that require neither inequality nor compulsion. In a strictly archical relationship, both persons are free and equal yet act differently toward each other on account of one being the source of the other, the one taking the *archic* role of the Father and the other taking the *eucharistic* role of the Son.

Obvious human analogues of relations between the Father and the Son are relations between parents and children, but not young parents and young children, between which there is of course inequality and some coercion. Think, rather, of a father in his golden years who has

---

25. John of Damascus, *Exact Exposition of the Orthodox Faith* 1.8, 9.

26. Gregory Palamas, *Chapter 132*, PG 150, 1213B–C, my translation.

27. LSJ, 992, and *American Heritage Dictionary*, 1973 edition, 1521.

28. The distinction of *archē* and *kratos*, understood as social rank and physical force, is the basis of my book *Eight Ways to Run the Country*.

raised his son to take over the family business and who now looks with pride and joy on his son's own success, believing that his own glory is only increased by his son exceeding him. Think also of the fully mature son who still shares his father's values and vision, who is now fully capable of running things on his own, but who still values his father's advice and honors his legacy, giving thanks to his father for all that he has and is. The two are now equally competent, and the son is no longer subject to his father, yet they are still father and son and therefore relate to each other differently—one as loving father, the other as grateful son.

## "That they may be one, even as we are one"

At the Last Supper, Christ prayed to the Father, saying, "And the glory which thou gavest me, I have given them, that they may be one, even as we are one" (John 17:22). These words (and those very like them in John 17:11) are often read only as a prayer for unity, unity itself being an aspect of divinity, but the words "even as we are one" could refer not just to the *fact* that the Father and the Son are one but also to the *way* in which they are one. In other words, Christ may be expressing his intention that his disciples become one by relating to each other *archically*, through godlike self-giving and thanks-giving, and that these distinct, reciprocal (not merely mutual) modes of relation are the "glory" given by the Father to the Son for the Son to give to his disciples.

Christ models both modes for us. Toward the Father, he is the thankful, obedient Son; toward us, he is the self-giving Lord and King who is our *archē kai telos*, our "beginning and end," both our origin or source (*archē*) and also our purpose or goal (*telos*) (Rev 22:13; cf. Col 1:18; Rev 3:14; 21:6). Christ is also the "head of the Church" and "savior of the body" (Eph 5:23). As the Divine Logos, he is the source of all creation, "by whom all things were made" (John 1:1–3). Thus, after declaring the Father to be the *archē* of the Son, Gregory Palamas says, "The Son is also *archē*, though they [the Father and the Son] do not constitute two *archēs*, but one. For the Son is [also] called *archē* in relation to creation."[29]

Ideally, we would imitate Christ in all our dealings with others, taking either the archic or the eucharistic role so as to be one the way God is one, sharing the same life, the same will, and the same interests equally. The Fall, however, has destroyed our original unity and set us at odds

---

29. Gregory Palamas, *Chapter 132*, PG 150, 1213B–C.

with each other over unequal conditions, differing interests, and conflicting wills, making unity all but impossible without subordinating some people to others—by force, by law, or by inequality, on the basis of which we may distinguish three forms of subordination:

- *Hierarchy*, based on natural, conditional, or circumstantial inequality—some people being smarter, stronger, wealthier, holier, luckier, or simply more active than others.
- *Subjection* (from the Latin *subicere* meaning "to put under"), based on acceptance of a customary or lawful order obliging natural, conditional, or circumstantial equals to submit one to another for the good of all.
- *Subjugation* (from the Latin *jugum* meaning "yoke"), based on the use of force, whereby some people impose their will on others.

Each of these three basic forms of subordination requires some degree of compliance or submission, which also appears in three forms:

- *Obedience*—when subordinates submit to superordinates.
- *Condescension*—when superordinates submit to subordinates, so as to please them (as when Christ turned water into wine to please his mother in John 2).
- *Deference*—when one person defers to another person not formally ordered under or over him.

Each of these subordinations and submissions has its place. God in fact ordains each of them for our own good at one time or another. But even men who do not fear God often fear the chaos that comes from anarchy and so opt instead for some form of subordination.

Political unions consist of all three subordinations: the forcible subjugation of those who misbehave, the lawful subjection of legal equals to civil authorities, and, inevitably, a social hierarchy of the rich, able, advantaged, and active over the poor, disabled, disadvantaged, and inactive. Inasmuch as rulers and the ruled share a common weal and relate as head and body in Christian fashion, their political union can also constitute a simultaneous archy, although archy itself admits no inequality, no imposition of will, no need for subjection, no subordination of any kind, being an order without suborder based on shared life, common interest, mutual concern, singular will, and reciprocal interaction. (The key word of the preceding sentence is the first word, *inasmuch*: Rulers and ruled only share a common weal to a limited degree—sometimes more, sometimes less.)

Families are also initially hierarchies, subjections, and subjugations on account of the immaturity of children, but as the children mature these subordinations give way gradually to a family archy, in which the parents continue to act as parents, supporting, encouraging, and guiding their children though they then be free, equal, and on their own. Parents never stop being parents because the essence of parenthood is not superiority or dominance but archic self-giving, which good parents continue to do for their children as long as they are able.

Churches are not subjugations because there is no force involved, but they are subjections inasmuch as members willingly submit to the authority of church leaders, and they are hierarchies inasmuch as church leaders are more able, more enlightened, or more holy. But ideally they are archies headed by men who give their lives for their flocks as Christ gave his life for the Church. This archic self-giving—in obedience to the New Commandment to love others as Christ loved his disciples—is ultimately what makes the Christian priest a spiritual father. Illumination is part of his priestly gift to people, but he imparts illumination less by theological instruction than by his example of fatherly self-giving, just as Christ manifested the glory of the Father less through his teaching, which requires interpretation, than through his self-sacrifice, which makes sense of his teaching. The priest's fatherhood does not depend on his intercession, mediation, spiritual superiority, clerical authority, or sacramental power. He need not be holier than others to perform his priestly office. He intercedes for the people, but the people also intercede for him. He does not stand between them and God but with them before God. He does not mediate between God and them, "For there is one God, and one mediator between God and men, the man Christ Jesus" (1 Tim 2:5).

Here we see a fundamental difference between Christian priesthood and pagan priesthood. Among pagans, priests alone were holy; they alone knew the secrets of their gods; they alone entered the temple; they alone performed the sacred acts, mediating between God and man; they alone had the power to perform these acts, which they could perform alone, without the participation of the people. The same cannot be said of Christian priests. Christian priests need not be holier or more enlightened than their people to still be priests; they do not keep the secrets of God to themselves but instead share them with the people as much as they and their people are able; they are not the only ones to perform sacred acts; the sacred acts reserved for bishops and presbyters require the people's participation; the only sacred acts bishops and presbyters may perform alone are the sacred acts any Christian may perform; and all Christians are, in fact, called to be priests, praying over and sanctifying material reality, mediating between God and creation. Whereas the pagan priest stood apart from other men, between them and God, the Christian priest stands at the head of an assembly, which stands together before God.

Other head-and-body associations (clubs, corporations, countries) may also exist as hierarchies, subjections, or subjugations on account of the Fall, but ideally they are archical unions more or less mirroring the relationship of the Father and the Son. Even military units are ideally archical within themselves. They function best when this is all they are. They become hierarchical only when inequalities of competence must be accommodated. They become subjections only when men disagree and leaders are obliged to "pull rank." They become subjugations only when force must be used to restrain bad behavior. Not all units become thus degraded. Some small, elite units can function merely archically, with no inequality of competence and no need to pull rank or use force. But take away their archical arrangement and they cease to be "units." To function as one, they must have one of their number to begin things, to give direction, to lead the way, and to commit himself to responsibility for the whole and give his life for it if necessary. That is the essence of *archē*.

## "Male and female created he them"

Man's imitation of Christ begins *en archē*, "in the beginning," when man is made male and female, the latter from the former. Both are made in the image of God (Gen 1:27), and both are given dominion over creation (Gen 1:28). Both therefore are meant to relate *archicly* toward creation and *eucharisticly* toward God, just as Christ, the Archetype of both, relates archicly toward creation and eucharisticly toward the Father.[30] But between the sexes, the man takes Christ's archic role and the woman takes Christ's eucharistic role. This natural, original relationship of the

---

30. As used here, *archic* and *archicly* refer to the way of relating by the source, whereas *archical* and *archically* refer more generally to relationships based on sourceness. In the same way, *eucharisticly* refers to the way of relating to one's source.

man and the woman, resembling the archical relationship of the Father, Son, and Holy Spirit, is seen in the following ways:

1. The Father is the beginning, source, and origin of the Son and Holy Spirit; the man is the beginning, source, and origin of the woman.
2. The Father does not create the Son or the Holy Spirit; the man does not create the woman.
3. The Godhead is complete in three distinct Persons; mankind is complete is two distinct sexes.
4. The Persons of the Trinity share a common divine nature; the man and the woman share a common human nature.
5. The Son is "one in essence" with the Father; the woman is "bone of my bones, and flesh of my flesh" (Gen 2:23).
6. The Trinity is of one will; the man and the woman at least began in a harmony of wills.
7. The Son and the Holy Spirit look ever unto the Father; the woman at first looked to the man, receiving from him her own name (twice: Gen 2:23 and 3:20), the names of the creatures, and the commandments of God.
8. The Father is the "head" of the Son; the man is the "head" of the woman (1 Cor 11:3).
9. The Father loves the Son and shares with him his very essence; the man is commanded to love his wife as his own flesh, giving his life for her as Christ gave his life for the Church (Eph 5:25–33).
10. The Son thanks the Father with humble service; the woman thanks her husband with the same (Eph 5:22–24, 33).
11. The Son comes "in the glory of his Father" (Matt 16:27) and is given "glory" by the Father (John 17:22); the woman is "the glory of the man" (1 Cor 11:7).
12. By the Son all things were made; by the woman the human race was multiplied.
13. Christ and the Holy Spirit are said to give life (John 6:33; 10:28; 17:2; 2 Cor 3:6; Gal 6:8); Adam named the woman "Life" (*Zoē*, Eve) "because she was the mother of all living" (Gen 3:20).

14. The Father is the *archē* of all, the Son is the *archē* of creation, and the man is the *archē* of mankind and the source of the woman, in the beginning and even now, for it is his genetic material, his X or Y chromosome, that determines whether a child will be male or female.

The fashioning of the woman from the man completed the creation of the world, which God declares "very good" only after the creation of man in both sexes (Gen 1:31). Procreation was not required for this completeness; procreation is instead what the man and the woman do when their archical union is complete, just as creation is what God does through the archical union of the Trinity. God was creating creatures in the image of God; he therefore created man as a loving union of archically related equals, blessing the first man with a mate made from him, like him, and for him, in the sense that without such a mate mankind could not know true love, which is to say, the archical love like that within the Trinity. Procreation was part of the plan but not the principal reason for male and female. The physical differences between the sexes are therefore secondary to the sexes' archical relation, since sexual distinction is less about procreation than about communion.

In fact, the story of Adam and Eve in Gen 2 and 3 says not one word about their physical differences. On the contrary, virtually every detail in both chapters communicates either the likeness of the primal pair or their archical relation, with no mention of any other kind of difference. The woman is fashioned from the man's own flesh and bone (Gen 2:21–23). Her name in Hebrew is taken from his: He is *ish*, she is *ishshah* (Gen 2:23).[31] God does not appear just to the man, for both the man and the woman are said to hear the voice of God and to hide from his presence (Gen 3:8). God also speaks directly to each, and each in turn answers him directly (Gen 3:9–13), showing that the man does not mediate hierarchicly between God and the woman, standing between her and God. God nevertheless addresses the man first as the archic head, calling for Adam (Gen 3:9) and questioning him before questioning Eve. As Eve's archic head, Adam should have answered for both himself and Eve, but in his fallen state he answers only for himself, saying, "I heard thy voice . . . I was afraid . . . I was naked . . . and I hid myself" (Gen 3:10), before blaming

---

31. Diodore of Tarsus says the Septuagint mistranslates Gen 2.23 by referring to the woman as *gynē* instead of *ē anthrōpos*, the feminine form of *o anthrōpos*. See Harrison, "Women, Identity and the Image of God," 210–11.

Eve, who answers only for herself, blaming the serpent for beguiling her without mentioning her tempting of Adam (Gen 3:13).

If every sex-specific detail of Gen 2 and 3 were deleted, there would be little left. Two whole chapters could be condensed into a single short sentence: God created humans, gave them dominion over creation, told them not to eat of the tree, and punished them when they did. Everything else about the creation, the commandments, the naming of creatures, the temptation, the transgression, the interrogation, and the sentencing relates to either the man or the woman and not to both.

Instead of the Fall as a simple matter of sensual desire or prideful disobedience, we can now see it as a series of anarchies unraveling the order of creation. In these acts of anarchy, the man and the woman each turn away from their *archē* and act contrary to their ordination as male and female, thereby destroying the natural relation between them. It begins with the Arch-anarchist himself, who through the serpent offers the woman equality with God. Why the woman? Because she fits Satan's own anarchistic outlook, his perverted vision of domination by the Creator justifying rebellion by the creature. Thus tempted, the woman turns away from the man to follow the serpent; the man then turns away from God to follow the woman. God could have punished Adam only for eating of the tree; instead, he finds Adam guilty of two charges, saying, "Because thou hast hearkened unto the voice of thy wife, and hast eaten of the tree" (Gen 3:17). To keep the man and the woman together, God commits the woman to the man's charge, saying, "thy turning [*apostrophē*] shall be to thy husband, and he shall rule over thee" (Gen 3:17). The alternative would have been to allow the man and the woman to go their separate ways, to live and die alone, never committing themselves to a loving relationship to give life to the world.

## Conclusion: Archē kai Telos

How different is the ancient Greek view of male and female as an unfortunate division occurring as a curse by the gods, as a two-phased fall from mind toward matter, or as the failure of a fetus to fully develop *in utero* by some accident of nature! Among the Greeks, the woman was an inferior being, a soul more burdened by its body. To escape the body, she had first to become a man through the practice of manly virtues. Marriage, for both men and women, was a distraction from the practice of virtue, burdening women even more with the demands of the body and turning men away from what is above and toward what is below. The only good of marriage was breeding, which was a concern only of lesser men, of the State, and of philosophers advising the State. Otherwise, it had no purpose and no meaning.

Early Christians inherited this view from the world around them through secular education and the attitudes of pagan elites, who self-identified as *Hellēnes* ("Greeks"). Some early Christians pushed such thinking to extremes, condemning marriage as fornication and proclaiming an end to male and female. Others allowed marriage only as a concession to weakness, seeing no need for further breeding and no significance to male and female beyond breeding. In various ways, these blamed marriage, male and female, and the pleasures of the body on the Fall, explaining the Fall as a turn away from an angelic life enjoying only intelligible pleasures, toward a bestial life obsessed with sensible pleasures. Obliged by dogma to allow marriage and accept the body, they tended nevertheless to blame the body for sin, to see male and female as a beastly add-on to human nature, and to see sexual intercourse as a source of all sin, a "mechanism of death," in the words of Zizioulas, perpetuating the cycle of pleasure and pain.[32]

But early Christians also inherited the Hebrew view of male and female as part of God's created goodness, fully intended by God not merely as a prevenient means of postlapsarian survival but as a naturally, distinctively human way of life, recognizing that man is neither an angel nor a beast, but a being between the two, sharing aspects of both, bearing a body and a soul as well as the image of God. Most early Christians defended both marriage and male and female and condemned those who disrespected both. They paid more attention to all that is said in Hebrew Scripture about Adam and Eve, men and women, and husbands and wives. They also habitually followed the Apostle Paul in regarding the first three chapters of Genesis as the basis of what Christians are to believe about male and female.

They were challenged to balance marriage and monasticism, and this they did by setting limits to both sexuality and asceticism to ensure that Christians practiced both safe sex and safe asceticism. These limits varied somewhat with time and place, with the West eventually insisting on clerical celibacy. But both East and West honored marriage as a

---

32. Zizioulas, *Communion and Otherness*, 58–59.

sacrament and exalted motherhood through the veneration of the Virgin Mother. They also both insisted on maintaining the distinction of male and female in church as well as in the world, treating male and female as a matter of both nature and calling—what we are and how we are to behave—*logos* and *tropos* in Maximian terms, sex and gender in modern terms, approximately. Thus the postmodern argument over essentialism vs. constructivism did not occur to them because they understood male and female as always a matter of both nature and nurture, what God intends and how man responds to God's intent.

Early Christians were not challenged to explain much about male and female. Today's Christians are challenged to explain much more. In meeting that challenge, the explanation of male and female set forth in this chapter, based on the Apostle Paul's analogy of the man and the woman to God and Christ (1 Cor 11:3), offers eight important advantages over all other explanations:

1. By identifying our fundamental modes of being not as masculine and feminine but as *archic* and *eucharistic*, we can relate male and female to divinity without sexualizing God or creation and thus read Gen 1:27 as a true Hebrew parallelism without imputing femininity to God or conjuring male and female deities.

2. We can therefore dismiss the needlessly narrow Greek Christian view of the image of God and of male and female, since from the beginning, as revealed in Holy Scripture, male and female was not just a bodily difference serving the single purpose of procreation in anticipation of the Fall; it was first and foremost a designation of different roles for the primal pair modeled on the Trinity, both roles expressing the distinctive image and likeness of the Christian God.

3. We can furthermore define a new category of relation that classes male-and-female relationships with other head-and-body relationships that all ought to imitate the Trinity, with self-giving heads and thanks-giving bodies, the model for Christian leadership and servanthood in any form.

4. We can include in this new category parent-child and senior-junior relationships, which also ought to follow the same pattern, with the young respecting their elders and even grown sons and daughters honoring their fathers and mothers.

5. We can see both Christ and the Theotokos setting the example for both men and women by each modeling both the archic and the eucharistic ways of relating: Christ models the archic as our Lord and King and the eucharistic as the grateful, obedient Son of the Father; the Theotokos models the archic as the mother of the incarnate Christ and the eucharistic as the New Eve.

6. We can avoid the simplistic Greek association of male and female with active and passive, understanding our archic and eucharistic ways of relating as both active and not passive.

7. We can bring much needed conceptual clarity to our relational terminology, distinguishing the ordered equality of natural archy from the ordered equality of economic subjection, the ordered inequality of hierarchy, the ordered inequality of subjugation, and the disordered equality of anarchy.

8. Finally, we can explain the subjection of the woman, as understood by the Apostles and Fathers, not as a matter of male dominance or female inferiority but as a matter of divine economy, a temporary expedient to keep the man and the woman together until they can regain their natural archical ways of relating.

In this archical view of human relations, subjection is merely a truss God uses to bind up what has been torn apart by the original sin of anarchy, until the sinews of faith and love grow strong enough to hold on their own. Archy is still the goal, the *telos* toward which we are all to strive. It is not such an impossible ideal for many relationships. In their years together, many married couples achieve a largely archical relationship, based on love, trust, and a life as one. In such relationships, the language of command, "Do as I say," gives way to the language of accord, "Let's do this," echoing God's own manner of speaking in Genesis 1:26: "Let us make man in our image, after our likeness." This is the first hint in Scripture of the plurality of persons in the Godhead, and it comes just as God turns to making man in His own image. Only then does God speak of "us" and "our."

How could this aspect of the image of God have appeared at creation without differentiation by archical relation? How could the first humans have learned to love each other without male and female?

The only love that appears in the beginning in the Greek Christian view is self-love for one's own body with its painful pleasures, yet in being male and female the first humans recognized their intimate relation, and by relating as male and female they experienced a *perichōresis*, an interpenetration of their persons physically and emotionally, and thereby became one in a deeply meaningful sense. The union of male and female made possible the revelation of God as Father and Son, for without male and female there would have been no fathers and no sons, as well as no Theotokos, no Mother of God. The differentiation of man as male and female and the fruitful union of their bodies seem thus to have been an absolute necessity for the communication of the Gospel, inasmuch as the Gospel is about a father so loving the world that he gives it his son (John 3:16). It is difficult if not impossible to imagine how the story could be told in any other way.

It is also still difficult if not impossible to see how the Greek Christian view and the Hebrew Christian view of male and female can be reconciled. Both can claim some support in Holy Scripture. Both have received the backing of some sainted Fathers. Both have been handed down through the ages as Church tradition and continue to influence Christianity down to our present day. But they differ in their fundamental assumptions about the image of God and the nature of male and female, and they point us in opposite directions—one toward shaking off the only body we know, with its "division" of male and female, the other toward loving others in that body by relating to them as what they are to us, including either male or female.

The difference in these two objectives derives directly from their different sources. In the spiritual philosophy of the Greeks, the fundamental conflict to be resolved was between mind and matter, souls and bodies, intelligibles and sensibles, whereas in the spiritual history of the Hebrews the conflict to be resolved was always between minds, between souls, between intelligibles. It was a history of God and man, man and woman, Hebrew and Egyptian, Israelite and Canaanite, Jew and Gentile. It was a history of relation, a series of lessons in love teaching man to love as God loves, "that they may be one, even as we are one" (John 17:22). The Hebrew Christian tradition continues this series of lessons as they pertain to male and female; the Greek Christian tradition does not.

# Bibliography

Ackerman, Susan. "The Personal is Political: Covenantal and Affectionate Love ('AHEB, 'AHABA) in the Hebrew Bible." *Vetus Testamentum* 52 (2002) 437–58.
Aimilianos of Simonopetra. *The Mystical Marriage: Spiritual Life according to St. Maximos the Confessor*. Translated by Maximos Constas. Columbia, MO: Newrome, 2018.
Allen, Prudence. *The Concept of Woman: The Aristotelian Revolution, 750 b.c.–a.d. 1250*. 2nd ed. Grand Rapids: Eerdmans, 1997.
Alter, Robert. *The Wisdom Books: Job, Proverbs, and Ecclesiastes: A Translation with Commentary*. New York: Norton, 2010.
Ambrose of Milan. *Concerning Virgins, Concerning Widows, On the Duties of the Clergy, On the Holy Spirit*. In vol. 10 of *Nicene and Post-Nicene Fathers, Series 2*, edited by Philip Schaff, translated by H. de Romestin. Buffalo: Christian Literature, 1896.
———. *Expositio evangelii secundum Lucan*. Corpus Scriptorum Ecclesiasticorum Latinorum 32. Vienna: Academiae Litterarum Caesareae, 1902.
———. *Hexameron, Paradise, Cain and Abel*. In vol. 42 of *Fathers of the Church*, translated by John J. Savage. York, PA: Fathers of the Church, 1961.
———. *On Virginity*. Translated by Daniel Callam. Toronto: Peregrina, 1980.
———. *Seven Exegetical Works*. In vol. 58 of *Fathers of the Church*, translated by Michael P. McHugh. Washington, DC: Catholic University Press, 1972.
*The American Heritage Dictionary of the English Language*. Edited by William Morris. Boston: Houghton Mifflin, 1973.
Andia, Ysabel de. "Pseudo-Dionysius the Areopagite and Maximus the Confessor." In *The Oxford Handbook of Maximus the Confessor*, edited by Pauline Allen and Bronwen Neil, 177–93. Oxford: Oxford University Press, 2015.
Andreopoulos, Andreas. "Eschatology in Maximus the Confessor." In *The Oxford Handbook of Maximus the Confessor*, edited by Pauline Allen and Bronwen Neil, 322–40. Oxford: Oxford University Press, 2015.
*Ante-Nicene Fathers*. Edited by Philip Schaff. Buffalo: Christian Literature, 1886–1989.
Antiphon. *The Older Sophists: A Complete Translation by Several Hands of the Fragments in Die Fragmente Der Vorsokratiker Edited by Diels-Kranz*, edited by Rosamond Kent Sprague. Columbia: University of South Carolina Press, 1972.
*Apostolic Constitutions*. In vol. 7 of *Ante-Nicene Fathers*, translated by Alexander Roberts and James Donaldson. Buffalo: Christian Literature, 1886.
Apostolic Fathers. In vol. 1 of *Ante-Nicene Fathers*, translated by Alexander Roberts and James Donaldson. Buffalo: Christian Literature, 1885.
Apuleius. *Florida*. In *The Works of Apuleius*. London: Bell and Sons, 1914.

Aristophanes. *Aristophanes Comoediae*. Edited by F. W. Hall and W. M. Geldart. Vols. 1–2. Oxford: Clarendon, 1907.

Aristotle. *Aristotle in 23 Volumes*. Cambridge: Harvard University Press, 1933–1981.

———. *History of Animals*. Translated by D'Arcy Wentworth Thompson. Adelaide: University of Adelaide, 2016.

Athanasius of Alexandria. *Against the Arians*. In vol. 4 of *Nicene and Post-Nicene Fathers, Series 2*, translated by Archibald Robertson. Buffalo: Christian Literature, 1892.

Augustine. *City of God*. In vol. 2 of *Nicene and Post-Nicene Fathers, Series 1*, translated by Marcus Dods. Buffalo: Christian Literature, 1887.

———. *Confessions*. In vol. 1 of *Nicene and Post-Nicene Fathers, Series 1*, translated by J. G. Pilkington. Buffalo: Christian Literature, 1886.

———. *De Genesi ad litteram*. In vols. 1–2 of *Augustine: The Literal Meaning of Genesis*, translated by John Hammond Taylor. New York: Newman, 1982.

———. *De Genesi contra Manichaeos*. In *Saint Augustine on Genesis*, translated by Roland J. Teske. New York: Fathers of the Church, 1991.

———. *Letters*. In vol. 1 of *Nicene and Post-Nicene Fathers, Series 1*, translated by J. G. Cunningham. Buffalo: Christian Literature, 1886.

———. *On the Good of Marriage, On the Holy Trinity, On Holy Virginity*, and *On the Works of Monks*. In vol. 3 of *Nicene and Post-Nicene Fathers, Series 1*, translated by C. L. Cornish. Buffalo: Christian Literature, 1887.

———. *On Marriage and Concupiscence*. In vol. 5 of *Nicene and Post-Nicene Fathers, Series 1*, translated by Peter Holmes. Buffalo: Christian Literature, 1887.

———. *Reply to Faustus the Manichaean*. In vol. 4 of *Nicene and Post-Nicene Fathers, Series 1*, translated by Richard Stothert. Buffalo: Christian Literature, 1887.

———. *The Soliloquies of Augustine*. Translated by Rose Elizabeth Cleveland. Boston: Little, Brown, and Co., 1910.

Baer, Richard A. *Philo's Use of the Categories of Male and Female*. Leiden: Brill, 1970.

Bailey, Derrick Sherwin. *The Man-Woman Relation in Christian Thought*. London: Longmans, Green & Co., 1959.

Balthasar, Hans Urs von. *Cosmic Liturgy: The Universe according to Maximus the Confessor*. Translated by Brian E. Daley. San Francisco: Ignatius, 2003.

———. *Theo-Drama: Theological Dramatic Theory, Vol. 2: Dramatis Personae: Man in God*. San Francisco: Ignatius, 1976.

———. *Theo-Drama: Theological Dramatic Theory, Vol. 4: The Action*. San Francisco: Ignatius, 1994.

———. "Women Priests? A Marian Church in a Fatherless and Motherless Culture." *Communio* 22 (1995) 164–70.

Bammel, C. P. "Adam in Origen." In *The Making of Orthodox: Essays in Honor of Henry Chadwick*, edited by Rowan Williams, 62–93. Cambridge: Cambridge University Press, 1989.

Barth, Karl. *Church Dogmatics III*. Translated and edited by G. W. Bromiley and T. F. Torrance. Edinburgh: T. & T. Clark, 1961.

Bartholomew, Craig G. *Ecclesiastes*. Grand Rapids: Baker Academic, 2009.

Basil of Caesarea. *Ascetical Works*. In vol. 1 of *Fathers of the Church*, translated by M. Monica Wagner. Washington, DC: Catholic University of America Press, 1950.

———. *Exegetical Homilies*. In vol. 46 of *Fathers of the Church*, translated by Agnes Clare Way. Washington, DC: Catholic University of America Press, 1963.

———. *Letters and Select Works*. In vol. 8 of *Nicene and Post-Nicene Fathers, Series 2*, translated by Blomfield Jackson. Buffalo: Christian Literature, 1895.

———. *Sermon 70*. In *The Ascetic Works of Saint Basil*, translated by W. K. L. Clarke, London: SPCK, 1925.

Beavis, Mary Ann. "Philo's Therapeutai: Philosopher's Dream or Utopian Construction?" *JSP* 14.1 (2004) 30–42.

Bedale, Stephen. "The Meaning of *kephalē* in the Pauline Epistles." *JTS* 5.2 (1954) 211–15.

Behr, John. "Marriage and Asceticism." *Sobornost* 29.2 (2007) 24–50.

———. *The Mystery of Christ: Life in Death*. Crestwood, NY: St. Vladimir's Seminary Press, 2006.

———. *The Nicene Faith: Part 2*. Crestwood, NY: St. Vladimir's Seminary Press, 2006.

———. "The Rational Animal." *JECS* 7.2 (1999) 219–47.

Berglund, Carl Johan. "Origen's Vacillating Stances toward his 'Valentinian' Colleague Heracleon." *Vigiliae Christianae* 71.5 (2017) 541–69.

Blomquist, Karin. "Chryseïs and Clea, Eumetis and the Interlocutress: Plutarch of Chaeronea and Dio Chrysostom on Women's Education." *Svensk Exegetisk årsbok* 60 (1995) 173–90.

Blosser, Benjamin P. *Become Like the Angels: Origen's Doctrine of the Soul*. Washington, DC: Catholic University of America Press, 2012.

Blowers, Paul M., and Robert Louis Wilken, eds. *On the Cosmic Mystery of Jesus Christ: Selected Writing from St. Maximus the Confessor*. Crestwood, NY: St. Vladimir's Seminary Press, 2003.

———. *Maximus the Confessor: Jesus Christ and the Transfiguration of the World*. Oxford: Oxford University Press, 2016.

Boersma, Gerald. "'Let Us Flee to the Fatherland': Plotinus in Ambrose's Theology of Ascent." *Nova et vetera* 14.3 (2016) 771–81.

Boersma, Hans. *Embodiment and Virtue in Gregory of Nyssa: An Anagogical Approach*. Oxford: Oxford University Press, 2013.

———. "Nuptial Reading: Hippolytus, Origen, and Ambrose on the Bridal Couple of the Song of Songs." *Calvin Theological Journal* 51 (2016) 227–58.

Börjesson, Johannes. "Augustine on the Will." In *The Oxford Handbook of Maximus the Confessor*, edited by Pauline Allen and Bronwen Neil, 212–34. Oxford: Oxford University Press, 2015.

Borodai, T. Iu. "Plotinus's Critique of Gnosticism." *Russian Studies in Philosophy* 42.1 (2003) 66–83.

Bosman, Philip R. "Utopia, Domestication and Special Status: Marriage and Family in the Stoic Tradition." *Acta Patristica et Byzantina* 21.2 (2010) 5–18.

Boyarin, Daniel. *Carnal Israel: Reading Sex in Talmudic Culture*. Berkeley: University of California Press, 1993.

Bradshaw, David. *Aristotle East and West: Metaphysics and the Division of Christendom*. Cambridge: Cambridge University Press, 2004.

Bradshaw, Paul F. *Ordination Rites of the Ancient Churches of East and West*. New York: Pueblo, 1990.

Brakke, David. *The Gnostics: Myth, Ritual, and Diversity in Early Christianity*. Cambridge: Harvard University Press, 2010.

Breck, John. *Scripture in Tradition: The Bible and Its Interpretation in the Orthodox Church*. Crestwood, NY: St. Vladimir's Seminary Press, 2001.

Brenton, C. L., trans. *The Septuagint with Apocrypha: Greek and English*. London: Bagster & Sons, 1851.

Broek, Roelof van den. *Gnostic Religion in Antiquity*. Cambridge: Cambridge University Press, 2013.

———. *Studies in Gnosticism and Alexandrian Christianity*. Leiden: Brill, 1996.

Brown, Francis, et al. *Brown-Driver-Briggs Hebrew and English Lexicon, Unabridged, Electronic Database*. http://biblehub.com.

Brown, Peter. *Augustine of Hippo: A Biography*. Oakland: University of California Press, 2000.

———. *The Body and Society: Men, Women, and Sexual Renunciation in Early Christianity*. New York: Columbia University Press, 1988.

Bynum, Caroline Walker. *The Resurrection of the Body in Western Christianity, 200–1336*. New York: Columbia University Press, 1995.

Cameron, Averil. "The Early Cult of the Virgin." In *Mother of God: Representations of the Virgin in Byzantine Art*, edited by M. Vassilaki. Athens: Benaki Museum, 1999. http://www.myriobiblos.gr/texts/english/cameron_virgin1.html.

Casiday, Augustine. *Evagrius Ponticus*. London: Routledge, 2006.

———. *Reconstructing the Theology of Evagrius Ponticus: Beyond Heresy*. Cambridge: Cambridge University Press, 2013.

Chadwick, Henry. *Early Christian Thought and the Classical Tradition*. New York: Oxford University Press, 1966.

———. *The Early Church*. New York: Dorset, 1967.

Chadwick, Henry, and J. E. L. Oulton, eds. *Alexandrian Christianity*. Philadelphia: Westminster, 1954.

Cicero. *Tusculanae Disputationes*. Translated by Charles Duke Yonge. New York: Harper & Brothers, 1877.

Clark, Elizabeth A. *The Origenist Controversy: The Cultural Construction of an Early Christian Debate*. Princeton: Princeton University Press, 1992.

———. *Women in the Early Church*. Collegeville, MN: Liturgical, 1990.

Clement of Alexandria. *Excerpta ex Theodoto*. Translated by Robert Pierce Casey. London: Christophers, 1934.

———. *Exhortation to the Heathens, The Instructor (Paedagogus), and The Stromata, or Miscellanies*. In vol. 2 of *Ante-Nicene Fathers*, edited by A. Cleveland Coxe. Buffalo: Christian Literature, 1885.

———. *Stromateis*. Books III and VII in *Alexandrian Christianity*, edited by Henry Chadwick and J. E. L. Oulton, translated by Henry Chadwick. Philadelphia: Westminster, 1954.

Cohen, David. "Law, Society and Homosexuality in Classical Athens." In *Sex and Differences in Ancient Greece and Rome*, edited by Mark Golden and Peter Toohey, 151–66. Edinburgh: Edinburgh University Press, 2003.

Constas, Maximos. "Maximus the Confessor, Dionysius the Areopagite, and the Transformation of Christian Neoplatonism." *Analogia* 1.2 (2017) 1–12.

Constas, Nicholas. "Weaving the Body of God." *JECS* 3 (1995) 169–94.

Cooper, Adam G. *The Body in Maximus the Confessor: Holy Flesh, Wholly Deified*. Oxford: Oxford University Press, 2005.

Corrigan, Kevin. *Evagrius and Gregory: Mind, Soul and Body in the 4th Century*. Burlington, VT: Ashgate, 2009.

———. *Love, Friendship, Beauty, and the Good: Plato, Aristotle, and the Later Tradition*. Eugene, OR: Wipf & Stock, 2018.

———. "'Solitary' Mysticism in Plotinus, Proclus, Gregory of Nyssa, and Pseudo-Dionysius." *Journal of Religion* 76.1 (1996) 28–42.

Costache, Doru. "Gender, Marriage, and Holiness in *Amb.Io.* 10 and 41." In *Men and Women in the Early Christian Centuries*, edited by Wendy Mayer and Ian J. Elmer, 351–71. Early Christian Studies 18. Strathfield, NSW: St Pauls, 2014.

———. "Living Above Gender: Insights from Saint Maximus the Confessor." *JECS* 21.2 (2013) 261–90.

———. "Mapping Reality within the Experience of Holiness." In *The Oxford Handbook of Maximus the Confessor*, edited by Pauline Allen and Bronwen Neil, 378–96. Oxford: Oxford University Press, 2015.

Crouzel, Henri. *Origen*. Translated by A. S. Worrall. Edinburgh: T. & T. Clark, 1989.

Cunningham, Mary. "All-Holy Infant: Byzantine and Western Views on the Conception of the Virgin Mary." *St. Vladimir's Theological Quarterly* 50.1–2 (2006) 127–48.

Cyprian of Carthage. *On the Dress of Virgins* and *Treatise 11*. In vol. 5 of *Ante-Nicene Fathers*, edited by A. Cleveland Coxe. Buffalo: Christian Literature, 1886.

Cyril of Alexandria. *Commentary on 1 Corinthians 11*. PG 74. Paris: Garnier fratres, 1879.

Cyril of Jerusalem. *Procatechesis*. In vol. 7 of *Nicene and Post-Nicene Fathers, Series 2*, translated by Edward Hamilton Gifford. Buffalo: Christian Literature, 1894.

Daley, Brian E. "Evagrius and Cappadocian Orthodoxy." In *Evagrius and His Legacy*, edited by Joel Kalvesmaki and Robin Darling Young, 14–48. Notre Dame: University of Notre Dame Press, 2016.

Daniélou, Jean. *The Ministry of Women in the Early Church*. Translated by Glyn Simon. London: Faith, 1961.

———. *Origen*. Translated by Walter Mitchell. New York: Sheed and Ward, 1955.

Davidson, James. *Courtesans and Fishcakes: The Consuming Passions of Classical Athens*. London: HarperCollins, 1998.

———. "Dover, Foucault and Greek Homosexuality: Penetration and the Truth of Sex." *Past and Present* 170 (2001) 3–51.

———. "Hebrew Bible Goddesses and Modern Feminist Scholarship." *Religion Compass* 6.6 (2012) 298–308.

Deddo, Gary W. *Karl Barth's Theology of Relations: Trinitarian, Christological, and Human: Towards an Ethic of the Family*. Eugene, OR: Wipf & Stock, 1999.

DelCogliano, Mark. "The Quest for Evagrius of Pontus: A Historiographical Essay." *American Benedictine Review* 62.4 (2011) 387–401.

Demosthenes. *Demosthenes with an English translation*. Translated by Norman W. DeWitt and Norman J. DeWitt. Cambridge: Harvard University Press, 1949.

Democritus. *Ancilla to the Pre-Socratic Philosophers: A Complete Translation of the Fragments in Diels, Fragmente der Vorsokratiker*. Translated by Kathleen Freeman. Cambridge: Harvard University Press, 1956.

Diamond, Eliezer. *Holy Men and Hunger Artists: Fasting and Asceticism in Rabbinic Culture*. Oxford: Oxford University Press, 2004.

*Didascalia Apostolorum*. Translated by R. Hugh Connolly. Oxford: Clarendon, 1929.

Dillon, John. *The Middle Platonists*. Ithaca, NY: Cornell University Press, 1996.

———. *The Roots of Platonism: The Origins and Chief Features of a Philosophical Tradition*. Cambridge: Cambridge University Press, 2019.

Diogenes Laertius. *Lives of Eminent Philosophers*. Translated by R. D. Hicks. Cambridge: Harvard University Press, 1925.

Douglas, Mary. *In the Wilderness*. London: Oxford, 2001.
———. *Purity and Danger: An Analysis of the Concepts of Pollution and Taboo*. London: Routledge, 1966.
Dover, K. J. "Classical Greek Attitudes to Sexual Behavior." *Arethusa* 6.1 (1973) 59–83.
———. *Greek Homosexuality*. Cambridge: Harvard University Press, 1989.
Edwards, Mark J. "Ammonius, Teacher of Origen." *Journal of Ecclesiastical History* 44.2 (1993) 169–81.
———. "Atticizing Moses? Numenius, the Fathers and the Jews." *Vigiliae Christianae* 44 (1990) 64–75.
———. *Catholicity and Heresy in the Early Church*. Farnham, UK: Ashgate, 2009.
———. "One Origen or Two? The Status Quaestionis." *Symbolae Osloenses* 89.1 (2015) 81–103.
———. *Origen against Plato*. Aldershot, UK: Ashgate, 2002.
———. "Origen in Paradise: A Response to Peter Martens." *ZAC* 23.2 (2019) 163–85.
———. "Origen's Platonism: Questions and Caveats." *ZAC* 12 (2008) 20–38.
Eller, Cynthia. *The Myth of Matriarchal Prehistory: Why an Invented Past Won't Give Women a Future*. Boston: Beacon, 2000.
Elshtain, Jean Bethke. *Public Man, Private Woman*. Princeton: Princeton University Press, 1981.
Empedocles. *Early Greek Philosophy*. Translated by John Burnet. London: A & C Black, 1920.
Engberg-Pedersen, Troels. "Philo's *De Vita Contemplativa* as a Philosopher's Dream." *Journal for the Study of Judaism in the Persian, Hellenistic, and Roman Period* 30.1 (1999) 40–64.
Ephrem the Syrian. *Selected Prose Works: Commentary on Genesis, Commentary on Exodus, Homily on Our Lord, Letter to Publius*. In vol. 91 of *The Fathers of the Church*, translated by Edward G. Mathews Jr. and Joseph P. Amar. Washington, DC: Catholic University of America Press, 1994.
Epictetus. *The Discourses of Epictetus, with the Enchiridion and Fragments*. Translated by George Long. London: Bell and Sons, 1890.
Epiphanius of Salamis. *The Panarion of Epiphanius of Salamis*. Translated by Frank Williams. Vols. 1–2. New York: Brill, 1994.
Eriugena, John Scotus. *Periphyseon*. In *Periphyseon ("The Division of Nature")*, revised by John J. O'Meara, translated by I. P. Sheldon-Williams. Washington, DC: Dumbarton Oaks, 1987.
Euripides. *Euripides, with an English translation by David Kovacs*. Cambridge: Harvard University Press, 2018. http://www.perseus.tufts.edu.
Eusebius. *History of the Church*. In vol. 1 of *Nicene and Post-Nicene Fathers, Series 2*, translated by Arthur Cushman McGiffert. Buffalo: Christian Literature, 1890.
Evagrius Ponticus. *Kephalaia Gnostika*. Translated by Ilaria L. E. Ramelli. Atlanta: Society of Biblical Literature, 2015.
Evans, Robert F. *Pelagius: Inquiries and Reappraisals*. New York: Seabury, 1968.
Evans-Pritchard, E. E. "Sexual Inversion among the Azande." *American Anthropologist* 72 (1970) 1428–35.
Evdokimov, Paul. *Woman and the Salvation of the World*. Crestwood, NY: St. Vladimir's Seminary Press, 1994.
Falcon, Andrea, and David Lefebvre, eds. *Aristotle's Generation of Animals: A Critical Guide*. Cambridge: Cambridge University Press, 2018.

Faye, Eugène de. *Origen and His Work*. Translated by Fred Rothwell. New York: Columbia University Press, 1929.
Fiorenza, Elisabeth Schüssler. *Jesus: Miriam's Child, Sophia's Prophet*. New York: Continuum, 1999.
Fontenrose, Joseph. *Python: A Study of Delphic Myth and Its Origins*. New York: Biblo & Tannen, 1974.
Ford, David C. "The Interrelationship of Clergy and Laity Within the Church according to St. John Chrysostom." *St. Vladimir's Theological Quarterly* 36.4 (1992) 329–53.
———. *Women and Men in the Early Church: The Full Views of John Chrysostom*. South Canaan, PA: Tikhon's Seminary Press, 1996.
Forde, Steven. "Gender and Justice in Plato." *The American Political Science Review* 91.3 (1997) 657–70.
Foucault, Michel. *The History of Sexuality, Vol. II: The Use of Pleasure*. Translated by Robert Hurley. New York: Random House, 1985.
Fox, Michael V. *Proverbs 1–9*. Anchor Yale Bible Commentary 18. New Haven: Yale University Press, 2000.
Fraade, Steven D. "Ascetical Aspects of Ancient Judaism." In *Jewish Spirituality from the Bible through the Middle Ages*, edited by Arthur Green, 253–86. New York: Crossroads, 1986.
Frankiel, Tamar. *The Voice of Sarah: Feminine Spirituality and Traditional Judaism*. New York: Biblio, 1990.
Freeman, Kathleen. *Ancilla to the Pre-Socratic Philosophers: A Complete Translation of the Fragments in Diels, Fragmente der Vorsokratiker*. Cambridge: Harvard University Press, 1956.
Frymer-Kensky, Tikva. *In the Wake of the Goddesses: Women, Culture, and the Biblical Transformation of Pagan Myth*. New York: Free, 1992.
Fuchs, Eric. *Sexual Desire and Love: Origins and History of the Christian Ethic of Sexuality and Marriage*. Translated by Marsha Daigle. Cambridge: Clark, 1983.
Gaca, Kathy L. *The Making of Fornication: Eros, Ethics, and Political Reform in Greek Philosophy and Early Christianity*. Berkeley: University of California Press, 2003.
Garrison, Daniel H. *Sexual Culture in Ancient Greece*. Norman: University of Oklahoma Press, 2000.
Giles, Kevin. *The Trinity & Subordinationism: The Doctrine of God & the Contemporary Gender Debate*. Downers Grove, IL: IVP Academic, 2002.
*The Gospel of Philip*. In *The Nag Hammadi Library: The Definitive Translation of the Gnostic Scriptures Complete in One Volume*, edited by James M. Robinson, translated by Wesley W. Isenberg, 139–60. San Francisco: HarperCollins, 1990.
*The Gospel of Thomas*. In *The Nag Hammadi Library: The Definitive Translation of the Gnostic Scriptures Complete in One Volume*, edited by James M. Robinson, translated by Thomas O. Lambdin, 124–98. San Francisco: HarperCollins, 1990.
Grant, Robert M. "Early Alexandrian Christianity." *Church History* 40.2 (1971) 133–44.
Greer, Rowan A. *Origen*. New York: Paulist, 1979.
Gregory of Nazianzus. *Selected Orations and Letters*. In vol. 7 of *Nicene and Post-Nicene Fathers, Series 2*, translated by Charles Gordon Browne and James Edward Swallow. Buffalo: Christian Literature, 1894.
Gregory of Nyssa. *Homilies on the Song of Songs*. Translated by Richard A. Norris. Atlanta: Society of Biblical Literature, 2012.
———. *The Life of Saint Macrina*. Translated by Kevin Corrigan. Eugene, OR: Wipf & Stock, 2001.

———. *On the Making of Man, On Not Three Gods, On the Soul and the Resurrection, and On Virginity.* In vol. 5 of *Nicene and Post-Nicene Fathers, Series 2*, translated by William Moore and Henry Austin Wilson. Buffalo: Christian Literature, 1893.

Gruber, Mayer I. *Hosea: A Textual Commentary.* London: Bloomsbury T. & T. Clark, 2017.

Grudem, Wayne. "The Meaning of the Word *Kephalē* ("Head"): A Response to Recent Studies." In *Recovering Biblical Manhood & Womanhood: A Response to Evangelical Feminism,* edited by John Piper and Wayne Grudem, 425–68. Wheaton, IL: Good News, 1991.

Gryson, Roger. *The Ministry of Women in the Early Church.* Translated by Jean Laporte and Marie Louise Hall. Collegeville, MN: Liturgical, 1976.

Guilland, Rodolphe. "Les Eunuques dans l'Empire Byzantin: Étude de titulature et de prosopographie byzantines." *Études Byzantines* 1 (1943) 197–238.

Guffey, Andrew R. "Motivations for Encratite Practices in Early Christian Literature." *JTS* 65.2 (2014) 515–49.

Gunton, Colin. *The Promise of Trinitarian Theology.* New York: T. & T. Clark, 2003.

Guthrie, W. K. C. *The Greeks and Their Gods.* London: Methuen, 1950.

———. *A History of Greek Philosophy.* Vol. 3. Cambridge: Cambridge University Press, 1969.

Hadas, Moses. "Observations on Athenian Women." *Classical Weekly* 29 (Feb. 3, 1936) 97–100.

Halperin, David M. "The Social Body and the Sexual Body." In *Sex and Differences in Ancient Greece and Rome,* edited by Mark Golden and Peter Toohey, 131–50. Edinburgh: Edinburgh University Press, 2003.

Harl, Marguerite. "La préexistence des âmes." In *Origeniana Quarta: Die Referate des 4. Internationalen Origeneskongresses (Innsbruck, 2–6 September 1985),* edited by Lothar Lies, 244–46. Innsbruck, AT: Tyrolia, 1987.

Harper, Kyle. *From Shame to Sin: The Christian Transformation of Sexual Morality in Late Antiquity.* Cambridge: Harvard University Press, 2013.

———. "*Porneia*: The Making of a Christian Sexual Norm." *JBL* 131.2 (2012) 363–83.

Harrington, Hannah K. "Leviticus." In *Women's Bible Commentary,* edited by Carol A. Newsom et al., 70–78. Louisville: Westminster John Knox, 2012.

Harrison, Verna. "The Allegorization of Gender: Plato and Philo on Spiritual Childbearing." In *Asceticism,* edited by Vincent L. Wimbush and Richard Valantasis, 520–34. New York: Oxford University Press, 1995.

———. "Male and Female in Cappadocian Theology." *JTS* 41.2 (1990) 441–71.

———. "Perichoresis in the Greek Fathers." *St. Vladimir's Theological Quarterly* 35 (1991) 53–65.

———. "Women, Identity and the Image of God." *JECS* 9.2 (2001) 205–49.

Hart, Mark. "Gregory of Nyssa's Ironic Praise of the Celibate Life." *Heythrop Journal* 33 (1992) 1–19.

———. "Reconciliation of Body and Soul: Gregory of Nyssa's Deeper Theology of Marriage." *Theological Studies* 51.3 (1990) 450–78.

Heger, Paul. *Women in the Bible, Qumran and Early Rabbinic Literature: Their Status and Roles.* Leiden: Brill, 2014.

Heine, Ronald E. "Origen's Alexandrian *Commentary on Genesis.*" In *Origeniana Octava: Origen and the Alexandria Tradition* 1, edited by Lorenzo Perrone, 63–73. Leuven: Peeters, 2003.

———. "The Testimonia and Fragments Related to Origen's Commentary on Genesis." *ZAC* 9 (2005) 122–42.
Herter, Hans. "The Sociology of Prostitution in Antiquity in the Context of Pagan and Christian Writings." In *Sex and Differences in Ancient Greece and Rome*, edited by Mark Golden and Peter Toohey, 57–113. Edinburgh: Edinburgh University Press, 2003.
Hesiod. *Theogony and Works and Days*. Translated by M. L. West. Oxford: Oxford University Press, 1988.
Hilary of Poitiers. *On the Trinity*. In vol. 9 of *Nicene and Post-Nicene Fathers, Series 2*, translated by E. W. Watson and L. Pullan. Buffalo: Christian Literature, 1899.
Hippolytus of Rome. *On the Apostolic Tradition*. Translated by Alistair Stewart-Sykes. Crestwood, NY: St. Vladimir's Seminary Press, 2001.
———. *Refutation of All Heresies*. In vol. 5 of *Ante-Nicene Fathers*, edited by Alexander Roberts and James Donaldson. Buffalo: Christian Literature, 1886.
Hipponax. Various fragments in *Greek Iambic Poetry from the Seventh to the Fifth Centuries BC*, translated by Douglas E. Gerber. Loeb Classical Library 259. Cambridge: Harvard University Press, 1999.
Holum, Kenneth G. *Theodosian Empresses: Women and Imperial Dominion in Late Antiquity*. Berkeley: University of California Press, 1982.
Homer. *Iliad*. Translated by Anthony Verity. Oxford: Oxford University Press, 2011.
———. *The Iliad with an English Translation by A. T. Murray*. Cambridge: Harvard University Press, 1924.
———. *The Odyssey with an English Translation by A. T. Murray*. Cambridge: Harvard University Press, 1919.
*Homeric Hymns, Epic Cycle, Homerica*. Translated by H. G. Evelyn-White. Loeb Classical Library 57. Cambridge: Harvard University Press, 1914.
Hopko, Thomas. "Galatians 3:28: An Orthodox Interpretation." *St. Vladimir's Theological Quarterly* 35.2–3 (1991) 169–86.
———. "God and Gender: Articulating the Orthodox View." *St. Vladimir's Theological Quarterly* 37.203 (1993) 141–83.
Hubbard, Thomas K. "The Paradox of 'Natural' Heterosexuality and 'Unnatural' Women." *Classical World* 102.3 (2009) 249–58.
———. "Popular Perceptions of Elite Homosexuality in Classical Athens." *Arion: A Journal of Humanities and the Classics* 3.6.1 (1998) 48–78.
Huffman, Carl. "Pythagoreanism." In *Stanford Encyclopedia of Philosophy* (Fall 2019 ed.), edited by Edward N. Zalta. https://plato.stanford.edu/entries/pythagoreanism/#4.
Hunt, Patrick. *Poetry in the Song of Songs: A Literary Analysis*. New York: Lang, 2008.
Hunter, David G. *Marriage, Celibacy, and Heresy in Ancient Christianity: The Jovinianist Controversy*. Oxford: Oxford University Press, 2007.
———. *Marriage in the Early Church*. Minneapolis: Fortress, 1992.
Irenaeus of Lyon. *Against Heresies (Adversus Haereses)* and *Fragments*. In vol. 1 of *Ante-Nicene Fathers*, edited by A. Cleveland Coxe. Buffalo: Christian Literature, 1885.
Jacobsen, Anders Lund. "Genesis 1–3 as Source for the Anthropology of Origen." *Vigiliae Christianae* 62 (2008) 213–32.
Jankowiak, Marek, and Phil Booth. "A New Date-List of the Works of Maximus the Confessor." In *The Oxford Handbook of Maximus the Confessor*, edited by Pauline Allen and Bronwen Neil, 19–83. Oxford: Oxford University Press, 2015.
Jenkins, Claude. "Origen on 1 Corinthians." *JTS* 9.36 (1908) 500–14.

Jerome. *Letters and Selected Works*. In vol. 6 of *Nicene and Post-Nicene Fathers, Series 2*, translated by W. H. Freemantle. Buffalo: Christian Literature, 1893.

———. *The Homilies of Saint Jerome*. In vol. 2 of *Fathers of the Church*, translated by Marie Liguori Ewald. Washington, DC: Catholic University of America Press, 1966.

———. *The Principal Works of Jerome*. In vol. 6 of *Nicene and Post-Nicene Fathers, Series 2*, translated by W. H. Freemantle. Buffalo: Christian Literature, 1899.

John Chrysostom. *Homilies on the Acts of the Apostles*. In vol. 11 of *Nicene and Post-Nicene Fathers, Series 1*, translated by J. Walker et al. Buffalo: Christian Literature, 1889.

———. *Homilies on the Epistles of Paul to the Corinthians*. In vol. 13 of *Nicene and Post-Nicene Fathers, Series 1*, edited by Talbot W. Chambers. Buffalo: Christian Literature, 1889.

———. *Homilies on Galatians, Ephesians, Philippians, Colossians, Thessalonians, Timothy, Titus, and Philemon*. In vol. 12 of *Nicene and Post-Nicene Fathers, Series 1*, edited by Alexander Gross et al. Buffalo: Christian Literature, 1889.

———. *Homilies on Genesis*. In vols. 1–3 of *Fathers of the Church*, translated by Robert C. Hill. Washington, DC: Catholic University of America Press, 1985.

———. *Homilies on the Gospel of Matthew*. In vol. 10 of *Nicene and Post-Nicene Fathers*, translated by George Prevost. Buffalo: Christian Literature, 1888.

———. *Homilies on S. Ignatius*. In vol. 9 of *Nicene and Post-Nicene Fathers, Series 1*, translated by W. R. W. Stephens. Buffalo: Christian Literature, 1889.

John of Damascus. *Exposition of the Orthodox Faith*. In vol. 9 of *Nicene and Post-Nicene Fathers, Series 2*, translated by S. D. F. Salmond. Buffalo: Christian Literature, 1893.

John Paul II, Pope. *Man and Woman He Created Them: A Theology of the Body*. Translated by Michael Waldstein. Boston: Pauline, 2006.

Justin Martyr. *Dialogue with Trypho, Discourse to the Greeks*, and *First Apology*. In vol. 1 of *Ante-Nicene Fathers*, edited by A. Cleveland Coxe. Buffalo: Christian Literature, 1885.

Kadari, Tamar. "Deborah 2: Midrash and Aggadah." In *Jewish Women: A Comprehensive Historical Encyclopedia*. https://jwa.org/encyclopedia/article/deborah-2-midrash-and-aggadah.

Karras, Ruth Mazo. "Active/Passive, Acts/Passions: Greek and Roman Sexualities." *American Historical Review* 105.4 (2000) 1250–65.

Karras, Valerie A. "Orthodox Theologies of Women and Ordained Ministry." In *Thinking Through Faith: New Perspectives from Orthodox Christian Scholars*, edited by Aristotle Papanikolaou and Elizabeth H. Prodromou, 113–58. Crestwood, NY: St. Vladimir's Seminary Press, 2008.

Katz, Marilyn. "Ideology and 'The Status of Women' in Ancient Greece." *History and Theory* 31.4 (1992) 70–97.

Keuls, Eva C. *The Reign of the Phallus: Sexual Politics in Ancient Athens*. Berkeley: University of California Press, 1993.

Kilby, Karen. "Perichoresis and Projection: Problems with the Social Doctrine of the Trinity." *New Blackfriars* 81.956 (2000) 432–45.

King, Christopher J. *Origen on the Song of Songs as the Spirit of Scripture*. Oxford: Oxford University Press, 2005.

Klawans, Jonathan. "Idolatry, Incest, and Impurity: Moral Defilement in Ancient Judaism." *Journal for the Study of Judaism* 29.4 (1998) 391–415.

Kochańczyk-Bonińska, Karolina. "The Philosophical Basis of Maximus' Concept of Sexes: The Reasons and Purposes of the Distinction of Man and Woman." In *Maximus the Confessor as a European Philosopher*, edited by Sotiris Mitralexis et al., 229–38. Eugene, OR: Wipf & Stock, 2017.

Koltun-Fromm, Naomi. *Hermeneutics of Holiness: Ancient Jewish and Christian Notions of Sexuality and Religious Community*. Oxford: Oxford University Press, 2010.

Kosman, Aryeh. "Male and Female in Aristotle's *Generation of Animals*." In *Being, Nature, and Life in Aristotle*, edited by James G. Lennox and Robert Bolton, 147–67. Cambridge: Cambridge University Press, 2010.

Kraut, Richard. *Aristotle on the Human Good*. Princeton: Princeton University Press, 1989.

Lambriniadis, Elpidophoros. "First without Equals: A Response to the Text on Primacy of the Moscow Patriarchate." *Ecumenical Patriarchate*, Feb. 14, 2014. https://bit.ly/3zriU8h.

Lampe, G. W. H. *A Patristic Greek Lexicon*. Oxford: Oxford University Press, 1961.

Lankila, Tuomo. "The Corpus Areopagiticum as a Crypto-Pagan Project." *Journal for Late Antique Religion and Culture* 5 (2011) 14–40.

Loraux, Nicole. "What Is a Goddess?" In *A History of Women: From Ancient Goddesses to Christian Saints*, edited by Pauline Schmitt Pantel, 11–45. Cambridge: Harvard University Press, 1992.

Leduc, Claudine. "Marriage in Ancient Greece." In *A History of Women: From Ancient Goddesses to Christian Saints*, edited by Pauline Schmitt Pantel, 235–95. Cambridge: Harvard University Press, 1992.

Lefkowitz, Mary R. *Women in Greek Myth*. Baltimore: Johns Hopkins University Press, 1986.

Lewis, C. S. *The Four Loves*. New York: Harcourt Brace Jovanovich, 1960.

Lewis, Nicola Denzey. *Introduction to "Gnosticism": Ancient Voices, Christian Worlds*. Oxford: Oxford University Press, 2013.

Liddell, H. G., et al. *A Greek-English Lexicon*. Oxford: Clarendon, 1940.

Limberis, Vasiliki. "The Council of Ephesos: The Demise of the See of Ephesos and the Rise of the Cult of the Theotokos." In *Ephesos: Metropolis of Asia*, edited by Helmut Koester, 321–40. Valley Forge, PA: Trinity, 1995.

Loader, William. *The Dead Sea Scrolls on Sexuality: Attitudes towards Sexuality in Sectarian and Related Literature at Qumran*. Grand Rapids: Eerdmans, 2009.

———. *Making Sense of Sex: Attitudes towards Sexuality in Early Jewish and Christian Literature*. Grand Rapids: Eerdmans, 2013.

———. *The New Testament on Sexuality*. Grand Rapids: Eerdmans, 2012.

———. *Philo, Josephus, and the Testaments on Sexuality: Attitudes towards Sexuality in the Writings of Philo and Josephus and in the Testaments of the Twelve Patriarchs*. Grand Rapids: Eerdmans, 2011.

Löhr, Winrich. "Christian Gnostics and Greek Philosophy in the Second Century." *Early Christianity* 3 (2012) 349–77.

Loraux, Nicole. "What Is a Goddess?" In *A History of Women: From Ancient Goddesses to Christian Saints*, edited by Pauline Schmitt, 11–45. Cambridge: Harvard University Press, 1992.

Loudovikos, Nikolaos. *A Eucharistic Ontology: Maximus the Confessor's Eschatological Ontology of Being as Dialogical Reciprocity*. Brookline, MA: Holy Cross Orthodox, 2010.

———. "Person Instead of Grace and Dictated Otherness: John Zizioulas' Final Theological Position." *Heythrop Journal* 52 (2011) 684–99.

Louth, Andrew. *Maximus the Confessor*. New York: Routledge, 1999.

Lucretius. *De Rerum Natura*. Translated by William Ellery Leonard. New York: Dutton, 1916.

Lysias. *Lysias with an English translation by W. R. M. Lamb*. Cambridge: Harvard University Press, 1930.

Mainoldi, Ernesto Sergio. "Why Dionysius the Areopagite? The Invention of the First Father." In vol. 96 of *Studia Patristica*, edited by Markus Vinzent, 425–40. Leuven: Peeters, 2017.

Manoussakis, John Panteleimon. "The Anarchic Principle of Christian Eschatology in the Eucharistic Tradition of the Eastern Church." *HTR* 100.1 (2007) 29–46.

———. "Marriage and Sexuality in the Light of the Eschaton: A Dialogue between Orthodox and Reformed Theology." *Religions* 7.89 (2016) 1–13.

Markschies, Christoph. "Gnostics." In *The Westminster Handbook to Origen*, edited by John Anthony McGuckin, 103–6. Louisville: Westminster John Knox, 2004.

Marre, Martine de. "Aristophanes on Bawds in the Boardroom: Comedy as a Guideline to Gender Relations in Antiquity." *Social Identities* 7.1 (2001) 37–65.

Martens, Peter W. "Embodiment, Heresy and the Hellenization of Christianity: The Descent of the Soul in Plato and Origen." *HTR* 108 (2015) 594–620.

———. "Origen's Doctrine of Pre-Existence and the Opening Chapters of Genesis." *ZAC* 16 (2012) 516–49.

———. "Response to Edwards." *ZAC* 23.2 (2019) 187–200.

Martimort, Aimé Georges. *Deaconesses: An Historical Study*. Translated by K. D. Whitehead. San Francisco: Ignatius, 1986.

Martin, Troy W. "The Covenant of Circumcision (Genesis 17:9–14) and the Situational Antithesis in Galatians 3:28." *JBL* 122 (2003) 111–25.

Maximus the Confessor. *The Ascetic Life, The Four Centuries on Charity*. Translated by Polycarp Sherwood. Westminster, MD: Newman, 1955.

———. *Commentary on the Our Father* and *Four Hundred Chapters on Love*. In *Maximus Confessor: Selected Writings*, translated by George C. Berthold, 33–126. New York: Paulist, 1985.

———. *On Difficulties in the Church Fathers: The Ambigua*. Vols. 1–2. Translated by Nicholas Constas. Cambridge: Harvard University Press, 2014.

———. *On Difficulties in Sacred Scripture: Responses to Thalassius*. In vol. 136 of *Fathers of the Church*, translated by Maximos Constas. Washington, DC: Catholic University of America Press, 2018.

———. *Questions and Doubts*. Translated by Despina D. Prassas. DeKalb: Northern Illinois University Press, 2010.

———. *Two Hundred Chapters on Theology*. Translated by Luis Joshua Salés. Yonkers, NY: St. Vladimir's Seminary Press, 2015.

Mayhew, Robert. *The Female in Aristotle's Biology: Reason or Rationalization*. Chicago: University of Chicago Press, 2004.

McLeod, Frederick G. *The Image of God in the Antiochene Tradition*. Washington, DC: Catholic University of America Press, 1999.

Meir, Tamar. "Miriam: Midrash and Aggadah." In *Jewish Women: A Comprehensive Historical Encyclopedia*. https://jwa.org/encyclopedia/article/miriam-midrash-and-aggadah.

Melzer, Arthur M. *Philosophy Between the Lines: The Lost History of Esoteric Writing.* Chicago: University of Chicago Press, 2014.
Menander. *The Plays and Fragments.* Translated by Maurice Balme. Oxford: Oxford University Press, 2008.
Mendels, Doron. "Hellenistic Utopia and the Essenes." *HTR* 72.3–4 (1979) 207–22.
Meredith, Anthony. *Gregory of Nyssa.* London: Routledge, 1999.
Methodius of Olympus. *The Banquet of the Ten Virgins (Symposium)* and *Discourse on the Resurrection.* In vol. 6 of *Ante-Nicene Fathers,* translated by William R. Clark. Buffalo: Christian Literature, 1886.
Meyendorff, John, *Marriage: An Orthodox Perspective.* Yonkers, NY: St. Vladimir's Seminary Press, 1975.
Mitchell, Brian Patrick. *The Disappearing Deaconess: How the Hierarchical Ordering of the Church Doomed the Female Diaconate.* Alexandria, VA: Eremía, 2021.
———. *Eight Ways to Run the Country: A New and Revealing Look at Left and Right.* Westport, CT: Praeger, 2006.
———. "The Problem with Hierarchy: Ordered Relations in God and Man." *St. Vladimir's Theological Quarterly* 54.2 (2010) 189–217.
Mitralexis, Sotiris. "Rethinking the Problem of Sexual Difference in *Ambiguum* 41." *Analogia* 2 (2017) 373–86.
Moltmann, Jürgen. *The Trinity and the Kingdom of God.* New York: Harper and Row, 1981.
Musonius Rufus. *Fragments.* Translated by Cora E. Lutz in "Musonius Rufus, the Roman Socrates," *Yale Classical Studies* 10 (1947) 3–147.
Neudecker, Reinhard. "Marriage and Divorce: The Pharisees and Jesus in the Light of Early Rabbinic Literature." *Sacra Scripta* 11.2 (2013) 262–86.
*Nicene and Post-Nicene Fathers, Series 1–2.* Edited by Philip Schaff and Henry Wace. Buffalo: Christian Literature, 1886–1900.
Niditch, Susan. *Judges: A Commentary.* Louisville: Westminster John Knox, 2008.
Nussbaum, Martha C. "Erôs and Ethical Norms: Philosophers Respond to a Cultural Dilemma." In *The Sleep of Reason: Erotic Experience and Sexual Ethics in Ancient Greece and Rome,* edited by Juha Sihvola and Martha C. Nussbaum, 55–94. Chicago: University of Chicago Press, 2002.
———. "The Incomplete Feminism of Musonius Rufus, Platonist, Stoic, and Roman." In *The Sleep of Reason: Erotic Experience and Sexual Ethics in Ancient Greece and Rome,* edited by Juha Sihvola and Martha C. Nussbaum, 283–326. Chicago: University of Chicago Press, 2002.
Nygren, Anders. *Agape and Eros.* New York: Harper and Row, 1969.
O'Carroll, Michael. *Theotokos: A Theological Encyclopedia of the Blessed Virgin Mary.* Wilmington, DE: Glazier, 1982.
O'Connell, Robert J. *The Origin of the Soul in Augustine's Writings.* New York: Fordham University Press, 1987.
Origen. *Commentary on the Epistle to the Romans.* In vol. 104 of *Fathers of the Church,* translated by Thomas P. Scheck. Washington, DC: Catholic University of America Press, 2012.
———. *Commentary on John.* In vol. 9 of *Ante-Nicene Fathers,* translated by Allan Menzies. Buffalo: Christian Literature, 1896.
———. *Commentary on Matthew.* In vol. 9 of *Ante-Nicene Fathers,* translated by John Patrick. Buffalo: Christian Literature, 1896.

———. *Commentary on the Song of Songs*. In vol. 26 of *Ancient Christian Writers*, translated by R. P. Lawson. Westminster, MD: Newman, 1957.

———. *Contra Celsus*. In vol. 4 of *Ante-Nicene Fathers*, translated by Frederick Crombie. Buffalo: Christian Literature, 1885.

———. *De Principiis*. In vol. 4 of *Ante-Nicene Fathers*, translated by Frederick Crombie. Buffalo: Christian Literature, 1885.

———. *Dialogue with Heraclides*. In *Alexandrian Christianity*, edited by Henry Chadwick and J. E. L. Oulton, translated by J. E. L. Oulton. Philadelphia: Westminster, 1954.

———. *On First Principles: Being Koetschau's Text of the De Principiis*. Translated by G. W. Butterworth. 1936, Reprint, Eugene, OR: Wipf and Stock, 2012.

———. *Fragments on 1 Corinthians*. In Claude Jenkins, "Origen on 1 Corinthians," *JTS* 9.36 (1908) 500–514.

———. *Homilies on Genesis and Exodus*. In vol. 104 of *Fathers of the Church*, translated by Ronald E. Heine. Washington, DC: Catholic University of America Press, 1982.

———. *Homilies on Leviticus 1–15*. In vol. 83 of *Fathers of the Church*, translated by Gary Wayne Barkley. Washington, DC: Catholic University of America Press, 1990.

———. *Orations*. In *Origen*, translated by Rowan A. Greer. New York: Paulist, 1979.

———. *On Prayer*. In *Alexandrian Christianity*, edited by Henry Chadwick and J. E. L. Oulton, translated by J. E. L. Oulton. Philadelphia: Westminster, 1954.

*On the Origin of the World*. In *The Nag Hammadi Library in English: The Definitive Translation of the Gnostic Scriptures Complete in One Volume*, edited by James M. Robinson, translated by H. G. Bethge and Bentley Layton, 170–89. San Francisco: HarperCollins, 1990.

Oster, Richard. "When Men Wore Veils to Worship: The Historical Context of 1 Corinthians 11.4." *New Testament Studies* 34.4 (1988) 481–505.

Ostrogorsky, George. *History of the Byzantine State*. Translated by Joan Hussey. New Brunswick, NJ: Rutgers University Press, 1969.

Pârvan, Alexandra. "Genesis 1–3: Augustine and Origen on the *coats of skins*." *Vigiliae Christianae* 66 (2012) 56–92.

Pascuzzi, Maria A. "Reconsidering the Authorship of Colossians." *Bulletin for Biblical Research* 23.2 (2013) 223–46.

*Patrologia Graeca*. Edited by J. P. Migne. Paris: Migne, 1857–1886.

*Patrologia Latina*. Edited by J. P. Migne. Paris: Migne, 1844–1864.

Pentiuc, Eugen J. *Long-Suffering Love: A Commentary on Hosea with Patristic Annotations*. Brookline, MA: Holy Cross Orthodox, 2002.

Perl, Eric D. *Theophany: The Neoplatonic Philosophy of Dionysius the Areopagite*. Albany: State University of New York Press, 2007.

Petra, Basilio. "Personalist Thought in Greece in the Twentieth Century: A First Tentative Synthesis." *Greek Orthodox Theological Review* 50.1–4 (2005) 1–48.

Petrey, Taylor G. *Resurrecting Parts: Early Christians on Desire, Reproduction, and Sexual Difference*. London: Routledge, 2016.

Philo of Alexandria. In *The Works of Philo: New Updated Edition*, translated by C. D. Yonge. Peabody, MA: Hendrickson, 1993.

Philolaus of Tarentum. Various fragments in *Ancilla to the Pre-Socratic Philosophers: A Complete Translation of the Fragments in Diels, Fragmente der Vorsokratiker*, translated by Kathleen Freeman. Cambridge: Harvard University Press, 1956.

Phipps, William E. "The Heresiarch: Pelagius or Augustine?" *Anglican Theological Review* 62.2 (1980) 124–33.

Pierce, Alexander H. "Reconsidering Ambrose's Reception of Basil's *Homiliae in Hexaemeron*: The Lasting Legacy of Origin." *ZAC* 23.3 (2019) 414–44.

Plato. *Plato in Twelve Volumes*. Cambridge: Harvard University Press, 1921–1969.

Plotinus. *Enneads*. In *Plotinus: Complete Works*, translated by Kenneth Sylvan Guthrie. 1918. Reprint, Kshetra, 2017.

Plutarch. *Plutarch's Lives*. Translated by Bernadotte Perrin. Cambridge: Harvard University Press, 1916.

———. *Plutarch's Morals*. Edited by William W. Goodwin. Boston: Little, Brown, and Co., 1874.

Pomeroy, Sarah B. *Goddesses, Whores, Wives, and Slaves: Women in Classical Antiquity*. New York: Schocken, 1995.

Porphyry. *Letter to Marcella*. Translated by Alice Zimmern. Grand Rapids: Phanes, 1986.

———. *Life of Plotinus*. In *Plotinus: Complete Works*, translated by Kenneth Sylvan Guthrie. 1918. Reprint, Kshetra, 2017.

———. *Selected Works of Porphyry*. Translated by Thomas Taylor. London: Rodd, 1823.

Price, A. W. *Love and Friendship in Plato and Aristotle*. Oxford: Clarendon, 1990.

Proclus. *The Commentaries of Proclus on the Timaeus of Plato*. Translated by Thomas Taylor. London: Valpy, 1820.

———. *Platonic Theology*. In *The Six Books of Proclus on the Theology of Plato*, translated by Thomas Taylor. 1916. Reprint, Kshetra, 2017.

Pseudo-Dionysius. *Dionysius the Areopagite: Works*. Translated by John Parker. London: Parker and Co., 1899.

———. *Pseudo-Dionysius: The Complete Works*. Translated by Colm Luibheid. New York: Paulist, 1987.

Qimron, Elisha. "Celibacy in the Dead Sea Scrolls and the Two Kinds of Sectarians." In vol. 1 of *The Madrid Qumran Congress: Proceedings of the International Congress on the Dead Sea Scrolls, Madrid, 18–21 March 1991*, edited by J. Trebolle Barrera and L. Vegas Montaner, 287–94. Leiden: Brill, 1991.

Quasten, Johannes. *Music & Worship in Pagan & Christian Antiquity*. Translated by Boniface Ramsey. Washington, DC: National Association of Pastoral Musicians, 1983.

Quispel, Gilles. "Origen and the Valentinian Gnosis." *Vigiliae Christianae* 28.1 (1974) 29–42.

———. "The Study of Encratism: A Historical Survey." In *Gnostica, Judaica, Catholica: Collected Essays of Gilles Quispel*, edited by Johannes Van Oort, 330–63. Boston: Brill, 2008.

Ramelli, Ilaria L. E. "Evagrius and Gregory: Nazianzen or Nyssen? Cappadocian (and Origenian) Influence on Evagrius." *Greek, Roman, and Byzantine Studies* 53 (2013) 117–37.

———. *Evagrius's Kephalaia Gnostika: A New Translation of the Unreformed Text from the Syriac*. Atlanta: Society of Biblical Literature, 2015.

———. "Origen in Augustine: A Paradoxical Reception." *Numen* 60 (2013) 280–307.

———. "Origen the Christian Middle/Neoplatonist: New Arguments for a Possible Identification." *JECS* 1 (2011) 98–130.

———. "Origen, Patristic Philosophy, and Christian Platonism Re-Thinking the Christianization of Hellenism." *Vigiliae Christianae* 63 (2009) 217–63.

———. "'Preexistence of Souls'? The Αρχή and Τέλος of Rational Creatures in Origen and Some Origenians." In in vol. 56 of *Studia Patristica*, edited by Markus Vinzent, 167–226. Leuven: Peeters, 2013.

Reid, Duncan. "Patristics and the Postmodern in the Theology of John Zizioulas." *Pacifica* 22 (2009) 308–16.

Ringrose, Kathryn M. *The Perfect Servant: Eunuchs and the Social Construction of Gender in Byzantium*. Chicago: University of Chicago Press, 2003.

Rist, John M. *Eros and Psyche: Studies in Plato, Plotinus, and Origen*. Toronto: University of Toronto Press, 1964.

———. "Plotinus on Matter and Evil." *Phronesis* 6.2 (1961) 154–66.

———. "Plutarch's *Amatorius*: A Commentary on Plato's Theories of Love?" *Classical Quarterly* 51.2 (2001) 557–75.

Rivas, Rubén Pereto. "The Two Versions of Evagrius Ponticus' *Kephalaia gnostika*: A New Discussion on Their Authenticity." *Adamantius* 24 (2018) 485–92.

Rogers, Justin M. "Origen in the Likeness of Philo: Eusebius of Caesarea's Portrait of the Model Scholar." *Studies in Christian-Jewish Relations* 12.1 (2017) 1–13.

Rousselle, Aline. "Body Politics in Ancient Rome." In *A History of Women: From Ancient Goddesses to Christian Saints*, edited by Pauline Schmitt Pantel, 296–337. Cambridge: Harvard University Press, 1992.

Runia, David T. *On the Creation of the Cosmos according to Moses: Introduction, Translation and Commentary*. Leiden: Brill, 2001.

———. "Philo of Alexandria." In *The Westminster Handbook to Origen*, edited by John Anthony McGuckin, 169–71. Louisville: Westminster John Knox, 2004.

———. "Philosophy." In *The Westminster Handbook to Origen*, edited by John Anthony McGuckin, 171–75. Louisville: Westminster John Knox, 2004.

———. "Why Does Clement of Alexandria Call Philo 'The Pythagorean'?" *Vigiliae Christianae* 49 (1995) 1–22.

Russell, D. A. *Plutarch*. London: Duckworth, 1973.

Russell, Norman. *The Doctrine of Deification in the Greek Patristic Tradition*. Oxford: Oxford University Press, 2004.

Salés, Luis Joshua. *Saint Maximus the Confessor: Two Hundred Chapters on Theology*. Yonkers, NY: St. Vladimir's Seminary Press, 2015.

Satlow, Michael L. "Philo on Human Perfection." *JTS* 8.39.2 (2008) 500–19.

Schindler, David L. *Heart of the World, Center of the Church: Communio Ecclesiology, Liberalism, and Liberation*. Grand Rapids: Eerdmans, 1996.

Scott, Mark S. M. *Journey Back to God: Origen on the Problem of Evil*. New York: Oxford University Press, 2012.

Sedley, David. "Hesiod's *Theogony* and Plato's *Timaeus*." In *Plato and Hesiod*, edited by G. R. Boys-Stones and J. H. Haubold, 246–58. Oxford: Oxford University Press, 2009.

Semonides. Various fragments in *Greek Iambic Poetry from the Seventh to the Fifth Centuries BC*, translated by Douglas E. Gerber. Loeb Classical Library 259. Cambridge: Harvard University Press, 1999.

Sherrard, Philip. *Christianity and Eros: Essays on the Theme of Sexual Love*. Limni, EL: Harvey, 2002.

Sherwood, Polycarp. *Maximus the Confessor: The Ascetic Life, The Four Centuries on Charity*. Westminster, MD: Newman, 1955.

Sherwood, Yvonne. *The Prostitute and the Prophet: Hosea's Marriage in Literary-Theological Perspectives*. Sheffield: Sheffield Academic, 1996.

Siewers, Alfred Kentigern. "Mystagogical, Cosmological, and Counter-Cultural: Contemporary Orthodox Apologetics for Marriage." In *Glory and Honor: Orthodox Christian Resources on Marriage*, edited by David C. Ford et al., 353–94. Yonkers, NY: St. Vladimir's Seminary Press, 2016.

Sihvola, Juha. "Aristotle on Sex and Love." In *The Sleep of Reason: Erotic Experience and Sexual Ethics in Ancient Greece and Rome*, edited by Martha C. Nussbaum and Juha Sihvola, 200–21. Chicago: University of Chicago Press, 2002.

Sissa, Giulia. "The Sexual Philosophies of Plato and Aristotle." In *A History of Women: From Ancient Goddesses to Christian Saints*, edited by Pauline Schmitt Pantel, 46–82. Cambridge: Harvard University Press, 1992.

Skehan, Patrick W., and Alexander A. Di Lella. *The Wisdom of Ben Sirach: A New Translation with Notes*. Garden City: Doubleday, 1987.

Skinner, Marilyn B. *Sexuality in Greek and Roman Culture*. Malden, MA: Blackwell, 2005.

Skliris, Dionysios. ""The Ontology of Mode in the Thought of Maximus the Confessor and Its Consequences for a Theory of Gender." In *Mustard Seeds in the Public Square*, edited by Sotiris Mitralexis, 39–60. Wilmington, DE: Vernon, 2017.

Smith, J. Warren. "The Body of Paradise and the Body of the Resurrection: Gender and the Angelic Life in Gregory of Nyssa's *De hominis opificio*." HTR 99.2 (2006) 207–28.

———. *Christian Grace and Pagan Virtue: The Theological Foundation of Ambrose's Ethics*. Oxford: Oxford University Press, 2011.

Sophocles. *Sophocles Fragments*. Translated by Hugh Lloyd-Jones. Loeb Classical Library 483. Cambridge: Harvard University Press, 1996.

Stansell, Gary. "David and His Friends: Social-Scientific Perspectives on the David-Jonathan Friendship." *Biblical Theology Bulletin* 41.3 (2011) 115–31.

Stephens, William. "What's Love Got to Do with It? Epicureanism and Friends with Benefits." In *College Sex—Philosophy for Everyone: Philosophers with Benefits*, edited by M. Bruce and R. M. Stewart, 75–90. Malden, MA: Wiley-Blackwell, 2010.

Sterling, Gregory E. "Philo's Hellenistic and Hellenistic Jewish Sources." *Studia Philonica Annual* 26 (2014) 93–97.

Stewart, Anne W. "Deborah, Jael, and Their Interpreters." In *Women's Bible Commentary*, edited by Carol A. Newsom et al., 128–32. Louisville: Westminster John Knox, 2012.

Sutton, Agneta. "The Complementarity and Symbolism of the Two Sexes: Karl Barth, Hans Urs von Balthasar and John Paul II." *New Blackfriars* 87.1010 (2006) 418–33.

Taylor, Joan E. "Virgin Mothers: Philo on the Women Therapeutae." *Journal for the Study of the Pseudepigrapha* 12.1 (2001) 37–63.

Tertullian. *Against Marcion, On the Resurrection of the Flesh*, and *On the Soul*. In vol. 3 of *Ante-Nicene Fathers*, translated by S. Thelwall. Buffalo: Christian Literature, 1885.

———. *Exhortation to Chastity, On Monogamy*, and *On the Veiling of Virgins*. In vol. 4 of *Ante-Nicene Fathers*, translated by S. Thelwall. Buffalo: Christian Literature, 1885.

Teske, Roland J. "Origen and St. Augustine's First Commentaries on Genesis." *Origeniana quinta* (1992) 179–85.

Theodoret of Cyrus. *Commentary on the Letters of St. Paul*. Translated by Robert Charles Hill. Vols. 1–2. Brookline, MA: Holy Cross Orthodox, 2001.

———. *Questions on Genesis*. In *Theodoret of Cyrus: The Questions on the Octateuch, Vol. 1: On Genesis and Exodus,* translated by Robert C. Hill, 2–221. Washington, DC: Catholic University of America Press, 2007.

Thornton, Bruce J. *Eros: The Myth of Ancient Greek Sexuality.* Boulder, CO: Westview, 1998.

Thunberg, Lars. *Microcosm and Mediator: The Theological Anthropology of Maximus the Confessor.* Chicago: Open Court, 1995.

Tollefsen, Torstein. *Christocentric Cosmology of St. Maximus the Confessor.* Oxford: Oxford University Press, 2008.

Topping, Eva Catafygiotu. *Sacred Songs: Studies in Byzantine Hymnography.* Minneapolis: Light and Life, 1997.

Törönen, Melchisedec. *Union and Distinction in the Thought of St. Maximus the Confessor.* Oxford: Oxford University Press, 2007.

Torrance, Alan J. *Persons in Communion: An Essay on Trinitarian Description and Human Participation.* Edinburgh: T. & T. Clark, 1996.

Tougher, Shaun. "Byzantine Eunuchs: An Overview, with Special Reference to Their Creation and Origin." In *Women, Men, and Eunuchs: Gender in Byzantium*, edited by Liz James, 168–84. London: Routledge, 1997.

———. *The Eunuch in Byzantine History and Society.* London: Routledge, 2008.

Toynbee, Arnold J. *Hellenism: The History of a Civilization.* London: Oxford University Press, 1959.

Trenham, Josiah B. *Marriage and Virginity according to John Chrysostom.* Platina, CA: Herman of Alaska Brotherhood, 2013.

Trible, Phyllis. "Depatriarchalizing in Biblical Interpretation." *Journal of the American Academy of Religion* 41 (1973) 30–48.

Trigg, John Wilson. *Origen: The Bible and Philosophy in the Third-century Church.* Atlanta: John Knox, 1983.

*Tripartite Tractate.* In *The Nag Hammadi Library: The Definitive Translation of the Gnostic Scriptures Complete in One Volume*, edited by James M. Robinson, translated by Harold W. Attridge and Dieter Mueller, 58–103. San Francisco: HarperCollins, 1990.

Turcescu, Lucian. "Person Versus Individual and Other Modern Misreadings of Gregory of Nyssa." *Modern Theology* 18.4 (2002) 527–39.

Tzamalikos, Panayiotis. *Origen: Cosmology and Ontology of Time.* Leiden: Brill, 2006.

Veyne, Paul. "La famille et l'amour sous le Haut-Empire romain." *Annales, E.S.C.* 33 (1978) 35–63.

Wang, Robin R. *Yinyang: The Way of Heaven and Earth in Chinese Thought and Culture.* Cambridge: Cambridge University Press, 2012.

Ware, Bruce A., and John Starke, eds. *One God in Three Persons: Unity of Essence, Distinction of Persons, Implications for Life.* Wheaton, IL: Crossway, 2015.

Ware, Kallistos. "Man, Woman and the Priesthood of Christ." In *Women and the Priesthood*, edited by Thomas Hopko, 5–54. Crestwood, NY: St. Vladimir's Seminary Press, 1999.

West, M. L. *The East Face of Helicon: West Asiatic Elements in Greek Poetry and Myth.* Oxford: Clarendon, 1997.

Wilson-Kastner, Patricia. *Faith, Feminism and the Christ.* Philadelphia: Fortress, 1983.

Wolff, H. W. *Hosea: A Commentary on the Book of the Prophet Hosea.* Translated by Gary Stansell. Philadelphia: Fortress, 1989.

Wybrew, Hugh. *Orthodox Feasts of Jesus Christ and the Virgin Mary.* Crestwood, NY: St. Vladimir's Seminary Press, 2000.

Xenophon. *Xenophon in Seven Volumes.* Cambridge: Harvard University Press, 1924.

Zachhuber, Johannes. *Human Nature in Gregory of Nyssa: Philosophical Background and Theological Significance*. Lieden: Brill, 2000.
Zehnder, Markus. "Observations on the Relationship between David and Jonathan and the Debate on Homosexuality." *Westminster Theological Journal* 69 (2007) 127–74.
Zizioulas, John D. *Being as Communion*. Crestwood, NY: St. Vladimir's Seminary Press, 1985.
———. *Communion and Otherness*. London: T. & T. Clark, 2006.

# Subject Index

*1 Enoch*, 88, 92
*2 Baruch*, 88
*2 Clement*, 108

Abraham, 70–74, 81, 85, 96, 164, 168, 170, 199
abstinence, 87, 175–76
Achilles, 30–31
Ackerman, Susan, 205, 223
Adam, 7, 65–70, 81, 88, 95–96, 98–99, 103, 108, 117–18, 128–29, 131, 137–39, 147–48, 152, 163–66, 177, 189–90, 192–93, 215–18, 224
adultery, 26–27, 33, 55, 83–84, 99, 105, 136, 156–57
Agamemnon, 31, 37–38
*agapē*, 4, 105, 121, 196, 235
Agapetae, 105
Aimilianos of Simonopetra, 203, 223
allegory, 93, 121, 127, 150
Allen, Prudence, 24–25, 35–36, 38, 54, 223
Alter, Robert, 89, 223
Ambrose of Milan, Saint, xxv, 2, 12, 80, 132–37, 139, 154, 179, 184, 186–87, 223, 225, 237, 239
Ammonius, 6, 112, 197, 228
anarchy, 207, 212, 217, 220
Anaximander, 36
Anaximenes, 36
Andia, Ysabel De, 142, 223
Andreopoulos, Andreas, xi, 142, 223
Antiphon, 38, 223

*apatheia*, 40
Aphrahat, 98
Aphrodite, 24–27, 31–35, 43–44, 109
    Ourania (Heavenly), 32, 44, 59
    Pandemos (Vulgar), 32, 34, 44, 59
*Apocryphon of John*, 109
Apollonius of Rhodes, 35
Apostolic Canons, 174, 182, 184, 186
*Apostolic Constitutions*, 167, 174, 186, 189, 223
Apuleius, 39, 223
Aquila, husband of Priscilla, 188
*archē*, xx, 17–18, 50–51, 119, 133, 161–62, 207, 209–11, 214, 216–17
archy, archic, archical, 207, 209–16, 219–20
Ares, 33, 35, 109
Aristippus of Cyrene, 39
Aristophanes, 26, 28, 35, 38–39, 224, 234
Aristotle, xiii, xxiv, 4, 36, 47–55, 57, 60, 95, 121, 196, 224, 226, 228, 232–34, 237, 239
    influence on Maximus the Confessor, 53–54, 140, 146–49
    on affection (*philia*), 47–49
    on generation, categorization, and sexual distinction, 49–54
    on *eros*, 49
    on marriage, 47–49
    on women, 50–51, 65
Athaliah, 80
Athanasius the Great, Saint, 13, 129, 170, 209, 224
Athena, 25–26

## Subject Index

Augustine of Hippo, Saint, xxv, 12–13, 98, 132, 135–40, 143, 154, 162–63, 165–66, 170–72, 180–81, 224–26, 235–37, 239

Bacchus, 183–84
Baer, Richard A., 95, 224
Bailey, Derrick Sherwin, 2, 224
Balthasar, Hans Urs von, xxi, 8–11, 15–17, 144, 224, 239
Bammel, C.P., 7, 117, 224
Barak, 77–80
Barth, Karl, 15–17, 224, 227, 239
Bartholomew, Craig G., 89, 224
Basil of Caesarea, Saint, 7–8, 124–27, 132–33, 154, 164, 182, 186, 224–25, 237
Bathsheba, 83, 85
beards, beardlessness, 29, 75, 182–84
Beavis, Mary Ann, 93–94, 225
Bedale, Stephen, 161, 225
Behr, John, xi, 8, 17, 130, 225
Berdyaev, Nikolai, 20
Berglund, Carl Johan, 212, 225
bestiality, 83–84, 99
Bilhah, 72–74, 82
bishops, 155, 158, 164, 175, 181, 214
Blomquist, Karin, 54, 225
Blosser, Benjamin P., 6–7, 118, 225
Blowers, Paul M., 10, 151, 225
Boersma, Gerald, 133, 225
Boersma, Hans, 7–8, 121, 126–28, 130, 134, 225
Borborites, 105
Börjesson, Johannes, 140, 225
Borodai, T.Iu., 122, 225
Bosman, Philip R., 55, 225
Boyarin, Daniel, 14, 95, 97–99, 225
Bradshaw, David, xi, 122, 208
Bradshaw, Paul F., 1990
Brakke, David, 109, 225
Breck, John, xxiii, 225
Broek, Roelof van den, 109, 122, 226
Brown, Francis, 226
Brown, Peter, 2, 7, 12, 67, 98, 106, 110–11, 113, 121, 124, 134–37, 139–40, 176, 179, 181, 226
Bulgakov, Sergei, 18, 226

Bynum, Caroline Walker, 226

Cameron, Averil, 104, 190, 226
Carnutus, 25
Carpocratians, 105
Casiday, Augustine, 8, 125, 226
castration, 113, 181–83
Chadwick, Henry, 108–9, 113, 123, 175–76, 224, 226, 236
Chanters (singers), 167, 187
childlessness, 88
Chinese philosophy, xxvi–xxvii, 22, 36, 240
Chrysippus, 28, 30, 40, 112
Cicero, 132, 136, 226
Clark, Elizabeth A., 8, 116, 119, 126, 138–39, 226
Clement of Alexandria, xiv, 2, 9, 12–13, 94, 106–10, 112, 123, 161–62, 169–70, 174–76, 181, 184–85, 204, 226, 238
Clement of Rome, Saint, 173
"coats of skins," 68, 96, 108, 114–15, 117–19, 127–28, 147–48, 197, 236
Cohen, David, 5, 28, 226
Collyridians, 189
*Community Rule*, 88
concubines, 27, 31, 47, 71, 82–83, 136, 158
Constas, Maximos, 142, 234
 as Nicholas Constas, 145, 191, 226, 234
*Consultations of Zaccheus and Apollonius*, 180
Cooper, Adam G., 10, 151, 226
Costache, Doru, 10–11, 144–45, 149, 151, 202, 227
Council *in Trullo* (Quinisext), xix, 8, 164, 174, 181, 184, 186–87
Council of Constantinople (II), Fifth Ecumenical, xix, 8, 116, 126, 173
Council of Constantinople (III), Sixth Ecumenical, xix, 8
Council of Elvira, 181
Council of Ephesus, Third Ecumenical, 191–92
Council of Gangra, 124, 184

Council of Nicaea (I), First Ecumenical, 182
Council of Nicaea (II), Seventh Ecumenical, xix, 8,
Crates the Cynic, 39–40, 55–56
cross-dressing, 92, 183–84
Crouzel, Henri, 7, 113, 115, 117–18, 121–22, 227
Cunningham, Mary, 191, 227
Cynics, 39–40, 54
Cyprian of Carthage, Saint, 107, 164, 186, 227
Cyreniacs, 39, 54
Cyril of Alexandria, Saint, 161–63, 186, 204, 209, 227
Cyril of Jerusalem, Saint, 12, 164, 186, 227

Daley, Brian E., 8, 125, 227
*Damascus Document*, 92
Damasus I, Pope, 181
Daniélou, Jean, 7, 121, 123, 227
David, King, 74, 80, 83, 85, 87, 205, 241
Davidson, James, 6, 227
deaconesses, 167, 189, 192, 234–35
deacons, 110, 125–26, 142, 158, 167, 175, 181
Dead Sea Scrolls, 14, 86–87, 92, 233, 237
  *See also* Qumran
Deborah, 77–80, 87, 232, 239
Deddo, Gary W., 15, 227
defilement, 4, 26, 59, 76, 82, 84, 86–87, 97, 104–5, 111, 113, 134–35, 145, 158, 177, 179, 181, 232
DelCogliano, Mark, 125, 227
Democritus, 38–39, 50, 227
Demosthenes, 27, 227
Diamond, Eliezer, 14, 98, 227
*Didascalia Apostolorum*, 184, 186, 189, 227
Dillon, John, 57, 94, 106, 227
Dinah, 73, 81, 86
Diocletian, 181
Diogenes Laertius (D.L.), xiv, 38–41, 47, 196, 227
Diogenes of Sinope, 39, 56

Dionysius the Areopagite, Saint, 141, 234
  *See also* Pseudo-Dionysius
Dionysus, 34, 43
divorce, 38, 71, 75, 84–85, 156–58, 235
dominion, sovereignty, 64–65, 162, 167–68, 204, 210, 214, 217
"double creation," 7, 10, 117–18, 128, 133, 148
Douglas, Mary, 76, 228
Dover, K.J., 2, 5–6, 26–27, 29–31, 227–28

Edwards, Mark J., xi, 6–7, 94, 118–19, 228, 234
Eller, Cynthia, 26, 228
Elshtain, Jean Bethke, 51, 228
Empedocles, 35, 38, 41, 50, 109, 228
Encratites, encratism, xxv, 9, 101–2, 105–7, 109, 112–13, 150, 155, 169, 170, 174, 180, 196, 230, 237
Engberg-Pedersen, Troels, 93, 228
Ephrem the Syrian, Saint, 13, 162, 165–66, 204, 228
Epictetus, 41, 56–57, 228
Epicureans, Epicureanism, 39–40, 54–56, 89, 196, 239
Epicurus, 40
Epiphanius of Salamis, 116, 119, 164, 169, 189, 209, 228
*Epistle to Diognetus*, 173
*eros*, 4, 13, 24, 34–36, 40, 43–44, 46, 49, 55–56, 59, 61, 94, 107, 121–22, 196, 229, 235, 238, 240
Eros (god), 24, 34–36, 43
esoteric writing, 30–31
Essenes, 92–94, 235
Eudorus of Alexandria, 57–58, 112
eunuchs, 50, 102, 113, 156, 181–83, 238, 240
Euripides, 30–31, 35, 38, 228
Eusebius of Caesarea, xiv, 6, 93–94, 113, 123, 209, 228, 238
Eustathius, Eustathians, 124, 179, 184
Evagrius Ponticus, xiv, xix, xxii, xxv, 6–9, 120, 125–26, 140, 142–43, 151–52, 154, 179, 197, 226–28, 237–38
Evans, Robert F., 138, 228
Evans-Pritchard, E.E., 28, 228

Evdokimov, Paul, 18, 228
Eve, 9, 68–70, 88, 95–96, 98–99, 108, 117–18, 131, 134, 137–39, 144, 147, 152, 163–66, 176, 189–90, 192–93, 215–18, 220

Falcon, Andrea, 228
Fates, 25–26
Faye, Eugène de, 7, 229
Fiorenza, Elisabeth Schüssler, xxiii, 229
Ford, David C., 12–13, 162, 175, 180, 204, 229
Forde, Steven, 47, 229
Foucault, Michel, 2, 5–6, 229
Fox, Michael V., 229
Fraade, Steven D., 14, 98, 229
Frankiel, Tamar, 99, 229
Freeman, Kathleen, 227, 229, 236
Frymer-Kensky, Tikva, 90, 100, 204, 229
Fuchs, Eric, 105, 137, 229

Gaca, Kathy L., 3, 40–41, 96, 229
*gamos,* 27–28, 144, 147
Garrison, Daniel H., 2–3, 23, 25, 27, 30–31, 34–35, 37, 39, 101, 229
gender, xvii–xviii, xxii, xxv–xxvi, xxviii, 5, 10–11, 17–18, 32, 37, 47, 73–74, 76–77, 80, 95, 126, 149, 152, 155, 182, 185, 192–94, 202–3, 219, 227, 229–31, 234, 238–40
Gibeah, 83
Gideon, 79, 82
Giles, Kevin, 17, 229
Gnostics, Gnosticism, xxv, 60, 101–2, 106–11, 113, 118, 122, 141, 150, 154, 171, 174, 204, 225–26, 229, 233–34, 236–37, 240
    *See also* Valentinus *and* Valentinians
gods (male), 24–27, 31
goddesses, 5, 24–26, 33, 63, 90, 100, 152, 204, 227, 229, 233, 237–39
Gomer, 74
*Gospel of the Egyptians,* 107–8
*Gospel of Philip,* 110–11, 113, 229
*Gospel of Thomas,* 107–8, 229
Grant, Robert M., 112–13, 136, 229
Greer, Rowan A., 229, 236

Gregory of Nazianzus, Saint, 7–9, 12, 20, 124–26, 147, 152–54, 186, 207, 209, 229
Gregory of Nyssa, Saint, xiv, xix, xxii, xxv, 1–2, 7–10, 13–14, 119–20, 126–33, 138, 140, 147–49, 151–53, 162, 172, 177–78, 197, 209, 225, 227, 229, 235, 240–41
    on "double creation," 10, 128, 133, 148
Gruber, Mayer I., 74, 230
Grudem, Wayne, 162, 230
Gryson, Roger, 160, 188–89, 230
Guffey, Andrew R., 106, 230
Guillaumont, Antoine, 6, 8
Gunton, Colin, 17, 21, 230
Guthrie, W.K.C., 36, 230
gynaeceum, 5, 183

Hadas, Moses, 5, 230
Hades, 24–25, 84
Halperin, David M., 5, 230
Harl, Marguerite, 7, 117, 230
Harper, Kyle, 3–4, 27, 101, 105, 135, 179, 230
Harrington, Hannah K., 75–76, 230
Harrison, Verna, 16, 95, 125, 169, 216, 230
Hart, Mark, 8, 130, 230
head-covering, 159–63, 185
Heger, Paul, 14, 98, 230
Heine, Ronald E., 114, 119, 230
Hephaestus, 33
Hera, 24–26, 33
Heracleon, 111–12, 122–23, 150, 225
Heraclitus, 23, 36
Herter, Hans, 26–27, 34, 231
Hesiod, xiv, 23–25, 28–29, 33, 35, 37–38, 66, 231, 238
Hestia, 24–25
*hetaira* (hetaera), 27, 33
hierarchy, xxv, 17–19, 141–42, 207–9, 212–14, 216, 220, 235
Hilary of Poitiers, Saint, 170, 231
Hipparchia, 39
Hippolytus of Rome, Saint, 106, 133, 167, 171, 175, 186, 225, 231
Hipponax, 38, 231

Holum, Kenneth G., 191–92, 231
Homer, xiv, 23, 25, 29–33, 35, 37–38, 231
homosexuality, xxi, xxiv, 2, 5–6, 28–31, 46, 74, 84, 91, 101, 105, 185, 226–28, 231, 241
Hopko, Thomas, 18, 232, 240
Hosea, xxii, 74, 87, 230, 236, 238, 240
Hubbard, Thomas K., 5, 36, 231
Huffman, Carl, 57, 231
Hunt, Patrick, 90, 231
Hunter, David G., 106–7, 113, 134, 174, 176, 179–81, 231

Ignatius of Antioch, Saint, 173
"image of God," xviii, xxvii, 10, 14, 16–17, 64–65, 95, 114, 124, 128–29, 131, 133, 147, 152–54, 159, 162–63, 175–76, 193, 195, 200, 203–4, 214, 216, 218–21, 230, 234
Irenaeus of Lyon, Saint, xiv, 77, 105–6, 110–11, 138, 164, 174, 176, 188, 190, 231
Isaac, 70–74, 96, 134, 199, 205
Isaiah, 87 141, 161

Jacob, 65, 70, 72–74, 81–82, 86, 96, 199, 205
Jacobsen, Anders Lund, 119, 231
Jael, 78–79, 239
Jankowiak, Marek, 140, 231
Jenkins, Claude, 231, 236
Jephthah, 78–79, 82
Jerome, Saint, 12. 119, 133, 138, 154, 167, 170–73, 180, 181, 186–87, 232
Jews, Judaism, xxiv, xxvi, 1–4, 12, 14, 20, 63–65, 70, 88–94, 97–99, 101, 103–4, 106, 108, 121, 159, 168, 171, 179, 198, 221, 228–29, 232–34, 237–39
John Chrysostom, Saint, 12–13, 94, 158, 162–63, 165–68, 170–73, 181–82, 185–86, 190, 229, 232, 240
  on the "image of God," 162, 204
  on marriage, 13, 172–73, 177–78, 181

  on Gal 3:28, 170–72
  on gender roles, 185
  on the spiritual equality of women, 170–71
  on the subjection of women, 163, 165–68, 188
John of Damascus, Saint, 151, 207, 209–10, 232
John Paul II, 15–17, 232, 239
John Scotus Eriugena, 151, 228
Josephus, xiv, 87, 233
Jovinian, Jovinianism, 134, 155, 180–81, 231
Julian of Eclanum, 139
Julius Cassianus, 108–9, 170
Justin Martyr, Saint, 104, 106, 170, 183, 185, 190, 232
Justinian I (emperor), Saint, xix, 116, 126, 141, 173, 181–82

Kadari, Tamar, 80, 232
Karras, Ruth Mazo, 5, 232
Karras, Valerie A., 12, 232
Katz, Marilyn, 5, 232
Keuls, Eva C., 5, 23, 232
Kilby, Karen, 17, 232
King, Christopher J., 232
Klawans, Jonathan, 86, 232
Kochańczyk-Bonińska, Karolina, 11, 233
Koltun-Fromm, Naomi, 14, 97, 233
Kosman, Aryeh, 51, 233
*kouroi, korai*, 30
*kratos*, 210
Kraut, Richard, 60, 233

Lactantius, 12
Lambriniadis, Elpidophoros, 19, 233
Lampe, G.W.H., 16, 179, 211, 233
Lankila, Tuomo, 141, 233
Leduc, Claudine, 26, 233
Lefkowitz, Mary R., 5, 233
Lewis, C. S., 32, 233
Lewis, Nicola Denzey, 233
Limberis, Vasiliki, 191, 233
Loader, William, 3, 14, 67, 86–88, 91–93, 95–97, 105, 233
Löhr, Winrich, 109, 233
Loraux, Nicole, 26, 233

Lossky, Vladimir, 20
Loudovikos, Nikolaos, xxi, 20–21, 142, 233
Louth, Andrew, 10, 145, 234
Lucretius, 40, 234

Mainoldi, Ernesto Sergio, 141, 234
Manichaeans, 136–37, 139, 179, 224
Manoussakis, John Panteleimon, xx–xxi, 234
Marcella of Rome, Saint, 186
Marcion of Sinope, Marcionites, 105–6, 234, 239
Markschies, Christoph, 122, 234
Marre, Martine de, 26, 28, 39, 234
Martens, Peter W., 7, 117–20, 228, 234
Martimort, Aimé Georges, 192, 234
Martin, Troy W., 169, 234
Mary, the Virgin, 9, 15, 18, 104, 107, 134, 155, 160, 167, 188, 190–94, 219, 226–27, 235, 240
  See also Theotokos
masturbation, 46, 82–83
Maximus the Confessor, Saint, xiv, xvii–xxii, xxiv–xxv, xxviii, 1, 5, 8–14, 20–21, 53–54, 102, 119–20, 140–52, 154, 162, 172, 178, 197–99, 201–3, 223–27, 231, 233–34, 238–40
  on equality of love, 198
  on "double creation," 10, 148
  on five fundamental divisions, 1, 9, 145–46, 151,
  on instantaneous fall, 147–48, 152, 197
  on means and extremes, 143, 147–48
  on pleasure and pain, 9, 144, 147–48
  reliance on Gregory of Nyssa, 1, 8–9, 147–48, 150–51
  view of marriage, 144–45
Mayhew, Robert, 234
McLeod, Frederick G., 204, 234
Meir, Tamar, 99, 234
Melzer, Arthur M., 130–31, 235
Menander, 38, 235
Mendels, Doron, 94, 235
Meredith, Anthony, 235
metempsychosis, 41, 45, 57

Methodius of Olympus, Saint, 12–13, 15–16, 19, 176–77, 181, 209, 235
Meyendorff, John, 235
Michal, wife of David, 74, 205
Middle Platonists, Middle Platonism, 54–56, 57, 94, 112, 118, 123, 227, 237
Miriam, xxiii, 76–77, 99, 164, 234
misogyny, 12, 37–38, 56, 89–90
Mitchell, Brian Patrick, xxv, 192, 227
Mitralexis, Sotiris, 11, 148, 233, 235, 239
Moltmann, Jürgen, 16–17, 235
monastics, monasticism, xvii, 4, 9, 12, 23, 102, 144, 137, 170, 170–71, 178–80, 186–87, 201–2, 224, 218
Moses, 11, 75–77, 82–84, 87, 94, 96, 99, 144–45, 157, 164, 228, 238
Muses, 25–26, 43
Musonius Rufus, 55–56, 235

Nag Hammadi, 107, 109–10, 121, 229, 236, 240
Nazarites, 87
Neoplatonists, Neoplatonism, xix, xxiv, 6, 57–60, 64, 99, 102, 122, 132, 136, 141–42, 151, 196, 198, 208, 226, 236–37
Nestorius, 190–92
Neudecker, Reinhard, 157, 235
Nicolaitans, 105
Niditch, Susan, 78–79, 235
nudity, nakedness, 29–31, 40, 47, 65–66, 70, 74, 82, 84, 91–92, 148, 216
Numenius of Apamea, 57–58, 94, 106, 112, 228
Nussbaum, Martha C., 4, 54, 235, 239
Nygren, Anders, 4, 235

O'Carroll, Michael, 192, 235
O'Connell, Robert J., 235
Odysseus, 30, 32
*On the Origin of the World*, 107, 236
Onan, Onanism, 82–84
Origen, xiv, xix, xxii, xxiv–xxv, xxviii, 2, 6–8, 13–14, 60, 111–35, 137–38, 140–41, 144, 150, 152, 154, 162, 174, 176, 189–90, 197, 209, 224–25, 227–32, 234–40
  on the body, 114–16

## Subject Index

on "double creation," 7, 117–18, 128, 133
on marriage, 112–13, 129
on the soul, xix, 6–7, 116–21, 124, 126, 129, 131, 152, 230, 238
Valentinian influence on, 119–24
Origenists, Origenism, 6, 102, 116, 119–20, 126, 131, 138, 140–41, 151–52, 155, 171, 179–80, 197
Oster, Richard, 159, 236
Ostrogorsky, Georges, 189, 236

Panaetius the Stoic, 55
Pan, 184
Pandora, 37
Parmenides, 38, 142
Pârvan, Alexandra, 137, 236
Pascuzzi, Maria A., 169, 236
Paul, Saint, the Apostle, 2–3, 16, 79–80, 103–4, 115, 141–42, 156–69, 171, 173, 175, 183, 180, 188, 190, 193, 196, 200, 204, 218–19, 232, 239
Paulinus of Nola, Saint, 12
Pausanias, 32–36
pederasty, 23, 28–29, 31, 43–44, 55, 91
Pelagius, Pelagianism, 13, 138–39, 187, 228, 237
Penelope, 31, 37
Pentiuc, Eugen J., 74
*Perichōrēsis*, 16–17, 221, 230, 232
Perl, Eric D., 141, 208, 236
Petra, Basilio, 20, 236
Petrey, Taylor G., 236
Pherecydes of Syros, 25
*philia*, 47–49, 55, 143
Philo of Alexandria, xv, xxiv, 3, 7, 9, 14, 58, 64, 67, 92–97, 99, 108–9, 112–14, 116, 119, 123, 127–28, 132–34, 137, 140, 143, 150, 197, 224–25, 228, 230, 233, 236, 238–39
Philolaus, 41, 236
Phipps, William E., 139, 237
*physis*, 36–37
Pierce, Alexander H., 133, 237 Pierce
Plato, xv, xxiv, 4, 6–7, 24–25, 28, 30, 32, 34, 37, 39, 41–50, 52, 55–57, 59–61, 66, 80, 94, 109, 114–16, 118–19, 123, 132, 143, 176, 185, 196, 226, 228–30, 234, 237–39
influenced by Pythagoreanism, 41, 57
on *eros*, 43–44, 46
on pederasty, 44
on unity and diversity, 57
on women, 44–47
Platonists, Platonism, 6–7, 55–59, 61–62, 94, 109–12, 116, 118, 123–24, 127, 133, 141, 150, 152, 197, 227, 235, 237
*See also* Middle Platonists *and* Neoplatonists
Pliny the Elder, 92
Plotinus, xxiv, 4, 6, 41, 58–62, 112, 122, 131–32, 136, 202, 208, 225, 227, 237–38
Plutarch, 27, 55–57, 106, 225, 237–38
polygyny, 73, 81, 83, 85
Pomeroy, Sarah B., 5, 26, 237
Porphyry, xv, xxiv, 58–60, 62, 109, 123, 132, 135–36, 140, 237
presbyters (Christian priests), 141–42, 181, 214, 164, 167
priesthood, Christian, 15, 141–42, 187–88, 191, 201, 210, 213–14
priesthood, Hebrew, 75, 77, 80, 84, 159, 191
priesthood, pagan, 213–14
Price, A.W., 45–48, 237
Priscilla, wife of Aquila, 187–88
Priscillianists, 179
Proclus, 4, 141–42, 208, 227, 237
Proclus of Constantinople, 192
Procopius of Gaza, 117, 119
procreation, xviii–xix, xxi, xxv, 9, 12–13, 28, 43–44, 46–49, 60–61, 96, 98, 101, 112, 133, 137–39, 147, 157–58, 174, 177–78, 203, 216, 219
*See also* progeny
progeny, 63, 71, 92, 97, 156, 202
prophesying by women, 159–63, 188–89
prostitutes, prostitution (harlotry), xxii, 23, 26–27, 34, 63, 74, 82–84, 91, 231, 238
Protevangelium of James, 104, 190–91

## Subject Index

Pseudo-Dionysius, xv, 4, 140–42, 151, 208–9, 223, 226–27, 234, 236–37
Pseudo-Justin, 172
Pseudo-Phocylides, 91
Pulcheria, Saint, 190–91
Pythagoras, 38, 41, 55, 94
Pythagoreans, Pythagoreanism, 3, 41, 54, 57–58, 94, 96, 106, 112, 121, 141, 150, 231, 238
  table of opposites, 36, 57

Quasten, Johannes, 187, 237
Quinisext Council. *See* Council *in Trullo*
Quintillianists, 164, 169, 189
Quispel, Gilles, 7, 107, 111, 122–23, 237
Qumran, 86, 88, 92, 98, 105, 330, 237
  *See also* Dead Sea Scrolls

Rabbinic literature, xxiv, 14, 74, 98–99, 230, 235
Rachel, 70, 72–73, 105
Ramelli, Ilaria L.E., 6, 8, 120, 125–26, 137, 237
rape, 26, 28, 30, 82–84, 86, 109
readers (lectors), 126, 167, 187
Rebecca, 70–74
Reid, Duncan, 20, 238
reincarnation. *See* metempsychosis
resurrection of the body, xix, 115–16, 127, 150–51, 197, 226
Reuben, 82, 105
Ringrose, Kathryn M., 182, 238
Rist, John M., 4, 56, 58, 238
ritual purity, uncleanness, 76, 83, 86–87
Rivas, Rubén Peretó, 8, 238
Rogers, Justin M., 113, 238
Rousselle, Aline, 27, 238
Rufinus of Aquileia, 114, 117
Runia, David T., 94, 112, 238
Russell, D.A., 55–56, 238
Russell, Norman, 112, 123–24, 238

sacraments, xxi, 111, 144, 157, 170, 172, 219
Salés, Luis Joshua, 238
Salome, Saint, 107–8
Samson, 74, 78–79, 82, 87, 205
Sarah, 70–72, 99, 229

Satlow, Michael L., 96, 238
Scott, Mark S.M., 7, 118, 238
Sedley, David, 37, 238
Semonides, 38, 238
Septuagint, 3, 68–69, 71, 79–80, 86, 99, 157, 161, 216, 226
sexualization,
  of the Greeks, 29–31
  of the Hebrews, 88, 90–92, 97–99
shame, 5, 66, 108, 77, 79, 135, 140, 176
*Shepherd of Hermas*, 173
Sherrard, Philip, 13, 238
Sherwood, Polycarp, 10, 198, 238
Sherwood, Yvonne, xxii, 238
*Sibylline Oracles*, 91
Siewers, Alfred Kentigern, 201–2, 239
Sihvola, Juha, 27–28, 47, 49, 239
silence of women, 164, 172, 186–88
Siricius, Pope, 179, 181
Sissa, Giulia, 52, 239
Skehan, Patrick W., 90, 239
Skinner, Marilyn B., 3, 29–30, 32, 40–41, 54, 239
Skliris, Dionysios, 11, 149, 151–52, 239
slaves, slavery, 84, 125, 165, 171, 182, 198, 237
  sexual slavery, 4, 23, 27–28, 101, 194
Smith, J. Warren, 8, 130, 239
Social Trinitarianism, 16–18, 21
Socrates, 38–39, 43, 45, 55
Sodom, 81–82
sodomy, 83
Solomon, 83, 88–90
sophianism, 18
Sophocles, 33, 38, 239
Speusippus, 57
Stansell, Gary, 74, 239
Stephens, William, 40, 239
Sterling, Gregory E., 94, 239
Stewart, Anne W., 78, 239
Stoics, Stoicism, 2–3, 25, 40–41, 53–55, 57, 94, 112, 123, 138–39, 196, 225, 235
subjection, xxiii, 16, 210–14, 220
  of women, 10, 36, 51, 60, 67, 69–70, 76–77, 80, 79, 163–68, 188–89, 191, 193, 202, 217, 220

## Subject Index

subordination, 15, 17–18, 25, 80, 164, 205, 207–9, 212–13, 229
subjugation, 16, 212–14, 220
Sutton, Agneta, 16, 239

Tamar, wife of Er, 82, 84
Tamar, daughter of David, 83
Tatian the Syrian, 106
Taylor, Joan E., 93, 239
teaching by women, 187–89
Tertullian, 12–13, 104, 106–7, 135, 138, 163, 172, 178, 181, 189, 239
Teske, Roland J., 137, 239
*Testaments of the Twelve Patriarchs*, 104, 233
Thales of Miletus, 23
Thecla, Saint, 104
Theodoret of Cyrus, 161–63, 188, 204, 239
Theodosius the New (II, emperor), Saint, 191
Theodotus, 110–11
Theophilus of Alexandria, 116, 119, 138, 174
Theophylact of Ochrid, Saint, 182
Theotokos, 190–94, 220–21, 233, 235
  See also Mary, the Virgin
*Therapeutae, Therapeutrides*, 93–94, 239
Thornton, Bruce J., 3, 27, 29–37, 41, 240
Thunberg, Lars, 9–10, 128, 143, 146, 148, 151, 240
Tollefsen, Torstein, 53, 240
Topping, Eva Catafygiotu, 187, 240
Törönen, Melchisedec, 53, 140, 240
Torrance, Alan J., 17, 21, 240
Tougher, Shaun, 182–83, 240
Toynbee, Arnold J., 22–23, 240
*Treatise of the Two Spirits*, 88
Trenham, Josiah B., 12–13, 129, 176, 178, 180, 240
Trible, Phyllis, xxiii, 240

Trigg, John Wilson, 123, 240
*Tripartite Tractate*, 121–23, 240
Turcescu, Lucian, xxi, 21, 240
Tzamalikos, Panayiotis, 7, 119–21, 240

Valentinians, Valentinianism, 7, 106, 108–12, 116, 119–24, 127, 150, 197, 225, 237
influence on Origen, 112, 116, 119–24, 197
Valentinus of Alexandria, 106, 111, 121–22, 124–25, 140, 150, 197
Veyne, Paul, 2, 240
virgins, virginity, 4, 8, 13, 18, 25–26, 81, 83–84, 86–88, 91, 93, 103–4, 107, 113, 127, 129–30, 134–35, 137, 155–56, 160, 163, 167, 173, 175–81, 186, 190–93, 202, 219, 223, 224, 226–27, 230, 235, 239–40

Wang, Robin R., xxvii, 36, 240
*War Scroll*, 91–92
Ware, Bruce A., 17, 240
Ware, Kallistos, 18, 240
Wilson-Kastner, Patricia, 16, 240
*Wisdom of Solomon*, 88
Wolff, H.W., 74, 240
Wybrew, Hugh, 191, 240

Xenophon, xv, 32, 41, 48, 240

Yannaras, Christos, 20
yinyang, xxvi–xxvii, 22, 36, 240

Zachhuber, Johannes, 128, 241
Zehnder, Markus, 74, 241
Zeno of Citium, 25, 39–40
Zipporah, 74, 87, 99
Zizioulas, John, xx–xxi, 18–20, 207, 218, 234, 238, 241

www.ingramcontent.com/pod-product-compliance
Lightning Source LLC
Chambersburg PA
CBHW070242230426
43664CB00014B/2384